PALESTINE IN TURMOIL

The Struggle for Sovereignty, 1933-1939

PALESTINE IN TURMOIL

The Struggle for Sovereignty, 1933–1939

Volume I: Prelude to Revolt, 1933-1936

MONTY NOAM PENKOWER

New York 2014

Library of Congress Cataloging-in-Publication Data:

A catalog record for this book is available from the Library of Congress.
ISBN 978-1-61811-315-3 (hardback)
ISBN 978-1-61811-367-2 (paperback)
ISBN 978-1-61811-316-0 (electronic)

Published by Touro College Press and Academic Studies Press.
Typeset, printed and distributed by Academic Studies Press.

Cover design by Adell Medovoy

On the cover:
British baton charge against Arab demonstrators, Jaffa, 1936.
Photograph courtesy of the Central Zionist Archives, Jerusalem.

Touro College Press
Michael A. Shmidman and Simcha Fishbane, Editors
43 West 23rd Street
New York, NY 10010, USA
www.touro.edu/touropress

Academic Studies Press
28 Montfern Avenue
Brighton, MA 02135, USA
press@academicstudiespress.com
www.academicstudiespress.com

To the Cherished Memory of

Rabbi Murry S. Penkower (1911 – 1998)
and Lillian Stavisky Penkower (1909 – 2004)

Table of Contents

Preface

In the spring of 1939, on the eve of the darkest night in Jewish history, eighty-three year old Louis D. Brandeis penned a simple, moving note. "What does the world propose to do with the Jews for whom exile is enforced? Unless civilization has so reverted to primitivism as to wish the destruction of homeless Jews, it must encourage the proved medium to solve in great measure the problem of Jewish homelessness." For the first Jew to be appointed to the U.S. Supreme Court, that "proved medium" rested on the soil of his people's historic homeland in Palestine, the biblical Promised Land. Jews had prayed to Zion three times a day throughout the two millennia of their dispersion and persecution, their hopes culminating annually at the close of Yom Kippur prayers and of the Passover seder in the cry "Next Year in Jerusalem!" Even the non-Zionist Irving Lehman, Presiding Judge of the Appellate Division of New York, when asked why he paid regular visits on Saturdays to the Palestine Pavilion's little court at the 1939 World's Fair in Queen's Flushing Meadows, replied *"Klein, aber mein"* (small but mine). Albert Einstein, guest speaker at the structure's opening ceremony that drew 100,000 spectators, had gone further in describing Zionism as a nationalism "whose aim is not power but dignity and health," the world's most eminent scientist viewing Palestine primarily as "the embodiment of the reawakening corporate spirit of the whole Jewish nation."[1]

Yet Palestine, already harboring a vibrant Jewish *risorgimento* and capable of absorbing far larger numbers beyond its more than 445,000 Jews, also bore witness in this same decade to the emergence of nationalism amongst an Arab population of close to 1 million.[2] What developed into a deadly upsurge began in October 1933 with the first demonstrations against the mandatory power and escalated after the police killing of Sheikh Iz al-Din al-Qassam in November 1935. The tensions smoldering just beneath the uneasy surface exploded spontaneously on April 19, 1936, in Jaffa, taking a toll that day of 9 Jews killed and 60 wounded. A general strike commenced under the sponsorship of the newly created Arab Higher Committee, to be quickly followed by the mounting carnage of Jewish civilians and British forces. While the murderous 1929 Arab riots against Palestinian Jews had a religious character, as Jewish Agency Executive chairman David Ben-Gurion emphasized to Brandeis in May 1936, Zionists confronted at present "*a serious political struggle*" whose perpetrators demanded Arab sovereignty and an end to the Jewish National Home.[3] The country's Arabs proceeded to engage for three years in an armed rebellion which, abetted by the surrounding Arab states and encouraged by Italian funds and German propaganda, brought the Palestine cauldron to a boil. Haj Amin al-Husseini, the Grand Mufti of Jerusalem, also orchestrated a terrorist campaign against his Arab opponents, all the while remaining impervious to any compromise with Zionist aspirations.

Great Britain, publicly pledged by the Balfour Declaration in November 1917 to facilitate the establishment of a Jewish National Home in Palestine and awarded a mandate there from the League of Nations five years later, sought to calm the roiling waters. It responded with a mixture of legislation, a Royal Commission that radically suggested partitioning the country into two independent polities, another commission that rejected that solution as impracticable, and armed retaliation against Arab assault. This maelstrom also drew the United States and other governments into confronting the Palestine imbroglio alongside the urgent plight of endangered European Jewry. In March 1939, carrying a suitcase stuffed with Franz Kafka's papers, Max Brod set out for Palestine on the last train to leave Prague, five minutes before the Nazis closed the Czech border.[4] Most of his trapped fellow Jews on the Continent, with the shadows closing in on them, would not be so fortunate. On May 17, 1939, stressing the needs of Imperial strategy and *réalpolitik*, London issued a White Paper sharply curtailing Jewish immigration and land purchase. Britain's granting in the next five years a maximum of 75,000 entry certificates to Jews—thereafter with Arab consent, Colonial Secretary Malcolm MacDonald explained to the Permanent Mandates Commission, was intended to bring the Jewish community up to one-third of the total population. Within ten years, a single Palestine commonwealth having an Arab majority should arise.[5]

The pages that follow examine the growing conflict between Arab and Jew in Palestine which first surfaced clearly in the pivotal years 1933-1939, and which proved to be an irreconcilable rift once the leadership of both peoples refused to accept minority status. A number of past studies discussed some aspects of this clash for supremacy, but a sustained narrative, one offering a broad perspective and rooted in extensive archival sources, remained to be written.

Several issues that previously have eluded comprehensive, scholarly inspection receive their due. First, the Palestinian settlement of sizable numbers of Jewish refugees from Germany's descent into barbarism, joined by many more Jews escaping antisemitism and poverty in Central Europe, dramatically altered the face of the yishuv. Second, these waves of immigration galvanized the Arab Revolt, a rebellion which had its genesis in the contentious, but regularly overlooked, response of Palestine's Arabs between the years 1933-1936 to the expanding Jewish presence. Third, these twinned, novel developments in turn stirred the intervention of Arab states in the region. Fourth, the larger international context of approaching global war, and particularly the reaction of foreign statesmen to Third Reich aggression, played an instrumental role in this drama; the world diplomatic framework demanded inclusion, too.

Various suggestions were advanced for resolving the Palestine conundrum, within and without the two contending camps. These alternatives are also explored in depth, as are the internal divisions and rivalries which beset both the Palestinian Jewish and Palestinian Arab communities. Secret talks between Jewish and Arab leaders, alongside Jewish Agency intelligence reports and recorded Arab telephone conversations, are highlighted in these chapters. The involvement of the United States government is revealed here, for the first time as well. Finally, the deliberations which took place at the meetings of the League of Nations (surprisingly absent in earlier analyses), the World Zionist Congress, the Pan Arab Congress, the Bludan Conference, the Evian Conference on Refugees, the Inter-Parliamentary Arab Congress, and the St. James Conference are all given the careful, definitive attention they merit.

Palestine in Turmoil: The Struggle for Sovereignty, 1933-1939, with volume I devoted to the years 1933-1936 and volume II to the years 1937-1939, is a prequel to my examination of Palestine and the Anglo-American alliance during World War II. That book, *Decision on Palestine Deferred: America, Britain and Wartime Diplomacy, 1939-1945*, relates in detail how those two governments' policy of drift and delay only aggravated the natural divide that had emerged by September 1939 between the two claimants to Palestine. The postponement by London and

Washington of confronting the vexing dilemma, a decision taken while Jews under the swastika fell victim to systematic slaughter, also meant death for the one people targeted by Adolf Hitler and the Third Reich for murder in the Second World War. The chapters in both studies comprise part of my attempt over the past four decades to analyze and explain the crucial nexus that exists between the Holocaust and the rise of the State of Israel, the most significant events in the contemporary Jewish experience. No comparable experiences reflect the hard antinomies of Jewish life—rupture and renewal.[6]

My focus also stems from the tragic fact that a crippling hold of anxiety and violence continues to grip the Holy Land. The past stalks the present, polarization abounds, and Arab-Jewish understanding appears farther away than ever. Moreover, the State of Israel is the sole community worldwide whose right to exist is still questioned. Despite all the remarkable successes wrought by the Zionist revolution in dramatically transforming Jewish life, Israel has become a stigmatized outcast, a pariah nation. Aside from daily facing lethal incitement and terrorism from implacable neighbors, Israel is the only commonwealth that is currently threatened with total extinction. On a broader scale, failure to achieve peace between Arab and Jew, bolstered by the increasing spread of Islamic fundamentalism, also threatens a globe that has witnessed wondrous strides toward freedom.[7] Perhaps a full, documented account of the origins of the militant confrontation that developed between Arab and Jew prior to Israel's rebirth, on May 14, 1948, can contribute to an appreciation of the historical complexities involved and, thereby, to some meaningful reconciliation and a redeeming ray of light.

Like its immediate sequel, this volume is the culmination of many years of effort and owes much to several individuals. The expertise and help of archivists on three continents were most welcome, and I have thanked them in my preface to *The Jews Were Expendable: Free World Diplomacy and the Holocaust*. Additional mention should be made here of Bernhardine Pejovic, now retired, for her aid as director of the League of Nations Archives and Historical Collections Section consultation room in Geneva; Helena Vilensky at the Israel State Archives in Jerusalem; and Lora Korbut, Archivist of the *New York Times* in New York City. Special thanks are due the late Julian Amery, the Sieff family, and Yosi Ahimeir for permission to examine the papers of Leopold Amery, Israel Sieff, and Abba Ahimeir. The writings of numerous specialists have been very beneficial. Grants from the National Foundation for Jewish Culture; the Memorial Foundation for Jewish Culture; the Littauer Foundation; the Eleanor Roosevelt Institute; the American Philosophical Society; the National Endowment for the Humanities; and the American Jewish Archives's Marguerite R. Jacobs Memorial Fellowship are much appreciated. Michael Popkin, professor emeritus of English at Touro College, reviewed the manuscript for clarity of prose. I am privileged to call him my former colleague and constant friend.

Most significantly, a dear family's affection and understanding over the years has proven of inestimable worth. My wife, Yael, is the quintessence of an *ezer k'negdo*. Our children and their spouses are daily sources of much pride and joy, while our grandchildren provide great delight. My sisters, brother, and brothers-in-law have always been supportive in wonderful ways. Lastly, my late parents, Rabbi Murry S. Penkower and Lillian Stavisky Penkower; my late father-in-law and mother-in-law, Abraham Goodman and Leah Stampfer Goodman Baruchi; my late son-in-law, Ari Kraut; and my late *mehutan*, Larry Roth, illuminated our lives with an incandescent glow. To them—each of cherished memory—these two volumes are dedicated.

Endnotes

1   Louis D. Brandeis, *Brandeis on Zionism: A Collection of Addresses and Statements* (Washington, D.C., 1942), 155-156; Meyer Weisgal, *...So Far: An Autobiography* (New York, 1971), 162-163; Albert Einstein, *The World As I See It* (New York, 1934), 167, 154. Einstein much preferred "reasonable agreement with the Arabs on the basis of living together in peace than the creation of a Jewish state," but added that "if external necessity should after all compel us" to assume "the burden" of political nationhood, "let us bear it with tact and patience" (*Out of My Later Years* [New York, 1950], 262-264). For the controversy that arose because the British government objected to

the Zionist flag being flown over the Palestine Pavilion, see L66/135, Central Zionist Archives, Jerusalem; Box 211, New York World's Fair 1939-40 collection, New York Public Library. Also see Barbara Kirshenblatt-Gimblett, "Performing the State: The Jewish Palestine Pavilion at the New York World's Fair, 1939/40," in *The Art of Being Jewish in Modern Times*, ed. B. Kirshenblatt-Gimblett and J. Karp (Philadelphia, 2008), 98-115.

2   F. J. Jacoby, ed., *The Anglo-Palestine Year Book, 1947-1948* (London, 1948), 33.

3   Ben-Gurion to Brandeis, May 7, 1936, microfilm #25, Louis D. Brandeis MSS., University of Louisville, Louisville, KY. In July 1937, the British Colonial Secretary put the Christian population (including Arabs) at 100,000 (W. Ormsby-Gore testimony, July 31, 1937, *League of Nations, Permanent Mandates Commission, Minutes of the Thirty-Second (Extraordinary) Session* [Geneva, 1937], 24).

4   Elif Batuman, "Kafka's Last Trial," *New York Times Magazine*, Sept. 22, 2010. Kafka had died from complications of tuberculosis 15 years earlier, and was buried in Prague's New Jewish Cemetery. His three sisters were killed in the Holocaust.

5   MacDonald testimony, June 17, 1939, *League of Nations, Permanent Mandates Commission, Minutes of the Thirty-Sixth Session* (Geneva, 1939), 95-140, 171-186.

6   Monty Noam Penkower, *Decision on Palestine Deferred: America, Britain and Wartime Diplomacy, 1939-1945* (London, 2002); Monty Noam Penkower, *The Jews Were Expendable: Free World Diplomacy and the Holocaust* (Urbana, 1983); Monty Noam Penkower, *The Holocaust and Israel Reborn: From Catastrophe to Sovereignty* (Urbana, 1994).

7   Monty Noam Penkower, *The Emergence of Zionist Thought* (Millwood, 1986); Monty Noam Penkower, *Radical Islam and the War Against Freedom* (New York, 2003).

1. The Gathering Storms

"Sieg Heil! Sieg Heil! Sieg Heil!" Roaring this cry, twenty-five thousand delirious members of the brown-shirted Nazi SA (Storm Troopers) marched in parade dress and nail-studded jackboots on the evening of January 30, 1933, starting from Berlin's Tiergarten through the Brandenburg Gate and down the Wilhemstrasse, as they paid homage to Adolf Hitler. The 43-year-old Austrian of peasant stock and Führer (leader) of the National Socialist German Workers' (Nazi) Party had been appointed Chancellor of Germany that morning by the President of the liberal, post-war Weimar Republic, Field Marshal Paul von Hindenburg. To Hitler's right at an open window of the Chancellery stood Hermann Göring, President of the Reichstag and second in the Nazi hierarchy. The torchlight parade with swastika banners proudly unfurled went on from dusk until far past midnight, as Hitler danced up and down, continually jerking his right arm outstretched with palm opened in the Nazi salute, his eyes full of tears. In a rambling monologue during the early morning hours of January 31, Hitler commented that he eagerly looked forward to the parliamentary election of March 5 against his "Red" adversaries, and averred that his chancellorship was inaugurating the final struggle of the "Aryan" white man for mastery of the earth. Joseph Goebbels, who had run the party's stormy election campaigns since 1930, wrote in his diary before retiring at 3 a.m.: "The new Reich has been born. Fourteen years of work have been crowned with victory. The German revolution has begun!"[1]

These votaries—particularly Hitler, the impassioned herald whom von Hindenberg, by then in his dotage, had denigrated earlier as "that Bohemian corporal"—had made no secret of their apocalyptic, racist convictions. The Nazi program, announced on February 24, 1920, included the demand for expanded "land and soil" (*Lebensraum*) to satisfy the needs of those of "German blood"—expressly excluding Jews as "Citizens of the State," the party promising to fight "against the Jewish-materialistic spirit within and around us." Hitler's *Mein Kampf* (1925)

expanded upon these themes, connecting world Jewry—"the personi-
fication of the devil"—to "any form of filth or profligacy," and asserting
that "by defending myself against the Jew, I am fighting for the work of
the Lord." The 1931 Boxheim Documents, outlining emergency decrees
for a future Nazi dictatorship, stated that Jews would be forced to emigrate or to starve to death on the spot. The articles and pornographic
caricatures in Julius Streicher's widely influential newspaper *Der
Stürmer* depicted the Jews as the origin of all evil, while one celebra-
tory SA street chant, added unofficially to the "Lied der Sturmsoldaten,"
contained this line: "When Jewish blood spurts from the knife, then
things go even better."[2]

Hitler's accession elicited other reactions. "It was a stupendous
demonstration," admitted Pulitzer Prize-winning American journalist
H. R. Knickerbocker to a friend about the mass of serried SA ranks,
"but I am very much afraid his frantically enthusiastic followers will
have a bad headache of disappointment in a few months." Ambassador
André François-Poncet beheld "the river of fire" flowing past the French
Embassy, "whence, with heavy heart and filled with foreboding, I watched
its luminous wake." While acknowledging that the Nazi party has been
"preaching hate and violence toward Jewish life and Jewish culture,"
the pro-Zionist American Jewish Congress declared that in the qualities
of "firmness of character, natural justice and intelligence" of "the great
German people," in "the sober commonsense of the parties at present
collaborating with Hitler," and particularly in President Hindenburg's
leadership, "we place our faith in this grave hour." The great majority of
Germany's approximately 525,000 Jews exhibited no apparent sense of
panic or urgency, speakers at a benefit for Jewish handicrafts in Berlin's
Café Leon considering one Zionist rabbi's remarks about the new leader
of the Reich as a major change to be "panic-mongering." An editorial
on January 30, 1933, in the newspaper of the Central Association of
German Citizens of the Jewish Faith stated: "The German Jews will not
lose the calm they derive from their tie to all that is truly German. Less
than ever will they allow external attacks, which they consider unjustified, to influence their inner attitude toward Germany."[3]

Recha Freier, the 41-year-old wife of an Orthodox rabbi in Berlin and
a mother of four children, thought otherwise. Influenced by Dov Ber
Borochov's initial advocacy of a Marxist-oriented Zionism to provide
Diaspora Jews "rootedness" in their own homeland, and shocked by

park posters in her native town of Norden proclaiming that "Jews and dogs are not allowed," this folklore researcher and teacher heard the appeal in February 1932 of some unemployed Jewish sixteen-year olds for advice as to their future. Meeting next with Enzo Sereni, an emissary from Kibbutz HaMeuhad's Givat Brenner, she shared her idea that these youngsters should be sent to Eretz Yisrael (the Land of Israel)— Palestine's historic Hebrew name—to live and to work. With his strong encouragement, Freier drew up lists of interested children, had a woman named Mrs. Berger of Danzig put the idea before Henrietta Szold in Jerusalem, and subsequently went to Palestine herself to explore transfer possibilities with the Histadrut labor organization.

Szold, who had founded Hadassah in 1912 in the United States and currently headed the Va'ad HaLeumi (National Council) Department of Social Welfare, categorically rejected Freier's plan. The educational facilities of the yishuv (Jewish community in Palestine) were "hopelessly inadequate," she argued, and the children already in the country had tremendous needs. Very disappointed at this reply, Freier found a receptive ear in Kibbutz Ein Harod's willingness to receive immediately what would soon be called a "Youth Aliya" group. Those opposed to Freier's ideas prevented her from obtaining immigrant certificates, but Dr. Siegfried Lehmann of the Ben Shemen agricultural school, financed by a Berlin Orphan Fund under the chairmanship of young businessman Wilfrid Israel, consented to receive eleven boys and one girl that October. Freier soon founded the *Jüdische Jugendhilfe*, and sought additional means to further her crusade for the migration of children from Germany to Palestine.[4]

At that same moment, a struggle for hegemony that was spearheaded by the political Left embroiled the yishuv, then under a mandate for Palestine which the Council of the League of Nations had accorded to His Majesty's Government (HMG) on July 24, 1922. The mandate noted that recognition had been given to "the historical connection of the Jewish people with Palestine" and to "the grounds for reconstituting their national home in that country," language identical to that of the principal Allied victors in the Great War of 1914-1918, meeting at the San Remo Conference in April 1920, in awarding the Palestine Mandate to Great Britain. Its origins lay in British interest, which had officially been conveyed on November 2, 1917, when Foreign Secretary Arthur Balfour wrote a letter to Baron Walter Rothschild giving HMG's public pledge to "use their best endeavours to facilitate the achievement" of establishing in Palestine "a national home for the Jewish people." From the Balfour Declaration up until 1920, no distinction was made between the two banks of the Jordan River, constituting in total about 1.5 percent of the entire Middle East. However, once French occupation forces in Syria ousted Feisal, son of Sharif Hussein of Mecca, from his Damascus throne and his hope for a Greater Syria, including Palestine (called "Southern Syria"), collapsed, the British installed Feisal as King of Iraq. The British also selected Abdullah, his older brother, to be Emir of Transjordan (the biblical name Eiver HaYarden given to the area of Eretz Yisrael east of the Jordan River). On September 16, 1922, HMG informed the League that all the provisions of the Palestine Mandate concerning the Jewish National Home were inapplicable to Transjordan. Reluctantly, the Jewish Agency Executive acquiesced in this separation.[5]

In Palestine, laborite leaders David Ben-Gurion, Yitzhak Ben-Zvi, Berl Katznelson, and like-minded colleagues of the Second Aliya (1904-1914) focused on creating a new Jewish socialist republic that would live in harmony with its Arab neighbors. (This Marxist interpretation, which Ben-Gurion put into practice when he was Histadrut secretary, denied the existence of a distinct Palestinian Arab national entity and of the Arab national movement.) The Ahdut HaAvoda party (1919) and its merger with the more moderate HaPoel HaTsa'ir into Mapai in 1930, together with the earlier creation of the Histadrut (1920) to forge a centralized workers' society rooted in agricultural communes, reflected these objectives. In the process, Ben-Gurion pioneered in de-legitimizing rivals like the left-wing of Poalei Zion, Communists, HaPo'el HaMizrachi, and Moshe Smilansky's Farmers' Federation, labeling competitors on different occasions as "renegades," "informers," and "enemies" of Zionism. The poet Uri Zvi Greenberg apparently first heard the vicious pun "this uncircumsized rabbi" (*arel zeh rav*) used against HaPoel HaTsa'ir's Haim Arlosoroff, then an opponent of union with Ahdut HaAvoda, while working in the editorial office of the Histadrut's *Davar* newspaper.[6]

Vladimir (Ze'ev) Jabotinsky's creation of the World Union of Zionist-Revisionists in April 1925, with its right-wing platform to transform Palestine gradually into a Jewish Commonwealth on both sides of the Jordan River, did not spark Labor's ire at first. The founder of the Jewish Legion during the Great War and of the first Hagana (defense) units in Jerusalem against Arab attack in 1920, Jabotinsky had by then resigned from the World Zionist Organization (WZO) executive, this exit to signal disapproval with what he viewed as the consistent concessions by WZO president Chaim Weizmann to the mandatory authorities. Jabotinsky, like Labor's leadership, sought to inherit the role of the dominant General Zionists, a loosely-knit, non-ideological bloc composed mainly of middle-class Jews, who would still enjoy a 51 percent electoral majority at the 1929 Zionist Congress. The Revisionists and Labor both railed against the employment of Arab workers, although Jabotinsky championed the bourgeoisie and urban settlement, and favored the individual over the collective. As late as February 1928, against the urging of former Labor members Abba Ahimeir, Yehoshua Yeivin, and Greenberg, a newly formed "Revisionist labor bloc" chose to press their interests within the framework of the Histadrut.[7]

The Arab riots of August 1929 affected this picture dramatically, altering the structure of the Zionist movement for decades to come. The then 160,000-strong yishuv, encouraged by the potential of an enlarged Jewish Agency for Palestine that drew in wealthy non-Zionists at Weizmann's urging, was shocked by the murder of 133 Jews in Hevron, Tsfat (Safed), and elsewhere, as well as 339 wounded, and by the tardy British military response. Ben-Gurion began to recognize the existence of an Arab national movement, revising his early class formula and its assumption that Jews and Arabs could live peacefully together in the framework of a Jewish Palestine as part of an Arab Federation. London's official reaction, culminating in the anti-Zionist tone of Colonial Secretary Lord Passfield's White Paper of 1930, which sought to freeze the yishuv's development, strengthened the shrill appeals of the political Left and Right within Palestinian Jewry. Protracted economic crises across Europe, bolstering the diametrically opposed forces of Communism and Fascism on the Continent, played their part as well. By the 1931 Congress, the General Zionists' percentage of the electorate had plummeted to 36 percent, while Labor raised its total since 1929 from 26 to 29 percent and the Revisionists tripled theirs to 21 percent.[8]

Radicalization, with neither Left nor Right prepared to compromise, now ensued. The Labor Party persistently charged Jabotinsky with irresponsibility and militarism, the disciplined, uniformed brown ranks of the Revisionists' Betar youth movement (the color actually chosen to evoke Palestine's soil) viewed as Fascist in nature. For his part,

Revisionism's chief ratcheted up critiques of Labor's leftist class-warfare philosophy as "poisonous," warning that the movement's success required both workers and private enterprise. By May 1930, Revisionist and Betar workers formed their own organization independent of the Histadrut; physical assaults that broke out between the opposing forces became a common occurrence. The ideological chasm separating the two camps appeared unbridgeable.[9]

The unyielding anti-Marxist stance of Ahimeir, views shared by Yeivin and Greenberg, sharpened this divide. Founder of the maximalist trend in Revisionism, Ahimeir seconded Otto Spengler's revulsion towards declining Western liberalism, and thought nationalism and Marxism irreconcilable. He found Mussolini's authoritarian rule as Duce in Italy especially attractive, with its violent opposition to Socialism and Communism, its romantic glorification of the leader and an elitist youth, and a corporate economy—virtues concomitantly trumpeted by the likes of Winston Churchill, George Bernard Shaw, and much of the West's business class. The severe economic crisis that hit the yishuv during the Fourth Aliya (1924-1928) further strengthened his conviction that Labor's leadership, with its gradualism and neglect of the middle class, had to be replaced. Ahimeir's provocative "From a Fascist's Notebook," columns published in the newspaper *Do'ar HaYom* from October 1928 on once he switched to the Revisionist camp, urged Jabotinsky to become Zionism's Duce *à la* Mussolini and pressed Betar youth to assume the role of a fighting avant-garde. The Jewish Nation, he opined, would be created not through the gradual methods of Labor, but thanks to "a messiah riding aboard a tank."[10]

The traumatic 1929 riots fueled Ahimeir's radical assumptions about the mandatory power. While Greenberg had already called in 1923 for "biryonim" (ruffians) who dreamt of the restoration of "the Kingdom of Israel" and in 1928 for a Jewish armed force to conquer Palestine, and Yeivin blasted the WZO executive for relying on England, Ahimeir championed Lenin, Mussolini, and Kemal Ataturk as models for national redemption. He characterized Weizmann's public suggestion of Palestine's being "shared by two nations" as completing "the work of destruction," requiring Jews to sever themselves from the WZO's "dead body." On October 9, 1930, Ahimeir and some of his followers demonstrated against visiting Colonial Office Under-Secretary Drummond Shiels, protesting that the latter had come to "dig Zionism's grave" with the approval of "the traitorous executive." He and four Betarim, accept-ing his order to be arrested and not flee the police, were manhandled and put in prison for one week. Not long thereafter, Ahimeir insisted that a war for independence resting on a dynamic minority, following the example of recent Jewish heroes like Sarah Aaronsohn, Joseph Trumpeldor, and Shalom Schwartzbard, could strive towards the ideal: a state in Eretz Yisrael matching the boundaries of King David's reign.[11]

This first call to revolt against Great Britain did not meet with Jabotinsky's approval. His abiding faith in British parliamentarian-ism, liberal values, and open diplomacy precluded the break demanded by Ahimeir and his small circle. The 1929 Arab riots led Revisionism's standard-bearer to press for a renewal of the Jewish Legion, all the while preferring that a Jewish commonwealth become part of Britain's dominions. Privately, he warned against the "hysteria" to be found in *Do'ar HaYom*, and refused to accept the mantle of Duce or follow Ahimeir's path, revolted as he was by any form of Fascism. Still, in November 1930, Ahimeir was chosen as a member of the Revisionists' central committee; under his influence, its Palestinian wing pressed for the party's withdrawal from the WZO if the movement refused to declare its ultimate objective to be the creation of a Jewish majority in Palestine. Two months later, Ahimeir and Greenberg joined other Revisionists as new members of the yishuv's third Elected Assembly (Aseifat HaNivharim).[12]

The 1931 Zionist Congress that summer, coming five months af-ter Prime Minister James Ramsay MacDonald reversed the Passfield White Paper with a letter on February 13 to Weizmann, proved to be a watershed for Jabotinsky's party.[13] Some General Zionists, the reli-gious–Zionist Mizrachi, and the so-called Radicals joined Jabotinsky in excoriating Weizmann. "You have sat too long at English feasts," railed Stephen Wise, Honorary President of the American Jewish Congress, in attacking Weizmann's record. Weizmann resigned from the WZO presi-dency, to be succeeded by Nahum Sokolow, after an ill-advised interview quoted him as saying that the development of Jewish civilization and culture did not require a majority in Palestine. A majority comprised of Mizrachi, the Revisionists, and the General Zionists Group B, against the desire of the Labor faction and General Zionists Group A, had achieved their wish that he be removed from office. Failing, however, to have the Congress endorse a Jewish majority and Jewish statehood on both sides of the Jordan River, Jabotinsky tore up his delegate card and stormed out of the hall. Moderate General Zionists such as Weizmann and national poet Chaim Nahman Bialik enjoyed some consolation: Arlosoroff, able defender of Weizmann's approach at the proceedings, became head of the Jewish Agency's political office.[14]

During the next year, Jabotinsky, denied return to Palestine from 1930 onward because of his caustic attacks against HMG, increasingly drew closer to the maximalists. Accepting Betar Jerusalem head Yosef Katznelson's analysis that the Arabs were but an instrument of London's anti-Zionism, Ahimeir and a few others, spontaneously organizing themselves under the name Brit HaBiryonim after the zealots who had fought both Roman rule and fellow Jews favoring compromise with the enemy (66-73 C.E.), tried to hamper a census of Palestine's population. Jabotinsky applauded the unsuccessful effort, which was begun in the fear that anti-Zionist High Commissioner John Chancellor sought to introduce a Legislative Council that would perpetuate the Jews' minority status; 123 protesters landed in jail. In October, Jabotinsky accused Britain of "treachery," and called upon Jewish youth to learn to fire weapons. *Hazit HaAm*, a newspaper founded by Ahimeir and Yeivin in January 1932, featured Jabotinsky among its major contributors. The following month, Revisionist youth inspired by the Biryonim halted a lecture at the Hebrew University by Norman Bentwich, inaugurating a chair in international peace studies, because the former Attorney General for Palestine backed Brit Shalom's support of a bi-national state based on parity with the country's Arab population. Jabotinsky hailed those fifteen arrested for their "adventurism," including Ahimeir, whom he publicly saluted as "our teacher and master." For the first time, the Revisionist leader advocated steps against restrictive immigration and paying taxes, together with favoring "disturbances" and serving time in prison. Encouraged, Ahimeir pressed Jewish youth to adopt "revolutionary Zionism" although he opposed Jabotinsky's public appeal for a worldwide petition to gain the political goals of Revisionism.[15]

Jabotinsky did not give total support to Ahimeir and like-minded Palestinian activists, led by Wolfgang von Weisl, as the fifth Revisionist World Conference in August 1932 made clear. While charging that "the present mandate has become unlawful," he refused to secede from the WZO. Jabotinsky categorically refused the youngsters' call for a dictatorial regime, avowing that he believed in "the ideological patrimony" of nineteenth-century liberal paragons Garibaldi and Lincoln, Gladstone and Hugo. When columns by Ahimeir and by Yeivin raised the possibility of political terror, and even described "German Nazism" (Hitler had won an impressive victory in the elections to the Reichstag that July) as another national liberation movement which should be emulated, the World Union promptly dissociated itself from the views expressed in *Hazit HaAm*. Jabotinsky went further in private, warning Yeivin that their "sans-culottisme," if victorious, would drive him from the Revisionist cause.[16]

The Zionist establishment, and Labor in particular, drew no distinctions between Jabotinsky and his right wing. *HaAretz*'s editor, Moshe Glickson, had equated Revisionism with Fascism from 1928 onward (he denied Ahimeir future entry to its columns that March), as did counterparts on *Davar*. Revisionism, Weizmann informed an American follower in 1931, represented "Hitlerism all over in its worst possible form." After a period of quiet, antagonism flared up in mid-1932 between Histadrut workers and Betar laborers in Herzliya and Tel Aviv, prompting *BaMa'aleh* to call for active retaliation against Betar "brutality"; in September the Jewish Agency Executive deprived the Revisionist party of its status as a "separate union." That fall, the Histadrut commenced a long but ultimately unsuccessful strike against the Frumin plant, opposed by Betar workers, which coincided with Jabotinsky's essay against the Labor federation's monopoly, "Yes, to Break." Furious, Ben-Gurion and the majority of his colleagues on the Histadrut's General Council backed resorting to violence against any who would not toe their organization's line.[17]

Shying away from the partisan strife, Arlosoroff focused at this point on Jewish settlement in Transjordan. That area, three-quarters of the original British-controlled Palestine, Colonial Secretary Winston Churchill had lopped off in 1922 and awarded to Abdullah. As soon as Arlosoroff assumed office, several Transjordanian sheikhs offered land for sale to the Agency's political department. Arab nationalists in their own legislature objected to the proposal, however, which apparently led Abdullah to come into contact eventually with Emanuel Neumann and Yehoshua Heshel Farbstein of the Agency Executive in Jerusalem. Without informing Arlosoroff, these representatives of the General Zionists and Mizrachi, respectively, met Abdullah on November 27, 1932, in the home of his confidant, Mohammed Bey El Unsi. The financially strapped Emir expressed the desire to "bridge the gulf which now separated the two races," offering a six-month option agreement on approximately 70,000 dunams of his own land in the central section of the Jordan Valley, and anticipating a binding contract for a long-term lease. A surprised Arlosoroff, who had thought the time not ripe for purchase, eventually backed the plan, which had gained Sokolow's approval. With Abdullah's signature on a contract drawn up by Agency lawyer Bernard (Dov) Joseph, the annual rent of £2,000 and a £500 payment to the Emir was settled on December 30. El Unsi, Neumann, and Farbstein signed the contract on January 5, 1933.[18]

Arlosoroff officially informed High Commissioner Arthur Wauchope of the transaction on January 20, noting that in their conversations during the past year Wauchope had told him (and Neumann) that the extension of Jewish economic activities to Transjordan was "inevitable." True, Wauchope acknowledged, but he had regarded this as a matter of "gradual development." He considered the present contract "most inopportune and very ill-advised," since Arab-Jewish relations in Palestine had "considerably changed overnight," and HMG could not guarantee the safety of Jewish settlers across the Jordan River. (That same day, an assembly in Nablus (Shekhem), sparked by the Pan-Syrian Istiqlal (Independence) Party's young, dynamic Akram Zu'aiter, cabled Wauchope to prohibit land sales to Jews and urged Abdullah not to lease the Ghore al-Kibd territory to Jewish groups.) Aware of vehement objections by the British Resident in Amman, Henry Cox, Arlosoroff countered that the new breed of Jewish halutzim (agricultural pioneers) would know how to defend themselves if needed; Wauchope insisted that the position on the western side of the River would have to be much more stable before he could give his approval to London. Abdullah, following a visit from octogenarian Palestine Arab Executive president (since 1920) Musa Kazim Pasha al-Husseini and Grand Mufti of Jerusalem Haj Amin el-Husseini, officially denied the "false rumors" about the lease to Jews. Wrote the staunchly pro-Zionist U.S. Supreme Court Justice Louis D. Brandeis to a "rather depressed" Neumann: "The crack in the Transjordan wall which you effected will be widened—and opportunity opened for Jew and Arab by the Jewish immigration."[19]

Although convinced that Neumann and Farbstein had acted independently of the pro-Weizmann political department in order to gain laurels for their own parties, Arlosoroff sought assurance that Wauchope would not do anything to "prejudice a positive solution in the future." While giving his consent, the High Commissioner refused to say when he thought the time would be ripe for the Agency to begin economic activities in Transjordan. Colonial Office Permanent Under-Secretary Arthur Cosmo Parkinson suggested a compromise on February 13 whereby the option would be allowed to go through and the lease taken up, with the proviso that Wauchope's consent should be obtained before any settlement work was begun there. Colonial Secretary Sir Philip Cunliffe-Lister and the High Commissioner agreed, with Wauchope telling Abdullah that HMG did not think the present year "a suitable juncture" for Jewish settlement east of the Jordan in light of security. (Concurrently, Cox was informed of Abdullah's hope that by facilitating Jewish entry he would obtain Jewish assistance to make him King of a combined Palestine and Transjordan.) "If Government attached so much importance to the excitement prevailing in the Arab press or in certain political circles," the disappointed Arlosoroff remarked to Wauchope on February 20, "a more propitious time would never come." Indeed, Wauchope saw no reason to hope that, if the option were extended for six months or even a year, the situation then would be "materially different" from the situation at the present time.[20]

The foundations for the Zionist leadership's longstanding connection with Abdullah had been laid thereby, but at the price of growing radicalization among the Palestinian Arab community. British intelligence reported that circles inclined to the increasingly popular King Abdul Aziz Ibn Saud of Saudi Arabia, who had ousted Abdullah's father from the Hejaz in 1925, feared that Jewish colonization in Transjordan would lead to its inclusion once more in Palestine. While the Istiqlal Party led the crusade of protest, the Arab Young Men's Congress (like the Istiqlal, established in 1932) sent deputations to Amman, and a mob demonstrated against the Emir in Es-Salt. Musa Kazim called a meeting in Jerusalem on February 24, which, after reiterating Zu'aiter's demands of a month earlier, resolved to boycott official mandatory gatherings and to announce a general strike shortly. On March 26, a Non-Cooperation Congress, held in Jaffa under the auspices of the Palestine Arab Executive, drew up measures to be taken against the government. Haj Amin, who played a decisive role in fanning the flames that ignited the Arab riots of 1920, 1921, and 1929, objected to civil disobedience and resignations while declaring that he would have no difficulty in resigning office whenever it would benefit "the nationalist movement." This stand, taken against the rival Nashashibi and Istiqlal parties (the first favoring Abdullah, the second Feisal) primarily resulted in the Congress's decisions never being implemented and left the Palestinian political public with "a sense of gloom." Still, the mounting agitation against Zionist settlement, which decisively influenced the British to check Jewish land transactions across the Jordan River, could not be denied.[21]

All Zionist thoughts of Transjordan shifted course on March 5. On that date, Germany's 39 million citizens, in a campaign marked by massive Nazi violence and intimidation against the Communist, Center, and Social Democrat parties, gave the Chancellor a 52 percent majority in the Reichstag (with the Nationalist bloc's 8 percent). Four days earlier, with reports received of many Nazi terrorist acts against Jews and the *New York Herald Tribune* stating that a St. Bartholomew's Eve Massacre was being planned on or before the election, Weizmann had reviewed with Prime Minister MacDonald and Foreign Secretary John Simon his remarks for a dinner the following evening. Emphasizing to the Parliamentary Friends of Palestine that Transjordan was derelict and barren because the Jews "had not yet penetrated thus far," the Zionist tribune decried the fact that in a great country like Germany the economic and political existence of all Jewish citizens was imperiled by "a policy which has imbibed anti-Semitism in its most primitive, one might say medieval, form as an essential part of its program." Weizmann could only counsel "courage and endurance" to Germany's Jews, adding that they and co-religionists elsewhere should know that the "full weight of enlightened public opinion, non-Jewish and Jewish, in all civilized nations, and particularly England," stood behind them in their struggle against "the forces of reaction." Not long thereafter, Göring publicly denied any intention of a pogrom against Jews, declared that he was not an antisemite, and informed the heads of major Jewish organizations that Berlin "only opposed Marxist Jews." Waiting for the onslaught to subside, German Jewry's Central Association announced: "Germany will remain German, and nobody can rob us of our native earth and Fatherland."[22]

For the first time in its history, the Zionist movement was confronted with the plight of an entire, endangered Jewish community. Stephen Wise heard from "W" in the American Embassy in Berlin that a number of Jews had been "beaten senseless" by uniformed Nazis. In nearly all of Germany's cities, a wave of terror and wholesale arrests of prominent Jews began. Jewish lawyers lost their jobs overnight and Jewish doctors found themselves expelled from hospitals. A crowd of 30,000 in Frankfurt's Palm Garden heard the Chief of Police announce that the "legal" cleaning up process against Jewish "contamination" would perhaps prove "rather unpleasant" for Jews, who could go to Palestine "and pull each other the skin over your heads." Authenticated reports reaching Arlosoroff, which he passed on to Wauchope, described how individual Jews were "done to death." Numerous suicides and desecration of cemeteries were reported. Speaking of German Jewry's "Hour of Shoa," *Davar* opined that that community "is facing destruction."[23]

On March 22, Göring ordered Martin Rosenblüth of the Keren HaYesod (the Agency's principal financial instrument), Revisionist-Zionist Richard Lichtheim, and Dr. Ludwig Tietz of the Central Association board to go to London. Tietz, founder of the first Jewish union for youth (1927), pioneered in efforts to retrain these youngsters for vocations and trades at a time when their families favored the professions. The three men were instructed to take steps to halt the newspaper stories in England and even more so in the United States about atrocities against Jews. The Nazi official particularly wished them to stop Wise's planned mass meeting in Madison Square Garden, or else "I shall not be able to vouch any longer for the security of the German Jews." They found sympathy and readiness to help, Rosenblüth reminisced later, but "only incredulity" in a secret meeting at the Board of Deputies of British Jews regarding their contention that Hitler's fight against Jewry was "only the beginning of an aggressive policy which one day would disturb the peace of Europe." Hearing the request of these visitors for moderation, the Agency office at 77 Great Russell St. urged Wise, whose rally in Madison Square Garden on March 27 would draw 40,000, to focus the protest against any German depriving Jews of their legal economic rights and carrying out a "dry pogrom," and to express the belief that the "first chapter of physical violence was about to be closed."[24]

In this ominous climate, Palestine's appeal as a haven soared. The Zionist Federation of Germany, hitherto a decidedly minority movement within the Jewish community, was besieged daily by 70-100 applicants (mostly of the "capitalist class") for immigration certificates.

More than 1,200 youngsters, Sereni subsequently reported to the Histadrut, joined Zionist farm collectives (hakhsharot) within a year in preparation for work in the biblically covenanted Promised Land. "The inexorable logic of economic pressure" on both sides of the Jordan "will eventually make for common endeavour between Jews and Arabs," Weizmann asserted at a dinner of the Agency's British section. Clement Attlee, speaking on that occasion as Deputy Leader of the parliamentary Labour Party, hailed the "steady uplift of both races" in Palestine. Three days later, Abdullah secretly extended the Ghore al-Kibd option for another six months.[25]

Weizmann pressed Cunliffe-Lister to support the colonization of 1,000 halutzim in Transjordan and to help the WZO develop the malarious Huleh Valley. With the German situation calling for the Zionists' "urgent attention" and practically no unemployment in Palestine, Arlosoroff urged Wauchope to grant 13,000 labor certificates for the next six months and lower the £250 requirement first set in 1925 for the capitalist category to £150. Jewish organizations that took care of German refugees in nearby countries asked the Agency to obtain certificates for those who did not fit into the regular categories. A joint Zionist and non-Zionist Palestine Campaign, launched in New York on March 30, heard Zionist Organization of America (ZOA) president Morris Rothenberg declare that Palestine offered the "most prominent solution for hundreds of thousands of our people seeking a refuge and longing to live a consciously Jewish life."[26]

By the month's end, parliamentary democracy in Germany had been abolished by law, with Jews the prime victims. On March 16, Heinrich Himmler, Bavaria Chief of Police and head of the SS (Hitler's Protection Guard), assisted by Reinhard Heydrich, established a concentration camp northeast of Munich in Dachau. One week later, a two-thirds majority in the Reichstag passed an Enabling Act which granted Hitler full power for a period of four years. To meet rising agitation in the United States and England over antisemitic "brown terror," Göring ordered some communal Jewish leaders to his office, where, given the alternative of being "shot down" in the streets upon their exit, they signed a statement denying persecution. On the night of March 28, Nazi headquarters proclaimed a systematic boycott of Jewish goods and Jews in the professions, to start on April 1, as a counter-action to the "lies and defamations of absolutely shocking perversity which have been let loose about Germany." Its organizer would be the rabidly anti-Jewish Gauleiter of Franconia, Julius Streicher. Ernst Hanfstaengl, Hitler's foreign press chief, informed Foreign Policy Association president James G. McDonald the next day that "every Jew has his SA. In a single night it could be finished." Hitler would soon tell McDonald privately that "I will do the thing that the rest of the world would like to do. It doesn't know how to get rid of the Jews. I will show them."[27]

Pressed by the American Jewish Committee, the American Jewish Congress, and B'nai Brith, which had been asked by Weizmann and the Anglo-Jewish Joint Foreign Committee (combining the Board of Deputies of British Jews and the Anglo-Jewish Association) to "consider appropriate means" of intervening vis-à-vis Germany, U.S. Secretary of State Cordell Hull moved cautiously. Wishing to respond against the assaults without encouraging the threat by Jewish spokesmen of an American boycott of German-made goods, he had Under-Secretary William Phillips get a message to German Foreign Minister Constantine von Neurath on the evening of March 31. If Berlin called off the boycott, Washington would publicly declare that reports of atrocities had been exaggerated. (Foreign Secretary Simon had agreed to write a letter in the same sense, von Neurath soon confided.) In Jerusalem, a majority of the Va'ad HaLeumi under Ben-Zvi's chairmanship demanded that immigration, rather than a boycott, be Jewry's response. The Agency asked Wauchope on March 31 that top immigration priority be given to German applicants, and that certificates be issued ahead of the next quota. The same day, the Grand Mufti secretly declared to the German consul in Jerusalem that Palestine's Muslims welcomed Hitler's regime and hoped for a boycott of the Jews in Germany. That night, von Neurath replied, in "great distress," that it was too late to halt the scheduled Nazi boycott, adding that Hitler had already ordered it to be limited to one day. The boycott would then be held in abeyance until April 5. If the "propaganda" abroad had not decreased, it would be resumed "with greater intensity."[28]

The U.S. chargé d'affaires in Berlin reported to Hull that the boycott had passed off "with surprising calm," but persecution of Jews did not let up. The headline of the Nazi party's *Völkischer Beobachter* on April 2 called the Jews "the enemy of the nation outlawed." Pamphlets and posters warned German mothers to protect their children: "The Passover festival of the Jews is approaching." A Law for the Restoration of the

Professional Civil Service on April 7 declared that only "Aryans" (primarily excluding Jews) qualified for these posts. Altogether, 20,000-25,000 German Jews were unemployed; about 15,000 refugees were scattered in countries bordering on Germany. Felix Warburg, a founder of the American Jewish Joint Distribution Committee (JDC) and a member of the Jewish Agency Council, possessed reliable reports that the boycott and outrages which went on "behind the scenes" had long been planned and promised, and were "simply throwing meat to the wolves."[29]

"It is a war of extermination that Hitler is waging," thought Wise, who privately lamented that newly elected U.S. President Franklin D. Roosevelt (FDR) "has not by a single word or act intimated the faintest interest in what is going on" with respect to German Jewry. *Foreign Affairs* editor Hamilton Fish Armstrong heard that the Germans were having quantities of arms manufactured in Belgium and slipped quietly to them by sea; *New York Times* correspondent Fredrick T. Birchall wrote home that the SA were marching with rifles, in contravention of the post-war Treaty of Versailles, and he concluded: "Hitlerites are not peaceable. It is the same old Germany." While Hull issued a limited statement that he would continue to watch the situation, McDonald told the renowned columnist Walter Lippmann that if a Franco-Polish occupation of Germany occurred, "my guess is that the first thing would be a wholesale slaughter of the Jews."[30]

To meet the growing emergency, the Jewish Agency Executive in London announced that it would seek to obtain authorization from the mandatory government to enable "some thousands of Jewish men and women from Germany, in addition to the steady stream of immigration from Eastern Europe, to enter Palestine in the course of the next few weeks." On April 4, *Jüdische Rundschau* editor Robert Weltsch courageously called on his fellow German Jews to "wear it with pride the yellow badge!", which was the symbol pasted on Jewish stores on April 1 to recall the antisemitic mark of shame which Jews had to wear in the Middle Ages. That same day, the Executive in Jerusalem informed the London office that it would explore the options of negotiating with Berlin over immigration and begin fund raising immediately for the absorption of German immigrants in Palestine. Arlosoroff urged the non-committal Cunliffe-Lister, then visiting the country, to provide special entry for Jewish workers and capitalists, and pressed Wauchope to approve 13,000 certificates in the half-year labor schedule beginning

April 1. The High Commissioner, worried over the possibility of "a turn of the economic tide" and taking note of approximately 9,000 illegal Jewish immigrants (Arlosoroff thought this number exaggerated) who had arrived in 1932 as "tourists" with a three-month permit and several hundreds who crossed the border from Syria, approved only 4,500 plus an advance of 1,000 for halutzim from Germany.[31]

With Weizmann and Neumann in attendance, Arlosoroff also hosted a few Transjordanian sheikhs on April 8 at Jerusalem's King David Hotel. Arlosoroff spoke of the prospect of mutual benefit to Jew and Arab in Transjordan, where "millions" could live comfortably. Noting that the two peoples had lived together "in friendship" during the Middle Ages, Weizmann also recalled his meeting in 1918 north of Akaba with Feisal, which had led to a signed agreement between them on January 3, 1919, whereby they would work together at the Paris Peace Conference for implementation of the Balfour Declaration and "large-scale" Jewish immigration along with an Arab State, the "definite boundaries" between that State and Palestine to be determined. The publicity accorded the gathering at the hotel sparked the Arab Executive in turn to boycott meetings with Cunliffe-Lister and General Edmund Allenby, conqueror of Palestine against the Turkish forces in 1917-1918. (This boycott greatly impressed the Colonial Secretary, one of whose secretaries stated afterwards "we had discovered the Arabs in Palestine".) It also issued a manifesto which hinted that the Arab "nation" would act to "halt the pressure and prevent the injustice" done to it if the necessary means were available. On April 26, Arlosoroff left for Berlin. His objectives included exploring the possibilities of immigration, of future Zionist activities, and of liquidating Jewish assets in Germany so that these could be transferred to Palestine.[32]

Arlosoroff did not know that the first meeting of the British Cabinet Committee on Refugees, on April 7, to discuss the burgeoning issue of refugees from Germany had already decided that, while the decision on entry to Palestine was strictly up to Wauchope, "there is no reason to suppose that room could be found in Palestine in the near future for any appreciable number of German Jewish refugees." Not surprisingly, Cunliffe-Lister concluded in his talks with the High Commissioner that no Jewish settlement in Transjordan could go forward in the next year. In addition, any approval from Wauchope thereafter would be given only to a private company independent of the Agency.[33]

The two British administrators gave some encouragement to Pinhas Rutenberg, who had successfully established the Palestine Electric Corporation in 1923 to harness the waters of the Jordan and Yarmukh Rivers for hydroelectric purposes. Rutenberg now proposed a £10 million project for urban development of large tracts for 4,000-5,000 Jewish families in Palestine's Jordan Valley and, after "perhaps five years," in Transjordan. Weizmann and Arlosoroff preferred to focus on a plan to drain the Huleh Valley marshes, which Rutenberg thought too costly and lengthy a process even for his rich corporation. The three finally agreed on April 15 that the Agency and Rutenberg's group would participate equally in Rutenberg's venture, but Cunliffe-Lister and Wauchope continued to raise the security factor as reason enough to push off settlement east of the Jordan "for the time being." A final agreement between the Executive and Rutenberg as to a division of responsibilities had not been signed by the time of Arlosoroff's departure.[34]

German Jewry's singular plight did nothing to mute Labor's acrimony against the Right for political control of the yishuv. "I am first and foremost interested in the destruction of Revisionism among youth and the masses," Ben-Gurion had emphasized to a correspondent in early January. At a public gathering in Tel Aviv on February 18, self-restraint was cast to the winds as he called Jabotinsky "Vladimir Hitler" for charging in a Berlin address that Zionism had fallen under Communist control, and he asserted that the "Jewish Hitlerites" in Palestine "pray for bloodshed." Betar's objection to a Histadrut strike against agricultural employers in Petah Tikva drew his fire, and that of HaKibbutz HaMeuhad's Yitzhak Tabenkin; *Davar* co-editors Moshe Beilinson and Berl Katznelson, Mapai's principal ideologue, along with some others, favored compromise. A particularly vicious attack on the seventh day of Passover against Betar-allied children by organized Labor forces in Tel Aviv elicited support from Eliyahu Golomb and Berl Repetur of Mapai's central committee (Katznelson submitted his resignation); the Tel Aviv worker's council, *BaMa'aleh*, and *Davar* also justified the violence against "Hitler-uniformed" provocateurs. Jabotinsky actually spearheaded an anti-Hitler crusade at that very moment, warning in two articles soon after the first official persecution of Jews in Germany that if the Führer's regime was "destined to stay, Jewry is doomed." On April 28, he called from the Polish radio in Warsaw for a worldwide boycott of the Third Reich and for a Jewish commonwealth in Palestine as the only adequate reply to the Nazi threat. Sixty-nine pro-boycott meetings throughout Eastern Europe would follow.[35]

Oblivious to this fratricidal struggle, the Zionist Organization of America formulated its own program of action. In light of Germany's relentless pursuit of a program against its Jewish citizens that "brings to life again the barbarism of medieval times," on April 9, the ZOA's Administrative Committee unanimously adopted a resolution calling on the Agency Executive to submit "the Jewish problem in its specific aspect as an international question" to the League of Nations for immediate consideration. Without relinquishing any civil rights to Jews in the lands of their birth or adoption, the ZOA appealed to the nations of the world "to consider in what manner the Jewish National Home may serve for the immediate relief of the appalling conditions that have been created by the forces of anti-Semitism." As Theodor Herzl, the founder of political Zionism, had postulated, the "Jewish problem" represented "an issue and a problem which affect the peace and stability of the entire world," and its solution lay in a national home in Palestine as articulated in the first WZO Congress's Basle Program of 1897, the Balfour Declaration, and the mandate. In addition to the mandatory government opening Palestine "immediately" to "a maximum number of refugees," the League and the United States, in conjunction with HMG and the Jewish Agency, should execute and finance a plan whereby the Promised Land could accept refugees to the limit of its absorptive capacity. The full text was addressed to Sokolow, sent to Weizmann and the London office, and ultimately printed on April 28 in the ZOA's *New Palestine* magazine.[36]

Related calls were heard in Great Britain. At a large protest meeting in London, Lord Mount Temple appealed for opening Palestine's gates "as wide as possible" to suffering German Jewry, whose very existence was "gravely threatened." Viscount Robert Cecil, assistant to Foreign Secretary Balfour when he had given HMG's pledge to Lord Rothschild to facilitate the creation of a Jewish national home in Palestine, noted to the Anglo-Palestine Club the urgency that "Jews ... have a national existence like other nations so that they can intervene and protect their nationals when necessary." In a House of Commons adjournment debate on April 13, which touched on the refugee question, Attlee argued that the British mandatory had a special responsibility to aid German Jewish refugees, and that Palestine could absorb a considerably larger population. In reply, Simon noted Wauchope's concessions: an immediate grant of 1,000 certificates and of blocks of 200 certificates to immigrants possessing at least £1,000; a "liberal review" of those commanding certain skilled trades and crafts and having a minimum of £500; and consideration for those German Jews already in Palestine towards admitting their parents or other relatives. One week later, non-Zionists Neville Laski and Leonard Montefiore, presidents of the Board of Deputies of British Jews and of the Anglo-Jewish Association, respectively, strongly urged Wauchope to have the next immigration schedule increased to the "maximum number possible" in view of the "tragic situation" of German Jewry.[37]

At the end of three months of Nazi rule, Sir Horace Rumbold and Hamilton Fish Armstrong both realized that Hitler would not be overthrown. In a long message on April 26 to his superiors at Whitehall, HMG's Ambassador to Berlin cautioned that *Mein Kampf* contained the principles which had guided Der Führer during the last fourteen years: "The fighting capacity of a race" depended on its purity; pacifism, personified in the internationalist Jewish race, was "the deadliest sin"; only brute force could insure the survival of a race. "I fear," emphasized the author of this five-thousand word dispatch, "that it would be misleading to base any hope for a return to sanity or a serious modification of the views of the Chancellor or his entourage." Owing to Hitler, Rumbold ended, the German people no longer felt humiliated or oppressed. Simon had concluded his remarks in the Commons on April 13 by stating that, while it would not help the German Jews for HMG to intervene on their behalf, he hoped that the debate's "friendly but firm remonstrance" might have an affect on Berlin. In fact, the debate elicited a sharp protest by the German Ambassador in London. Armstrong, too, understood that "the Nazis are Germany." After an hour's solo harangue by Hitler in a private interview on April 27, the editor of *Foreign Affairs* feared that what the world currently needed—"steady, intelligent, conciliatory pressure in the right direction"—was "not inherent in the character of this man."[38]

The prescient Brandeis grasped early on what this fundamentally portended for Jews. Only eight days after Hitler's election, he had told Wise that "the Jews must leave Germany." He had also urged Wise, despite the American Jewish Committee and B'nai Brith canceling their participation in the previous month's Madison Square Garden rally after

Hull's intercession, to make the protest meeting "as good as you can." On April 25, McDonald had told a meeting of half a dozen Christian ministers and Wise about his interview with the German Chancellor, and declared: "Hitler will not rest until he has destroyed the Jewish people." The next day, Brandeis confided in Harvard University law professor Felix Frankfurter his hope that Roosevelt, then focused on the Great Depression in the United States and on a World Disarmament Conference, would respond soon to German Jewry's crisis: "it is becoming a disgrace to us all that America does not act." Wise later heard that while FDR had been prepared in early March to issue a presidential order admitting victims of religious and political persecutions to America, advisors James and Eric Warburg, Felix's nephews, had told FDR that the stories of German atrocities against Jews were exaggerated. Writing three days later to Frankfurter, Brandeis thought that the Jews of Germany "had better make up their minds to move on, all of them." The German nation was "crazy now," but life there "will never be safe, and it has been distinctly degrading to the present generation of Jews." The Associate Justice grimly concluded: "Hitlerism shows that the Allies were right in 1914, in opposing with all available force German aggression. If only they had not been wrong in 1919."[39]

The process of *Gleichschaltung* (coordination), by which the life of the German nation was to be brought under the complete control of the Nazi party, moved steadily forward. The dreaded Gestapo (Secret Police), created by Göring in his capacity as Interior Minister of Prussia, came into being. Communist property was confiscated and free trade unions smashed, numerous members dispatched to Dachau and Oranienburg. On May 10, sparked by student groups with the support of newly appointed Minister of Popular Enlightenment and Propaganda Goebbels, the Nazis committed to the flames some 25,000 books by Jewish authors, and others which they declared to be written "in a Jewish spirit." Among those condemned in what Saul Friedländer has termed "rituals of exorcism" were the works of the popular German-Jewish poet Heinrich Heine, who had reluctantly converted to Protestantism a century earlier as "the ticket of admission into European culture." In his tragedy "Almansor," written in 1821, Hassan says to the hero: "This was a prelude only; where they burn books they will eventually burn people." "Hitler is a fanatic on the subject of Jews," wrote Rumbold home the next day after their first formal meeting. On May 13, the *Manchester Guardian* railed against the Nazi "purge" of Jewish professors from the universities. Increasingly, legislation removed Jews from government service and industry; quotas limited attendance of Jewish children in schools; Jews could not enter many parks and beaches. Aside from "the mad dogs who are in the Government now," wrote Felix Warburg to Anthony de Rothschild in London, "the poison has gone through the whole nation, and the worst of it is that the children's minds have been warped." Watching this "suicide of a culture," the British Jew and Socialist thinker Harold Laski understood, "for the first time with sympathy, why Candide was content to cultivate his garden."[40]

With their fellow Jews not afforded the luxury of Voltaire's Candide, the Agency Executive officially expressed its "deep resentment" on May 3 that Wauchope had just rejected their request for 13,000 labor certificates in favor of a drastic cut of 5,500 for the new six-month immigration schedule. This figure was 1,800 lower than what had been approved by Albert M. Hyamson, an observant Jew who had restricted Jewish entry to Palestine ever since his appointment in 1921 as Immigration Commissioner. Aside from the present development in Palestine warranting a much larger number, the Executive pointed out, the "ruthless policy of economic extermination" to which German Jewry was subject made it "imperative" that the mandatory power utilize "to the utmost degree" all the absorptive opportunities available through the yishuv's efforts. Two days later, Neumann and Moshe Shertok (later Sharett), Arlosoroff's assistant, unsuccessfully tried to have the High Commissioner reverse this "arbitrary curtailment" before he departed for a month's leave in London. Wauchope is "a gentleman," "is keen," and "is a Scotchman," concluded Neumann: "He gives us little, for all his good manners and kind words." Eric Mills, to succeed Hyamson one year later, thought it "short-sighted" to think that Palestine could "accomplish miracles of absorption on behalf of the distressed Jewry of Europe." Writing to Norman Bentwich, he added:

> I suppose Austria is likely to follow in these matters, and this would add to our local difficulties. I wish the Jewish Agency would do more to check illegal immigration in

Palestine.... I'm sure if they took statesman-like lines regarding these matters they could help us more than they do, and might make the calculation of the economic capacity of the country a simple matter.[41]

The violent persecution of Jews in Germany also led the Va'ad HaLeumi, which called a special meeting on May 10 of yishuv representatives, to change its original, quietist attitude. Tel Aviv Mayor Meir Dizengoff spoke first, asserting that since the Nazi regime sought to "destroy the entire Jewish race," the movement should actively work towards uniting Jewry in "a war against Germany." Arthur Ruppin, the father of yishuv settlement, focused on saving Jewish youth; Zionist bard Chaim Nahman Bialik, in agreement, urged that the WZO bring about world awareness that Eretz Yisrael offered the largest haven. Ultimately, the Va'ad HaLeumi's declaration championed Jewish rights everywhere, while announcing that "the only radical solution for the Jewish problem is the re-establishment of the Jewish National Home in the historic birthplace of the Jewish people." It called on "enlightened public opinion" to firmly protest the German Government's "trampling upon" the equality of man, and on Jewish organizations everywhere to "join in the defensive struggle" against "the regime of tyranny." The administration was asked to open wide the doors of Palestine, and the League of Nations to raise an emergency international loan for "the re-patriation of Jews now made homeless to the country of their national birth."[42]

Reporting to his British superiors one week later on this Va'ad HaLeumi shift, the Deputy Inspector-General of the mandatory police's Criminal Investigation Department (C.I.D.) observed that feeling within the Palestinian Jewish community "against German Hitlerism is acute," and that many young "national extremists" affiliated with the Brit Trumpeldor (Betar) and the Revisionist Party were involved. The last observation reflected the accelerating rift between the yishuv's dominant political parties. Jabotinsky had refrained from replying to Ben-Gurion's false charge about personally incitement in Berlin against the Left, but sternly informed *Hazit HaAm*'s editors on May 17 that their finding in Hitlerism some form of a "national movement" was "sheer ignorance." Should the editors not halt unconditionally "this outrage," he would demand their expulsion from the Revisionist party and break off personal relations with anyone so involved. Four days earlier, members of Brit HaBiryonim had burned the door of Germany's consulate in Jerusalem, followed on the morrow by removing the swastika-laden flag atop the consulate in Jaffa (Yafo) and, two weeks later, in Jerusalem. These activities, Ahimeir replied to Jabotinsky, clearly revealed that the maximalists were fighting Hitler in their own fashion.[43]

The Revisionists' boycott crusade also translated into strong attacks in *Hazit Ha'Am* on Arlosoroff, a target of their vitriol ever since he had defended Weizmann at the 1931 Zionist Congress and became the Agency Executive's political director. Beginning in 1932, the maximalists' newspaper assailed the thirty-three year old "wunderkind" for approving the transfer of Jewish lands to "the students of the Mufti and Jamal al-Husseini" (secretary of the Arab Executive and Haj Amin's cousin), flying from Jerusalem to Kibbutz Deganya Bet and back with Wauchope while Britain was "liquidating" Zionism, and refusing to share diplomatic affairs with less compromising members of the Agency Executive. They also accused "this uncircumcised rabbi" of acceding to the mandatory's wish to set up a pro-Arab Legislative Council (which Arlosoroff opposed), as well as closing the gates of Eretz Yisrael to the middle class and Betar loyalists. The Revisionists viewed as particularly abominable the announced negotiation between "the Jewish diplomat" and Nazi authorities in May 1933 for a "ha'avara" (transfer agreement) scheme, enabling German Jews to liquidate some of their property through the export of German goods to Palestine. Thus the headlines that soon followed: "From the Liberal Apostasy in Germany to the Socialist Apostasy in Eretz Yisrael" and "The Jewish S.D. is Sabotaging Our War on Hitlerism."[44]

Arlosoroff had set out from Palestine at the end of April to attain "the liquidation of Jewish fortunes in Germany for transfer to Palestine." Traveling to Berlin, he secured official approval for arranging, in conjunction with the Nazi regime and the WZO, a gradual shift of Jewish funds abroad; *Jüdische Rundschau* received permission to publish the full outline of his scheme, including ten new school settlements in Palestine for children, a vocational reconstruction program there for youth, and a development corporation for adults to service thousands in industry and agriculture within a few years. The "war of destruction against German Jewry," Arlosoroff proceeded to warn audiences across Europe, raised the question of the Jewish tragedy worldwide, and demanded a quick and vigorous response which, by necessity, would reveal a "radical change" regarding Zionism. A central apparatus had to be set up without delay in Palestine and in Germany, he informed a small group at Soklow's London home, with one or two Americans or Britons dispatched to work out a plan of action with the Third Reich government. He also sought support from the Colonial Secretary on June 1 for the transfer scheme, only to meet with Cunliffe-Lister's immediate, "markedly negative" response that British exports to Palestine would suffer thereby.[45]

The Arab Executive reacted quickly, sending a letter to nationalist leaders in Syria to commence an active campaign of protest against the immigration of German Jews to the Near East, and to Palestine in particular. (Aside from another possible land sale in Transjordan, offers to purchase land were then reaching the Jewish Agency from Lebanon, backed by Maronite Patriarch Antoine Arida in a power struggle in that country against the Muslims and the Greek Orthodox.). According to an Agency intelligence report, Musa al-Alami, one of Wauchope's Private Secretaries with special responsibility for advising him on Arab affairs, hosted a meeting on May 23 in his own home, including Musa Kazim, Husseini, and Istiqlal leader Auni Bey Abd al-Hadi, at which a messenger from Feisal spoke of a plan for annexing Palestine and Transjordan to Iraq under Feisal's sovereignty. Each would retain control of internal affairs, but unite for political and military purposes. Abd al-Hadi also submitted a petition to the League seeking to end Jewish immigration and land purchases, opposing any Legislative Council, and claiming the Palestinian Arabs' "full rights to independence and liberty in a union with other Arab countries."[46]

Haj Amin, in the meantime, headed a delegation to Iraq before traveling to India in order to raise funds for the establishment of the Muslim University in Jerusalem that had been decided upon at the 1931 Pan-Islamic Congress, which he had initiated. At a major reception in Baghdad, Haj Amin noted that the Supreme Muslim Council under his aegis had resolved to establish universities in all the countries of Islam. At the moment, he called for raising funds to "save the Haram [the Mosque of Omar area and Jerusalem in general] from the claws of the Zionists and the Imperialists before the menace will spread all over the Holy Land and from there all over her neighboring countries."[47]

On June 6, the Arab Executive announced its decision to boycott all celebrations for the birthday of King George V. The resolution explained that Palestine "has never been a part of the British Empire," and Arab honor would suffer otherwise because "Britain has forced an unconstitutional status on Palestine, and only oppression and loss of rights have been the lot of the people under British auspices." The same day, the sixth Transjordan Congress, with Husseini, Abd al-Hadi, and ten other Palestinian Arab delegates in attendance, resolved to "prohibit and prevent" the permanent stay of any Jews in Transjordan. Those assembled also called for united efforts by the Arab countries against "Zionist imperialism" and for an Arab confederation. Passing through on his way to London, Feisal told Musa Kazim and others in an Arab Executive delegation which had aired its grievances to the Iraqi monarch that "Palestine is Arab and will remain Arab."[48]

Soon thereafter, the Colonial Office received an informal suggestion from Iraqi Foreign Minister Nuri Sa'id that Feisal and Weizmann meet to "ease the situation" in Palestine. A "very doubtful" Deputy Under-Secretary Sir John E. Shuckburgh found it difficult to believe that such a talk would result in the improvement of Arab-Jewish relations there. Professing to be unaware of Nuri's suggestion, Feisal indicated that, if approached, he would be prepared to see Weizmann (then visiting the United States), but did not know "if there was anything which they could usefully discuss." George Rendel, chief of the Foreign Office's Middle East Department, agreed with Shuckburgh, suspecting that the Iraqi object appeared to be to place Feisal in a position to meet Weizmann as a special favor to HMG and then subsequently "make undesirable capital" out of the matter. Sir Francis Humphrys, Britain's Ambassador to Iraq, dismissed the idea, too, as perhaps "an Oriental manoeuvre" on Feisal's part. Nuri's suggestion was dropped.[49]

On June 15, one day after he returned from Europe, a very depressed Arlosoroff insisted before Mapai's central committee that the ha'avara concept had to be implemented quickly; the world, he believed, was responsible for Jewry's fate. The next morning, Revisionist vilification against him came to a head with Yohanan Pogrovinsky's article in *Hazit Ha'Am*, "The Alliance of Stalin–Ben-Gurion–Hitler." Publishing this attack three weeks after Yitshak Lufban's inciting essay "Satan's Ally" in Mapai's *HaPoel HaTsa'ir* directly linked Hitler to Jabotinsky, the former secretary of both Zionist philosopher Ahad Ha'Am and Bialik took Arlosoroff (called here "the Red suckling" and "the Red diplomat of Mapai") to task for sacrificing Jewish honor for the sake of money to Nazi coffers. This step, Pogrovinsky went on, reflected the WZO leaders' decision to copy the pact of "Stalin their mentor" with the "most deranged antisemites—Hitler and Göring," and corroborated the accusation by Marx, "antisemitism's high priest," that Jews were prepared to sell everything. At a time when Jewish blood spilled onto German streets, and Communists filled German prisons and concentration camps, the "ha'avara" proposal by Labor's representative had no parallel for "ugliness and degradation" in the last century. It appeared, Pogrovinsky suggested, that Stalin had given approval to Arlosoroff, Ben-Gurion, and others of the Soviet dictator's Mapai "hasidim" to follow his footsteps. Jews in Eretz Yisrael and the world over would receive this "unforgivable" agreement with "scorn and revulsion." Always knowing how to evaluate properly those who sold the honor of their people and their Torah, the writer concluded, the Jewish nation "will also know today how to respond to this villainy, which is being carried out in broad daylight and before the entire world."[50]

Pogrovinsky and other Revisionists could not have known that Arlosoroff had long abandoned his earlier belief that Zionism could be fully implemented with British cooperation and Arab understanding. Telling his wife Sima that he was preparing his political testament for the next ten years, Arlosoroff spent several nights during the spring of 1932 drafting ideas that crystallized in a lengthy, confidential letter to Weizmann on June 10 about his doubts and perplexities. Opting for a transitory period whereby "the organized revolutionary rule of a Jewish minority government" would "usurp the state machinery, the administration, and the military power" in Palestine, ideas that approached some of Jabotinsky's views, Arlosoroff favored a systematic policy of development, immigration, and settlement that would insure the yishuv's future. Receiving no reply from Weizmann, he continued to press Wauchope for greater immigration, development, and additional Jewish representation in the mandatory government. Refusing to equate Revisionism with Fascism, unlike more militant colleagues in Mapai, he also sought some compromise in the Histadrut-Betar Petah Tikva labor dispute.[51]

On Friday morning, June 16, Arlosoroff saw a number of callers, met with Jewish National Fund president Menahem Ussishkin regarding the removal of Arabs from Wadi Hawarith (Emek Hefer), and lunched with Wauchope. The two men then visited the village of Ben Shemen, where the German children's success in agriculture and farming obviously touched the High Commissioner. At 4 p.m. a car took Arlosoroff to his Tel Aviv home, from which he sent a message to the WZO newspaper *HaOlam* in London, discussing the imminent Zionist Congress. With Jewry's plight growing like "an ever rising, engulfing wave," he noted, the events in Germany had again proven that "the Jewish question is an urgent, international problem." The movement needed a striking platform. "We dare not at this time degrade the Congress into an arena of unrestrained party obstinacy and unchecked rivalry," the Agency Executive's political director stressed. Rather, those assembled should speak "nobly, clearly, and as one soul." He also posted a letter to the Mapai office in Prague containing this proclamation: "The Congress had to be transformed into a mighty demonstration of our national existence without submission and of our uncompromising national will.... Eretz Yisrael must be the transmitter of the Jewish nation's battles at the period of the greatest crisis in its life." Arlosoroff then went with Sima to dinner at the Kaete Dan pension nearby, following which the couple set out for a walk on the beach.[52]

A little after 10 p.m., two men accosted Arlosoroff and Sima as they strolled on that moonless night. Shining a flashlight in his face, the taller individual asked Arlosoroff in rudimentary Hebrew what the time was. "Why are you bothering us?" he angrily retorted. At that moment, the shorter man fired one revolver shot, felling the 34-year-old Arlosoroff to the sands. Sima's screams sent the assailants rushing up the hill to an old Muslim cemetery, where they were lost to sight. After a while, the profusely bleeding Arlosoroff was taken by a private car to the municipal Hadassah hospital; his wife had gone earlier to the Kaete Dan pension to telephone for an ambulance and to contact British deputy inspector of police Captain Harry P. Rice. When the stricken man arrived at the hospital, no doctor was present who could carry out an emergency operation. Lacking the proper apparatus for a blood transfusion, a nurse administered a painkiller to Arlosoroff, who called out for Sima and spoke briefly to Dizengoff. From time to time, he lost consciousness. Only at 12:30 a.m. did operation procedures begin. Summoned from his home, Dr. Felix Danziger discovered that the tube for a saline drip, which should have been ordered immediately, was leaking. He removed the bullet, which had damaged one of the arteries supplying the intestines, but the loss of blood was far too great.

As soon as the transfusion needle pierced his arm, Arlosoroff died. The clock read 12:45 a.m. Danziger stripped off his surgical gloves, flung the implements on the floor, and cried: "It wasn't the Arab who killed Arlosoroff but rather this pigsty!"[53]

A shocked yishuv united to mourn, but the political truce proved short-lived. Official statements from Left and Right bemoaned this enormous loss for the Zionist cause and called for a full investigation. Their respective ranks contributed to the more than 30,000 who attended the funeral on Sunday, as black crepe draped Tel Aviv's major buildings and consular flags flew at half mast. The day of the funeral, Jabotinsky declared that he thought Arabs responsible. As secretary of the Histadrut, Ben-Gurion had wired from Vilna on June 17 to colleagues that young Revisionist "biryonim thirsty for our blood" had killed Arlosoroff, but Labor should "not seek revenge." The next day, however, Ben-Gurion publicly averred in Warsaw that he did not believe Jewry had a party dedicated to "political terror," his characterization of the murder. The atmosphere dramatically shifted with the arrest on June 19 of Avraham Stavsky, a member of Betar, followed by Sima's claim the next day that he had held the flashlight on her husband's face. In his own eulogy of Arlosoroff at the end of the traditional seven-day mourning period, Berl Katznelson cautioned Labor not to emulate the way of brutal power lauded by other parties. On that same occasion, Bialik implored the yishuv to purge Revisionist-related phrases like "fist," "ruffian," and "blood and fire" from its vocabulary, and to keep its camp pure.[54]

Jabotinsky immediately responded to the news of Stavsky's arrest with a public statement, announcing his belief in the young man's innocence, and castigating those who pronounced him guilty well before a court's verdict had been rendered. He accused "a large section of Jewry" of "a shameful pogrom and blood-libel campaign" against Stavsky and the Revisionists for the sake of "party vendetta and electioneering speculation." "We will stand by this innocent man as my generation stood by Mendel Beilis," he ended, also paying tribute to Arlosoroff's last utterance: "I do not believe that the murderer was a Jew." The next day, Warsaw's Revisionist newspaper, *Moment*, carried his lengthy essay in Yiddish, entitled "With Coolness and Steadfastness." It highlighted the fact that the police had only produced the questionable "proof" that Arlosoroff's widow could identify a person whom she had seen on a dark night and for a fleeting moment. The allegation that a link existed between the murder and Revisionist critiques of Labor policy was absurd, Jabotinsky postulated, especially given the far greater incitement by leftist proponents of "the class war" against the Jewish "bourgeoisie" (Revisionists and the middle class) in Eretz Yisrael. These malicious tactics, aimed to assure victory at the upcoming World Zionist Congress elections, he considered intolerable.[55]

Ben-Gurion led the counterattack with a blistering "I Accuse!" Halting an intensive tour across Poland since early April to canvas votes for the Congress, Ben-Gurion openly declared his suspicion that "a poisoned Jewish hand" had committed the murder. Previous attacks against the workers' party by Jabotinsky, his close associates, the poet Uri Zvi Greenberg, and Revisionist organs like *Hazit HaAm* "create the atmosphere in which political killers are educated." The Revisionists, Ben-Gurion went on, assailed Communists and Marxists, attempted to harm him during a Warsaw appearance, praised the Nazi party when Hitler came to power, and spoke regularly of Labor "traitors." Behind closed doors, Zalman Aharonovitz (later Aranne) and Ben-Zvi of Mapai's central committee spoke of "a war of destruction" to be conducted against that party after the investigation ended, while Yosef Sprinzak insisted that the war be extended to all, such as the historian Joseph Klausner, who encouraged Betar and Ahimeir. Histadrut workers in Petah Tikva, B'nei Brak, and Tel Aviv insisted that they did not wish to work with Betar "killers." The poets Avigdor HaMeiri and Avraham Shlonsky blamed Jabotinsky and Ahimeir's Brit HaBiryonim for raising the flag of militancy and its accoutrements as the symbol of Jewish rebirth. Yitzhak Lufban, editor of *HaPoel HaTsa'ir*, labeled the Revisionists a party marked by "cunning," "impurity," "poison," and "a will for destruction," a "dictatorial" group that had to be expelled from the WZO.[56]

Some raised the possibility that Moscow or Berlin had engineered the murder. The first report by the secretary of the Agency Executive about Arlosoroff's death observed that Sima's testimony tended to strengthen the opinion of those who suspected Palestine's Communists, that party recently having suffered one of its greatest defeats in being unable to halt the evacuation of the Bedouin at Wadi Hawarith. Furious that the move had transpired smoothly, they organized the uprooting of trees a night earlier at Netanya. The moment also coincided with the third anniversary of the day that Arabs were executed for their role in the lethal 1929 riots against the yishuv. Ruppin also recorded in his diary the yishuv's first reaction that the murderers were Jewish and Arab Communists. Soon thereafter, a Jewish teacher in Damascus relayed to the Agency the confession of two White Russians to a friend that they had fulfilled their "mission" against Arlosoroff, revenge initiated by the German community in Haifa. One month later, a rabbi traveling by train to southern Bessarabia heard a German passenger tell a fellow countryman that a Nazi agent had killed Arlosoroff because Hitler had ordered the death of some fifty "popular" anti-German world leaders, including that "dirty" Zionist "minister." The account of that dialogue ultimately reached Jabotinsky.[57]

Ben-Zion Katz remained uncertain. On June 26, the veteran journalist appealed in *HaAretz* for a thorough investigation. He had already heard from a close contact of Agency treasurer Eliezer Kaplan that Arlosoroff, at the hospital, had told Kaplan that Jews were not the killers—a fact which Kaplan transmitted the next day to a private meeting in Tel Aviv presided over by Dizengoff. The first and major police queries, Katz declared, should be directed to Arabs, who had killed three Jews in Yagur and two in Nahalal (a terrorist group led by Sheikh Iz al-Din al-Qassam). The second possibility, first briefly raised by Katz three days earlier in that newspaper and here characterized as a "dubious conjecture," was that, as with other peoples, two or three crazed Jewish zealots could be responsible for a political murder. His friends and fellow writers, Yehoshua Ravnitski and particularly Alter Druyanov, also General Zionists, objected to the second suggestion. Bialik, however, congratulated Katz for the article. Before long, Katznelson would publicly cite Katz's article as proof that Jews could have been the killers.[58]

Initially, Katznelson had told Katz that the Revisionists were Arlosoroff's only strong enemies, but they would do nothing so terrible without Jabotinsky's approval, and he thought that the Revisionist leader would never countenance such a thing. By mid-July, however, he took issue with the appeal by Mizrachi religious-Zionist advocate Daniel Sirkis to halt Histadrut sewing of hatred against the Revisionists and the slide to civil war, since no Jewish group or party was capable of this terrible act. What of Revisionist constant smearing of Labor, Katznelson queried, resorting to such epithets as "embezzlers," "followers of the Red rag and the Evsektsii," calling their institutions "mosques," "selling their nation for money," "descendants of Josephus Flavius," "Sanbalatim"? Jabotinsky and his acolytes, in his view, had introduced the fratricidal conflict, insisting that the enemy must be destroyed.[59]

Jabotinsky's foes branded him personally culpable. Ben-Gurion candidly admitted to a Lithuanian newspaper that he was "less interested in whether Stavsky is the murderer or not, than in Jabotinsky," who, as the head and mentor of Betar, bore "all the general responsibility." General Zionist leader Yitzhak Gruenbaum, certain of Stavsky's guilt, signed a proclamation by left-wing Zionists in Poland that Jabotinsky's party should be banished from Jewish life. Even the moderate Weizmann wrote to his wife Vera after Stavsky's arrest that he had predicted murders before the Congress in light of the "terrible propaganda against workers and all this Fascism in Palestine"; Arlosoroff's killing seemed likely enough after years of the Revisionists' "savage demagogy."[60]

In Ben-Gurion's eyes, Zionism's current primary concern involved a thorough cleansing against the "filth" and "malignant leprosy" of those who, although "steeped in Arlosoroff's blood" (sic), yet sought to rule. Since mid-March, he had thought that the next Congress would prove critical: if Revisionism triumphed, all of Labor's activity in Eretz Yisrael would "likely be destroyed to the foundation." Hence his unequivocal program, presented on July 9 in a long letter to the Histadrut, opposing surrender to the "philanthropic lords" and "the impure": if an undisputed anti-Revisionist majority emerged from the Congressional elections, it should create a commission to examine the Revisionists' "war-like ways," this leading within two years to the entire collapse of "the house of cards of the party of strikebreakers and murderers."[61]

The results of the elections to the eighteenth World Zionist Congress boosted Ben-Gurion's hopes considerably. On July 19, the *Palestine Post* reported that Labor had gained 70 percent of the ballots cast across the country, resulting in 34 out of 50 delegates. Worldwide, out of a total of 535,113 votes, the Revisionists would garner 96,818. This compared with 55,848 votes in 1931, but their number of delegates (46) now comprised six fewer than were at the previous Congress due to the tremendous increase of 300,000 ballots cast overall. Of the more than 300 delegates poised to attend, Labor represented 44 percent, commanding a clear majority when joined to allies like Gruenbaum and some other General Zionists. Ben-Gurion's vision that the Labor movement should shift its focus "from class to nation," a thesis articulated in his book of that title, appeared on the cusp of realization. Jabotinsky's forecast in April that the Congress would proclaim a Jewish State on both sides of the Jordan River, condemn class warfare in Palestine, and even demand a legal self-defense organization proved badly mistaken. So, too, did his public statement one month before the Congress convened that a big "Judenstaat front" might be created, including Revisionists, and that "no blood-libel attempts will be permitted, of course."[62]

Weizmann, who equated Revisionism's anti-Labor middle-class economics as "nothing but Fascism," privately hailed Labor's signal success at the polls. A far greater fear, however, seized his imagination: "I cannot but feel that the mere fact that suspicion (if it is no more than suspicion) has fallen on Jews is a terrible and humiliating sign of the depths to which political controversy has sunk in our midst today." The architect of the Balfour Declaration concluded that he would not attend the Zionist gathering, since the Revisionists had not been excluded, and he expected "no good to come of it." His suspicions and those of Revisionism's staunchest enemies received apparent confirmation with a wave of arrests on July 23, three days after the judicial inquiry into Arlosoroff's death began. Primarily on the testimony of a young woman who had recently deserted Betar, Rivka Feigin, the police rounded up Ahimeir (in whose Tel Aviv apartment Stavsky had been arrested), more than thirty Betar members, and a few prominent Revisionist Party spokesmen. All but two were released within a month. Ahimeir, whose Brit HaBiryonim came under police investigation as of August 8, would be charged on August 24 with advising and inciting the crime. Five days later, Sima identified Zvi Rosenblatt, one of the Betar youngsters behind bars, as the killer.[63]

Jabotinsky responded quickly to the mass arrests. He cabled an S.O.S. to British member of Parliament Josiah Wedgwood about the "wicked crusade" being conducted against the Revisionists. Particularly galling was the Agency Executive's hiring of the top four Jewish lawyers in Palestine to represent Sima Arlosoroff. (One, Bernard Joseph, would maintain close contact with Bekhor Shitreet, head of the mandatory's police investigation.) Convinced that Ahimeir and all the others arrested, like Stavsky, had no connection to the murder, whose origins he claimed lay at the door of past Arab terrorism, Jabotinsky worked strenuously to raise the necessary funds to hire the London barrister and former Jewish Legion colleague Horace B. Samuel. He also wrote a slew of articles in *Moment* casting grave doubts regarding the police's inquiry, beginning with the assertion that Stavsky had quietly departed a Jerusalem hotel for Tel Aviv sometime after 8:30 p.m., killed Arlosoroff two hours later, and again slipped unnoticed into his bed early the next morning. An Arab tracker's later evaluation of Stavsky's alleged shoe prints in the sand, he observed, also appeared highly inconclusive.[64]

Unbeknownst to the Revisionists, the Labor Party chieftains had commenced their own inquiry, augmenting the official investigation. Behind this silent effort, spearheaded by Shaul Meirov (later Avigur), Eliyahu Golomb, and Dov Hos of the Hagana military command, lay an unshakable article of faith: Stavsky and his comrades were guilty. They aided the police in coaching Sima to identify Stavsky and Rosenblatt, refusing to accept the early conclusion of Avraham Tehomi (the former Hagana commander in Jerusalem who had created the secessionist Hagana Bet in 1931) that Stavsky was innocent, and that no connection existed between the murder and Jabotinsky's adherents. They communicated regularly with two Jewish police officers attached to the case, Captain Shitreet and Inspector Yehuda Tenenbaum (later Arazi), as did the Jewish Agency with C.I.D. head Rice. No one in Mapai dared to question the guilt of the accused; party member Dov Sadan (formerly Stock) confessed only years later in a private letter that he was not called to testify for the defense about Ahimeir's actual presence in Jerusalem the night of the murder because "some quick hand intervened." A few non-Revisionist voices tried to stem the tide, including Ravnitski, Druyanov, and essayist Moshe Carmon, to little avail.[65]

Notwithstanding the decision by Shitreet, the Hagana's investigative committee, and Katznelson not to rely on the highly suspect revelations of prime witness Feigin, Mapai was convinced that documents taken by Shitreet from Ahimeir's desk and shared with the committee proved the presence of a Jewish terrorist band in Palestine. Taking their case to the WZO's Va'ad HaPo'el (Executive Committee) prior to the opening of the Congress, Ben-Gurion, Katznelson, and other Mapai loyalists focused on stigmatizing the Revisionists as affording protection to terrorist groups within the movement. Jabotinsky lieutenant Joseph Schechtman deplored the use of unfounded gossip and quotation out of context, a proposed inquiry meant to divert the Congress from external politics and dangers facing Jewry. Mizrachi's Meir Berlin (later

Bar-Ilan) expressed hesitation about an inquest, as did General Zionists Yitzhak Schwartzbart and Yehoshua Suprasky. A commission of six, after reviewing a file of "evidence" provided by Golomb to Katznelson, concluded that a tribunal should examine the definite existence of a terrorist group within the yishuv. The laborites present also claimed that Revisionists could not join the Congress presidium. Two lawyers disagreed with the council's decision (U.S. delegate Wise privately dubbed it "lynch judgment"), warning against pronouncing judgment on a matter which was *sub judice*, but Mapai's unyielding stance won the day. The eighteenth World Zionist Congress would now open on August 21 in Prague, Arlosoroff's murder hovering over all.[66]

This gathering, where the Revisionists (to cite Jabotinsky's apt recollection) were "pilloried as organically connected" with Arlosoroff's assassination, signaled Labor's decisive triumph. While Katznelson appealed for "cleansing the camp" of blood, Labor's resolution that "the Party in which people who are being officially suspected of organizing the murder of one of our comrades grew up" should not sit on the presidium passed by a majority of two. By a vote of 197-62, the General Council was instructed to appoint a commission that would investigate "tendencies" that ran counter to "the fundamental principles of Jewish ethics" and endangered Zionism, having the authority to "eradicate" from the movement any "elements" responsible. This innuendo, coupled with rumors (quickly proven false) that Ahimeir had confessed to the crime, ruled out Jabotinsky's request that the Congress objectively investigate the alarming rise of party and class warfare in Palestine. Defeated, he sent a "triple Tel Hai" Betar salute to "innocent brothers" in prison, Ahimeir, Stavsky, and Rosenblatt. Weizmann refused to attend the Congress, he told a Labor delegation, because he did not wish to "sit with killers"; Sokolow was re-elected president, with Ben-Gurion, Kaplan, Gruenbaum and Shertok, who assumed Arlosoroff's post, joining the Executive for the first time.[67]

No free discussion of the German-Jewish crisis took place. Jabotinsky only ventured to say that world Jewry had to "react with all means of just defense ... against this attempt to destroy the Jewish people." For the first time in Zionist history, among the forty-six countries represented there were no delegates from Germany. Ruppin called for the emigration of 200,000 German Jews during the next five to ten years, Palestine to receive between 25 to 50 percent of the total. In a relatively mild censure, the Congress resolutions (the Revisionists alone abstaining) acknowledged that "not the 600,000 Jews of Germany alone, but the very existence of the Jewish people has been endangered and its honour attacked." "Real and lasting salvation for German Jewry" rested in "a great effort to settle large numbers" in Palestine, "where they will bring their possessions, their culture, and their ability in order to enrich the land and the nation." The delegates appointed the London-based Weizmann to head a Central Bureau for this purpose, "in unison with the Executive." Given the troubled relations between Weizmann and the majority of the Executive, Ruppin was to direct a parallel, autonomous "German Department" of the Jewish Agency in Jerusalem. That department would also create an Office for Youth Aliya under Henrietta Szold's direction.[68]

The Congress's emphasis on emigration ruled out a boycott of the German economy. In addition to strong support in Poland from Jabotinsky's disciples and the masses, East European-born Jews had spontaneously rallied to calls from Lord Melchett in England, the pro-Zionist American lawyer Samuel Untermyer, and the U.S. Jewish War Veterans to respond to the Nazi *Judenpolitik* by means of economic pressure. Understandably, yishuv leaders sympathized with this appeal, but they had received early warnings from Kurt Blumenfeld and other German Zionist spokesmen about its endangering the Jewish community there. Hearing similar concerns and calls for emigration expressed by Chief Rabbi Leo Baeck, banker Max Warburg (Felix's older brother), and Wilfrid Israel of the Central Bureau of Relief and Reconstruction, the Anglo-American Jewish establishment, centered in the American Jewish Committee, B'nai Brith, the Board of Deputies of British Jews, and the Anglo-Jewish Association, favored "quiet diplomacy" and opposed an organized boycott campaign. The American Jewish Congress, usually supportive of public protest and demonstrations, vacillated. Finally, pressed by the American Jewish Congress's Administrative Committee in mid-August, Wise came out in support of the boycott while attending the opening in Prague of the International Executive for a projected World Jewish Congress.[69]

Shertok, like his late mentor Arlosoroff, insisted that a political movement, which "cannot act according to feelings only," had to back a transfer of the emigrants' capital. "Building the country is our war with Germany," he told the Histadrut Executive Committee, "and this should be our focus." Most of the Agency Executive agreed, but, given the controversial dilemma that Jewish circles faced in boycotting Jewish goods, they took what Yoav Gelber has characterized as a "passive" and limited role in the negotiations leading to the Transfer Agreement. Initially, with the Executive's approval, Sam Cohen, a businessman working on behalf of the Zionist Federation in Germany and the Association of German Immigrants in Palestine, had pursued talks with Third Reich officials whereby the privately owned HaNoteah Company in Palestine could import building materials, pipes, and agricultural machinery in exchange for money in blocked Reichsmark accounts. The Anglo-Palestine Corporation Bank, under director Sigmund Hoofien, was to be the trustee representing the interests of German Jews who wished to transfer their assets to Palestine via deposit in these accounts. Ultimately, Hoofien obtained the approval of the two big Jewish banks in Germany to set up a trust company there, which enabled Ruppin to help arrange for every emigrant to bring £1,000 in bills of exchange and 20,000 Marks' worth of goods, with the possibility of more. On August 28, the German Foreign Office, Ministry of Economics, and the Reichsbank signed a contract for transfer with Hoofien and the German Zionist Federation.[70]

His Majesty's Government remained wary. Weizmann viewed strengthening the yishuv population to 400,000 as the "Archimedes point on which you can apply a lever to lift the weight of the problem which is likely to crush us all!" On a related note, Lord Lugard and Otto Van Rees of the League of Nations' Permanent Mandates Commission championed Jewish settlement in Transjordan. Expressing reservation, however, Palestine Chief Secretary M. A. Young noted security issues, and added that a great part of Transjordan's 43,000 square kilometers was desert. Wauchope objected to any resettlement of Palestinian Arabs there, reminding Cunliffe-Lister of the strong reaction of the Wadi Harawith Arabs against the mandatory's offer of suitable land in the Beisan and Jenin sub-districts. Mandatory officials thought the illegal Jewish immigrants in Palestine a "very serious" issue, closing their eyes at the same time to the unchecked infiltration from Transjordan and the northern border, particularly Syria's Hauran region, of countless hundreds of Arabs who, as Young publicly conceded, "did not require passports."[71]

Other examples of Great Britain's inclination abounded. A projected

Government loan of £2 million earmarked a sizeable portion for Arab cultivators allegedly "displaced" by Jewish purchases of land, although even the two French Reports commissioned by HMG concluded that the number, as noted in the London *Times*, was "inconsiderable." This favoring of Arab cultivators, moreover, came at a time when Jewish contribution to the country's revenue (then at a great surplus) reached almost 40 percent. Preoccupied with the delicate state of Anglo-German relations, Sir Robert Vansittart, Permanent Undersecretary at the Foreign Office, advised Laski and Bentwich that successful political action to aid Germany's Jews was hopeless, since Hitler was "completely fixed" in his antisemitic ideas. For the reluctant Colonial Office, any British initiative with the League on the refugees' behalf would imply a willingness to help, such as supporting a considerable immigration to Palestine.[72] The summer closed on a somber note for Zionist aspirations.

Come September, reports of visitors to Hitler's Germany indicated only darkest night for the Jews. Without doubt, McDonald informed the Joint Foreign Committee, the Nazis regarded the Jews "as vermin, as bacilli which poisoned the life blood of Germany, as an element which must be destroyed and crushed by being prevented from taking any part in the political, economic or cultural life of the State." Shocked that even "fine people" in the Third Reich felt little real horror over the outrages against Jews, publisher Henry Haskell of the *Kansas City Star* felt that "Germany is lost to western civilization for the present." After a private meeting with Hitler, the illustrious American professor of German literature John Firman Coar informed U.S. Ambassador William E. Dodd that Hitler "talked wildly about destroying all Jews," and that "Germany was showing the world how to rid itself of its greatest curse." Göring, Wise informed Brandeis, had told a Berlin friend that "we will not consider *Regelung der Judenfrage* [settlement of the Jewish question] until two or three hundred thousand Jews are out." In a long letter to New York Governor Herbert Lehman, Jacob Billikopf, executive director of the Jewish Federation of Charities, wrote of "Aryans" telling him about 260 Jewish men in Nuremberg who were forced on July 19 to clear a plot of ground by pulling up the grass with their teeth; of the expropriation of Jewish property and many Jews sent to concentration camps; of statues of prominent Jews now removed from parks; of the idolization of Hitler; and of the "complete unanimity" of opinion regarding the one item in the Nazi program that was being "sadistically pursued" as "a sacred dogma": "Jewry must be destroyed!"[73]

Lehman brought Billikopf's letter to a private meeting with Roosevelt on September 14. Upon appointing Dodd, FDR had confided to the University of Chicago professor of American history that while the German authorities were treating the Jews "shamefully" and American Jewry "are greatly excited," the government could only intervene for U.S. citizens "who happen to be made victims." Whatever could be done to "moderate the general prosecution" by unofficial and personal influence "ought to be done," he added. Now, accompanied by Secretary of the Treasury Henry Morgenthau, Jr., Lehman asked for a presidential statement that acknowledged the "tragic conditions" of the Jews. Roosevelt countered that "denial of human rights" would be preferable, as it could not provoke Berlin's reply that this was an interference in internal affairs. Lehman found the alternative wording "perfectly agreeable," and immediately had Frankfurter advised of his sense that "the Chief" was sympathetic and would act, though "when is uncertain." Roosevelt soon told Lehman that he sent the "intensely interesting" Billikopf letter to Hull and Phillips. The office of Western European Affairs Division chief Jay Pierrepont Moffat had just drawn up "a cagey reply" to the Jewish Telegraphic Agency (JTA)'s request for a message from Hull for the Jewish New Year, expressing sympathy "without intervening in any way in German affairs." Four days after hearing Coar report directly to him, Moffat got word to McDonald that "it seemed extremely difficult to know how we could do anything" about the League's possible intention of recreating the post of High Commissioner for Refugees to aid the persecuted Jews.[74]

Fully aware of German Jewry's travail, and greatly concerned about a shortage of workers in Palestine, Shertok and Ben-Zvi submitted an official request on September 13 for 24,500 labor certificates in the next immigration schedule. The figure was "so much in excess" of what both Wauchope and Hyamson had contemplated, the High Commisioner responded, that a discussion of the matter would take some time; a decision would therefore have to be postponed until he returned in mid-October from London and holiday. While prepared to offer an advance of 1,000 certificates, Wauchope cautioned that the final decision had to look farther ahead than the next six months while also considering the German-Jewish situation. Ben-Zvi pointed out that Jewish distress in some other countries was reaching much the same proportions as that in Germany; in Salonica, Jews were driven out of their traditional stronghold of work, and refugees from Bukhara were stranded in Afghanistan. Their detailed memorandum, Shertok noted, did not include the industrial works to be carried out with the proceeds of the British campaign headed by Weizmann for German Jewry, for which an allocation of £50,000 had been made, or the Jewish share among the 500 laborers needed for the works of the Iraq Petroleum Company.[75]

Shertok quickly relayed a report to Agency Executive member Selig Brodetsky in London, adding that the labor shortage "is assuming well nigh catastrophic proportions," at least from "our national point of view." Arab labor, he explained, was making inroads in zones of Jewish settlement and increasing in building projects executed by Jews, while a growing number of contracts were not being put in hand solely because of the lack of Jewish laborers. The 1,000 advance would not solve the problem, especially as the yishuv was expected to face a "serious gap" of workers in November and December. The whole issue should be raised in the Colonial Office, he suggested, in the hope that if a "desired psychological effect" was produced, it would be reflected in its correspondence with Wauchope, and perhaps achieve some positive results.[76]

The increasing momentum of Jewish entry into Palestine, about 20,000 in the last eight months, began seriously to alarm Arab leaders. Ben-Zvi protested to the Chief Secretary about a series of virulent articles for several weeks in the Arab press opposing Jewish immigration and threatening the Jews. Rutenberg privately worried about "the eastern imagination of simple-minded human beings, overheated, agitated by endless reports of great speeches, of great Jews, about their ambitious intentions, of the great invasion of all the German Jews into Palestine and Transjordan. Fear and rage, accumulated under high pressure of political agitation and daily suffering. Who knows what it will result in?" A C.I.D. report observed that the activities of the Arab Young Men's movement in Iraq and Syria were spreading in Palestine. Szold noticed the growing restiveness in all circles of the Arab population, seeing youth organizations arranging meetings and adopting resolutions, with their elders doing the same "with even more éclat." Defending two Arab men, part of a terrorist gang, who were sentenced to death for the murder of a farmer and one of his children in Nahalal the previous December, their counsel pleaded for mercy on the ground that the crime occurred because of the mandatory's "reprehensible" Balfour Declaration policy. On October 8, the Arab Executive called for demonstrations in different towns on alternative Fridays against Jewish immigration. Chief Secretary J. Hawthorn Hall, the Officer Administering the Government (O.A.G.) in Wauchope's absence, forbade an announced procession of the Supreme Muslim Council in Jerusalem for five days hence, and suggested to Musa Kazim that a statement of their grievances be transmitted instead to the League of Nations.[77]

The Arab Executive decided to adhere to its plan. A crowd of thousands, headed by Kazim, assembled in the Haram and, after the midday Friday prayer on October 13, moved to the Church of the Holy Sepulchre in token of Muslim-Christian solidarity. They then proceeded through the streets of Jerusalem's Old City, in defiance of the government order. A scuffle broke out between the assembled and the police, leaving 11, including 5 policemen, injured. For the first time, noted the C.I.D., the Arab criticism was directed against the British authorities in Palestine; placards against Zionism were not conspicuous. The executive of the Arab Youth Congress (formed in December 1932) passed a resolution that Arabs should write to the Arab kings pointing out the danger to Palestine and the Holy Places, and demonstrate throughout the Arab world; moderate opinion in the Arab Executive was forced to accept this view. The marchers believed that HMG would only yield to force, the report concluded, and that riots were the only means of ridding themselves of foreign rule. A similar demonstration was called for in Jaffa on October 26.[78]

The Jaffa protest, with others in Jerusalem, Haifa, Beersheba, Lydda, Gaza, and Nablus, exacted a far fiercer toll. Wauchope warned the Arab Executive on October 25 that he would order force against any demonstrators, then noted that the administration was reducing illicit Jewish immigration and that Palestine's economic absorptive capacity would continue to regulate legal entry. The Executive, having assured the Arab public that the processions would be peaceful, went forward nonetheless two days later. Activists of the Youth Congress threw paving stones and brandished sticks when blocked from reaching the district commissioner's office, and the police, after an initial baton charge, fired on the crowds. Official casualty figures showed 1 policeman and 24 Arabs were killed or died of wounds, with 28 policemen and 205 civilians wounded. "The entire world will know," wrote the renowned Palestinian Arab educator Khalil al-Sakakini in his diary, "that the Arab nation is not easy prey." The next day, a mass meeting was held in the Omayyad Mosque in Damascus, and the French authorities made a large number of arrests. Wauchope assumed emergency powers. The inauguration of Haifa harbor on October 31 took place behind barbed wire entanglements under heavy guard with the briefest of ceremonies.

A general Arab strike continued from October 29 to November 3, during which time Wauchope ordered a censorship of the Arab press because of untrue statements of excessive police brutality which were likely to "mislead people in a dangerous way and in a dangerous direction." A British report, based on closed hearings, exonerated the Palestine police from having acted without restraint, pointing out that the proximity of Jewish settlements to the scenes of disturbances laid a heavy responsibility on the police, whose duty it was to prevent development of race riots. Thanks to Wauchope's earlier securing the goodwill of the villagers by rescinding the heavy agricultural tax which had been imposed upon them by the Turkish rulers, the 100,000 fellahin (rural peasants) were not drawn into the struggle. Arab leaders still pressed for the right to hold peaceful demonstrations, which, to the Jewish Agency's astonishment, Wauchope eventually granted.[79]

All the while, the widening political divide within the yishuv over Arlosoroff's murder grew. Undeterred by the World Zionist Congress resolutions, Ben-Zion Katz pursued his own crusade for truth, increasingly convinced that the Revisionists accused were innocent. A week before the Congress convened, two of his articles along these lines, previously published in *Moment*, had seen print in Palestine under the title *Lo Ukhal L'Hahashot* (I Cannot Be Silent). No legal charges followed, and the pamphlet gained wide circulation. At the summer's end, Bialik, who believed that Jabotinsky's downfall at the Congress offered the reform of Zionism, expressed to Katz his "100 percent certainty" that Jews did not kill Arlosoroff. Confidentially, the poet added that a Hebrew school principal was told by Captain Alfred Riggs of the C.I.D. that the entire police investigation was "a bluff": the killing was a haphazard incident, not a political assassination. Unknown to Katz and Bialik, Inspector Tenenbaum resigned at that same moment from the police force after Rice refused to accept his conclusion that the three Revisionists had no connection with the murder. Tenenbaum's secret report failed to sway Hagana officials Meirov, Hos, and Golomb; Golomb quickly challenged Katz in *Davar*. That did not stop Mizrachi's Sirkis from accusing Labor of mounting a "blood libel," recalling what had occurred against Alfred Dreyfus and Sacco-Vanzetti, and instigating civil war at the Congress. Druyanov's articles continued in a similar vein, earning Professor Klausner's private commendation.[80]

A simultaneous police investigation of Ahimeir and twenty others for illegal activity via the Brit HaBiryonim provided grist for Labor's mill. Shitreet, relying mainly on Tenenbaum, made public a few papers seized from Ahimeir's desk which suggested a secret Revisionist underground bent on terrorism. *Davar* and *HaAretz* highlighted Ahimeir's essay "Megilat HaSikrikin" (The Sicarii), dedicated to the memory of Charlotte Corday and Dora Kaplan, as the proof text for his sanctioning murder on behalf of "communal objectives" that dramatically alter the course of history. Defenders replied that the draft consisted of private philosophical musings composed in 1926, including Ahimeir's having judged this phenomenon "a very dangerous disease," and that Brit HaBiryonim's public activities never embraced murder. Hardly persuaded, Labor publications noted excerpts from Ahimeir's diary for 1931 that spoke, for example, of "the amount of blood spilt as the measure of a great revolution or war," dismissing Ahimeir's entry of June 6, 1933, which described how he declined the plea of young followers to form "a secret revolutionary organization" because he wished to retire to a life of "cabinet quietness." On October 3, Ahimeir and six of his comrades were charged with belonging to an illegal group and inciting rebellion.[81]

Jabotinsky remained steadfast, doing all in his power to strengthen the defense and his party's ranks. During the Zionist Congress, he had derided the rumors about Ahimeir's confession as a leftist provocation, and later publicly called its intervention in a matter *sub judice* "a crime." He obtained the necessary funds to hire lawyer Samuel, to whom he subsequently sent detailed memoranda about numerous flaws in the prosecution's case. Supportive articles by Katz, Ravnitski, Druyanov, and Farmers' Federation head Smilansky, the latter having heard from Tenenbaum and another police officer that the three accused were innocent, bolstered his hopes. Immediately after the Congress debacle, which included the departure of the moderate wing (to be called the Jewish State Party) from his own ranks, Jabotinsky declared that one million

Jews had to be brought to Palestine without delay. The Revisionist Union, its new executive announced on October 18, would launch a worldwide petition movement and unite Jewry in a campaign against the Third Reich. The following week, Betar issued a secret "Directive No. 60" against accepting its share from the paltry mandatory six-month allotment of 5,500 Palestine certificates even while negotiating with private employers outside of the labor schedule. The WZO, in turn, denounced these independent steps as breaches of Zionist discipline.[82]

Yet for all the internal strife threatening the yishuv's stability, it was far outweighed by unmistakable signs of rising Arab militancy. Ruppin could only see a solution for the future in giving the Jews autonomy in the valleys, with the same accorded to the Arabs in the hills and the lower Jordan Valley. Not so easily dealt with were hundreds of hostile Bedouin protestors outside Tulkarm, who were dispersed by a squadron of British airplanes at noon flying very low. Nor Arab leaders arrested for the October demonstrations like Husseini, who, upon his November 5 release from Acre prison on bail with Istiqlalist Abd al-Hadi and Yaqub al-Ghusayn of the Arab Youth Congress, exhorted the Arab people to observe a strict boycott of the Jews and engage in strong action against land sales to them. Those who did not would be considered traitors, editorialized the pro-Mufti newspaper *al-Jamia al-Arabiya*, a daily which disseminated the virulent antisemitic *Protocols of the Learned Elders of Zion*; *Falastin*, a newspaper close to the Nashashibi clan, urged the Arab press to begin a spirited boycott campaign in this regard.[83]

Foreign correspondents took notice as well. German newspapers published (exaggerated) stories of street battles of Arab vs. Jew in Tel Aviv. Moscow official daily *Izvestia* applauded the Arab proletariat masses—unlike the landowning bloc of the Arab Executive Committee—for actively opposing "British imperialism" and the "Jewish Zionist bourgeoisie." (Several Communists were arrested by the mandatory authorities, and widely distributed party pamphlets in Yiddish and Arabic called on the fellahin, the Bedouin, and the "national revolutionaries" to struggle for freedom.) The London *Times* noted the influence of the late King Feisal, who had died prematurely in September, and the progress toward independence in Iraq, when a massacre by the army in August of some 3,000 Assyrian Christians served as proof to Palestinian Arabs that Baghdad had really shaken off British control. Increasing Jewish immigration, the *Times* added on November 6, also contributed to "a paroxysm of exasperation" against British rule.[84]

One week later, Haj Amin called on the British Ambassador to Iraq. After telling of his journey through India to Kabul, and from Quetta to Meshed (in Khorasan) and thence back to Baghdad via Tehran, the Mufti expressed his appreciation for all the help given him by British representatives, as well as his deepest regret at the assassination of King Nadir Shah of Afghanistan, whom he held in "high esteem." He "deplored" the recent disorders which had occurred in Palestine, leading Sir Francis Humphrys to rejoin that if the Arabs put forward their case in "an orderly and constitutional manner," Wauchope would give them an "attentive hearing." Rioting would put them seriously in the wrong, however, and alienate much of the sympathy and friendly feeling the British people felt for them. The Mufti replied that he did not doubt the desire of Wauchope and the British people to see that justice was done to Palestine's Arabs, but the Jews were "everywhere rich and powerful, while the Arabs were poor and had no means of organizing propaganda in support of their case." For example, Dr. Weizmann and the Zionists had induced HMG to reject the recommendation of the Shaw Commission and subsequent Hope-Simpson Report (the basis of the Passfield White Paper) to curtail Jewish immigration; at the present rate they would soon become the majority and reduce the Arabs status to that of "a helot minority." Humphrys urged his visitor to have "complete confidence" in Wauchope, who had recently stressed in a Haifa speech Britain's determination to "protest and foster" Arab interests equally with that of the Jews. Haj Amin took his leave, repeating his intention to use his influence to prevent any recurrence of the recent rioting.[85]

The radicalization of Palestine's Arabs made its mark on Wauchope, as the Jewish Agency soon discovered. Despite Shertok's reiterating the reasons for a large labor certificate schedule and Ben-Gurion's warning that large masses of Polish Jewry were living "on the brink of starvation," the High Commissioner focused on Arab unemployment and particularly on the Jewish illegals in Palestine. His Executive Council drew up measures to constrict this entry, Wauchope subsequently informing Shertok that the question of immigration could not be satisfactorily dealt with until their numbers had been "very greatly reduced." Rather than the requested 24,500 certificates, he approved 5,500, which came as "a severe disappointment" to the Agency. Palestine was our last and only hope," Ben-Gurion stressed to Wauchope on October 20: "The future of our people depended on its success, and here the factor of time was fateful," for "if a political catastrophe were to break out in Europe, the storm would not pass over this country."[86]

Wauchope and the Agency leadership were rapidly nearing an impasse. The High Commissioner stood his ground on the 5,500 certificates, and even considered sending to Cyprus two boats that had just arrived with 1,882 immigrants and tourists. Eventually he approved their de-embarkation in Haifa port, but without a guarantee for their safety against protesting Arabs. The Hagana successfully carried out this task, as it did the transfer of eight containers of weapons that had been shipped from Belgium and Italy under the label "machinery parts." For Ben-Gurion, Germany represented only "the prelude," since he viewed the Jewish communities of Eastern Europe, confronted by economic privation and growing antisemitism, to be "without hope." Before long, he advised Weizmann, the yishuv could absorb at least 100,000 Jews annually. In light of Jewry's present condition, "aliya" (immigration to Palestine) was the central political question in Zionism today, Ben-Gurion concluded.[87]

British caution had also manifested itself during a discussion in early October at the League, when the Assembly's Sixth Committee addressed the issue of mandates. Christian L. Lange welcomed the "exceptional prosperity" prevailing in Palestine, "doubtless due to in large measure" to Jewish immigration and the influx of capital, which also benefited the Arab population. The problem of the thousands of Jewish refugees in Germany, the Norwegian delegate remarked, might "to a large extent" find its solution in their establishment in Palestine. Observing that 25,000-30,000 Jews coming to Palestine this year might furnish a partial solution of the German-Jewish refugee problem, Poland's Edouard Raczynski hoped that the mandatory power would "do the utmost to facilitate Jewish immigration so far as was compatible with the capacity of the country to absorb the immigrants." William G. A. Ormsby-Gore, responding for the United Kingdom, agreed that Palestine's favorable economic condition was largely due to the efforts and capital of the Jewish immigrants, whose entry of 15,305 in the first six months of 1933 represented a tripling of the number which had arrived in the same period for 1932. At the same time, the machinery whereby "equilibrium was assured" in the matter of Jewish immigration should not be changed. Moreover, the mandatory could not "arrest" the immigration of Jews from other countries. Palestine was a small country, Ormsby-Gore emphasized, and could not furnish the "entire and unique solution" of the problems at issue. Finally, it was important "not to disturb the relations between the Jews and the non-Jewish population in Palestine, which were constantly improving [sic]."[88]

This attitude also manifested itself in regard to the League's High Commissioner for Refugees (Jewish and other) Coming from Germany, a newly designated title which James McDonald assumed on October 27. Foreign Secretary Simon had informed Ormsby-Gore at the beginning of October that HMG would not accept any exceptions made by the League to the principle that Palestine's economic absorptive capacity determined immigration there, nor would London bear any expenses tied to activities to solve the German refugee problem. (Ormsby-Gore did join Czechoslovakia's Edouard Beneš and numerous other delegates in vigorously attacking Third Reich delegate Friedrich von Keller's statement that the Jews were not a minority in Germany, and paid tribute to the services rendered in the different countries, such as Benjamin Disraeli in England, by "persons of Hebrew origin.") Simon later repeated these instructions to Cecil, who was appointed the British representative to the High Commissioner's Governing Body, adding that there would generally be "very little scope for immigration of persons of a white race" into the majority of Great Britain's colonial empire. In Simon's view, the mandate had already, "with many difficulties," developed a means for effecting Jewish immigration through the Jewish Agency, and placing Palestine within McDonald's purview "would enormously complicate an already complicated situation." The energetic American expressed "annoyance" at this exclusion, reported Bentwich, his choice for assistant. McDonald insisted on his right to submit to London demands for admitting German Jewish refugees under a separate and distinct quota, to no avail.[89]

The mandatory tightened the screws further on immigration. It introduced new measures on November 2, the 16th anniversary of the Balfour Declaration, of deporting Jews and Arabs in individual cases who had entered Palestine illegally and of expelling all unauthorized immigrants who entered after that date. As Hall put it to Shertok and Agency Executive member Werner Senator, the mandatory sought to "deter newcomers of this category from staying on indefinitely." Since

Wauchope definitely intended not to give the Agency any more certificates for the current six-month schedule, Hall suggested that the Agency spread the distribution over a longer period than a mere month or so. This decision was "a calamity," answered Shertok, since it arrested the growth of the Jewish National Home. The government opposed speeding up Jewish immigration, Hall retorted; a "setback" might occur, since the general atmosphere was still tense and people might be deterred by rioting from making new capital investment, even as rents were "shooting up to quite inordinate heights."[90]

From London, Agency Executive secretary Arthur Lourie warned Shertok that the recent Arab disturbances, and especially the publicity given to them, had been "vastly more successful" than past riots in strengthening the Government's hands as regards Jewish immigration. On November 10 Wauchope informed Ben-Gurion and Shertok that there would be no supplementary schedule within the present half year; if Jews needed workers, they should employ Arabs. It was the "essence" of Zionism, Ben-Gurion responded, that they could build up a strong community "capable of a healthy existence" only by employing Jews to the "maximum extent possible." Rejecting Ben-Gurion's contention that the High Commissioner's decisions were actuated by political motives, Wauchope insisted that what he decided was always the result of careful consideration free from both Arab and Jewish pressures.[91]

Wauchope's response when meeting with six Arab mayors three days later, soon published as an official communiqué, reflected the changing stance. Ragheb Nashashibi of Jerusalem declared that the riots were inevitable, and he called for preventing Jewish immigration, a representative government, and more Arab employment. Nablus's Suleiman Tukan expressed Arab fears that Jewish progress in Palestine would lead to their "banishment or enslavement." British promises to the Jews had been fulfilled, argued Hassan Shukri of Haifa. In reply, Wauchope agreed that the Arabs had "a legitimate grievance" against unauthorized immigration, and he listed the mandatory's new measures to check this phenomenon. The delegation was informed that he had also deducted 1,000 certificates from the last schedule on the supposition that so many Jewish tourists would in all probability remain in Palestine without authorization. Recognizing the fact of Arab unemployment, Wauchope announced that he would appoint an investigative committee to clarify the situation. Certain that Palestine's citizens would have "complete faith in the main defender," Nashashibi ended by asking Wauchope not to permit "the people of the disturbances" to rule in Palestine, and he pledged that the mayors would not hamper the administration's work.[92]

Ben-Gurion, Shertok, and Ben-Zvi immediately protested Wauchope's statement, which Ben-Gurion deemed "a very severe shock for our people." The Agency intended to issue a rejoinder, he informed Wauchope during their interview of November 15, saying that it regarded his communiqué as "a radical departure" from McDonald's letter in February 1931 to Weizmann. The latter document had recognized the Agency's right to employ Jewish labor on Jewish works; said that Arab unemployment was not a factor in assessing immigration for the needs of Jewish capital and for the share due the Agency on Government works; and declared that temporary employment was to serve as a basis for immigration. Wauchope countered that he was not stopping immigration, but the administration was facing great difficulties and "had to proceed with caution." The difference between them was that while Ben-Gurion wanted to go "too fast," Wauchope wanted to proceed "more slowly." Ben-Gurion responded: "We did not mean to go too fast, but only as fast as possible. We wanted immigration to proceed to the fullest possible extent of the country's absorptive capacity." Jewish entry into Palestine, he stressed, was "the hinge upon which the destiny of our people turned." Although scores of Jews had been murdered by Arab rioters four years ago, that had not frightened the yishuv; it was prepared for sacrifices. The Zionists, Ben-Gurion added, had not injured Arabs or taken employment away from them. The same day, the Jerusalem Executive's own statement concluded that the "artificial curtailment" of Jewish immigration into Palestine, "the very blood of the Jewish National Home," was a matter "in which the Jewish people will not acquiesce."[93]

Privately, Weizmann viewed the restrictions as "a temporary unpleasantness and annoyance," but a far greater concern occupied his thoughts. Writing to Warburg on November 20, he noted that, in spite of everything, from 35,000 to 40,000 Jews would enter Palestine this year, a "colossal" immigration. The Balfour Declaration still stayed "at the foundation of every house, at the root of every new tree, and on the visa of every new immigrant." At the same time, Weizmann concluded on a very bleak note:

The world is gradually, relentlessly, and effectively being

closed to the Jews, and every day I feel more and more that a ring of steel is being forged round us, every one of us, and unless we hurry up to make out of Palestine and some of the surrounding neighborhood a powerful Jewish centre, I would advise every Jew not to marry and not to increase the race [*sic!*]. It is all inescapable, and every ounce of my energy—whatever it may mean—is going towards the consummation of that end. Everything else is a palliative, a half-measure, and merely postponing the evil day—a short respite.[94]

He took up the cudgels when talking to Cunliffe-Lister four days later, beginning their brief conversation by noting the "ugly situation" that was developing between the Agency and the High Commissioner. The regular police roundup of a few "illegal" settlers was keeping the yishuv "in a state of nervousness and ferment," and some general understanding had to be worked out on the subject, possibly tightening up the regulations for the future; deportation was "most undesirable." Cunliffe-Lister emphatically denied rumors of HMG establishing in practice a sort of *numerus clausus* for Jewish entry, and said that the government's policy remained unchanged. Weizmann noted Wauchope's response to a delegation headed by Ben-Zvi, published in the London *Times* the previous day, especially that "the hardship to which the Jews might be exposed in other countries was not a consideration which could be allowed to affect policy in Palestine." Everyone realized that Palestine was the one country in which the exiles "stood a reasonable chance of being permanently and satisfactorily absorbed," Weizmann argued, and Wauchope's statement was "calculated to paralyze our work." Cunliffe-Lister, who had once remarked that he felt himself fortunate in being able as Colonial Secretary to carry on the pro-Zionist tradition of his godfather, Lord Balfour, responded that he was quite sure this was not Wauchope's intention. The two men agreed to take up this and the question of Jewish settlement in Transjordan, especially as Arabs from Transjordan were infiltrating into Palestine, in their next meeting.[95]

On November 30, Ben-Gurion joined that important conversation, which took place after dinner in Weizmann's home at 16 Addison Crescent, in London's fashionable West Kensington district. Palestine today for Jews was not only an ideal, Weizmann led off, "but a vital necessity—life itself." The country could absorb 40,000-50,000 immigrants a year, presenting the real possibility that during the next four or five years Jews might become a community of some half a million— and then "all your troubles will be over." The Arabs would recognize the Jewish National Home as a fait accompli, he and Ben-Gurion explained, and cease their opposition to the Jews and to the mandatory government. Ben-Gurion pointed out that the great strides in Palestine's industry and agriculture justified the Agency's application for almost 25,000 certificates, especially "after the German collapse." Cunliffe-Lister worried about reverting to the economic crisis of 1926-1927 if the building trade boom proved temporary, but Ben-Gurion pointed to the great increase in the area of plantations and new industries since then. The two Zionist leaders questioned Wauchope's figure of 20,000 Arab unemployed, while Weizmann said that he could not ask American Jews during his next trip to give funds to have German Jews absorbed in Palestine by providing employment for thousands of Arabs in Jewish settlements.

Recalling his trip in April to Palestine, Cunliffe-Lister disclosed his impression at the time that "the Arabs would in future fight not against the Jews but against the Government." Imagine the outcry in England, he went on, if ten British officials in Palestine were killed by Arab rioters. The public and press would demand that HMG should "leave the whole thing alone." The "man in the street" had not the slightest interest in the implementing of the Balfour Declaration and MacDonald's letter to Weizmann. The Colonial Secretary then remarked ominously: The government had given "an enormous number of promises during the War; many of these contradictory, and very few of them are ever likely to be fulfilled." But Britain needed allies in Palestine, Weizmann replied, and we were "the most closely bound" to her in friendship. It was costing about £750,000 a year to maintain British troops in Palestine "to keep the Jews there," Cunliffe-Lister countered, and the Muslims in India, the only element on which Britain could really rely, opposed Zionism. Weizmann again mentioned that HMG had strategic interests in Palestine which had to be safeguarded, such as the Haifa harbor, the oil pipeline from Iraq and the airway ports, whether there was a Jewish National Home or not; the larger and more firmly rooted the Jewish population, the easier Great Britain's task there would be.

Two main conditions were needed for bringing permanent peace to

Palestine, Ben-Gurion declared: a big Jewish community together with economic cooperation and assistance for the fellahin and Arab workers. The hard conditions of Arab laborers were improving largely due to the yishuv's influence, he asserted. The fellahin had taken no part in the last troubles, and relations between the kibbutzim (agricultural settlements) and their Arab neighbors were, in general, excellent. Moreover, there was no assurance that Arabs employed by Jews would necessarily take no part in riots. Sir Philip reverted to his concern about future Arab attacks against the British, to which Weizmann replied that he had always been "very apprehensive" of such a contingency. To avoid it, he would "gladly" see the Jews take over the defense of the country for themselves. Cunliffe-Lister did not reply to this. Weizmann added that he could see little prospect of the permanent establishment of Jewish refugees outside Palestine, although, with French cooperation, something might be done in parts of the French mandated territory in Syria and Lebanon. Cunliffe-Lister said that he would like Weizmann to see former Prime Ministers Stanley Baldwin and David Lloyd George, and on that note the three-hour conversation ended.[96]

In Jerusalem, seeking to win back Arab confidence in Government and lay the foundation for "a permanent peace" in the future, Wauchope met with Haj Amin on the afternoon of December 5. Nothing but "a curative remedy which will go to the root of the evil" would improve conditions, the Mufti began. The situation was "dangerous," the prevalent Arab feeling one of "despair." The immediate remedy could be found within the Palestine Mandate, although this did not mean that he accepted it or that his views or those of the Arabs about their aspirations had changed. An economic survey of Palestine should determine if the Jewish National Home had reached the stage of completion, the crucial issue over which the Arabs and HMG had reached "a deadlock." Pending the announcement of the Royal Commission's recommendations, Jewish immigration and land transfer to the Jews should be stopped.

As to the recent bloodshed, the Mufti continued, all the Arab casualties should be looked on as innocent; even if guilty, a death penalty should not be inflicted on them. The administration had a duty to compensate their families and dependants, as it had done after the 1929 riots, a "just" action that would "remove the idea of revenge" from the minds of the Arabs and help to win over their confidence. The mandatory should also help the Arabs in reclaiming their lands, which were in danger of passing over to the Jews, reimbursing the Supreme Muslim Council between £100,000-£150,000 for having bought lands and given them to Arabs dispossessed because of Jewish purchases. Unless HMG took a definite move on these lines, he asserted, it would be difficult to visualize how far his efforts to work "hand in hand" with the British would be successful. Wauchope thanked Haj Amin for this "frank talk," said that he had already thought of establishing a statistical bureau to study the entire land issue, and added that he would consider the question of paying some form of compensation to families of Arab casualties. He hoped that the Council and the administration Treasurer, W. J. Johnson, would agree as soon as possible regarding the Waqf (the Muslim religious endowment) claims to certain tithes and arrears.[97]

In that same interview, Haj Amin also expressed Arab disillusionment with HMG's proposed Legislative Council. Ever since assuming office five years earlier, Wauchope had sought to create this institution for the country's inhabitants. The idea had first been proposed by Churchill in his July 1922 White Paper on Palestine, providing representation on a 5:1 ratio of Arabs to Jews, with Herbert Samuel, Palestine's first High Commissioner, acting as president and the British having a majority. (That White Paper had asserted that Jews were in Palestine "as of right," Jewish immigration would be subject to Palestine's economic capacity, and the Balfour Declaration was not "susceptible to change.") When the Arabs rejected the Council, as well as an appointed Advisory Council and an Arab Agency akin to the Jewish Agency in 1923, HMG vested legislative authority in the High Commissioner. During the summer of 1929, Chancellor attempted to revive the scheme, yet Arab riots in August and September and the unrest that ensued in their wake halted any possible implementation. The Jewish Agency consistently rejected the proposal, insisting on parity in representation, while the Palestine Arab Executive, Haj Amin, and Abd al-Hadi gave their reserved approval. The October 1933 demonstrations, however, spurred Haj Amin to advise Wauchope of finding a solution within the framework of the mandate.[98]

Musa Alami elaborated further on Haj Amin's proposal with a second one. These two proposals were undoubtedly coordinated, a conclusion corroborated by the fact that Alami was a brother-in-law, close friend, and a plantation-owning partner of Husseini's. Once the Colonial Secretary declared that the Jewish National Home had already been established, Alami's memorandum read, the government would establish an autonomous canton allowing for free Jewish immigration in the coastal plan from Athlit to a point south of Tel Aviv. This canton would be part of a Palestinian state under the guidance of the mandatory. A Legislative Council for the whole country would be formed with full legislative power, the High Commissioner retaining the right of veto as to immigration, land, Jewish culture, and Imperial defense. At the same time, Alami warned that Palestinian Arab youth preferred "open war," feeling that if only "slow death" could be expected from the current government policy, "it would be better to be killed in an effort to free us from our enemies."[99]

Neither Wauchope nor the Colonial Office fully endorsed these views, but the prospects of the Jewish National Home remained uncertain. On December 9, a prolonged clash between the police and Revisionist-Zionist youth in Tel Aviv against British measures to deport illegals left 18 (including police) injured, 5 seriously, and resulted in the arrests of 7 protesters. The Jewish Agency officially condemned the "shameful incident," asserting that violence could not be justified against policemen performing their duty. Aware that the cautious Wauchope sharply differed with him over the question of "pace" in light of Arab militancy, Ben-Gurion urged his colleagues to focus on doubling the yishuv's current population to 500,000 in the next 4-5 years, thereby (as Weizmann and Ben-Gurion had declared to Cunliffe-Lister) "solving the Arab question"; even Herbert Samuel, critical of the Agency's stance towards Palestine's majority population, accepted this assumption. On December 19, Wauchope encouraged Shertok to renew the option on Abdullah's lands, but warned "casually" that Jewish settlement in Transjordan would not be possible within the next five years. As for Pan-Arabism, French Consul-General d'Aumale agreed with Shertok that its "more extreme tendencies" had come to the fore after Feisal's death in September, reflecting hostility to the British, the French, and the Jews—"all people who wore hats instead of tarbushes."[100]

The crisis facing German Jewry left less room for doubt. James Gerard's review in the *New York Times* of the abridged edition of *Mein Kampf*, Hitler's manifesto published in the United States and Britain that autumn, noted that the main message was still clear: "It is with sadness, tinged with fear for the world's future, that we read Hitler's hymn of hate." Robert Dell, Geneva correspondent of the *Manchester Guardian*, concluded that the Third Reich's antisemitic action would go on "until the Jews have been entirely eliminated or reduced to a handful of beasts of burden." Weizmann heard from a German with contacts in "the most intimate" Nazi circles that, according to Goebbels, in four or five years there would be "only a few Jewish beggars left in Germany." Julius Streicher's Der *Stürmer*, whose masthead trumpeted "The Jews Are Our Misfortune," more blatantly declared that a vast plan was being formulated for their "final extermination." A confidential JTA evaluation reported that Jewish prisoners in the Brandenburg and Bavarian concentration camps were singled out for especially brutal treatment, and that many sealed coffins were being returned of Jewish prisoners who, after being seized from their homes by SA members, suddenly "committed suicide."[101]

"Nothing but foreign intervention will save the Jews in Germany," Dell concluded, but appeals to conscience for help from that quarter went wanting. At the first meeting of McDonald's Governing Body in Lausanne, Weizmann hailed the Zionists' successful endeavor in Palestine just when "a wave of anti-Semitism is sweeping over the world." Other than a brief reference in Cecil's closing address, however, no delegate from the 14 nations present dealt with Palestine, nor was any country prepared to provide "either room or money" for the refugees. One month earlier, Rabbi Baeck had sent McDonald an estimated budget of the German Jewish community's needs, kept as low as possible in the hope that those requirements would not grow—"a hope which, as far as it is possible to judge at the present moment, will not be fulfilled." Towards the end of December, McDonald released a statement putting the number of Reich refugees at 60,000, and pointing out that the number would likely continue to increase. Concurrently, HMG Ambassador to Rome Sir Eric Drummond advised Alberto Theodoli, President of the League's Permanent Mandates Commission, that Britain, while recognizing that there should be a Jewish National Home in Palestine, did not wish "to alienate the Arab element."[102]

Many hoped for a public word of support from the White House. When asked by ZOA president Rothenberg for advice about FDR's giving public expression that Palestine offered "the fullest opportunity for asylum" to the German Jewish refugees, Brandeis replied that this would "hardly make a favorable impression" on the mandatory government and in League circles when the United States had "done nothing" towards opening its own doors. Roosevelt had been moved by a passage in Billikopf's September letter about an old man, patriarchal in appearance, who lifted his eyes from a prayer book in the Nuremberg synagogue and asked the American visitor: "Does your grosser Führer know what is going on?" Reports from Lehman, Frankfurter, and others did reach the Oval Office, yet FDR chose not to accede to Lehman's September request or to the appeal on October 17 from Frankfurter that he broadcast in German, "saying some plain things that need to be said," against the attack on Jewry and the larger significance of the "forces of violence and chauvinism of the Hitler regime." On December 28, two months after Hitler decreed that the Third Reich leave both the League and the World Disarmament Conference, Roosevelt used the occasion of an address before the Woodrow Wilson Foundation to call on every nation to take steps towards "real peace in the world." "Germany" and "Jews" found no place in the President's text.[103]

Viewing the current scene in Palestine and abroad, Ruppin was filled with foreboding. In his estimate, the Zionist enterprise had absorbed 35,000 Jewish immigrants in 1933, and the Jewish population had risen to 230,000-250,000. That, he realized, was "definitely a step forward." If the Agency could work at this pace for another five years, almost 500,000 would be reached, and then the yishuv would "no longer have to live in fear, as we do today, that a serious Arab revolt would ruin all our work." Yet Ruppin's diary entry for the last day of 1933 ended somberly: "There is much political unrest amongst the Arabs. I am therefore not optimistic as I enter the next year. Every disturbance in Palestine frightens away capital, and without capital a large immigration is impossible."[104] The highest annual figure of Jewish immigration in the mandate years to date had been reached, but the gathering storm in Germany put Jewish existence itself at grave risk, while another in Palestine threatened to shatter the boldest of dreams—peace in the Holy Land.

Endnotes

1   William L. Shirer, *The Rise and Fall of the Third Reich* (New York, 1959), 17-
     20, 249-262; Konrad Heiden, *Der Fuehrer, Hitler's Rise to Power*, trans. R.
     Manheim (Boston, 1944), chap. 21; Robert Payne, *The Life and Death of Adolf
     Hitler* (New York, 1973), 244-247; Joachim C. Fest, *Hitler*, trans. R. and C.
     Winston (New York, 1975), 369; *JTA*, Jan. 31, 1933.
2   Y. Arad, Y. Gutman, and A. Margaliot, eds., *Documents on the Holocaust*
     (Jerusalem, 1981), 15-18, 22; Adolf Hitler, *Mein Kampf*, trans. R. Manheim
     (Boston, 1971 ed.); Alfred Werner, "Twenty Years After," *Jewish Spectator*
     (Jan. 1953): 22; *JTA*, Apr. 25, 1932; Randall L. Bytwerk, *Julius Streicher*
     (New York, 1983); Jürgen Matthäus, "Antisemitic Symbolism in Early Nazi
     Germany, 1933-1935," *Leo Baeck Institute Yearbook* 45:1 (2000): 183-204
     (specifically p. 189). Hitler's eschatological vision was adumbrated further
     in 1928, the volume seeing print years later under the title *Hitler's Zweites
     Buch—Ein Dokument aus dem Jahr 1928* (Stuttgart, 1961), and translated as
     Hitler's Secret Book (New York, 1961).
3   Knickerbocker to Thompson, Jan. 31, 1933, Box 4, H. R. Knickerbocker
     MSS., Special Collections, Butler Library, Columbia University, New York
     City; Shirer, *Rise and Fall of the Third Reich*, 20; Statement of the American
     Jewish Congress, Feb. 3, 1933, B'nai Brith files, American Jewish Congress
     Archives (hereafter AJC), Center for Jewish History (hereafter CJH), New
     York City; Saul Friedländer, *Nazi Germany and the Jews*, 1, *The Years of
     Persecution, 1933-1939* (New York, 1997), 14-15.
4   Recha Freier, *Likrat Aliyat HaNoar* (Tel Aviv, 1947); Freier reminiscence,
     n.d. A256/411, Central Zionist Archives (hereafter CZA), Jerusalem;
     Naomi Shepherd, *A Refuge from Darkness: Wilfrid Israel and the Rescue of the
     Jews* (New York, 1984), 46-47, 69-70; Brian Amkraut, *Between Home and
     Homeland: Youth Aliya from Germany* (Tuscaloosa, 2006), 21-22. Two years
     later, while expressing her "deep appreciation" for Freier's "fruitful and fertile
     idea," Szold defended her initial response: Szold to Freier, July 3, 1935, *Youth
     Aliya Letters Written by Henrietta Szold*, vol. 2, ed. Zena Harman, Hadassah
     Archives (hereafter HA), New York City. For Borochov, see Monty Noam
     Penkower, *The Emergence of Zionist Thought* (Millwood, NY, 1986), chap. 10.
     For Sereni, see Ruth Bondy, *The Emissary: A Life of Enzo Sereni*, trans. S. Katz
     (Boston, 1977). The Hebrew word "*Aliya*," immigration to Palestine, also car-
     ries the spiritual connotation of "going up" to Eretz Yisrael.
5   Isaiah Friedman, *The Question of Palestine: British-Jewish-Arab Relations,
     1914-1918* (New York, 1973); Daniel Pipes, *Greater Syria, The History of an
     Ambition* (New York, 1990), chap. 2; Aaron S. Klieman, *Foundations of British
     Policy in the Arab World: The Cairo Conference of 1921* (Baltimore, 1970);
     Bernard Wasserstein, *The British in Palestine: the Mandatory Government and
     the Arab-Jewish Conflict in Palestine, 1917-1929* (Oxford, 1991). The Balfour

Declaration added that Great Britain would act without prejudicing "the civil and religious rights of existing non-Jewish communities in Palestine, or the rights and political status enjoyed by Jews to any other country." The original document is in the British Museum, London. After crushing the Bar Kokhba revolt (132-135 C.E.), the Romans changed the Hebrew name of Eretz Yisrael (the name given by the conquering Israelite tribes to the Land of Cana'an, that name derived from the Cana'anites, who had inhabited certain parts of it) to Palaestina, after the Philistines who inhabited the country's coastal area. Throughout the period of Turkish rule, the Arabic pronunciation Falastin was used.

6 Ze'ev Tzahor, "The Struggle Between the Revisionist Party and the Labor Movement—1929-1933," *Modern Judaism* 8 (Feb. 1988), 16; Shabtai Tevet, *Kin'at David*, 2 (Jerusalem, 1980), *passim*; *HaPo'el HaTsa'ir*, Apr. 18, 1924; *Kuntres*, Aug. 11 and 21, 1925; Sept. 24, 1925; Oct. 2, 1925; Anita Shapira, *Berl, Biografia*, vol. 2 (Tel Aviv, 1981), 392.

7 Tzahor, "The Struggle," 16; Ze'ev Jabotinsky, *BaSa'ar* (Jerusalem, 1953), 23-29, 33-42; Ya'akov Goldstein, *B'Derekh L'Hegmonia, Mapai—Hitgabshut Mediniyuta (1930-1936)* (Tel Aviv, 1980), 173, 176. Ahimeir's original family name was Haisinovits; he changed it to "brother of Meir" in memory of an older brother who died in the service of the Red Army during the Russian Revolution. His first name was an acrostic in Yiddish for Abraham son of Isaac.

8 Tzahor, "The Struggle," 15-16. The Jewish Agency had been recognized in Article 4 of the Mandate accorded by the League of Nations as speaking for "all Jews who are willing to assist in the establishment of the Jewish national home." The expanded Jewish Agency, approved by the sixteenth Zionist Congress in 1929 by a vote of 230 to 30 with 45 abstentions, had been opposed by several leading Zionists, including Jabotinsky, Yitzhak Gruenbaum, and Nahum Goldmann, out of concern that a mixed Zionist and non-Zionist body would retard the implementation of the Zionist program and endanger its political character. For the Passfield White Paper, see note 13 below.

9 Jabotinsky, *BaSa'ar*, 57-62, 65-68, 71-74; Goldstein, *B'Derekh L'Hegmonia*, 177-280, 169.

10 Yosef Heller, "'HaMonism Shel HaMatara' O 'HaMonism Shel HaEmtsa'im'?: HaMakhloket HaRa'ayonit V'HaPolitit Bein Ze'ev Jabotinsky L'Vein Abba Ahimeir, 1928-1933," *Zion*, 52 (1987): 318-324; Abba Ahimeir, "Im Ein Ani Li Mi Li," *HaAretz*, Nov. 15, 1927; Abba Ahimeir, "MiPinkaso Shel Fashistan," *Do'ar HaYom*, Oct. 28, 1928; Abba Ahimeir, "HaDiktatura HeLeumit BaOlam HaGadol," *Do'ar HaYom*, Jan. 29, 1929; Shaw, cited in *Do'ar HaYom*, Feb. 22, 1928; John P. Diggins, *Mussolini and Fascism: The View From America* (Princeton, 1972). For Greenberg and Yeivin, see Yosef Ahimeir and Shmuel Shatski, eds., *Hinenu Sikrikim* (Tel Aviv, 1978), 33-54.

11 Heller, "'HaMonism'," 328-329, 337-339; Uri Zvi Greenberg, "HaTsiyonut HaArtila'it V'HaMekonenim B'Shuleha," *HaOlam*, July 27, 1923; Uri Zvi

Greenberg, *Hazon Ehad HaLigyonot* (Tel Aviv, 1928); Norman Rose, *Chaim Weizmann: A Biography* (New York, 1989 ed.), 288-289; *Do'ar HaYom*, Oct. 10, 1930; Binyamin Zeroni, *Gaon V'Nadiv V'Akhzar* (Tel Aviv, 1992), 19-21. For Yeivin's early stance, see *Do'ar HaYom*, Jan. 20 and 27, 1929; Mar. 25 and 28, 1929; Apr. 9, 19, and 21, 1929. Sarah Aaronsohn (1890-1917), a leader in the band called NILI (an acrostic for the biblical phrase "Netsah Yisrael Lo Yeshaker," *Samuel* I, 15:29) that provided key intelligence information to the British in their campaign to capture Palestine during World War I, committed suicide to escape further torture by her Turkish captors. Joseph Trumpeldor (1880-1920), an ex-Russian officer and Palestinian *halutz*, died during the defense of Tel Hai against Arab attack. Shalom Schwartzbard (1886-1938) was acquitted after assassinating in 1926 Simon Petlyura, the Ukrainian leader largely responsible for the murder of thousands of Jews in pogroms after World War I. Ya'akov Cohen's poem "Biryonim" (1903), the first unequivocal call for war to redeem Eretz Yisrael, ended with this refrain: "In blood and fire Judah fell, and in blood and fire Judah will arise!"

12   Abba Ahimeir, *Brit HaBiryonim* (Tel Aviv, 1972), *passim*; Heller, "'HaMonism'," 334-335, 339-342.

13   Lord Passfield (Sidney Webb), as Colonial Secretary, had announced a renewed attempt to create a Legislative Council, asserted that there generally remained no new land available for agricultural settlement, and deprecated unrestricted Jewish immigration. This document was based upon the findings of the Hope-Simpson Report, inspired by High Commissioner John Chancellor. Written under the pressure of public opinion, MacDonald's letter of February 13, 1931, to Weizmann negated the anti-Zionist passages of the Passfield White Paper. *Palestine: A Study of Jewish, Arab and British Policies* (New Haven, 1947), 656-660; Rose, *Chaim Weizmann*, 282-286. The Arabs called that communication, which was read in the Commons and published simultaneously in the London *Times*, the "Black Letter."

14   Rose, *Chaim Weizmann*, 286-293; Joseph Schechtman, *Fighter and Prophet, The Jabotinsky Story, The Last Years* (New York, 1960), 147-154; Emanuel Neumann, *In the Arena: An Autobiographical Memoir* (New York, 1976), 100-102. Given Arlosoroff's following the political line of Weizmann thereafter, Palestine's Revisionists began calling him "Chaim the Second." Abba Ahimeir, "Pegishot Im Arlosorov," *Herut*, Jan. 15, 1965.

15   Heller, "'HaMonism'," 345-351; Ahimeir and Shatski, *Hinenu Sikrikim*, 20-22; A255/834, CZA. Ahimeir wanted the name "Agudat S'A" (the Sarah Aaronsohn Group), but Greenberg insisted on Brit HaBiryonim. Yosi Ahimeir lecture, Hebrew University Conference, May 17, 2006, Jerusalem. The Arabs rejected the Brit Shalom program of the 1920s to early l930s as a camouflaged Zionist front. Other than the support of important intellectuals like Shmuel Hugo Bergman, Rabbi Binyamin (Yehoshua Radler-Feldman), Arthur Ruppin, Chaim Kalvarisky-Margalioth, and Gershom Scholem, its influence on the yishuv was minimal.

16 Schechtman, *Fighter and Prophet*, 160-162; Heller, "'HaMonism',", 352-261. Despite his differences with Ahimeir, von Weisl, who took over the management of *Doar HaYom* as of the summer of 1930, concluded that Ahimeir "created the Jewish hero who is a patriot who inexorably, soberly, incorruptibly brings and demands sacrifices for the freedom of the Jewish fatherland, for the Jewish state" (*JTA*, May 18, 1934). The *sans-culottes* (those who did not wear the knee breeches of the middle and upper classes) were workers who demanded direct democracy and other militant reforms during the period of the National Convention (1792-1795) in the French Revolution. For excerpts of Yeivin's earlier letter to Jabotinsky, n.d., see file V243/2, Histadrut Archives, Makhon Lavon, Tel Aviv.

17 *HaAretz*, Mar. 26, 1938, and *passim*; Anita Shapira, "HaVikuah B'Tokh Mapai Al HaShimush B'Alimut, 1932-1935," *HaTsiyonut* 5 (1978), 144-147; *Goldstein, B'Derekh L'Hegmonia*, 172; Jabotinsky, *BaSa'ar*, 45-53.

18 Shertok and Neumann addresses, Aug. 27, 1933, Political Committee, World Zionist Congress, S25/10125, CZA; Memorandum, Nov. 27, 1932; Agreement and Abdullah to Mohammad Bey, Dec. 30, 1932; El Unsi to Neumann and Farbstein, Jan. 3, 1933; Neumann to Szold, Jan. 8, 1933; Memo, Feb. 2, 1933; all in Jewish Agency files, Zionist Archives (hereafter ZA), New York City (now at the CZA); Jewish Agency Executive Jerusalem (hereafter JAEJ), Jan. 3, 1933; Neumann to Edmond de Rothschild, Jan. 11, 1933, A126/518; both in CZA; Neumann, *In the Arena*, 123-127; David Ben-Gurion, *Zikhronot* 1 (Tel Aviv, 1971), 564-567; Anita Shapira, "Parashat HaOptsia Al Admot HaEmir Abdullah B'Ghore al-Kibd—Reishit HaKesher Bein HaHanhala HaTsiyonit V'HaEmir Abdullah," *Tsiyonut* 3 (Tel Aviv, 1973), 295-304, 319-331.

19 Arlosoroff-Wauchope interview, Jan. 20, 1933, Jewish Agency files, ZA; Jan. 22 and 29, 1933, JAEJ; both in CZA; Arlosoroff-Johnson interview, Jan. 23, 1933, ZOA assorted files, ZA; Neumann to Szold, Jan. 18, 1933; Brodetsky-Parkinson interview, Jan. 25 and 30, 1933; all in Jewish Agency files, ZA; Jewish Agency to London, Jan. 24, 1933, Chaim Weizmann Archives (hereafter WA), Rehovot, Israel; *Davar*, Jan. 26, 1933; Neumann, *In the Arena*, 127-130; Yoav Gelber, *Jewish-Transjordan Relations, 1921-1948* (London, 1997), 45-50. For Neumann's disagreeing with Arlosoroff's not pressing for an immediate approval so that plans could go forward, see Neumann to Zionist Executive, Feb. 20, 1933, Jewish Agency files, ZA. When sending a check to Neumann to proceed, Brandeis had commented to associate Robert Szold: "Empire Builders must take risks" (Wise to Mack, Jan. 25, 1933, Box 115, Stephen Wise MSS., American Jewish Historical Society [hereafter AJHS], CJH).

20 Arlosoroff to Weizmann, Feb. 2, 1933, file 1/1, Maurice Hexter MSS., American Jewish Archives (hereafter AJA), Cincinnati, Ohio; Arlosoroff-Wauchope interview, Feb. 14, 1933, Jewish Agency Confidential files, ZA; Parkinson-Brodetsky interview, Feb. 13, 1933, L9/339 and Wauchope-Arlosoroff interview, Feb. 20, 1933, L9/351, both in CZA; Cox memorandum,

Feb. 1933, Foreign Office (hereafter FO) files, 371/16926, Public Record Office (hereafter PRO), Kew, England; Arlosoroff to Wauchope, Feb. 22, 1933 and Wauchope to Arlosoroff, Feb. 25, 1933, both in Jewish Agency files, ZA.

21   C.I.D. reports, Jan. 28, 1933, Feb. 1933, and Apr. 22, 1933; all in FO 371/16926, PRO; Zvi Elpeleg, *The Grand Mufti Haj Amin al-Husseini, Founder of the Palestinian National Movement*, trans. D. Harvey, ed. S. Himelstein (London, 1993), 32; Yehoshua Porath, *The Palestinian Arab National Movement, 1929-1939: From Riots to Rebellion* (London, 1977), 41-42. For the earlier riots, see chap. 3, note 81, and for Haj Amin's role, see Yehoshua Porath, *The Emergence of the Palestinian Arab National Movement, 1918-1929* (London, 1974), 129-131, 266-271; Elpeleg, *The Grand Mufti*, 6, 19, 21; also, for 1929, H. Keith-Roach, *The Pasha of Jerusalem: Memoirs of a District Commissioner Under the British Mandate*, ed. P. Eedle (London, 1994), 122-123. For the emergence of a younger Palestinian Arab movement more militant than the Arab Executive Committee, see Mustafa Kabha, *Itonut B'Ein HaSe'ara, HaItonut HaPalestina'it K'Makhshir L'Itsuv Da'at Kahal, 1929-1939* (Jerusalem, 2004), 91-93.

22   Wise to Mack, Mar. 1, 1933, Box 115, Wise MSS; Weizmann-MacDonald and Weizmann-Simon interviews, Mar. 1, 1933; Weizmann address, Mar. 2, 1933; all in WA. Diary, Mar. 3, 1933, Richard Meinertzhagen, *Middle East Diary, 1917-1956* (London, 1959), 148; Weizmann to Lola Warburg, Mar. 4, 1933, WA; *HaOlam*, Mar. 9, 1933; Central Association statement, Mar. 9, 1933, cited in Matthäus, "Antisemitic Symbolism," 186. The St. Bartholomew's Day Massacre, which began in Paris on August 24, 1572, and spread to other sections of France, was directed by Catherine de Medici against the Protestant Huguenots. Its result was the resumption of civil war between Catholics and Protestants for freedom of religion and for control of the king of France.

23   "W" to Harry, Mar. 14, 1933, Box 82, Stephen Wise MSS, microfilm #2375, AJA; Goldmann to Wise, Mar. 20, 1933, file 214A, World Jewish Congress Archives (hereafter WJCA), New York City, now in AJA; Arlosoroff to Wauchope, Apr. 7, 1933, ZOA assorted files, ZA; Chief of Police speech, Mar. 22, 1933; Mar. 21, 1933 report, both in Box 84, Julian Mack MSS, ZA; *Davar*, Mar. 17, 1933. Also see Benny Morris, "Response of the Jewish Daily Press in Palestine to the Accession of Hitler, 1933." *Yad Vashem Studies* 27 (Jerusalem, 1999), 363-407.

24   Rosenbluth report, n.d., A222/34, CZA; Martin Rosenbluth, "With an Eye to the Future," *Independent Jewish Press Service*, Sept. 19, 1941; Richard Lichtheim, *Toldot HaTisyonut B'Germania* (Jerusalem, 1951), 167-169; Shepherd, *A Refuge from Darkness*, 69, 78-80; Daniel Frankel, *Al Pi Tehom, HaMediniyut HaTsiyonit U'Sh'eilat Yehudei Germania, 1933-1938* (Jerusalem, 1984), 47-49; Laski speech, Mar. 26, 1933, Minutes, Board of Deputies of British Jews Archives (hereafter BDA), London; Zioniburo to Wise, Mar. 27, 1933 and Locker to Wise, Apr. 4, 1933, both in F38/1081, CZA. Frank Cohen, an independent oil broker in Texas and Oklahoma, covered the

expenses for the rally. He and his wife Ethel, later sponsors of the ESCO (an acrostic of Ethel S. Cohen) Foundation for Palestine, subsidized the study that was published as *Palestine: A Study of Jewish, Arab and British Policies* by Yale University Press in 1947. Autobiographical Memoir, Box 4, ESCO Archives, Special Collections, Butler Library, Columbia University.

25   Confidential report, March 1933, L9/440, CZA; Sereni to Histadrut, 1933 letters, file P145/7, Enzo Sereni MSS., Central Archives for the History of the Jewish People (hereafter CAHJP), Jerusalem; *Palestine Post*, Mar. 14, 1933; Abdullah to Neumann and Farbstein, Mar. 17, 1933, Jewish Agency files, ZA. Of the more than 53,000 German Jews who would reach Palestine between 1933 and 1941, the great majority were young and more than 18,000 of these had been trained in the *hakhshara* programs (Frances R. Nicosia, "Jewish Farmers in Hitler's Germany: Zionist Occupational Training and Nazi Jewish Policy," *Holocaust and Genocide Studies* 19.3 [winter 2005]: 365-389).

26   Weizmann–Cunliffe-Lister interview, Mar. 7, 1933, F38/1081; Arlosoroff–Wauchope interview, Mar. 23, 1933, A44/37; HICEM to Agency, Mar. 29, 1933, S49/381; all in CZA. *New York Times*, Mar. 30, 1933 (sent by Campbell to Foreign Office, in FO 371/16927, PRO).

27   Alan Bullock, *Hitler: A Study in Tyranny* (New York, 1971 ed.), 146-149; "Enforced Denials of Ill Treatment," *JTA* report received Apr. 25, 1933, file 153, David Mowshowitz MSS, YIVO Archives, CJH; Mildred Wertheimer, "The Jews in the Third Reich," *Foreign Policy Reports*, 9:16 (Oct. 11, 1933): 174-175; *Advocate for the Doomed: The Diaries and Papers of James G. McDonald, 1932-1935*, ed. R. Breitman, B.M. Stewart, and S. Hochberg (Bloomington, IN, 2007), 28, 48.

28   Mar. 2, 1933 cable, file C11/12/14/1, BDA; Diary, Mar. 23-Mar. 31, 1933, J. Pierrepont Moffat MSS, Houghton Library, Harvard University, Cambridge, MA; Meeting of Vaa'd HaLeumi, Mar. 30, 1933, J1/7235, and Senator to Hyamson, Mar. 31, 1933, S25/2419, both in CZA; Jeffrey Herf, *Nazi Propaganda for the Arab World* (New Haven, 2009), 16; Strictly Confidential record, Apr. 1, 1933, Memoranda, vol. 22, Moffat MSS; Goebbels speech, reported on Apr. 2-3, 1933, file 131, Mowshowitz MSS.

29   Diary, Apr. 2, 1933, Moffat MSS; *Manchester Guardian*, Apr. 10, 1933; *Documents on the Holocaust*, 39-42; Memorandum, Apr. 1933, WA; Warburg to Meyer, Apr. 3, 1933, Box 298, Felix Warburg MSS, AJA.

30   C.H. Voss, ed., *Stephen S. Wise: Servant of the People* (Philadelphia, 1970), 184-185; Diary, Apr. 20, 1933, Hamilton Fish Armstrong MSS, Department of Rare Books and Special Collections, Princeton University Library, Princeton, NJ; Birchall to James, Apr. 28, 1933, file 11-Germany, Arthur Hays Sulzberger MSS, *New York Times* Archives, New York City; *New York Times*, Apr. 29, 1933; *Advocate for the Doomed*, 69. The mention of Passover related to the "blood libel." See note 80 below.

31   "To the Jews in All Countries," Apr. 1933, Jewish Agency files, ZA; *Documents on the Holocaust*, 44-47. Jewish Agency to London office, Apr.

4, 1933, S25/9809; Arlosoroff–Cunliffe-Lister, Apr. 12, 1933, L9/338; Apr. 19, 1933, JAEJ; Arlosoroff-Wauchope, Apr. 14, 1933, L9/339; all in CZA. Haim Arlosorov, *Yoman Yerushalayim* (Tel Aviv, 1949), 306-307; Arlosoroff to Wauchope, Apr. 22, 1933, file XIV/1, Jewish Agency files, ZA. German Jews were ordered to attach the yellow star to their clothing as of the autumn of 1941.

32   Meeting with Sheikhs, Apr. 8, 1933, WA; Shertok talk to Congress Political Committee, Aug. 27, 1933, Z4/234/2; Apr. 23 and 25, 1933, JAEJ; both in CZA. For the Weizmann-Feisal contacts, see Rose, *Chaim Weizmann*, 194, 199. For the arguments over plans to aid German Jewry, including Weizmann's role in heading the financial campaign, see Yoav Gelber, "The Reactions of the Zionist Movement and the Yishuv to the Nazis' Rise to Power," *Yad Vashem Studies* 18 (Jerusalem, 1987), pp. 53-57; Meeting, Apr. 27, 1933,Va'ad HaLeumi, J1/7235, CZA.

33   Meeting, Apr. 7, 1933, Cabinet papers 96/33, PRO; Eli Shaltiel, *Pinhas Rutenberg*, 2 (Tel Aviv, 1990), 411.

34   Shaltiel, *Pinhas Rutenberg*, 412-418, 423-425. "In the heat of the moment," Cunliffe-Lister even said that Transjordan was now closed to the Jews for twenty years because of Arab agitation. Shertok report, Aug. 27, 1933, Z4/234/2, CZA. Weizmann would subsequently—but privately—blame Rutenberg's intervention for the mandatory's delay in approving the Huleh Valley's development. Jewish settlement only beginning there in 1939, and (because of World War II and Israel's War of Independence) drainage operations carried out in the years 1951-1958. This irrigated land would be transformed into a highly fertile region in the State of Israel.

35   Ben-Gurion, *Zikhronot*, 563; *Davar*, Feb. 18, 1933; David Ben-Gurion, *Tenuat HaPoalim V'HaRevisionistim* (Tel Aviv, 1933); Ben-Yeroham, *HaAlila HaGedola, Lifnei Retsah Arlosorov U'LeAharav* (Tel Aviv, 1982), 232-234, 250; Yitshaq Ben-Ami, *Years of Wrath, Days of Glory: Memoirs from the Irgun* (New York, 1982), 100; Shapira, "HaVikuah," 148-155; Schechtman, *Fighter and Prophet*, 214-217. For the Tel Aviv Council's conclusion that the assault on Passover stemmed from political incitement, see file 1/3-A/8H, Jabotinsky Archives (hereafter JA), Tel Aviv. For the protest of the city's chief rabbis over that attack, see *Mikhmanei Uziel*, ed. S. Katz and E. Barnea, vol. 5 (Jerusalem, 2007), 263.

36   Apr. 9, 1933, ZOA Administrative Committee files, ZA; ZOA Statement, Apr. 1933, WA; Rothenberg to Zioniburo, London, Apr. 13, 1933, F38/1081, CZA; *New Palestine*, Apr. 28, 1933. For Herzl and the Basle Program, see Penkower, *The Emergence of Zionist Thought*, chap. 5.

37   London *Times*, Apr. 2, 1933; *Palestine Post*, Apr. 3, 1933; *Parliamentary Debates, House of Commons*, 276, cols. 2744-2812; Laski-Montefiore to Wauchope, Apr. 20, 1933, BDA.

38   Oct. 21, 1944, Joint Historical Research Section report, FO 371/39222, PRO; Diary, Apr. 20 and 27, 1933, Box 99, Armstrong MSS.

39   *Stephen S. Wise*, 194, 186; Cyrus Adler and Aaron M. Margalith, *American Intercession on Behalf of the Jews in the Diplomatic Correspondence of the United Stateas, 1840-1945* (New York, 1943), 365; Wise to Lipsky-Schultz, June 7, 1938, Box 67, Wise MSS; *"Half Brother, Half Son": The Letters of Louis D. Brandeis to Felix Frankfurter*, ed. M.I. Urofsky and D. Levy (Norman, OK, 1991), 519-520.

40   Shirer, *Rise and Fall of the Third Reich*, 281-283; Friedländer, *Nazi Germany and the Jews*, 56-58; Philip Kossoff, *Valiant Hero: A Biography of Heinrich Heine* (London, 1983); Martin Gilbert, *Sir Horace Rumbold: Portrait of a Diplomat, 1869-1941* (London, 1973), 379-380; *Manchester Guardian*, May 13, 1933; Warburg to Rothschild, May 29, 1933, microfilm 1916, Felix Warburg MSS, AJA; Laski to Holmes, May 13, 1933, in *Holmes-Laski Letters: The Correspondence of Mr. Justice Holmes and Harold J. Laski, 1916-1935*, 2, ed. Mark de Wolfe Howe (Cambridge, MA, 1953), 1440. While Heine's oft-quoted line referred to Christians in Spain burning a Koran while forcibly converting the Moors in the early sixteenth century, he also hinted thereby at Romantic nationalist student groups in Germany who burned "unpatriotic" books in October 1819. In 1832, the concluding passage of Heine's *Religion and Philosophy in Germany* warned that Christianity had "subdued to a certain extent the brutal warrior-ardor of the Germans, but it could not entirely quench it; and when the Cross, that restraining talisman, falls to pieces, then will break forth again the ferocity of the old combatants, the frantic Berserker rage whereof Northern poets have said and sung so much.... German thunder ... rumbles along somewhat slowly. But come it will, and when ye hear a crashing such as never before has been heard in the world's history, then know that at last the German thunderbolt has fallen" (*Heinrich Heine: A Biographical Anthology*, ed. H. Bieber, trans. M. Hadas, [Philadelphia, 1956], 331).

41   Neumann to Director of Department Immigration, May 3, 1933, and Neumann to Brodetsky, May 4, 1933, both in Jewish Agency files, ZA; May 7, 1933, JAEJ; Neumann to Szold, May 17, 1933, file Z1, Robert Szold MSS, ZA; Mills to Bentwich, May 8, 1933, A255/603, CZA.

42   May 10, 1933, Va'ad HaLeumi meeting, J1/7235; Va'ad HaLeumi statement, May 11, 1933, A126/602; both in CZA.

43   Deputy Inspector-General report, May 19, 1933, FO 371/16926, PRO; Schechtman, *Fighter and Prophet*, 214-217; Ahimeir diary, June 2, 1933, RG 69, P-22/3, Israel State Archives (hereafter ISA), Jerusalem.

44   *Hazit HaAm*, Jan. 9, 1932; Feb. 23, 1932; June 14, 1932; July 12, 1932; Nov. 18, 1932; Apr. 21, 1933; June 3 and 9, 1933. SD here referred to the Social Democratic Party in Germany. Greenberg had brought the pun "uncircumcised rabbi" into the Revisionist press in Poland: Ahimeir diary, Mar.-Apr. 1931, RG 69, P-22/3, ISA.

45   Arlosoroff at Jewish Agency Executive London (hereafter JAEL), May 8, 1933, Z4/302/29B; Arlosoroff memorandum, May 1933, S25/9706; both in CZA;

New Judea, July-Aug. 1933, 170-172; meeting, June 1, 1933, A145/203; S.B. (Brodetsky) memorandum, June 1, 1933 meeting, S25/9706; both in CZA.

46 Epstein to Shertok, May 16, 18, and 23, 1933; Almajali-Neumann talk, May 23, 1933; Gad's report, May 24, 1933; all in Jewish Agency files, ZA. *League of Nations, Permanent Mandates Commission, Minutes of the Twenty-Fifth Session* (Geneva, 1934), 134-135.

47 Chizik to Brodetsky, June 14, 1933, J1/6334 I, CZA. For the 1931 Islamic Congress, see Porath, *The Palestinian Arab National Movement*, 9-13. While Muslims consider the Haram al-Sharif (Noble Sanctuary) the third holiest site in Islam after Mecca and Medina, Jews have venerated the same area for 2,000 years as their holiest space, called the Har HaBayit (Temple Mount).

48 *Palestine Post*, June 4, 1933; Kirkbride to Foreign Office, June 8, 1933, FO 371/16932, PRO; *JTA*, June 15, 1933.

49 FO 371/16932; CO 733/2466/17547; both in PRO. Shortly after Feisal's departure for Europe, rumors spread of a scheme to annex Transjordan to Iraq as a step against throwing open Transjordan to Jewish immigration. Most Arabs thought that such Jewish settlement would mean the country's annexation to Palestine (Cox report, July 1933, FO 371/16926, PRO).

50 *HaPo'el HaTsa'ir*, June 23, 1933; *HaOlam*, June 22, 1933; *Hazit Ha'Am*, June 16, 1933. Pogrovinsky subsequently heard from Jaffa district police commander Euan William Lucie-Smith that a translation of the article into English had been prepared in the office of Bernard Joseph, then serving as the Jewish Agency's legal liaison with the British, with the highly significant addition of the word "physically" inserted after the original Hebrew "how to respond" (Abba Ahimeir, *HaMisphat* [Tel Aviv, 1968], 85-86). Joseph would work on the case of Arlosoroff's murder for a year. See memorandum, October 30, 1934, file P-772/10, ISA. Following the trial, he became legal advisor to the Agency's political department. For Ahad Ha'am's cultural Zionism, see Penkower, *The Emergence of Zionist Thought*, chap. 6.

51 Sima Arlosoroff report, n.d., Record Group 30.10, file G-8007/6, ISA; Arlosorov, *Yoman Yerushalayim*, 233-240; Arlosoroff-Wauchope interview, Mar. 23, 1933, A44/37, and Arlosoroff-Wauchope interview, Apr. 14, 1933, L9/339, both in CZA; Goldstein, *B'Derekh L'Hegemonia*, 171-172; Shapira, "HaVikuah," 151. It has been asserted that Arlosoroff was also criticized by some Arabs and Jews for supporting bi-nationalism via an agreement with Abdullah (Edwin Black, *The Transfer Agreement* [New York, 1984], 144-148). Arlosoroff did not favor bi-nationalism, while the unsuccessful negotiations for Jewish settlement in Transjordan, having no connection whatsoever to a bi-nationalist Palestine, were begun and carried out by Neumann and Farbstein.

52 Haim Shorer, "Arlosorov," *Davar*, Aug. 5, 1966; ? to Klausner, Apr. 4, 1949, A493/99, and Medzini to JAEL, June 17, 1933, S46/445, both in CZA; Raya Adler (Cohen), "The Tenants of Wadi Hawarith: Another View of the Land Question in Palestine, *International Journal of Middle East Studies* 20 (1988):

197-220; *Palestine Post*, July 6, 1933. The Hefer Valley, the central section of the Sharon Valley in the coastal plain of Israel, consisted of sand dunes and swamps. Bedouin mainly occupied the area until its acquisition by the Jewish National Fund in 1929. After the drainage of its swamps, it became one of the country's most fertile regions. The city of Netanya, named after the U.S. philanthropist Nathan Straus, was founded in 1929 on the valley's southwestern corner.

53   Medzini to JAEL, June 17, 1933, S46/445, CZA; Shabtai Tevet, *Retsah Arlosorov* (Tel Aviv, 1982), 75-78; Tom Segev, "The Makings of History/ Whodunit," *HaAretz*, June 29, 2008. In her very first report to a police officer at the hospital, Sima Arlosoroff had also thought that Arabs were the killers (Tevet, *Retsah Arlosorov*, 80).

54   *Yediot Iriyat Tel Aviv, 1933*, 2:9 (Tel Aviv, 1933), 301-302; *HaAretz*, June 18, 1933; *Davar*, June 18, 1933; H. Ben-Yeroham, *HaAlila HaGedola*, 57, 24; Tevet, *Retsah Arlosorov*, 105; *Davar*, June 26, 1933.

55   *Davar*, July 7, 1933 (a Jewish Telegraphic Agency statement reprinted from *Moment*, June 21, 1933); Ze'ev Jabotinsky, *BaSa'ar* (Jerusalem, 1953), 91-101. For Jabotinsky's taking the libel as a personal affront, see A. Remba, ed., *Shimshon Yunichman* (Tel Aviv, 1962), 14-15, 197. Menahem Mendel Beilis (1874-1934) was the victim of a blood libel in Czarist Russia, charged with murdering a young Christian boy for Jewish ritual purposes. Worldwide protest ensued; a Russian jury acquitted the innocent man in 1913.

56   *Davar*, July 7, 1933; Mapai Central Committee, June 20 and 29, 1933, Labor Archives, Bet Berl, Kfar Saba, Israel; Betar secretariat to Histadrut Va'ad HaPoel, June 21, 1933, file G-23/22/7, ISA; Avigdor HaMeiri, "Ovdei HaSatan," *Turim*, June 29, 1933; Avraham Shlonsky, "Lo Tirtsah," *Turim*, July 28, 1933; Hanan Hever, *Moledet HaMavet Yafa: Estetika U'Politika B'Shirat Uri Zvi Greenberg* (Tel Aviv, 2004), 29; Ben-Yeroham, *HaAlila HaGedola*, 48, 28-30. A few years later, Klausner sent Ahimeir a copy of his article on the zealot leaders Yohanan from Gush Halav and Shimon Bar-Giora with the inscription: "To the zealot of our generation" (Ahimeir and Shatski, *Hinenu Sikrikim*, 10).

57   Medzini to JAEL, June 17, 1933, S46/445, CZA; A. Ruppin, *Memoirs, Diaries, Letters*, ed. A. Bein, trans K. Gershon (London, 1971), 264; Goldschmidt to Lulu, June 21, 1933, file G-22/7123, ISA; Lipstuk to Jabotinsky, Aug. 17, 1933, JA. The Communists quickly blamed "Zionist Fascists" for the murder, and specifically Stavsky of Jabotinsky's party, which "hates Arab nationalists and workers" (Statement, June 23, 1933, A192/1103, CZA).

58   *HaAretz*, June 23 and 26, 1933; Ben-Zion Katz, *Al Itonim V'Anashim* (Tel Aviv, 1983), 157-158. For al-Qassam, see chap. 3.

59   Katz, *Al Itonim V'Anashim*, 157; *HaMatara*, June 30 and July 7, 1933; *Davar*, July 6 and 14, 1933; *Kings* I, 21:19. The *Evsektsii* were the Jewish Sections in the Communist Party after the Bolshevik Revolution. Josephus Flavius abandoned the Jewish revolt in 67 C.E. to join the Roman enemy, and

later authored an account of the rebellion in *The Jewish War*. Sanballat was a satrap of Samaria who opposed Nehemiah and obstructed the rebuilding of Jerusalem after Cyrus of Persia had permitted Jews to return from the Babylonian exile to Eretz Yisrael (*Nehemiah*, chaps. 4, 6).

60 Ben-Yeroham, *HaAlila HaGedola*, 24, 36-42, 71-72; *The Letters and Papers of Chaim Weizmann*, vol. 16, ed. G. Sheffer (Jerusalem, 1978), 3-4; *BaMa'aleh*, July 14, 1933.

61 Ben-Gurion, *Zikhronot*, 586-588, 645-647. The "philanthropic lords" referred to the equal representation given to wealthy non-Zionists in the enlarged Jewish Agency, which Weizmann had achieved in order to obtain urgently needed funding for the Zionist enterprise.

62 *Palestine Post*, July 19, 1933; Ben-Gurion, *Zikhronot*, 644; David Ben-Gurion, *MiMa'amad L'Am* (Tel Aviv, 1933); Joseph Schechtman, *Fighter and Prophet: The Vladimir Jabotinsky Story, The Last Years* (New York, 1961), 191-192; *Hazit HaAm*, Apr. 7, 1933. For Ben-Gurion's ideological shift, see Roni Stauber, "Nationalism and Statism in Ben-Gurion's Weltanschauung," *Studia Judaica* 15 (2007), 57-66.

63 *The Letters and Papers of Chaim Weizmann*, 16-17; Tevet, *Retsah Arlosorov*, 149-178, 185-186.

64 Jabotinsky to Ya'akobi, July 24, 1933, JA; *JTA*, July 24, 1933; Ben-Yeroham, *HaAlila HaGedola*, 89-90; Ze'ev Jabotinsky, *Mikhtavim* (Tel Aviv, n.d.), 98-102. For Joseph's active role, see Ben-Yeroham, *HaAlila HaGedola*, 77, 267, 277, 292, 313, 315, and note 50 above. Jabotinsky and the ex-Russian officer and Galilee pioneer Joseph Trumpeldor had pressed for a Jewish Legion during World War I to join the Allies in an effort to liberate Palestine from Ottoman rule and, thereby, strengthen Zionist claims at the eventual peace conference. Ultimately, the 38th, 39th, and 40th Battalions of Royal Fusiliers under British command, made up of Jewish volunteers from abroad, were consolidated into the "First Judean Regiment." After a successful campaign, the wary British disbanded the regiment.

65 Tevet, *Retsah Arlosorov*, 123-127; Tehomi statement, Apr. 1978, file 5/3/232-P, JA; Sadan's 1968 letter to Shlomo Grodzinski (file 26-713/1, Genazim Archives, Tel Aviv), briefly noted by Anita Shapira, *Berl, Biografia*, 2 (Tel Aviv, 1981), 741, note 112, is quoted extensively by Yosef Ahimeir in A. Bekher, ed., *B'Ikvot Ne'elamim, LeParashat Arlosorov* (Tel Aviv, 1989), 24-25; *Davar*, July 1933; *Do'ar HaYom*, July 10, 1933, Aug. 4, 25, and 30, 1933; *Davar*, Sept. 15, 1933; *Do'ar HaYom*, Oct. 8, 1933. For the Hebrew novelist Yehuda Burla's attack on Ravnitski, see *Davar*, Aug. 17, 1933. For Hagana Bet, see chap. 5, n18.

66 Tevet, *Retsah Arlosorov*, 150-154, 158-160; *Davar*, Aug. 16, 1933; Benkover to Mapai Central Committee, Aug. 10, 1933, A116/64; Va'ad HaPoel meetings, Aug. 17-22, 1933, Z4/287; both in CZA; Wise to Jabotinsky, Oct. 29, 1934, file 22/3/1-A, JA.

67 Schechtman, *Fighter and Prophet*, 192-196; *Davar*, Sept. 1, 1933; L9/93;

Aharonovitz letter, Aug. 24, 1933, A116/64; both in CZA; Weizmann to Hexter, Aug. 23, 1933, WA. For Labor's debate about Weizmann's return to the presidency, see Mapai meeting, Aug. 22, 1933, A116/64, CZA. Shertok personally felt that his precedessor's death left in its wake a "dark abyss" and an "unforeseeable future." Shertok to Sima Arlosoroff, Aug. 12, 1933, A44/39, CZA. An official British observer at the Congress emphasized that "mutual recrimination" prevented serious discussion of practical problems; Wise found Labor "exploiting" the Arlosoroff murder "in order to destroy Revisionism," with the Revisionists "hopelessly resolved to carry on the fight" (Gurney to Simon, Sept. 21, 1933, FO 371/16927, PRO; Wise to Mack, Aug. 30, 1933, Box 115, Wise MSS).

68   Schechtman, *Fighter and Prophet*, 193; *New Judea*, Sept. 1933; *JTA*, Aug. 27, 1933; Gelber, "Reactions," 66-68; Szold-Lowenthal interview, Dec. 29, 1935, Henrietta Szold MSS, HA. For an overview of the Youth Aliya department's work thereafter, see Refael Gat, "Mifal Aliyat HaNoar 1933-1939," *Katedra* 37 (1986): 149-176.

69   Emanuel Meltzer, "HaHerem HaKalkali HaYehudi HaAnti-Germani B'Polin BaShanim 1933-1934," *Gal-Ed* 6 (1982), 149-166; Schultz to Kallen, May 3, 1933, file 610, Horace Kallen MSS, YIVO Archives; Untermyer to Waldman, May 4, 1933, and Waldman reply, May 9, 1933; both in German-Jewish Situation files, American Jewish Committee Archives (hereafter AJCA); Cohen to Adler, May 4, 1933, B'nai Brith files, AJCA; Frankfurter to Proskauer, May 18, 1933, Box 137, Felix Frankfurter MSS., Library of Congress (hereafter LC), Washington, D.C.; Emergency Session, May 20-22, 1933, AJC; Adler to Laski, June 7, 1933, Laski files, Cyrus Adler MSS, AJCA; Interview with Baeck and others, June 11, 1933, file 75, Mowshowitz MSS; June 14, 1933, Joint Foreign Committee, Chronos file, AJCA; Laski address, June 1933, file 75, Mowshowitz MSS; Proskauer to Untermyer, June 28, 1933, Box 3, Louis Strauss MSS, AJHS; June 29, 1933 conference with Israel, Joint Foreign Committee files, Meeting with Baeck and Hirsch in Cologne, July 3, 1933, B'nai Brith files, and Board of Deputies meeting, July 23, 1933, Joint Foreign Committee files, all in AJCA; Aug. 3, 1933, Administrative Committee, AJC; Aug. 17, 1933, AJC Administrative Committee meeting; both in file 211A, WJCA. For the Congress's pro-boycott resolution, see Tanenbaum statement, Aug. 20, 1933, Box 13, Joint Boycott Council MSS, New York Public Library, New York City. For Israel's future activities, see Shepherd, *A Refuge from Darkness*.

70   Histadrut Executive Committee, Sept. 25, 1933, Makhon Lavon; Gelber, "Reactions," 70-83; Ruppin, *Memoirs, Diaries, Letters*, 264; *Documents on the Holocaust*, 54-55; London *Times*, Sept. 2, 1933; Frankel, *Al Pi Tehom*, 120-127; Yfaat Weiss, "The Transfer Agreement and the Boycott Movement: A Jewish Dilemma on the Eve of the Holocaust," *Yad Vashem Studies* 26 (1998): 129-171. Reporting to the Political Committee of the Zionist Congress, Hoofien believed that the Transfer Agreement would "definitely" enable

2,000 Jewish families to settle in Palestine with their goods and property "in the near future" (Meeting, Aug. 29, 1933, Z4/234/2, CZA). The subject was further discussed at length in that forum four days later (Meeting, Sept. 2, 1933, Ibid.).

71   Weizmann to d'Avigdor-Goldsmid, Aug. 14, 1933, WA; *League of Nations, Permanent Mandates Commission, Minutes of the Twenty-Third Session, June 19-July 1, 1933* (Geneva, 1933), 98-99, 103; Wauchope to Cunliffe-Lister, July 26, 1933, FO 371/16928, PRO; Hexter–Farbstein–Shertok–Wauchope interview, July 5, 1933, L9/339, CZA; Medzini to Executive, Aug. 13, 1933, file ZOA misc., ZA.

72   Ben-Zvi–Wauchope interview, Aug. 25, 1933, file ZOA misc., ZA; London *Times*, July 23, 1933; Vansittart-Laski-Bentwich interview, June 22, 1933, file 75, Mowshowitz MSS; Aug. 4, 1933 minute, FO 371/16756; Aug. 3-5, 1933 minutes, FO 371/16727; both in PRO; Billikopf to Lehman, Sept. 1, 1933, file 244, Oscar G. Villard MSS, Houghton Library; Billikopf to Mack, Sept. 14, 1933, Jacob Billikopf MSS, file 18/3, AJA.

73   McDonald address, Sept. 6, 1933, Chronos file, AJCA; Haskell to Billikopf, Sept. 10, 1933, Jacob Billikopf file., Philip Bernstein MSS, University of Rochester, NY; W.E. Dodd, Jr. and M. Dodd, eds. *Ambassador Dodd's Diary, 1933-1938* (London, 1941), 37; Wise to Brandeis, Sept. 19, 1933, in *Stephen Wise*, 194; Billikopf to Lehman, Sept. 1, 1933, file 244, Oscar G. Villard MSS; Billikopf to Mack, Sept. 14, 1933, file 18/3, Jacob Billikopf MSS.

74   *Ambassador Dodd's Diary*, 19; JMW memorandum, Sept. 14, 1933; Lehman to Billikopf, Sept. 18, 1933; Roosevelt to Lehman, Sept. 27, 1933; all in file 16/2, Billikopf MSS. Moffat to Hull, Sept. 19, 1933, Memoranda, vol. 22; Diary, Sept. 18 and 23, 1933; both in Moffat MSS.

75   Shertok–Ben-Zvi–MacMichael interview, Sept. 13, 1933, file XIV/1, Jewish Agency, ZA. One year later, pipelines were completed from Kirkuk to Al Hadithah, and from there, to both Tripoli and Haifa; the Kirkuk oil field of the Iraq Petroleum Company was brought online the same year.

76   Shertok to Brodetsky, Sept. 14, 1933, file XIV/1, Jewish Agency, ZA.

77   Senator at meeting of *aliya* emissaries, Sept. 3, 1933, S6/8003; Ben-Zvi to Chief Secretary, Sept. 1, 1933, L9/349; both in CZA. C.I.D. reports, Aug., 10, 1933, and Sept. 12, 1933, both in FO 371/16926, PRO; Rutenberg to M. Warburg, Sept. 25, 1933, file A9009/55, Pinhas Rutenberg MSS, Israel Electric Company Archives, Haifa; Szold to sisters, Oct. 6 and 12, 1933, H. Szold MSS; C.I.D. report, Oct. 23, 1933, FO 371/16926, PRO.

78   Antonius to Crane, Oct. 28, 1933, Charles Crane MSS, Institute of Current World Affairs Archives, Alicia Patterson Foundation, New York City; London *Times*, Oct. 14, 1933. The C.I.D. estimated the crowd at 2,000, while Shertok gave a figure of 5,000 to the Jewish Agency Executive. C.I.D. report, Oct. 23, 1933, FO 371/16926, PRO; Ben-Gurion, *Zikhronot*, 668.

79   Antonius to Crane, Oct. 28, 1933, Crane MSS; London *Times*, Oct. 26, 1933; Elizabeth MacCallum, "Great Britain and the Race Problem in

Palestine," *Foreign Policy Reports* 10:12 (Aug. 29, 1934): 165-166; London *Times*, Nov. 7 and 8, 1933; Khalil al-Sakakini, *KaZeh Ani, Rabotai!*, trans. G. Shilo (Jerusalem, 1990), 169-170; Mackereth to Simon, Nov. 9, 1933, FO 371/16932, PRO; Ann Mosely Lesch, *Arab Politics in Palestine, 1917-1939, The Frustration of a Nationalist Movement* (Ithaca, 1979), 106, 214-215; Weldon C. Matthews, *Constructing an Empire, Constructing a Nation: Arab Nationalists and Popular Politics in Mandate Palestine* (London, 2006), 208-219; Ben-Gurion remarks at ZOA Administrative Committee, May 19, 1935, ZA. The Arabs soon exercised the right of peaceful demonstrations in a number of centers on January 17, 1934, without untoward incident.

80   Ben-Zion Katz, *Lo Ukhal L'HaHashot* (Tel Aviv, 1933); Katz, *Al Itonim V'Anashim*, 159-160; David Tidhar, *BeSheirut HaMoledet* (Tel Aviv, 1966), 423; Tevet, *Retsah Arlosorov*, 178-190; *Davar*, Sept. 14, 1933; *HaYesod*, Sept. 1933; Klausner to Druyanov, Oct. 3, 1933, A10/27/3, CZA. Three years later, the C.I.D.'s Assistant Inspector-General confirmed Riggs's confidential disclosure about the three accused Revisionists, writing in his published memoir: "We knew perfectly well that none of these men had been implicated in the crime." The voluminous depositions, he added, were inspected by Charles Leach of Scotland Yard, and his final report would be "a tremendous asset" to the defense" (Joseph F. Broadhurst, *From Vine Street to Jerusalem* [London, 1936], 236). The blood libel, charging Jews with murdering Christian children before Easter to use their blood for the baking of matza (unleavened bread) for Passover, began in Norwich, England, in 1144, and spread thereafter worldwide. The Italian-born philosophical anarchists Nicola Sacco and Bartolemeo Vanzetti were electrocuted in 1927 after a seven-year court case on the false charge that they had murdered a paymaster in Massachusetts.

81   *Davar* and *HaAretz*, Sept. 9, 1933; Ben-Yeroham, *HaAlila HaGedola*, 200-205; Heller, "'HaMonism',", 321-322; Ahimeir diary, Mar.-Apr. 1931, and May 24, 1931, RG 69, P-22/3; Ahimeir diary, June 10, 1933, file P-772/10; both in ISA. Challenging Glickson's argument earlier that no distinction ought to be made between private and public murder, Ahimeir had pointed to Schwartzbard's killing of pogromist Petlyura as a positive act (*Do'ar HaYom*, Nov. 4, 1928). The *sicarri*, carrying short daggers, killed Jewish leaders who openly cooperated with the Roman enemy; Uri Zvi Greenberg's poem "Sikrikin" (1929) urged the yishuv's youth to follow their example. Charlotte Corday murdered the Jacobin journalist Jean Paul Marat in 1793, while Dora Kaplan wounded Lenin in 1918.

82   Schechtman, *Fighter and Prophet*, 196-197, 211-213; Makhon Jabotinsky, *Pirsumim* 2 (Tel Aviv, Oct., 1955); Moshe Smilansky, *T'kuma V'Shoa* (Tel Aviv, 1953), 122-126; *Davar*, Sept. 10, 1933; *Din V'Heshbon HaExecutiva* (London, 1935), 34-35; Brodetsky letter, Jan. 16, 1934, A45/24, CZA. Also see Aviva Halamish, *B'Meirutz Kaful Neged HaZeman* (Jerusalem, 2006), 200-212.

83   Ruppin, *Memoirs, Diaries, Letters*, 265; London *Times*, Nov. 3, 1933; *Palestine Post*, Nov. 12, 1933; Efraim Karsh, *Palestine Betrayed* (New Haven, 2010),

19. The *Protocols of the Learned Elders of Zion*, an antisemitic forgery which sought to demonstrate that an international Jewish conspiracy was bent on world domination, was authored anonymously in Paris by a Russian secret police officer at the end of the nineteenth century. The text, widely circulated during the Russian civil war of 1919-1921, was publicized in the West by Russian émigrés associated with the anti-Bolshevik White armed forces. While Philip Graves exposed it in the London *Times* as closely similar to a French political pamphlet that attributed ambitions of world power to Napoleon III, it was translated into many languages. The *Protocols* found the largest number of adherents in Germany, and the Nazi Party propagated this theme from the start.

84 Gershom Scholem, *A Life in Letters, 1914-1982*, ed. and trans A.D. Skinner (Cambridge, MA, 2002), 251; *Izvestiya*, Nov. 3, 1933, in FO 371/16932, PRO; London *Times*, Nov. 5-7 1933. For the Iraqi slaughter of the Assyrians, see *Palestine: A Study of Jewish, Arab and British Policies*, 757-759, and *www.aina.org*, which cites *The Assyrian Tragedy* (Feb. 1934) and attributes this book to Mar Eshai Shimun, Catholicos Patriarch XXIII. William Saroyan, of Armenian parentage, wrote the short story "Seventy Thousand Assyrians" (1934) out of sympathy for these victims. The Simmele massacre in northern Iraq inspired the Jewish researcher Raphael Lemkin, his distress compounded by the slaughter of Armenians by Turks during World War I, to coin the word "genocide." The international Polish jurist began to examine these acts as crimes in an effort to deter and prevent them, and he presented his first proposal to outlaw such "acts of barbarism" to the Legal Council of the League of Nations in Madrid the same year. The proposal failed, however, and his work incurred the disapproval of his own government, which was at the time pursuing a policy of conciliation with Nazi Germany. Lemkin was forced to retire from his public position in 1934. Ten years later, having escaped from Nazi-occupied Poland to Sweden, he published a large (712 pp.) volume titled *Axis Rule in Occupied Europe: Laws of Occupation, Analysis of Government, Proposals for Redress*, in which the term "genocide" made its first appearance.

85 Humphrys to Simon, Nov. 16, 1933, FO 371/16932, PRO. Nadir Shah had urged a large-scale campaign, under British influence, against the non-Pashtun living in the country. Thousands of Afghanis were killed or imprisoned during his reign. Frank Clements, *Conflict in Afghanistan, A Historical Encyclopedia* (Santa Barbara, CA, 2003).

86 Ben-Gurion, *Zikhronot*, 668-673; Wauchope to Shertok, Oct., 19, 1933, J1/6334I, CZA; Executive Council, Oct. 17, 1933, file M-4753/28-29, ISA; Ben-Gurion–Shertok–Wauchope interview, Oct. 20, 1933, ZOA-Great Britain file, ZA.

87 Hall to Agency, Oct. 26, 1933, ZOA-Great Britain file, ZA; Shertok to Brodetsky, Oct. 23, 1933, file C14/10, BDA; Shertok memorandum, Nov. 2, 1933, J1/6334I, CZA; Reptur statement on 1933 disturbances, n.d., file P28/30, Ben-Zion Dinur MSS, CAHJP; Ben-Gurion, *Zikhronot*, 673-675.

88 *League of Nations, Journal of the Fourteenth Session of the Assembly* (Geneva, October 2, 1933), 85-86.

89 Simon to Ormsby-Gore, Oct. 3, 1933, FO 371/16757, PRO; *League of Nations, Journal of the Fourteenth Session of the Assembly*, Oct. 4, 1933, 118-120; Simon to Cecil, Dec. 1, 1933, FO 371/16758, PRO; Hyman to Warburg, Nov. 13, 1933, microfilm #1918, Warburg MSS; Bentwich-McDonald interview, Nov. 11, 1933, McDonald file, Oscar Janowsky MSS, AJHS; *New York Times*, Nov. 27, 1933. For the creation and subsequent fate of this new office, see Monty Noam Penkower, "Honorable Failures Against Nazi Germany: McDonald's Letter of Resignation and the Petition in its Support," *Modern Judaism* 30.3 (Oct. 2010): 247-298.

90 Hall-Shertok-Senator interview, Nov. 7, 1933, ZOA-Great Britain files, ZA. Immigrants who had entered prior to that date and were currently employed or financially independent would not be deported unless they were undesirable for other reasons.

91 Lourie to Shertok, Nov. 9, 1933; ZOA-Great Britain files, ZA; Ben-Gurion, *Zikhronot*, 676-696.

92 Ben-Gurion, *Zikhronot*, 696-700.

93 Ben-Gurion, *Zikhronot*, 700-702; Jewish Agency Executive statement, Nov. 15, 1933, ZOA-Great Britain files, ZA.

94 Weizmann to Warburg, Nov. 20, 1933, Z4/17026a, CZA.

95 Weizmann–Cunliffe-Lister interview, Nov. 24, 1933, WA; London *Times*, Nov. 23, 1933; M. MacDonald-Brodetsky-Lourie interview, Nov. 14, 1933, ZOA-Great Britain files, ZA.

96 Ben-Gurion, *Zikhronot*, 705-708.

97 Haj Amin-Wauchope interview, Dec. 5, 1933, Colonial Office files (hereafter CO) 733/257/37356/I, PRO.

98 Ibid.; Halperin to Hadassah, January 13, 1936, Rose Jacobs MSS, HA; Norman Rose, "HaVikuah Al HaMoeitsa HaMehokeket BaShanim 1919-1936," in B. Oded, A. Rapaport, and Y. Shatzmiller, eds., *Mehkarim B'Toldot Am-Yisrael V'Eretz-Yisrael*, vol. 2 (Haifa, 1972), 217-245; Porath, *The Palestinian Arab National Movement*, 143-147. The 1922 White Paper, mainly formulated by Samuel, also declared that the Balfour Declaration's terms "do not contemplate that Palestine as a whole should be converted into a Jewish National Home, but that such a Home should be founded in Palestine." The Zionist Executive (including Jabotinsky) accepted this reluctantly, while the Arab Executive rejected it outright.

99 Porath, *Palstinian National Movement*, 148; Tagar, "HaMered HaAravi," 94.

100 London *Times*, Dec. 11, 1933; *Palestine Post*, Dec. 12, 1933; Ben-Gurion, *Zikronot*, 708-711, 718, 720-722; Shertok-d'Aumale interview, Dec. 20, 1933, F38/1081, CZA. A British police report also noted that the idea of expelling any Jew from the national home was "abhorrent to all sections" of Palestinian Jewry, while the Arabs were trying to purchase land for needy Arabs. Summary, Dec. 19, 1933, FO 371/17878, PRO.

101 *New York Times*, Oct. 15, 1933; Robert Dell, *The Truth About the Jews in Germany* (New York, 1933[?]); Weizmann report, Dec. 18, 1933, L13/154a, CZA; *JTA* confidential reports, Nov. 29, 1933, and Dec. 22, 1933, General and Emergency Germany General files, American Jewish Joint Distribution Committee Archives, New York City.

102 Dell, *The Truth About the Jews in Germany*, 9; Weizmann address, Dec. 6, 1933, and Weizmann report, Dec. 18, 1933, both in L13/154a, CZA; Baeck to McDonald, Nov. 20, 1933, file C1605/15, League of Nations Archives (hereafter LNA), Geneva; *New York Times*, Dec. 24, 1933; Drummond to Simon, Dec. 13, 1933, FO 371/16932, PRO.

103 Billikopf to Hyman, Sept. 25, 1933, microfilm #1919, Warburg MSS; Rothenberg report, Dec. 7, 1933, Morris Rothenberg MSS, ZA; *Roosevelt and Frankfurter: Their Correspondence, 1928-1945*, ed. M. Freedman (Boston, 1967), 164; Roosevelt address, Dec. 28, 1933, Box 149, Sumner Welles MSS, Franklin D. Roosevelt Library (hereafter FDRL), Hyde Park, New York.

104 Ruppin, *Memoirs, Diaries, Letters*, 265. For *Filastin*'s strong opposition at this time to the possibility of partitioning Palestine into a Jewish and an Arab zone, see "Palestine—Sur le project de division de la Palestine en deux zones, juive et arabe," *l'Oriente Moderne* (Feb. 1934), 79-80.

2. Racing Against Time

One year after Hitler's rise to the chancellorship, the "cold pogrom" against those whom he called "Jewish maggots" went on unabated. It made no difference that Jews constituted less than one percent of the total German population and were even decreasing in ratio, or that some 12,000 had died as soldiers for the Fatherland in the years 1914-1918. Nor the fact that not one Jew could be found in the German federal cabinet in Germany or in any of its state cabinets, in the high administration of the federal railways, the Reichsbank, or the Prussian State Bank. In all, there were only 15 persons who had had a Jewish grandfather or grandmother among the 500 highest federal officials of all sorts in Germany; the last Reichstag had only one Jewish representative out of 608 members. Addressing the Cologne Chamber of Commerce, banker Kurt von Schröder, a leading member of the Third Reich's Economic Council, expressed the wish that all industrial and commercial affairs be placed under "purely Aryan leadership." Although skeptical of High Commissioner McDonald's efforts for refugees, Ambassador Dodd acknowledged on February 7, 1934, that "Hitler is never going to cease trying to ban all Jews from the Reich." Reporting two weeks later about the objection of a Leipzig schoolteacher and her principal to a young girl's reading in assembly a vicious antisemitic poem by Dietrich Eckhart, whose ideology had an early and decisive influence on Hitler, the *Berliner Tagblatt* approved of their dismissal for an "intolerable" misconception of their duties. "We must multiply this little incident to cover a thousand towns and villages," concluded Hamilton Fish Armstrong, and especially consider "the effect on the mass of German children whose hearts are being hardened and spirits warped."[1]

Viewing this "crushing attack" by a "totalitarian state" against the Jews, who represented "the very embodiment" of individual freedom and intellectual liberty, Weizmann asserted that only on Palestine's soil could Jewry reestablish and maintain those values now being threatened with extinction. England, he wrote to the British journalist and Christian Zionist Herbert Sidebotham on January 2, had therefore "no mean chance to help in this great process" of reconstruction of a community which, joining its strategic and economic position to its spiritual values, "fits so appropriately into the orbit of that great confederation of nations known as the British Empire." He was "heartily sick" of talk about whether they would have a Jewish state or not, on one side of the Jordan or both. Such discussion, Weizmann felt, constituted "Jerusalem of the upper regions." Focusing, from the vantage point of a practicing chemist, on politics as the art of the possible, the Zionist leader called for an annual immigration that would bring the yishuv up to a half million in four to five years. With Polish Jewry "destroyed," Russian Jewry "disappearing," American Jewry "on the edge," and German Jewry "declining," he told a Zionist General Council meeting in London on January 14, achieving this immigration would mean that the foundations of the Jewish National Home were "well and truly laid, and that it would not be wiped out any more."[2]

From Jerusalem, Ben-Gurion expanded on the same point in a long letter to Brandeis on January 5. Aside from the German-Jewish catastrophe, he worried that the "germ of the poisoning Nazi propaganda against Jews" was spreading slowly in England and France. Given the settlement during the last year of over 40,000 Jews in Palestine, where an acute shortage of labor prevailed, the country could now absorb 50,000 Jews per annum. Raising the Jewish population to about half a million would not yet be the "National Home," nor would that be the solution of the Jewish problem. A close settlement of at least 5-6 million Jews on both sides of the Jordan was possible, Ben-Gurion went on, but 500,000 would force the Arabs *"bon gré mal gré"* to come to terms with the yishuv. Attaining this number was "a political question of the first magnitude," because "another world war might be in store for us in a few years' time" in light of the looming German and the Japanese perils. If in such an emergency Palestinian Jewry were found wanting in strength and numbers, "we might be wiped out altogether, and all the labour of generations will come to naught." The Colonial Secretary was "assailed with doubts," and no other government would quarrel with His Majesty's Government (HMG) for the yishuv's sake, yet Zionists would find nowhere else "better and truer friends" than those they already had in England. A "friendly hint" from the American government "might help us a good deal," Ben-Gurion closed, but he was not qualified to express an opinion on this subject.[3]

Writing a similar letter to Anthony de Rothschild, Ben-Gurion added that Cunliffe-Lister had expressed worries about Arab opposition, although the Colonial Secretary did not mention "many actions of the Revisionists which were liable to undermine completely British trust in Zionism." These included the Revisionists' clash in Tel Aviv with the police the previous month over restricted immigration and, with the start of the New Year, Jabotinsky's launching a petition to King George V, the British Parliament, and other parliaments and prime ministers. On January 24, the Jewish Agency denounced the world-wide petition, which called for opening Palestine's gates to Jewish entry, as sabotaging Zionist politics, "harmful to the Zionist Movement and to the interests of the Jewish National Home." In exercising its right and duty of criticizing HMG "whenever circumstances so demand," the Agency based its policy "on relations of mutual cooperation" between the mandatory power and the Jews. In response to Betar's secret directive "No. 60" to boycott Agency certificates, the Agency also took steps to annul, at least temporarily, all aliya privileges for Betar members.[4]

The investigation of Arlosoroff's murder further exacerbated tensions between the yishuv's political Left and Right. A seeming breakthrough occurred in January, when Abdul Medjid El-Kurdi, in prison for another murder charge, confessed to Rice and then to Shitreet that he and companion Issa Darwish had been involved in killing the Jewish leader. Hearing of this startling news from the C.I.D.'s Riggs, Jewish police officer Shlomo Rosenstein had it transmitted to defense lawyer Samuel, who unsuccessfully raised the issue in court. After members of the Arab Executive visited his cell, Abdul Medjid then claimed that Stavsky and Rosenblatt had offered him a substantial bribe to confess the murder. BaMa'aleh and broadsides printed on Davar's machinery immediately pounced on the "unclean and bloody" Revisionists, who vehemently denied the allegation. Samuel accused the police of manipulating Sima's testimony, and proposed that the killing was connected to an intended sexual attack on Mrs. Arlosoroff by the two Arabs, much as Arabs had raped a Jewish woman near the same spot and then killed her and her male companion in 1931. Mapai and the Histadrut, with Ben-Gurion at the helm, relied on the widow's testimony. Jabotinsky retorted at the end of February that while the Jewish "jackals" in Eretz Yisrael dreamt that Jews would be convicted, the "clams" of the yishuv permitted the intrigue, more brazen than the Dreyfus and Beilis cases, to go unchallenged.[5]

Illegal Jewish immigration and Arab unemployment continued to preoccupy Wauchope. In a confidential letter to Sir Osmond d'Avigdor Goldsmid, chairman of the Jewish Colonization Association (ICA), the High Commissioner observed that "a certain set back" in Palestine's present period of prosperity had to be considered aside from the country's immediate labor requirements. Cunliffe-Lister had agreed, too, that taking Arab unemployment into account was not only right, but strictly in accord with MacDonald's 1931 letter to Weizmann. If the Zionists would employ a proportion of Arab labor, this would not only reduce Arab unemployment, it would also inspire "a better feeling" with the Arabs. Estimating the numbers of unsanctioned Jewish immigrants at 10,000 in 1933, Wauchope noted that 99 Jews and 178 Arabs had been deported in the last five months, and the "strongest measures" against all illegals would be taken from now on. He permitted peaceful Arab demonstrations against the mandatory, Wauchope informed Shertok on January 18, because "there was a great deal to be said in favour of a policy of letting off steam." He thought it "a mistaken policy" for yishuv newspapers to persistently impute weakness to the administration. This would make the Jews themselves "more nervous," while leading the Arabs to believe that HMG was truly weak and "liable to change its policy under threats." To Jewish and Arab leaders alike, Wauchope stressed that he was fully prepared to assume full responsibility for the country's internal security.[6]

Falastin's advocacy of an impending conference of Christian Arabs caused Shertok additional concern, particularly when sources in the Italian Consulate informed him that Charles R. Crane stood behind this campaign, with the Pope's approval, to gain support in the western Christian world against Zionism. Inheriting his father's millions from the manufacture of toilet bowl fittings, this Chicago businessman had visited Palestine and Syria with Henry King at the request of President Wilson, and then co-authored a report in August 1919 that recommended to the U.S. delegation at Versailles that Jewish immigration to Palestine be strictly limited and Palestine be included in a Syrian state. Crane subsequently became a fervent opponent of the Soviet regime ("a Jewish Empire, killing, starving and generally mistreating Christians") and an unqualified admirer of Saudi Arabian monarch Abdul Aziz Ibn

Saud, whom he visited in 1931 and then helped start oil explorations in Saudi Arabia. In January 1933, Arabs cabled a request to Crane that he provide financial assistance to enable them to buy back the land which Abdullah had leased to the Jewish Agency. That July, he advised Dodd to "let Hitler have his way," seeing Germany as "the real political bulwark of Christian culture." A private audience with Hitler, whom Crane later praised as "a man of great power with a definite, clear program that he is pushing through with the greatest energy," found both men having a passionate hatred of Jews and of certain foreign powers.[7]

Meeting with a highly appreciative Haj Amin in February 1931 and again in March 1933, Crane had proposed talks with the Vatican to plan an offensive against "the political Jews everywhere" who "aimed at the eventual destruction of religious life." On November 24, 1933, Crane reported to a distinguished group of Muslim clerics in Cairo that he had found Cardinal Eugenio Pacelli, the Papal Secretary of State, "very receptive and interested" in a Catholic-Muslim "united front" to counter an organized world campaign against faith and religion. (A few months earlier, in meeting with McDonald, Pacelli had defended his Concordat of understanding with the Nazi government, and indicated that the Vatican would not do anything to protest the persecution of German Jews.) The Papal Secretary went so far as to suggest that the Mufti might meet the Latin Patriarch in Jerusalem and initiate con- versations. In Crane's opinion, the clerical group was told, one phase of that world crusade was the return of the Jews to Palestine after an absence of nearly 2,000 years, aided by British force. They were not "the old Hebrews from whom prophets had come," but "an altogether differ- ent sort of Jew, who were impregnated with communistic and atheistic ideas." Their arrival in the Holy Land was "primarily another move in the anti-God campaign which they had started in Russia and elsewhere, and by which they hoped to achieve the annihilation of established religion and indeed of all belief in God." The gentlemen present "fell in with this view," thanked Crane warmly, and begged him "not to forget us."[8]

To George Antonius, Crane's Arabic translator in the Middle East ever since their first meeting in 1919, the group soon expressed their readiness to enter into immediate negotiations with "the other party." The Lebanese Greek-Orthodox Christian regularly reported to the el- derly American about the plans of the Mufti, the Muslim Congress, and the Arab Executive, as well as his own contacts with Bentwich, Hebrew

University Chancellor Judah Magnes, and historian Hans Kohn, all Jewish champions of a bi-nationalist Palestine, and his talks with Wauchope and Cunliffe-Lister. In the autumn of 1932, gaining access to "jealously guarded" archives, Antonius began working on a history of the Arab nationalist movement, including interviews with Feisal and other leading personalities. Crane, quick to finance this pioneering endeavor via an Institute for Current World Affairs in New York City, received letters from Antonius in the latter half of 1933 warning that the Zionists were "exploiting up to the hilt" the "anti-Jewish pressures of the Hitler Government"; that "each tide of Jewish settlers on the land" drove off Arab cultivators"; and that the Arabs gradually saw HMG as "the real enemy," reasoning that "if it were not for the subservience of the British, the Jews would be powerless." To the visiting pro-Soviet, anti-Zionist American journalist Louis Fischer, Antonius talked about an emerging and unifying nationalism in the entire Arab world, with the Jews "building a rich new home in the crater of a volcano."[9]

Antonius shared some of his views with Leo Kohn on January 31, hosting the Agency's newly appointed Political Secretary in the beautiful home, half way up Mt. Scopus, which the Mufti had presented to him. Antonius sought to compare the Arab nationalist cause with the Irish struggle against the British, about which Kohn had written. He averred that Arab revolutionaries, just like Arthur Griffith and Michael Collins, had risen above sectarian divisions to show a "statesmanlike attitude" towards minorities, "though this might not yet be visible to the public eye." He considered the Arabs to be "the aggrieved party." The mandate "must be revised," although "there is nothing in the Balfour Declaration that any fair-minded man could not subscribe to." Not going into details about these revisions, Antonius charged that the Jews already had their National Home with Tel Aviv, colonies all over the country, and the Hebrew University, and that relations between Jews and Arab were "worse than they had ever been." To emphasize the inherent extremism of the Zionism ideal, he remarked rather suddenly: "You know, if I had been a Zionist, I would have insisted on every Arab being removed from Palestine." Realizing that he had gone too far, Antonius then said "I really meant to say, if I were a Revisionist." "How much easier would it have been," he observed, "if the Zionists had gone to northern Syria, where there is so much more scope for development and where conditions are so much simpler." "Surely," Kohn rejoined, "there were some historical reasons which could not be ignored." Antonius nodded his head "rather doubtfully," and with that their lengthy conversation came to a close.[10]

Kohn correctly concluded from remarks by Antonius, as well as by Immigration Commissioner Eric Mills, that the Mufti faction now favored the creation of a central Legislative Council even with initial safeguards for Palestine's Jewish minority. In January, Wauchope moved forward to this end by initiating a Municipal Corporations Ordinance, under whose terms citizens prepared to elect their own local representatives for the first time since 1927. In an interview with the High Commissioner on February 9, Shertok and Ben-Zvi insisted on equality in the electoral committee for Jerusalem and an even division of seats in its municipal government. Two weeks later, Shertok warned Wauchope that the reappointment of Mayor Ragheb Nashashibi, "a type of *ancient régime*" despot whose neglect of the Jewish sections of the city and "gross irregularities" in general method had led the City Council's three Jewish members to resign five years earlier, would again result in the yishuv's non-cooperation. In addition, the Agency faulted the amended Ordinance for continuing to limit the vote to Palestinian citizens and permitting the owners of houses in the Old City, nearly all of them non-Jews, to vote without paying taxes. Both amendments threatened to turn the Jewish majority in Jerusalem (50,000 to 30,000 non-Jews) into a minority. The demand, maintained all along by the yishuv organizations, that the vote be extended to non-citizens prevented them from conducting at the same time a campaign for naturalization. Had such a campaign been undertaken, the position of the Jews in Jerusalem, Jaffa, and Haifa would have been much stronger at the time.[11]

The Zionists took heart with the February 19 arrival in Haifa's newly opened port, aboard the *SS Martha Washington* of the Lloyd Triestino Line, of the first German-Jewish Youth Aliya group assembled and trained for settlement in Palestine by Recha Freier's *Jüdische Jugendhilfe* with the support of HehHalutz and Wilfrid Israel's associates. Despite lengthy bureaucratic formalities and a steadily pelting rain, a welcome change from the devastating drought of the three preceding years, good humor prevailed as the twenty-five boys and eighteen girls made their way to Ein Harod. Now an integral part of the kibbutz's six-hundred members, among them ninety Jewish refugees recently come from Germany, the youngsters burst spontaneously into Hebrew song. After lunch came the inevitable, lively Hora dance of the halutzim, and then the newcomers made for housing in temporary wooden barracks. The group's leaders, Szold reported to the Central Bureau for the Settlement of German Jews into Palestine, expressed regret that eighteen more had not come, ten of whom had been denied certificates because they had passed their seventeenth birthday. Under the title "Palestine Gathers in the Exiles," Hadassah National President Rose Jacobs concluded: "The Jew, unhampered and unchained, freed from inhibitions imposed by alien majorities, will once more create new values of the spirit and new social forms in his Homeland. May this be in our day!"[12]

Weizmann, chairman of the Central Bureau, had just met Benito Mussolini to solicit the Fascist leader's help. A first meeting after World War I had left Weizmann with the impression that his host was not hostile to Zionism but suspicious that HMG were using the Zionists in order to cut across Italian control of the eastern Mediterranean. A second meeting in April 1933 was followed by a far more significant encounter on February 17, 1934, just when the Duce was at odds with Hitler over Austria. Mussolini showed much sympathy with his guest's cause, stating for the first time "You must create a Jewish state." Consenting that this "is the Archimedian fulcrum," Weizmann would not, however, exchange Rome for the Zionists' alliance with London. On a future occasion, he told the Colonial Secretary why almost all Jews and Zionists attached no value to Mussolini's "enticement": "Rome has destroyed Jerusalem; she will never build it up." He was also aware that Italy's Count Theodoli consistently posed in the Permanent Mandates Commission as the great defender of Arab rights and of the Catholic Church against the alleged Jewish introduction of "flagrant atheism" and excessive liberalism into the Holy Land. Still, Weizmann needed Italian goodwill in the international arena, as well as for boat departures from ports to Palestine and for intervention, as he had first urged Mussolini in June 1933, with those "who control the present destinies of Germany" regarding the "appalling problem" of Jews in the Third Reich.[13]

As for Mussolini's proposal concerning a "State of Zion" along the Mediterranean coast, Weizmann argued that Jews had to make up at least half of Palestine's population before territorial solutions could be discussed. According to Weizmann's interview two days later with British Ambassador Drummond, he had advised Mussolini that a division within Palestine already existed, with 75 percent of the Arabs in the hill districts and Jews mainly settled on the coast and in the plain.

This reflected Weizmann's endorsement of Palestine's partition during a talk with the director of the League's Mandates Section three months earlier, an idea which Britain's Foreign Office found "impractical" and the Colonial Office insisted should not be encouraged in order to give Italy "any special interest" not shared by the other Allied powers at the San Remo Conference.

Weizmann also explained to Drummond that he was "considerably troubled" by the large influx of German Jews into Palestine, for they were "difficult to absorb," and he did not see how the hundreds of thousands of Jewish refugees who had sought refuge in France, Poland, and Czechoslovakia could possibly be admitted into Palestine. The Zionist herald's concern surfaced as well in an Italian Foreign Ministry official's reports that, according to Weizmann, a settlement with the Arabs had to be put off until the Jewish population reached half a million. Further, Weizmann had candidly remarked to him that it would take "more than a few years" to mold the "Tower of Babel" which now constituted the yishuv into "an organic society": "Turn the Zionist community into a State? Internal strife would soon finish it off!"[14]

Given the gravity of the hour and looking to the near future, Ben-Gurion focused on immigration as Zionism's central problem. "The Hitler regime threatens the entire Jewish people," he had warned the fourth conference of the Histadrut in January. The Third Reich government could not survive for long without "a war of revenge" against France, Poland, Czechoslovakia, and the other neighboring countries where Germanic communities lived, or against Soviet Russia "with its wide expanses." Insofar as the future could be told, Jewry now faced "as great a danger of war as confronted the world prior to 1914," and that war "will be more disastrous and more terrible than the last." Perhaps four to five years stood between Jewry and "that dreadful day," which was why during that period the yishuv had to double its numbers. As for the Arabs, Mapai's Council was informed on March 22, Ben-Gurion would first offer parity in the government under the mandate, with neither Jew nor Arab dominating the other. Attaining a Jewish majority would then result in a Jewish state in Palestine, including Transjordan, to be joined to an Arab Federation. The latter proposal Ben-Gurion had already advocated in articles for *HaPoel HaTsa'ir* (1930-1931) and in his book *Anahnu U'Sh'kheineinu* (We and Our Neighbors).[15]

Considering his own formula far better than a Legislative Council with no real power given to either Arabs or Jews, Ben-Gurion, after consulting with Shertok, decided to broach the idea to Musa al-Alami that same month. From this talk with an Arab who, in Ben-Gurion's words, "had a reputation as a nationalist and a man not to be bought by money or by office, but who was not a Jew-hater either," Ben-Gurion and Shertok realized for the first time that the Arabs would oppose the Jews despite the benefits provided them by the Zionist movement. He would "prefer the land to remain poor and desolate even for another hundred years," Alami remarked, "until the Arabs themselves were capable of developing it and making it flower." While Arabs were also benefiting from Jewish development, the situation of the masses was "desperate." Their economic positions were "collapsing one by one," Alami observed. Why should the Arabs agree to a Jewish state including Transjordan, and why accept parity when they were four-fifths of Palestine's population? Ben-Gurion concluded that Alami was "sincere, straightforward and sensible." According to Alami's subsequent recollection, he also cited to the Agency officials many Zionist publications which "betrayed both expansionist designs and hatred of the Arabs." The three men parted on friendly terms, Alami favorably impressed by Ben-Gurion's forthrightness but also admitting to himself that he had been "incredibly naïve" in the past, not realizing that even these leaders, who were not "reckoned extremists," had made it "crystal clear that they were aiming at nothing less than the complete control of the country."[16]

At this point, factional rivalries and radicalizing pressures undermined the possibility of a united Palestinian Arab camp. The Husseini and Nashashibi families continued to bicker. As president of the Palestine Arab Executive, the elderly Musa Kazim had hesitated to confront the British openly, but "drifted with the political currents" and lent the name of the Executive to the protests initiated by youth groups and Istiqlal activists. On March 25, his 26-year-old son, Abd al-Qadir al-Husseini, met with almost thirty others in Jenin to decide on future strategy. Three years earlier, al-Husseini had founded a secret militant group of youngsters in Jerusalem known as al-Jihad al-Muqaddas (Holy War Society), who took first steps to prepare themselves for armed struggle. Their most important decision now was to reorganize into five-man cells and to elect a committee to assist their leader. The next day Musa Kazim died, after which the Arab Executive disintegrated swiftly.[17]

Some sheikhs questioned the handling of Waqf funds by Haj Amin, whose recent voyage to raise money in India had not been a success, and asked Wauchope for an impartial investigation. Abdullah continued to distrust the Mufti, particularly after the latter's trip to request Ibn Saud's support. "How can Haj Amin," he asked Shertok, "expect me to assist him in fighting his enemies—the Zionists—when he himself is throwing in his lot with my arch-enemy, the Wahhabi King?" At the same time, the C.I.D. reported that the Istiqlal groups in Damascus and associates in Haifa were calling for further agitation (unlike the Mufti). Even *Falastin*, noted for its generally moderate tone, carried an article which spoke of the "accelerated annihilation of the Arabs." The Arab leaders, concluded this report, were "more desperate" than ever before.[18]

Political rivalries within the yishuv and what he considered the many "non-productive" Jewish immigrants who recently entered Palestine particularly worried Weizmann. "If not for the British police there would have been a fratricidal war in the literal sense of the word," he wrote to close friend Israel Sieff on March 9. Three days later, during a meeting with Wauchope, Weizmann expressed great uneasiness over the number of "luftmensch" arrivals from Germany. When the High Commissioner expressed his fear of admitting too many immigrants in one year lest an economic setback occur, Weizmann quickly explained that the doors should be "thrown wide open" to all Jewish workers, where demand currently far exceeded supply. Further, he argued, the cause of suffering Jewry outside of Palestine and the urgent need to increase the yishuv's population to half a million warranted this request.

Asked about dividing Palestine into "two zones," Weizmann said that in the long run it all depended on the future of Transjordan. The Agency had renewed its option on Abdullah's Ghore al-Kibd territory two months earlier. "Neither I nor Cunliffe-Lister had changed our minds that the time was not yet ripe for Jewish settlement there," Wauchope replied, asking if Weizmann had changed his. Weizmann responded that he looked on the Huleh as "the bridgehead," and asked if the High Commissioner could arrange a meeting between Abdullah and himself. This would mislead the Emir, Wauchope countered, "and only lead to the hands of the clock being put further back." Mussolini had asked him the same question about partitioning Palestine, Weizmann remarked, and he would reply to Wauchope with the same response that he had given Il Duce: "He would give the answer five years hence."[19]

The possibility of Jewish refugee settlement in Transjordan and adjacent lands attracted James Rosenberg, who first met Neumann on March 14 at the suggestion of Brandeis ally Judge Julian Mack. A non-Zionist lawyer who served on the executive boards of the American Jewish Joint Distribution Committee and the American Jewish Committee and had first recommended McDonald for High Commissioner, Rosenberg considered emigration to be the only "lifesaving" answer to the Nazi policy of "complete extermination" of the Jews. Weizmann's strong opposition to the Neumann-Farbstein effort surprised him. He wrote a long letter seeking Warburg's support, seeing Transjordan, with fewer than 300,000 Arabs, as the natural agricultural hinterland to an increasingly industrialized Palestine, and offering an effective way to break "what is now perhaps threatening to become a united Arab front against Jews." The "greatly enhanced standard of living" of Palestine's Arabs over the past ten years, as against the "poverty, destitution and degradation" of the Arabs in Transjordan, had impressed the Emir and the sheiks. Developing the port of Akaba, thereby giving Britain access to India independent of the Suez Canal, and the entire Wady-el-Araba from there to the Dead Sea on both sides of the Jordan would benefit both Arabs and Jews. (Brandeis had written a memorandum along these lines a year ago July, similar to Warburg's own proposal, favoring a corporation with a first $1 million provided that HMG gave its approval.) James McDonald demurred, however. After consulting with Bentwich, he warned Rosenberg of British concerns about arousing a "serious Arab movement" which would affect Palestine, considering that "Arab national feeling is extremely sensitive throughout the Middle East."[20]

Seeking an advance on the immigration schedule as soon as the last batch of certificates had run out in the third week of February, Shertok pressed Wauchope for 3,000 certificates in light of the growing shortage of labor. Practically no Jews could be found in public works like the Haifa port, industry was handicapped, and construction and agricultural projects had been delayed. Skilled and unskilled workers were urgently needed, and even Arab labor and a continued influx of Arabs from across Palestine's borders did not solve the problem. On March 15, Wauchope decided to grant only 1,350, on the condition that 1,000 were allotted to Germany. Shertok immediately observed to Chief Secretary Hall, much as Weizmann had told Wauchope three days earlier, that many of the German refugees were unsuitable for manual labor, while only 400 labor immigrants were ready to leave Germany in the course of the next month. The Agency wanted the very maximum of 30 percent allotted for Germany; it would be much easier to bring over thousands of workers from Poland and other countries. The occupational character of the Jewish people abroad was not exactly "of the character Palestine was demanding. If that were the case, there would have been no need for Zionism." Students, shop assistants, and petty traders in the Diaspora, Shertok explained, had been transformed in Palestine to acquire their skills in the various branches of manual labor. Just before leaving for a visit to Iraq, Wauchope decided that 500 of the advance were to be given to Germany, keeping a 30 percent allotment for that country if the new schedule was not larger than the previous one and more certificates, although not at the same rate, if it were larger.[21]

The meager advance appeared to mock German Jewry's plight. Lloyd George was "sorry to hear" that reports of Hitler's "toning down his attack on Israel" had no foundation, bringing British barrister and popular writer Philip Guedalla to reply: "My impression is that the offensive is gradually passing into a war of starvation. If so, I feel that Abdul Hamid was kinder to the Armenians." The general situation, Wilfrid Israel reported to the Joint Foreign Committee on March 21, seemed to be heading towards "a social revolution or an intense militarization of every phase of life—whichever way it goes, the Jewish question will be revived and used as an excuse." An anti-Jewish boycott day, fixed for March 23, was cancelled only because the German Foreign, Finance, and Economic Ministers got the president of the Chamber of Commerce in Berlin to persuade Hitler against the measure. Streicher pleaded unsuccessfully to have his way in Nuremberg, but signs in the townships all around the city continued to carry signs that "no Jews are welcome." On the night of March 25-26, Jewish houses were attacked in Ellwangen, Mitelfranken, and Fürth; the entire male Jewish population in Gunsenhausen was beaten, and some died.[22]

Three days later, Cunliffe-Lister submitted to the cabinet a lengthy memorandum on Palestine marked "VERY SECRET." While the situation in Palestine appeared "outwardly calm" after the Arab disorders and riots of five months earlier, he began, "it is fundamentally unaltered." Wauchope had to maintain his considerable influence with the Mufti, "unquestionably the most influential Muslim in Palestine today." If the Mufti were "to throw in his lot with the extremists [sic], I should regard the position as much more serious." The Colonial Secretary evidently knew not of Haj Amin's unshakeable conviction that the Jews "corrupt morality in every single country, destroy all religions and sympathize with [communist] Russia ... rob people's property, steal money by usury, and distort the prophets' preaching." It was therefore very desirable to arrive at a settlement of the Muslim claims to Waqf funds quickly. Cunliffe-Lister found "very satisfactory" the official report on the "disturbances" between October 13 and November 3, 1933, which exonerated the police from the Arab charge of their using unreasonable force and highly praised the conduct of individual officers in charge at Jerusalem, Jaffa, and Haifa. Special measures were being taken to combat illicit immigration, which had assumed "alarming proportions" the previous year.

Cunliffe-Lister then turned his attention to the contending people of Palestine. There was no use "blinking the fact" that Arabs and Jews were "diametrically opposed" on the whole subject of immigration. Arabs wished a complete embargo, while Jewish extremists made claims to unlimited entry and had "avowed determination" to make Palestine a Jewish state. Arab hostility was not merely aimed at Jews, but at HMG as "the authors" of immigration. In assuming the country's absorptive capacity, Wauchope "must take a reasonably long view," including the normal increase of the Arab population. Out of an Arab population of over 750,000 according to the 1931 Census, Cunliffe-Lister observed in this respect, there were about 150,000 male Muslims under the age of 15. The High Commissioner also had to have regard for Arab unemployment.

How to resolve the enmity between Arab and Jew? In the Colonial Secretary's opinion, the only real solution could be found in the Jews abandoning the principle of exclusive Jewish labor and showing in practice that Arabs benefited directly by Jewish land purchase and industrial development. A meeting hosted by Cunliffe-Lister in London that past summer, attended by Wauchope, Weizmann, Rutenberg, Sokolow, Anthony de Rothschild, and Lord Reading, had found all participants in accord that no Jewish settlement in Transjordan could occur until the High Commissioner was satisfied that it could take place with "safety and goodwill." They had further agreed that Arabs should be employed in the Zionist development schemes for the Jordan and Huleh Valleys, and were "inclined to agree" that the Agency would have to modify its policy of only employing Jews—a position from which Weizmann had since receded. As to the Legislative Council, Cunliffe-Lister wished that the proposal had never been made, but "we are unfortunately absolutely committed by undertakings given in Parliament and to the Permanent Mandates Commission to make another attempt." The reform of local government was beginning, but the Council would not have executive authority. Still, several influential Arabs had told him that they would proceed to try to "mould the legislation which came before us." Concluding, Cunliffe-Lister admitted that he had no concrete proposals to make presently as to the Council, but these must "in due course" be put forward.[23]

The Colonial Secretary shared some of his thoughts with McDonald on April 9, beginning with why he would have to oppose "in every possible way" Jewish settlement in Transjordan. Doubting that the so-called concession secured by the Agency from Abdullah for agricultural lands was seriously intended by the latter, he quoted the sheiks as saying to their followers, "It is all right for us to lease out land to the Jews; after they have settled on it, you will be free to kill them. Then we will have our money, and you will have the land back again." He had persuaded Weizmann not to continue these negotiations, and repeated that premature Jewish activities in Transjordan might lead to the killing of British soldiers in Palestine, in turn possibly arousing British public opinion to demand that any British government close Palestine's doors for "a considerable time to come." Sir Philip then complained to McDonald of illegal Jewish immigration, which Laski and associates had in fact requested HMG to denounce. He hesitated to do this, however, and had insisted instead that the Agency authorities be "more severe themselves"; Weizmann had promised his cooperation. McDonald's only suggestion was that Cunliffe-Lister speak again to Weizmann with "added emphasis." McDonald reported to Warburg the gist of the conversation, which corroborated his earlier strictures to Rosenberg, in the strictest confidence. On April 11, the cabinet asked Cunliffe-Lister to draw up detailed proposals for creating the Legislative Council.[24]

The yishuv also had to contend with dramatic developments, centered in the person of Chief Rabbi Avraham Yitzhak Kook, relating to the Arlosoroff murder investigation. Shitreet conveyed the gist of what he had personally heard from Abdul Mejdid in January to Sephardi Chief Rabbi Ya'akov Meir, who in turn passed on the information to a British district court magistrate named Joseph Moshe Valero and to

Meir's Ashkenazi counterpart, the greatly respected Avraham Yitzhak Kook. Kook had hailed Jabotinsky as "a courageous, mighty spirit" after the latter was imprisoned in 1920 for defense activity against Arab assaults; he defended Jewish eternal rights to the Western ("Wailing") Wall following the Arab riots of 1929; he intervened shortly thereafter to get Moshe Segal released from jail when the Betar member became the first to defy British law against blowing a *shofar* at the conclusion of Yom Kippur prayers alongside the Western Wall. He also denounced the Passfield White Paper, declared settlement in Eretz Yisrael to be a divine injunction equal to all other biblical commandments, and told Wauchope that "illegal immigrants" were actually "returning natives." Yet when Katz pressed Kook to intervene, the Chief Rabbi always responded that he relied upon Mordekhai Eliash, his former student and an observant Jew, who had served for a time as one of the four Jewish Agency appointees on the legal team to represent Sima Arlosoroff.[25]

A faith in British justice and especially in Eliash explains Kook's early response, notwithstanding the entreaties of Rabbi Natan Milikovsky (Netanyahu) that he intervene on behalf of the Revisionists. Kook cherished Milikovsky, an outstanding Zionist preacher in Yiddish who had converted thousands across Siberia and Poland to the cause before and during World War I. When Milikovsky's oldest of nine children, Ben-Zion, a Revisionist who edited the magazine *Betar* with Klausner, told him that he saw Ahimeir in Jerusalem on the evening of Arlosoroff's murder, the father commenced his own investigation. He pressed Kook to intercede, but the Chief Rabbi preferred to wait for the court's verdict. Ahimeir's personal plea to Kook also went unanswered. Kook's doubts surfaced at a private meeting of illustrious yishuv personalities on the evening of March 13 in Tel Aviv, where, in tandem with the city's Chief Rabbis, Ben-Zion Uziel and Shlomo Aronson, he called for a truce between the warring political parties without arriving at judgment. It was finally decided that a proclamation should be issued against the rising political violence, and also to consider creating a committee to gather funds for the Stavsky-Rosenblatt-Ahimeir defense team.[26]

Milikovsky's tenacity at this point proved to be critical. In the course of a conversation with Betar official Yosef Katznelson, the latter bitingly challenged his praise of Jewish ethics, noting that even Kook had done nothing about the court case against the Revisionists. Greatly troubled, Milikovsky went straight to Kook's home with his son Ben-Zion and opened a discussion that lasted for three hours. He insisted that Kook break his silence; charged that Jews were worse than the Arabs, whose religious leaders spearheaded their political wars; and noted the eminent Jews of past generations who had sacrificed their own lives to save the innocent. When these arguments failed, Milikovsky stood up, all atremble, white with fever, and shouted:

> Please remember! In this city of Jerusalem, one innocent man was already hanged. And the Jewish people have paid for this with 1,800 years of servitude, tears, and blood. Do you wish to create in Jerusalem a new Jesus, to revive the crucified one from Nazereth?

Knitting his eyebrows, an agitated Kook asked for further explanation about the prosecution's charges. Milikosvky responded with a paragraph-by-paragraph analysis of Katz's *Lo Ukhal L'Hahashot*. Ultimately receiving the Chief Rabbi's approval to create a defense committee and his pledge to help with whatever Milikovsky requested, the overjoyed visitor set to the task with limitless fervor.[27]

Kook took the lead from then on, expressing to a small group the certainty "more than 100 percent" that the accused, whom Kook called "Prisoners of Zion," were innocent. Direct reports about the accused from "Reb" Aryeh Levin, who visited the three men in jail every Sabbath morning, strengthened the Chief Rabbi's resolve. On April 24, a public announcement, appearing in the first issue of Ben-Zion Netanyahu's newspaper *HaYarden*, requested funds for the defense of "our imprisoned three brothers" on trial in Jerusalem. The signatories included Kook, Uziel, Aronson, Klausner, Smilansky, Milikovsky, Berlin, Sirkis, Suprasky, and the eminent educator David Yellin, among others. Another manifesto, the authors of which included Dizengoff and Druyanov, called upon all factions in the yishuv to desist from political violence and civil war. At the private March 13 meeting, Bialik had criticized the current "baseless war" in the yishuv, attacked the education of the Left for transmitting "hatred and poison against their opponents to the hearts of small children," and supported aiding the defense "to raise it to its proper place and to honor it." Now, his name was conspicuously absent from both declarations.[28]

The next day, Ben-Gurion and Shertok made their appeal to Wauchope for 20,000 certificates in the next six-month schedule. After reiterating the argument of substantial labor shortages, which held back the yishuv's development, Shertok noted that agricultural labor was "irresistibly drained" by the better-paid occupations in the cities, and they had to safeguard Jewish positions in the orange plantations. Only about 100 out of the 2,000 new people who found employment in the Jaffa and Haifa ports were Jews, he added. As to Wauchope's concern about Arab unemployment, aside from the Agency's insistence on Jews employing Jews, the very fact that so many Arabs from outside Palestine were finding work showed that this concern was unfounded. Unlike Polish peasants in France and Italian laborers in Germany who regularly returned home, "outsiders were tempted to stay on indefinitely" in Palestine. A wide margin of unused capital existed in the country, and the process of investment and industrial expansion was steady. Wauchope did not seem to agree, however, with Ben-Gurion's insistence that the Agency be given the discretion to allot certificates in individual cases to people who were not of the skilled labor category. To their great disappointment, the High Commissioner also intended again to deduct a number of certificates on account of illicit settlement, currently averaging 500 per month, and was considering another deduction due to the 2,000 Palestinian young people coming of age and entering the labor market per year.

The Agency's discussion with the mandatory power about the admissible size of immigration had been going on for over two years, Ben-Gurion pointed out. Palestine's "tremendous development" had arisen from its economic possibilities and the "dire need" felt by the Jewish masses to migrate to Palestine, an urge which would not diminish. They were not only concerned about the quantitative size of the immigration, but "full of anxiety for the fate of Jewish labour in which they saw a basis of their national existence in Palestine." Their aim was not only to bring over "as many Jews as possible," but to bring them to "a healthy life by rooting as many of them as possible in the soil and in agricultural work." If small schedules continued, they stood to lose not only positions of employment created by Jewish capital, but also possibility of colonization. The settler's earnings as a wage laborer constituted an important element in the financing of any Zionist settlement scheme presently being undertaken. As the interview drew to a close after almost two hours, Shertok cut to the heart of the matter: "They might have put up with a slower pace," which Wauchope desired, "if they had the time safely stored away with them. The trouble was that they were running a hard race against time."[29]

McDonald's most recent sightings regarding the "Jewish Question" in Europe confirmed Shertok's cardinal observation. That same evening, Wilfrid Israel informed McDonald of Streicher's promise to "eradicate the Jews altogether" in Franconia; Israel foresaw a new German crisis approaching in which "one cannot safely ignore the possibility of another panicky exodus." One week earlier, George Messersmith, U.S. consul in Berlin, had cautioned McDonald that only when the Hitler government "is faced with the choice of destruction or yielding is there any chance that it will substantially moderate its Jewish policy." In Vienna, where newspapers printed selections from the *Protocols of the Learned Elders of Zion* and the city's 85,000 East European Jews faced what Laski termed a "completely hopeless" position, McDonald found Jewish leaders who were marked by timidity and insecurity over possibly antagonizing the increasingly right-wing regime of Austrian Premier Engelbert Dollfuss. The refugee situation in Czechoslovakia was "very serious" because the country was, as Foreign Minister Eduard Beneš put it to him, "an island of parliamentarianism surrounded by a sea of dictatorships." In Warsaw, McDonald was deeply impressed by Jabotinsky's honesty, "extraordinary mentality," and courage, but also by the fact that only the "strong arm" of sixty-six year old Marshal Józef Pilsudski held in check the "fanatical hatred" of the anti-Jewish Polish youth. Similar currents were "only too evident" in Rumania, Hungary, and "of course" in Austria. McDonald was also struck by the "unbelievable poverty" in Warsaw's Jewish living areas, and he noted "how piteously" the HehHalutz youth movement in Europe looked to Palestine, for them "the solace now and the hope for the future."[30]

Seeking to fulfill such expectations, Weizmann spoke to the French High Commissioner in Beirut about additional Jewish settlement in Syria. The French authorities were frightened, however, of German Jews as possible carriers of German influence; of "Zionist settlements" leading to a changing of frontiers; and of the Jews' arrival upsetting their desire to be left to peace ("*pas d'histoires*"). Some of the Arab newspapers in Damascus were less friendly than those of Beirut regarding his visit to Syria and Lebanon, Weizmann wrote to a British acquaintance on April 30, although Maronite Patriarch Arida gave him his blessing and promised "every possible support." The same day, Ruppin recorded that the head of Berlin's Jewish community was "extremely surprised" by Palestine's absorptive capacity, and by finding that hundreds of German Jewish refugees whom he encountered all felt "more or less settled." His diary entry concluded on an uncertain note: "The prosperity of Palestine in the midst of a world crisis is really fantastic. Will it last? Or is it only a fool's paradise?"[31]

On May 1, *Der Stürmer* published a special number with the front-page headline THE JEWISH MURDER PLOT AGAINST NON-JEWISH HUMANITY IS UNCOVERED. Accompanied by a drawing of two hideous-looking Jews collecting the blood of two naked Christian boys whom they had just murdered, one holding a blood-stained knife while a cross stands in the background, the issue endorsed the blood libel. Recalling that "legends and lies about the alleged custom of ritual murder by the Jews" had been "over and over again exposed," the Archbishop of Canterbury expressed his astonishment publicly "that such a publication, recalling the worst excesses of medieval fanaticism, should have been permitted in any civilized country." To the *New York Times* correspondent Frederick T. Birchall, this offered proof positive that the Nazi attitude toward the Jews "is *not* being modified, *it won't be modified*, in fact it *can't* be modified under this regime, for the regime depends on the spirit of men like Streicher." Close on the heels of Streicher's outburst, Goebbels' speeches sought to make the Jews responsible for Germany's present economic difficulties, then threatened them with a terrible vengeance in the event of these woes becoming even more acute. William Kube, Gauleiter of Brandenburg, using what the London *Times* called "robust language," compared Jewish influence to that of "plague, syphilis and consumption." Brutal assaults on Jews and numerous arrests followed these incitements to violence.[32]

McDonald's efforts to seek havens for the stateless refugees fleeing such Nazi terror filled him with pessimism, and he shared with Warburg the reflections of "a rather tired individual who…is somewhat depressed by the apparent lack of basis for a real program." At the second session of his Governing Body on May 2, McDonald reported that the conditions for admission into the countries adjacent to Germany had been made more severe. No viable large scheme of settlement in other countries had yet emerged, with Palestine, having absorbed 10,000 German Jews, essentially the only area which offered "an immediate opportunity for refugee colonization on an appreciable scale." Rebuffed by junior officials in Berlin regarding the withdrawal from the country of personal assets, the payment of pensions and social insurance contributions, and the heavy "flight tax," he appealed to the governments of the world. A reluctant London agreed finally to make an unofficial representation if Dodd would do likewise. Yet Roosevelt, informed of McDonald's current belief that Germany was not moderating its attitude towards Jews and in other respects, had already told him in January, "I did not see that there was anything I could do." McDonald's talks with Mussolini, Pacelli, chief of the French foreign ministry Alexis Saint-Léger, and Under-Secretary of State Phillips yielded nothing. Jewish groups differed amongst themselves regarding how to taking action. Another reality, McDonald observed to Baron Robert de Rothschild, could not be denied: "I had undertaken to try to help a people who were a drag on the market; the Jews were at the moment unpopular everywhere, and this condition obviously did not simplify one's task."[33]

Nor did Wauchope make things easier for the Zionists, authorizing on May 1 only 5,600 entry certificates for the next six-month schedule, without any explanation. As a "punishment" against illegal immigrants, 800 had been deducted from the original grant of 6,400. Considering that Ben-Gurion and Shertok had asked the High Commissioner in their interview on March 14 for 20,000, the Agency's response escalated. It officially noted that Zionist achievements had decisively contributed to the country's marked economic progress during the past two years, causing the government's revenue surplus to grow by £1 million in one year, and that a severe labor shortage continued to prevail in Palestine. Public demonstrations ensued. Wauchope counseled the Agency to be satisfied with a moderately large and continuous immigration, and in a personal note he quoted from Francis Bacon's 1625 essay "Of Plantations": "Cram not in people, by sending too fast company after company … but so as the number may live well in the plantation, and not by surcharge be in penury." The Aseifat HaNivharim (Elected Assembly), after a two-day meeting which the Revisionists boycotted in opposition to the Va'ad HaLeumi's causing "defeat after defeat," unanimously called for a half-day general strike against the new schedule. In addition,

Ben-Zvi's anxiety about rumors of a sizeable government allotment to allegedly "displaced" Arab cultivators, which he had first discussed with Wauchope the previous August, received confirmation when the Colonial Office's £2 million loan set aside £250,000 for this purpose.[34]

For Brandeis, Britain's decisions reflected an attitude that for a long period had been "so persistently adverse" to Jewish interests as to suggest that the "acts and refusals" of the mandatory administration and the Colonial Office were manifestations of a policy "to retard and largely prevent Jewish development." Writing to Frankfurter on May 13, the Justice explained that his faith in the British-Jewish enterprise was based upon a conviction that HMG had as much to gain as the Zionists from "the Jewish penetration of the Near East." The Jews had to have an outlet there, in Palestine and Transjordan now, and later in Iraq. "There is a force driving Jews as irresistible as gravitation," he went on, "the torrent must play itself out somewhere." France seemed to want Jewish settlement in Syria, and some "of our people"—a possible reference to Weizmann's recent visit to Beirut—believed that if England blocked Zionist aspirations, "we must seek French territory." Frankfurter was therefore asked to act as "unofficial ambassador without a portfolio" to be of as much help as he could in this and other connections.[35]

On May 23, the day of the general strike, a Va'ad HaLeumi-Aseifat HaNivharim delegation expressed to Wauchope the yishuv's feelings of bitterness at the inadequate schedule and the delays experienced by applicants for capitalist and dependent certificates. A recent anti-picketing amendment to the Prevention of Intimidation Ordinance, educator Ben-Zion Mossinsohn observed, prevented the Jewish workman in effect from having his full share in the Jewish economy. Histadrut executive member Zalman Rubashov (later Shazar) stressed the organization's desire to safeguard their full rights to Jewish labor without combating Arabs. Asserting that the Jews were here to build and had dispossessed no one, and that Palestine was the "only refuge" for persecuted Jewry, Uziel added that they regarded the English nation as "the emissary of Providence" to enable the Jews to return to their land. Ben-Zvi pointed to the country's state of prosperity, and declared that it was "impossible" for them to be satisfied with such immigration schedules. There were 900 Arab villages in which not a single Jew was employed, but the law did not allow Jews in their own 140 settlements to oppose any Arab who wished to work there.

In reply, Wauchope emphasized that no one, Jew or non-Jew, regretted the suffering of Jews outside of Palestine more than he did, but Palestine's absorptive capacity had to remain "the crucial test" of immigration. It was also his duty to "look ahead." The flourishing yishuv proved that HMG was not checking the growth of the population (in the last two years, Jewish immigration had swelled from 4,000 to 10,000 and from 10,000 to 40,000, exclusive of tourists who settled without permission). He realized the "great pressure" today that made Jews long to enter Palestine. He did appreciate Mossinsohn's sincerity in saying that East European Jewry considered Wauchope's stopping any Jew entering Palestine "the illegal act," and looked forward to their further talks together.[36]

In addition to these challenges, the Arlosoroff murder investigation continued to roil the yishuv. On May 16, the day that Ahimeir was acquitted of "conspiracy to murder," the ailing Milikovsky sent Kook a hastily written message of "mazel tov," and asked for action. Hailing the verdict as "a day of salvation from above," the "eternally faithful student" advised Kook to write or cable a blessing to the freed man. Kook did so, his letter (thanks to Milikovsky's advice) opening with the salutation "dear author." When Ahimeir then began a hunger strike after being kept in jail for Brit HaBiryonim activity, Milikovsky prevailed upon Kook to beseech the greatly weakened prisoner to halt his four-day fast. Kook promptly followed up, assuring Ahimeir of his certainty that the mandatory would soon "recognize its obligation" to free him completely. A highly appreciative Ahimeir complied with the request; *HaYarden* featured this correspondence. Furious, all Labor newspapers, together with *HaAretz* and *HaOlam*, blasted the use of "our brothers" and particularly Kook's resort to "dear author." On the Ashkenazi Chief Rabbi's doorstep appeared the slogan: "Woe the nation whose priests [Kook was of the Jewish priestly class] defend murderers." Although greatly distressed at these vindictive attacks, Kook declared that "dear author" was not, as HaPo'el HaMizrachi's *Netivot* newspaper excused it, a "slip of the pen."[37]

In Ben-Gurion's judgment, this mounting civil strife could likely result in schism once the court rendered judgment on Stavsky and Rosenblatt. With the yishuv facing "near destruction," he considered the situation more worrisome than "the hard blow" dealt by Wauchope's reduced schedule. (The Tel Aviv City Council, noting that a clash between Revisionists and police during the general strike had resulted in 50 wounded, settled on a compromise resolution which censured the "irresponsible men who bring ruin on the city with their actions.") Addressing Mapai's Central Committee on May 27, Ben-Gurion emphasized that the party had to solidify its ranks in Eretz Yisrael and beyond, especially in Poland and the United States. The next Zionist Congress would be decisive for the movement, he believed, witnessing either the exit of Labor or of the Revisionists from the WZO. Three days later, Ben-Gurion advised the party's Political Committee that even if the two young Betarim were acquitted, we should declare that the entire murder had yet to be revealed, since "apart from them two other men prepared the killing" and "we would not be quiet or rest until we discovered the murderers." The members present agreed that he would draft a proclamation in this vein; Mapai's forces would guard their institutions and members while maintaining strict neutrality whatever the court's decision. The government, in any event, should not be brought into the inter-yishuv political struggle.[38]

For Judah Magnes, the conflict continued to hamper serious discussion on the vital issue of Arab-Jewish relations. Too many Zionists denied that an Arab national movement existed, he told the ZOA's Administrative Committee on May 24. Young Palestinian Arabs, returning from university studies abroad, had forced the October demonstrations upon the old-time leaders; these men, such as the sincere Arab nationalist Alami, could not be bought as in Turkish days. A general cultural awakening was taking place, and the unlettered Arab was "just as keen about political discussion" as his educated brother, including talk about an Arab Federation of millions. Ibn Saud, one of the greatest Arab princes in centuries, has become in many ways an Arab hero. The Arab leaders in Palestine had reached "a state of national passion" where they were now ready to march at the head of a procession, even to go to prison.

If we had been able to retain Arab friendship over the years, Magnes went on, the whole Arab world, not only Transjordan, might be opened to our people. If we do not cooperate with a "very genuine" Arab national movement, "we will lose through sheer numbers." Why not try to work out a policy of cooperation in every phase of our undertakings? he challenged the group. If Zionists come in the spirit that the Arab is our enemy, the yishuv "will suffer a catastrophe such as Jewish history has never seen." Some Arabs were ready to talk of parity, equal rights, irrespective of population; the Jews did not necessarily have to be the majority. If the Jew could get from the Arab "one political idea," he concluded, that the Jews are in Palestine as of right and not on sufferance, "then all the other problems could be worked out."[39]

One week later, Hall addressed these and related matters before the Permanent Mandates Commission. After explaining the measured response of the administration to the Arab demonstrations of the previous October, the Chief Secretary observed that the January 17 processions had passed off "quite peacefully." Wauchope was taking steps toward the grant of self-government, beginning with advisory committees and a Municipal Corporations Ordinance. The government was "mindful of its dual obligation under the mandate," and adhered strictly to the economic absorptive capacity principle. Although there "might have been no sensible improvement politically" in relations between Jews and Arabs, Hall conceded, some progress in the economic and agricultural spheres had been made, "and there were grounds for hope." The government could undertake to maintain order "in any contingency" with the means at its disposal. The High Commissioner, responsible for the present and future welfare of the country "as a whole," was bound to take "a longer and more cautious view than the Jewish Agency" as regards immigration. In light of "strong public opinion" in Transjordan against Jewish settlement, he added, the mandatory felt that it would be unwise to approve this at the present time. In the end, Commission members Pierre Orts and Count de Penha Garcia concluded that protesting petitions from Jews and Arabs did not call for any special recommendation to the Council.[40]

On June 8, the court's final verdict freed Rosenblatt, but sentenced Stavsky by a vote of 3-1 to death (Justice Valero was the dissenting voice), in turn throwing Kook and his circle into unremitting activity. Telegrams were sent to Jewish communities abroad and to prominent individuals like the Archbishop of Canterbury. A long proclamation to the yishuv was also drafted, in which Kook inserted the words "innocent and righteous" regarding Stavsky; aside from Kook, Meir, and Uziel (but not Aronson), thirteen other illustrious Torah sages would append their names ten days later. On June 19, the same day that Ahimeir was sentenced to twenty-one months' imprisonment with hard labor (his three Brit HaBiryonim co-defendants received lesser sentences), one hundred and ten leading yishuv citizens headed by Dizengoff issued a manifesto averring that "a terrible crime" had occurred against Stavsky, and expressing their belief that the truth would eventually emerge victorious. Assailed by Labor, Kook issued more proclamations while Sirkis and an ill Milikovsky diligently canvassed signatures and funds for Stavsky's legal appeal. His certainty assured once lawyer Eliash privately heard Abdul Majdid repeat on June 19 his initial confession, Kook firmly defended his activities. Thus did he retort during a stormy interview with southern Jerusalem district governor Major J. F. Campbell:

> The Law of God permits trespass of God's command-
> ments for the purpose of saving life.... How much more
> so are we permitted, for the saving of life, to trespass the
> law of the State, which is the law of man.... I have suf-
> ficient reason and sufficient information at my disposal
> to convince me beyond a shadow of doubt that Stavsky
> is wholly [sic] blameless and innocent.[41]

Positive that Stavsky had committed the crime because of Revisionist indoctrination, Ben-Gurion now contemplated some punitive action against Kook. At Mapai's Central Committee on June 13, he lashed out against *Do'ar HaYom*, *Hazit Ha'am*, and *HaYarden*—as well as Kook—as "a small group of communal prostitutes [sic] who hated workers, joined by some innocent individuals." Those who educated Stavsky should be put in the dock and "destroyed," he concluded, for they endangered the hope of the Jewish people and of Zionism. Two weeks later, Ben-Gurion proposed that the authority of the Chief Rabbinate's office should be abolished, Palestinian Jewry demanding of the mandatory that "we be freed of our binding obligation to this institution in matters of marriage, inheritance, etc." Shertok advised that some of that office's jurisdiction be curtailed, while Yisrael Meriminski (later Merom) advocated the "nullification of religion" from the yishuv's body politic. Kaplan countered with a suggestion that action be taken against the rabbis without arousing the question of their authority, thereby "preventing a *kulturkampf*." The final vote on the three resolutions stood as follows: 7—Kaplan; 6—Ben-Gurion; 1—Meriminski.[42]

Even as the yishuv fixated on Stavsky's fate, some Zionist establishment figures pursued various avenues on behalf of their cause.

Weizmann dispatched a "personal and urgent" letter to Mussolini, begging him to draw Hitler's attention to how the Third Reich policy of "racial persecution" of Jews had not only caused "the deepest anxiety" among Jews and even non-Jews abroad, but had harmed Germany's economic and foreign position. The Agency Executive's Berl Locker, speaking in London on behalf of the Zionist Socialist movement, explained to the British Labour Party its rightful grievances against HMG. On June 20, Shertok noted to Wauchope that "a great deal of tension" existed in the yishuv as a result of the uncertainty felt with regard to the ultimate aims and objects of British policy in Palestine and the Middle East generally, in the mind of some Englishmen resembling Chesterton's "blind man in a dark room looking for a black hat that isn't there." People were becoming "deeply irritated" at the mandatory's immigration schedules. When the High Commissioner expressed alarm at the great lack of unity among the yishuv, Shertok responded that these internal difficulties were also largely due, according to the final analysis, to the difficulties the Agency was having with the administration. Wauchope did not reply to this, but in a confidential letter to another correspondent he averred that "it is just because Palestine is, as you say, a matter of life and death that Government must not risk taking leaps." He concluded: "May it not be wiser to make sure of the foundations, to allow the mortar to dry, before attempting to raise the whole superstructure?"[43]

Advocates for the Palestinian Arab cause were not idle either. On June 2, the mayors of the Arab municipalities suggested to Herbert Samuel, currently head of the Liberal Party, that the Jews make the first step toward an understanding with Arab moderates. Samuel was not certain that any success would attend these efforts, Hexter informed Warburg, "but was all for our making this *démarche*." Daniel Oliver, a Quaker educator in Syria, and school headmaster Khalil Totah of Ramallah traveled to London on a special mission to bring "peace and friendship" between Palestine's Arabs and Jews. Oliver called for concessions on both sides, but admitted that the Arabs would not mind if the country "went back to grass so long as they got their independence." Totah asked prominent Zionist writer Israel Cohen point blank: "Which would you rather have—the Balfour Declaration or Arab friendship?" He charged that cases of Arabs employed in Jewish settlements were the exception, and the average earnings of Arab workers were less than they used to be. Cohen responded that the number in the first instance may have reached up to 10,000. Certain Jewish settlements even employed more Arabs than Jews, and the fact that at least a few thousand Arabs had come in from neighboring countries to take advantage of labor opportunities provided by the Palestinian Jewish enterprise indicated beyond a doubt that the yishuv's work had improved the economic welfare of the country's Arabs. Not long thereafter, another representative commended to the British Labour Party's Advisory Committee on Imperial Questions the findings of the Shaw Commission and the Passfield White Paper when explaining why the country's Arabs "are apprehensive and in a state of great national tension."[44]

Events, quickly unfolding in July, placed European Jewry in their own state of tension. The great blood purge of June 30 directed by Göring and Himmler with the army's support against the SA, in which scores of high-ranking Nazi leaders and some officers were summarily murdered because of an alleged plot against Hitler and the regime, placed Germany "outside the European family of nations for the time being." So editorialized the London *Times*, while Messersmith saw the events as final evidence of Hitler's "capacity for cruelty" and his belief in "terror as the only worthwhile instrument with which to carry through his will." Visiting Berlin at that same moment, American Jewish Committee Executive Secretary Morris Waldman concluded that since "the situation has volcanic possibilities, we Jews on the outside should say nothing." From Haifa, Stefan Zweig wrote to Sigmund Freud that "as long as Göring, Goebbels and Hitler himself can still carry on unscathed, little is changed at the basis of the whole system, and evil and infamy remain unvanquished in the world." In Austria, where the situation of the Jewish refugees was reported to McDonald as "catastrophic," a Nazi putsch one month later (in which Dollfuss was assassinated) failed only because Mussolini mobilized his forces on the Brenner Pass. In Poland, a new National Radical Party, said to be a revolt by the youth against the older leaders of the parliamentary opposition National Democrat Party, arose with a program based entirely upon Hitlerism; a wave of anti-Jewish disturbances soon followed.[45]

Wauchope dug in his heels, however, on the matter of Jewish immigration. Before departing for London, Shertok asked on July 3 for a sizeable supplementary labor schedule in view of the "acute" shortage of workers. The High Commissioner persisted in his fears of Arab unemployment and a decline in Palestine's prosperity, such as in the building trade. This feeling, he wrote in reply, "may be evidence of a dull imagination but not of ill will," certain that "you and others appreciate the motives that actuate me." He even contemplated doubling the amount by law which enabled every Jew who possessed £1,000 to enter the country unless there were "some weighty reasons to the contrary." Such a decision would lead to "most serious results," Shertok shot back, stifling investment and restricting "very considerably" the already limited opportunities for Jews to establish themselves in Palestine. Ben-Gurion got no further when asking Wauchope on July 17 that a supplementary 7,116 certificates for agricultural workers be granted. Once again, the High Commissioner insisted that for the sake of the country and the Jewish National Home he had to be "very careful in my steps," asserting "there is no assurance that the country can absorb a large mass immigration." (Ultimately, Wauchope approved an additional 1,200 on the condition that the larger part would be allotted to Germany and to workers.) Suggestions from Immigration Commissioner Mills, Ben-Gurion observed at Mapai's Central Committee the next day, also hinted at a retreat from the economic absorptive capacity formula.[46]

Palestinian Arab leaders stood firm as well. They received encouragement when the Jerusalem District Court, while upholding the convictions for 18 Arabs who had taken part in the Jaffa riots of October 27, offered to all but one the option of release on probation. The terms of July 4 included signing bonds in the amount of £100 each to be "of good conduct for three years"; the freed men got permission to "indulge in lawful political activity." One week later, the Mufti returned home after successfully mediating with others a territorial feud between Ibn Saud and Yemen's Imam Yahya. The *Palestine Post* reported that cries of "Long live Haj Amin, the Hitler of Palestine" welcomed him on his route from Gaza to Lydda to Jerusalem, and patriotic inscriptions were erected in villages along the Jaffa-Jerusalem highway and the Old City's Damascus Gate. Nazi propaganda in the region, which had commenced in May following the visit of Interior Minister Wilhelm Frick, now surfaced in Palestine, Cairo, Beirut, and Baghdad.

Soon thereafter, Ahmad al-Samih al-Khalidi, principal of Jerusalem's Government Arab College, independently shared with Magnes his plan for the cantonization of Palestine, this "final solution" having an Arab numerical majority versus "a rich and enlightened Jewish minority." A "reasonable fixed quota" in land and population had to be preserved.

The two cantons would become League members, with the Arab one attached to Transjordan under Abdullah's sovereignty. The friendship of the Arab world, al-Khalidi declared, should be in the long run "more precious" to Jews than "obtaining millions of dunams or introducing thousands of immigrants. It is no use trying to quicken the [Zionist] experiment." A "drastic change" in the Jewish policy towards the Arabs was essential: "The move should come from your side," he concluded.[47]

Ben-Gurion undertook such an initiative, meeting with Abd al-Hadi on July 19 for three hours until midnight in Magnes's home. The Istiqlal leader insisted that Palestine was an Arab country. The Jews, "foreigners" in this country, purchased most of the good Arab lands at exaggerated prices, and the harm it caused Arabs ran counter to the mandate. Abd al-Hadi disputed the argument that Jewish settlement had raised the fellahin's wages and crop yields, but in any case maintained that the Arabs would need the land in a generation or two, when their numbers would be greater. The Zionists sought an agreement on the basis that if the Jewish right to return to their land were recognized by the Arabs, the Jews would recognize the right of the Arabs to remain on their land, Ben-Gurion observed. However, if Abd al-Hadi opposed all Jewish land purchases, "there was of course no possibility of a mutual understanding." The only result would be "tragedy and the shedding of innocent blood by both parties."

Our ultimate goal over a period of forty years, Ben-Gurion posited, was a Jewish state in Palestine on both sides of the Jordan as a community of four million with an Arab population of two million, the Zionists prepared to help the Arabs to bring about "the rebirth and unity of the Arab people." According to Ben-Gurion's account, Abd al-Hadi "became enthusiastic" about this; the Zionist may have misread what might have been the Arab nationalist's loud sarcasm when Abd al-Hadi responded that if the Jews could help Arab unity he would then agree to five to six million Jews in Palestine, and "go and shout in the streets and tell everyone he knew, in Palestine, in Syria, in Iraq, in Damascus and Baghdad." The Jews would not fight against the English, Ben-Gurion said frankly, but would build up the Arab economy and raise the cultural-educational level—all of which "preceded and conditioned political liberation." The Zionists "were neither desirous nor capable of building our future in Palestine at the expense of the Arabs," he insisted, but one truism had to be appreciated: "For us, the Land was everything, *and there was nothing else.* For the Arabs, Palestine was only a small portion of the large and numerous Arab countries." According to Ben-Gurion, the two adversaries "parted on very friendly terms." Abd al-Hadi's recollection ended rather differently, with him saying "The homeland is not sold for a price, and therefore it is not possible, Mr. Ben-Gurion, for us to come together."[48]

Earlier that same day, Shertok made his case to Cunliffe-Lister for a supplementary labor schedule. The Colonial Secretary had already been asked by McDonald for a special allocation as "an exceptional measure" for refugees, and informed the Board of Deputies of British Jews that the rate of immigration continued to be governed by the High Commissioner's evaluation of Palestine's economic absorptive capacity. Repeating this to Frankfurter, Cunliffe-Lister had added in confidence a personal belief that the Jews "must gradually penetrate" into Transjordan, but he did not wish the Jewish National Home "to rest too much on British bayonets: that isn't the kind of a Jewish Palestine that you and I want." His legal advisors, Shertok was told, had said that no legal provision existed for granting a supplementary schedule. Above all, assessing the country's capacity rested solely with Wauchope. Temporary employment, for which the Agency was claiming immigration permits, presented a very serious problem. An unemployment crisis might occur, and the problem of "a proper selection" of immigrants also had to be considered. He was optimistic about Jewish growth and welcomed any contact which could be established between the Jews and the Arabs, but "extremists on both sides must be left out of account." In his view, the most hopeful thing was that the Jews should be able to persuade the "main bulk" of Palestine's Arabs that they were obtaining direct benefit from employment through the Jews.[49]

The British appeal court's unanimous verdict on July 20, freeing Stavsky due to the lack of evidence corroborating Sima Arlosoroff's testimony while noting that the conviction would have been upheld in England and much of the empire, provided ammunition both for the Right and for the Left. Praising British justice, Jabotinsky gave thanks to Horace Samuel, Kook, Dizengoff, Katz, and others who had also toiled for the three accused; *Do'ar HaYom* asserted that the Jewish people sighed with relief because it was "washed clean of the grave accusation of murder within its midst." Milikovsky reminded a jubilant victory celebration that the Agency Executive's hands were stained with blood, but truth had triumphed. *Davar's* lead editorial, on the other hand, stressed that Stavsky was "not innocent but unpunishable" only because Palestinian law required two reliable witnesses to convict. Mapai broadsides on Tel Aviv's streets quickly declared that Stavsky and Rosenblatt remained the murderers, and insisted that Arlosoroff's death would be avenged with war against "the party of the Biryonim." With Ben-Gurion's support, a melee broke out when Labor youth disrupted the service after Stavsky and Rosenblatt were called to the Sabbath Torah reading in Tel Aviv's Great Synagogue. Once the police restored order, Stavsky and Rosenblatt walked home amidst throngs which shouted "Long live Chief Rabbi Kook!" and "Long live the truth!"[50]

Fully aware that continued civil war could destroy the yishuv, some appealed for healing the breach between Jew and Jew in the Holy Land. Katz's new pamphlet *HaEmet Kodemet LaShalom* (Truth Precedes Peace) urged that only an objective inquiry could resolve the contentious issue. All who set the good of their people above all, opined the *Palestine Post*, must work for "a pure and constructive policy in upbuilding the Jewish National Home," repudiate violence, and scorn party hate. Years might pass before the truth of the murder emerged, *HaAretz* editorialized, but Palestine's Jews now had to devote their entire thoughts "to our internal cleansing," rearing for Arlosoroff a lighthouse of peace "to send its rays into the hostile shadows and the threatening decadence." Mizrachi's *HaTor*, a consistent critic of attacks against Kook, pleaded for a return to quiet lest the yishuv witness "a third destruction." *Do'ar HaYom* hoped that the court's decision would mark the end of "a long and threatening nightmare," and the beginning if not of complete unity, then at least an armistice.[51] Given Labor's immediate response to the verdict, however, even this prudent wish appeared illusory.

Ben-Gurion also had to contend with Wauchope's insistence on establishing a Legislative Council, which the two began discussing on the night of July 29. Noting that HMG also had to deal with world Jewry where Palestine was concerned, Ben-Gurion argued that the Zionists, having lost faith in the eighteenth-century Emancipation's promise of civil rights and in Diaspora minority existence, felt that the "historical hope" of past Jewish generations for return to their national homeland "must find its fulfillment" in this generation. A Legislative Council, which meant an Arab state if based on the present population, was inconsistent with the fundamental idea of the Balfour Declaration and the

Palestine Mandate. Prior to any constitutional change, two preliminary conditions were essential: the safeguarding of certain elements that constituted the basis of the Jewish National home, including Jewish immigration, land purchase, settlement, and a share in government works, and Arab-Jewish mutual understanding. The Arabs, in and outside Palestine, would "reckon with us," Ben-Gurion declared, "when we have become a factor that cannot be ignored and cannot be destroyed." A yishuv population of a half million, "only a question of three-four years," would create "a practical basis" for that understanding, after which constitutional changes could be introduced.

The next morning, Wauchope countered by noting that the mandate had made HMG responsible for the development of self-governing institutions, and the 1922 Order-in-Council provided for a Legislative Council. While watching over the interests of the National Home, the Cabinet continued to favor this objective, and it "cannot be postponed any longer." Ben-Gurion and Weizmann had asked for a Jewish population of 500,000 first, but he believed that the yishuv was now "quite strong" and "already safe," and their proposal of parity "cannot be accepted." Ben-Gurion retorted that Prime Minister McDonald had agreed in July 1931 to "parity" as meaning "an equal share" between Jews and Arabs as "entities," and had stated to him and Professor Lewis B. Namier that Palestine "ought to be mainly for the Jewish people." Summarizing his talk with Abd al-Hadi, Ben-Gurion then added that the Jews, while returning to the East, were bringing with them European civilization. They wished Palestine to serve as "the bridge between East and West," and saw no better representative of western civilization than England. If the Cabinet decided to set up a Legislative Council, Wauchope responded, the necessary steps would be taken "to safeguard the interests of the minority," and he would proceed even if the Jews did not participate. "That was the basis of our opposition," Ben-Gurion riposted. The mandate and the Balfour Declaration recognized our rights "not as a minority but as a nation." The Arabs wanted Palestine to remain Arab, but for them "it is only a small strip in a vast territory inhabited by them. To us this country is everything, it is the only corner in the world that we look upon as our homeland."[52]

Two weeks later, sitting under an ancient oak tree in the courtyard of Alami's home in Sharafat, a village near Jerusalem, Ben-Gurion thrashed out with his host the basic questions relating to a Jewish-Arab agreement. To meet Arab fears of being dispossessed if the land passed to Jewish ownership, he proposed that the yishuv would teach the Arabs modern work methods, open schools and teachers' colleges, and establish factories with joint capital and labor. The two peoples should participate in the government's executive branch on a parity basis, and local autonomy given by the British in the towns and villages. An independent Jewish state combining Palestine and Transjordan would eventually be connected with an Arab Federation.

The Arabs, Alami responded, thought that such a federation would consist of three major states: Syria and western Palestine, Iraq and Transjordan, and Arabia—Hejaz, the Negev, and Yemen. French occupation and Feisal's death precluded this possibility for the present, yet a union of Iraq, Transjordan, and Palestine, along with the Kingdom of Saudi Arabia, was feasible. He considered the Istiqlal a small group without influence, except among the youth, "because the leaders were not trusted"; the Nashashibi opposition leaders were "corrupt" and not influential. The Mufti, "really not so terrible," was held in high esteem in the Muslim world. Alami therefore suggested that Ben-Gurion meet secretly with Haj Amin, and if nothing came of it, whatever was discussed between them for the past three hours that afternoon would be "null and void." Ben-Gurion countered with the proposal that the meeting with Haj Amin be postponed until he consulted with his colleagues abroad, and after he first met the Syrian Istiqlal leaders Ishan Bey al-Jabri (Alami's father-in-law) and Shakib Arslan, the exiled Druse nationalist who headed the "Syrian Palestinian Delegation" at Geneva.[53]

Ben-Gurion found a far less encouraging reception during an interview with Wauchope on August 15. He was informed that "a Legislative Council would be set up." The Government had to honor its pledge; the total number of Jewish members would not come up to the level of parity. Ben-Gurion reiterated that the Palestinian Jewish community would not take part in this venture. As for Wauchope's assurance that the Council would be precluded from discussing immigration and land, he noted that any economic measure might have a decisive influence on these matters. Despite the High Commissioner's veto power, the administration would not always be able to resist a majority decision; "pressure from the Arab side" had led the government in 1921 and 1930 to halt Jewish immigration. The Jews did not feel that all the pledges bearing on the establishment of the National Home were being carried out, an additional concern that was "aggravating" the Council issue. Ben-Gurion repeated his own vision of an Arab-Jewish agreement, but Wauchope again balked at the idea of Transjordan being joined to Palestine as a Jewish state and ultimately becoming an integral part of the British Empire as a self-governing dominion. Nor did the High Commissioner alter his stance on a larger immigration schedule, arguing that "if a war broke out, say six years hence," the stream of capital into Palestine would stop, and "terrible distress was bound to overtake us at that time" for Jew and Arab. Finally, "Zionism required peace and quiet in this country, and therefore it was necessary to proceed cautiously."[54]

By then, Palestinian Arab leaders had signaled to Wauchope their readiness to accept a parliamentary regime. After the violent demonstrations of October-November, the Arab mayors had raised the question with him of establishing a Legislative Council according to the terms of the mandate, emphasizing that if there were a national government the inhabitants would recognize their responsibility towards it and bloodshed would have been avoided. That December, Haj Amin and Alami had suggested to the High Commissioner a possible solution to be found within the mandate framework, as had al-Khalidi on his own initiative. After Wauchope proposed a Council in the summer of 1934, a number of Arab leaders met in Lebanon and decided to accept it. Al-Difa'a reported their statement that "we will find in it a temporary remedy, whose benefit will be greater than its harm." An article in Al-Jamia Al-Islamiya, which saw the Council as preventing the creation of the Jewish National Home, observed that "the Arab movement" in Palestine "believes that if a moderate government were set up, composed of local inhabitants, which would safeguard British interests in Palestine, its political situation would not be worse than that of Iraq." Kazim's death and the formal dissolving of the Arab Executive in August created a leadership vacuum. The resulting anarchy, combined with the yishuv's adamant opposition to the Legislative Council, persuaded Haj Amin and his rivals that its creation was something to be desired.[55]

All contenders for Kazim's mantle were now preoccupied with establishing political parties and "testing their strength," Haj Amin in the vanguard. When Fakhri Nashashibi organized an inaugural meeting of Palestinian Arab workers on July 28, the Mufti's group charged that it had ties to the Histadrut and did not intend to work for Arabs. A C.I.D. report on August 6 indicated that Haj Amin and many others held that the only solution for Palestine was an Arab confederacy and a world Islamic bond, he claiming to have secured Ibn Saud's sympathy for that objective. These steps recalled the Supreme Muslim Council's first open venture into political activity against the yishuv during 1929 and 1930, and Haj Amin's convening of a large General Islamic Congress in Jerusalem in 1931 as a challenge to the authority of the Arab Executive. The same day, the *Palestine Post* reported that that the Mufti had himself "stimulated or taken under his wing" the movement to form Arab contingents of "unofficial gendarmes" to police Palestine's frontiers against Jewish illegal immigrants. (In July, a first combined venture, initiated by Hagana leader Eliyahu Golomb and HehHalutz's Yehuda Braginski, had successfully brought 350 halutzim from Poland, Lithuania, and Latvia aboard the *Velos* to the shores of the Promised Land.) On August 14, Arabic posters with the swastika advocating a boycott of all Jewish stores suddenly appeared in Arab shop windows in Jerusalem and Haifa, with walls carrying Arabic swastika posters. The next day, a clash between the Abu Ubayda boy scouts from Tulkarm, who patrolled the Netanya coast, and Betar youth resulted in the serious wounding of one scout and the arrest of four Jews for questioning.[56]

On August 20, Wauchope informed Antonius that he had adopted many of the features of Antonius's draft eighteen months earlier on the Council, but thought that the two subjects of immigration and the sale of land should be forbidden in the new body's deliberations. This would probably "wreck the scheme from the point of view of its acceptability," Antonius replied, while the grant of veto and certification (which he had first proposed) by the High Commissioner could insure the mandate's implementation. Cunliffe-Lister would probably not go "to such lengths" as Antonius had recommended, Wauchope remarked confidentially, and what about Jewish opposition? "They would oppose any and every form of it until the last moment," Antonius answered. Laughing and saying that this "summed up his own view," Wauchope added that he had also adopted Antonius's recommendation on enlarging the Executive Council to appoint a Muslim, a Christian Arab, and a Jew. He did not take issue with Antonius's earlier recommendation that in the enlarged 32-member Council, aside from 7 in the Executive and 6 nominated by Wauchope, the 19 returned by the electorate should be 12 Muslims, 3 Christians, and 4 Jews. A delighted Antonius wrote to an American friend that the Council Wauchope hoped to announce in November upon his return from London might help "to reduce the present inequality and resulting waste," and, "by setting well-defined limits of the play and inter-play" of British, Jewish, and Arab forces, "it may provide real equilibrium, without which no real progress can be hoped."[57]

Wauchope's discussion with Ben-Gurion the next day reflected the deadlock between the two men. The High Commissioner did not see Jews settling in Transjordan this year or next, and he expressed reservations about the Agency's hopes for development in the Huleh Valley and the Negev. Wauchope again insisted that the jump from 1,000 Jewish immigrants in 1930 to 40,000 three years later demanded "a slower advance" in the future. Ben-Gurion noted that Wauchope's new suggestion for the projected Legislative Council suddenly introduced a problem of three faiths as separate entities (Muslim, Christian Arab, and Jew), instead of a problem of two races (Arab and Jew). Yet "the Jews were not only a religious body. They were a nation, and not one amidst three," he insisted. The proposed arrangement, according the Jews minority status, could only be seen as "striking a fundamental blow in our condition and threatening our future. Clearly, not one Jew would agree to participate in a Legislative Council under these conditions."

"We were still far from our goal," Ben-Gurion declared. He hoped Wauchope realized that "ever since the German disaster, Jews do not feel secure in any other country in the world, even in countries where their rights have not been harmed," except Palestine. A quicker and larger immigration would enable the Zionists to save a greater number of Jews and to arrive at an Arab-Jewish understanding. The Arabs, he understood, "naturally wished to guard all of the country for themselves." To the degree that Jewish numbers increased, "an agreement will also arise between us." This, Ben-Gurion concluded, not the Council, offered "the more certain way to peace in this land."[58]

Two final talks with Alami at the month's end, Ben-Gurion informed Magnes, "clarified the fundamental lines of an Arab-Jewish pact." Guarantees would certainly be given to allay the fears of Haj Amin and others that the Jews would not touch the Mosque of Omar in the Old City of Jerusalem. Ben-Gurion insisted that a Jewish state had to include Palestine and Transjordan, and that Jewish immigration would not be restricted. In exchange, a joint plan could accelerate Arab economic and cultural development in Palestine and in Iraq, which had an abundance of fertile land and water. In the transition period, participation in the executive branch would be on a parity basis, with an ultimate Jewish commonwealth linked to an Arab Federation. Alami emphasized that the solution to the Jewish-Arab dispute could only be found in "a general Arab framework." A first step would require negotiating with the Mufti and outside of Palestine with the Istiqlal. If agreements were reached, then a general Arab Congress would be convened to include delegates from Syria, Palestine, Iraq, Saudi Arabia, and Yemen.

On August 31, after reporting to Haj Amin, Alami told Ben-Gurion that the content of their talks had come as "a bombshell" to the Mufti. The latter had "no objection, so long as it would be possible to safeguard the religious, economic and political interests of the Arabs of Palestine." Still, he would have to give the plan further consideration; Arab public opinion was "far removed" from such a proposal. Alami advised that Ben-Gurion first meet Jabri and Arslan, for they and the Mufti attached "great weight" to each other's opinion. Afterwards, a general public declaration should be made. In the meantime, the talks had to remain absolutely secret. On September 2, Ben-Gurion sailed for London.[59]

The following day, the *Palestine Post* reported that Cunliffe-Lister had approved Wauchope's proposals to cope with illegal immigration. A "marine preventive force" and a special force of constables would be established for "intensive patrolling" of the frontiers, augmented by units of the Transjordan Frontier Force, a para-military border guard of Arabs under British command as of 1926. This official dispatch came on the heels of the mandatory's expelling 17 young Polish Revisionists who had been caught by police while trying to disembark from the Greek vessel *Ionian*. (The other 100 of their group successfully dispersed on August 25 in Tel Aviv.) Several months earlier, Jabotinsky, the first champion of this endeavor with his March 1932 essay in Yiddish "On Adventurism," had sent three representatives to Danzig to explore the possibilities of arrival in Palestine via the sea. "The most urgent matter for us is un-authorized Aliya," he wrote to associate Shlomo Jacobi in London on September 9. "I ascribe *tremendous* importance to this task—especially politically.... It would be the best demonstration of craving for Palestine one could imagine: a 'personified petition'." Avraham Stavsky, now a free man, set out to explore appropriate landing sites on Palestine's coastline and then left for Eastern Europe in order to arrange future transports.[60]

This novel phenomenon caught the Zionist establishment on the horns of a dilemma. In its evening edition for September 1, *Davar's* lead article bemoaned the vicious attacks of authorities against immigrant families, coming aboard boats ever since the First Aliya forty years ago, as "a desecration of the Divine name." Editors Berl Katznelson and Moshe Beilinson openly embraced this cause. The success of the *Velos*, whose HehHalutz organizers were directly tied to Mapai, augured well for future efforts. Alongside *Davar's* lead article appeared the poem "Hayinu K'Holmim" ("We Were as Dreamers") by Natan Alterman, writing under the pseudonym A. Nun, which spoke of consequent hope for the Almighty's returning "the exiles of Zion." At the same time, the Agency had to respond to a second *Velos* attempt on September 13, when the Hagana brought 48 of another 350 travelers to safety before the boat escaped from British surveillance and sailed beyond Palestine's territorial waters. Shertok, responsible for daily contacts with the administration, could not have the Agency openly endorse this traffic. Nor did he wish to grant the passengers entry certificates from the allotted schedule, since the precedent could encourage future trips without the supervision of the established Zionist organizations. Still, Shertok and three other colleagues on the Agency Executive would oppose a clear denunciation of the practice when Hexter advanced this step one month later.[61]

Shertok also contended that same month with picketing activity by Jewish workers against the hiring of Arabs in construction and industrial sites. Hall, serving as chief administrator in Wauchope's absence, warned that Jamal al-Husseini and his friends were thinking of counteracting this with pickets of their own, and he feared for inevitable clashes. Jewish labor was engaged in "a defensive battle," Shertok responded on September 7, and the yishuv overwhelmingly supported this "last resort" tactic owing to the principle that Jews should employ Jews. He realized that it looked "distasteful" to the Arabs and produced reactions which he was "most anxious" to avoid. The Jews were being "driven by instinct of self-preservation," however. Given the growing gap between the demand for labor and its supply, the availability of cheap labor in Palestine, and the continued influx of poor Arabs from outside the country, Jewish labor was threatened with "displacement on a very large scale." Hall conceded that the number of Hauranis and

Transjordanians in Palestine stood at 10,000 to 15,000, but observed that the mandatory was now adopting strong measures to evict them and to prevent "further influx." This would not provide a "radical solution," Shertok countered, since the current labor shortage and further progress of Jewish capital would continue to draw cheaper Arab labor from beyond Palestine unless "a biggish" Jewish labor schedule was permitted "to fill the void." The Agency was not "prepared to pay any price" to avoid troubles in Palestine, he ended, to give up their presence here or to sacrifice any vital interest.[62]

Jerusalem's municipal elections were yet another of Shertok's concerns. Hall vehemently deprecated the Agency's support of Dr. Husayn Fakhri al-Khalidi, "for all practical purposes identified with the Mufti," who had resigned as the senior medical officer of the Department of Health in order to challenge Nashashibi for the mayoralty. Shertok replied that they welcomed an individual of "higher moral standards and more modern conceptions." Moreover, since the government regarded Nashashibi's appointment as a certainty, all the more reason for a Jewish Vice-Mayor if it wished to see cooperation on the City Council between Jews and Arabs. This individual ought to be salaried, unlike a past Christian-Arab vice-mayor, as it would be a full-time appointment. Moreover, requesting the vice mayoralty was "a major concession" on their part. Shertok very strongly hoped that the Jews, more than half of the city's population, would be a majority on the Council after five years, and then the Agency would urge their claim to the position of Mayor. Ultimately, Khalidi was appointed to the post, the Jewish sections of Jerusalem (except for the Revisionists) backed a "united front" ticket for the first time, and the Council now consisted of six Jews out of twelve members. The Jews rejoiced over Nashashibi's defeat, all the while realizing that the Legislative Council now loomed up as "a serious menace to the Jewish National Home." Wrote Szold to her sisters: "There's no averting it. It has been impending these twelve years."[63]

Ben-Gurion's attention focused on the meeting in Geneva with Jabri and Arslan, which took place in Arslan's lavishly decorated apartment on the evening of September 23. Hearing the gist of his conversations with Alami, Arslan immediately responded that the Arabs had to remain the majority in Palestine, Jewish economic aid was not urgently needed, and the Arab nations, as had already occurred in Iraq, would gain their independence in time without help from the Jews. According to Jabri's subsequent account, the two Syrian nationalists charged that very little was being offered "in return for the Arab nation of twenty million souls accepting this humiliation of countersigning the evacuation of the land, every grain of which is saturated with the blood of their fathers, and which is so holy from the religious aspect." Better, they noted, for Ben-Gurion "to continue with reliance on British bayonets, and to create the Jewish Kingdom, but at least he should not contemplate an agreement with the Arabs."

In Ben-Gurion's account, Arslan asked: Why did not the Jews, if they needed a Jewish state, go into one of the larger, unpopulated countries? Ben-Gurion answered: Similar advice had been offered the Zionists when Prime Minister Joseph Chamberlain proposed Uganda in 1903, but they rejected it because of what "Eretz Yisrael had meant to the Jewish people for some four thousand years." Arslan denied as well the Jews' right to settle in Transjordan, was certain that England had no interest in creating a Jewish Palestine, and even if such an entity should be created, the Arabs "would never acquiesce." "We would stop them," his later version added, "without knowing how." According to Ben-Gurion, Jabri told him on the way to the railroad station that "the last word had not been spoken, and that the discussion would continue."[64]

Ben-Gurion also had to respond to a public offer on July 31 by the Revisionist World Executive to Mapai of immediate negotiations, rooted in halting physical violence on both sides without compromising on principles. Jabotinsky, having initiated what he called "a spectacular gesture" in the face of considerable opposition among his colleagues, pointed out to Sirkis on September 9 that the Left could not agree to peace because "our very existence" endangered Mapai and the Histadrut. His party wished for peace, but not on conditions that would "be a death blow to the unique character of the Revisionist movement," which had awakened hope" in groups that "despaired from Weizmannization and the rule of the Left." The offer itself had gone unanswered for some time; a *Davar* editorial spoke of the authors as "swindlers and hypocrites," and advised that much was not to be expected from such discussions. The Revisionists had also not joined the Jewish ticket for Jerusalem's municipal elections, suspecting a British ruse to create a Legislative Council and protest continued Arab control of the Old City. That area, so Klausner put it to a receptive Ussishkin, symbolized "the values of the Sancta of the Nation, the remnants of our freedom in the past and the hints of our freedom for the future." In Mapai meetings, Ben-Gurion continued to vilify the Revisionists as "Nazis" and as a false messianic "Frankist" movement, characterizations echoed by his colleagues. Finally, on September 21, the WZO's London Executive invited the Revisionists to send two delegates to negotiate about peace in the Zionist camp.[65]

Milikovsky, never allied with any party, unsuccessfully tried to reconcile the opposing factions. Katznelson did not encourage his suggestion that Kook arbitrate a peace between Labor and the Revisionists. Kook himself had retreated into silence regarding Stavsky's escape from the hangman's noose, secreting his innermost thoughts about the venomous attacks which he had quietly suffered in an untitled poem that would not surface for seventy-one years. "I am the man who has seen affliction," "savage men filled me with bitterness," and similar phrases are followed by "R[abbi] 'Ya'akov Meir' appeared as a blood avenger," "loosened the fetters of wickedness," and "delivered me from the netherworld beneath." At Milikovsky's intervention, Kook invited Ben-Gurion to his home. The skeptical Agency Executive member replied that Kook could meet him at his office in Jerusalem, while Mapai's Central Committee concluded that the Histadrut could dialogue over "Hebrew labor"—not peace. Kook instead received Katznelson and David Remez, and then tried to convince the Farmers' Federation to hire Jewish workers. He also issued a Jewish New Year's message on "Repentance and Peace," and reiterated the need for unity in a message to the jubilee celebration of Hovevei Zion. In the Mapai inner circle, *HaPoel HaTsa'ir* editor Yitzhak Lufban, Aharonovitz, Tabenkin, and Pinhas Lubianker (later Lavon), opposed any contact with the Ashkenazi Chief Rabbi; Golda Meyerson (later Meir), and Rubashov backed Remez and a bitter Katznelson.[66]

While this strife raged within the yishuv, the situation in Germany had hardly improved. In the small towns, Leo Baeck told the Agency Executive's Brodetsky, who was then visiting the Third Reich capital, the Jews lived "on the edge of a volcano in constant terror." He warned that the young Jews had to be gotten out; new legislation would likely result in the unemployment of between ten to fifteen thousand Jews under the age of twenty-five. Captain Frank E. Foley, the Chief Passport Officer attached to the British Embassy, remarked to Brodetsky that "Germany is for many years to come completely hopeless from the Jewish point of view," the children's life "is in most cases a hell," and the young men and women "have no prospects at all." Further, the lack of harmony among the countries surrounding Germany, even as Warsaw flirted with Berlin, checked any effective action to curb the rising military power of the Reich. Hitler had consolidated his position, McDonald wrote to a friend on September 16, and every week saw the strengthening of the German military machine. "The whole country is being mobilized," he emphasized, "first for the economic struggle and ultimately for a struggle of a different order."[67]

Political developments in Poland gave further cause for anxiety. In September, Foreign Minister Józef Beck denounced the League's continued protection of minorities (which included 3.3 million Jews) within his country. The British and French representatives immediately registered strong protests, Anthony Eden quoting from Shakespeare's *Othello* when averring that no State had any more valued possession than its good name for the just and impartial treatment of every section of its citizenry: "Good name in man and woman, dear my Lord, is the immediate jewel of their souls." Such sentiments carried little weight, however, against aroused nationalistic feeling and intense antisemitic propaganda within Poland, much coming from the Reich. Almost half of that country's Jews were "bordering on economic ruin" according to an October report from Joseph C. Hyman, Executive Director of the American Jewish Joint Distribution Committee.[68]

Nor were conditions promising elsewhere on the Continent. France's Joseph Avenol, Secretary-General of the League, left little doubt that he would not risk the "slightest jeopardy" to the League's relations with Germany in order to help McDonald's efforts. The day after Austrian chancellor Kurt Schuschnigg declared, following an interview with Laski and Nahum Goldmann, that Austria treated its Jewish citizens as equals, his government issued a decree segregating Jews from Catholics in the country's public schools. A new wave of antisemitism broke out in Rumania, where hundreds of thousands of Jews faced "abject poverty." A right-wing dictatorship in Latvia placed its Jews in a "very unsatisfactory and threatening" position. The restrictions on withdrawal of property from the Reich steadily intensified, destitution increasing among the emigrants because their resources were exhausted. A new wave from Germany of stateless Jews of Polish and Russian origin, in "a state of indescribable misery," soon began arriving in Czechoslovakia.[69]

Powerless to stem what McDonald characterized as "the present anarchic winds" blowing across Europe, on October 4 Weizmann tried to persuade Cunliffe-Lister against raising the Legislative Council at this juncture. Relying on a memorandum just submitted by the Agency Executive in London to the Colonial Office, including the suggestion that HMG convene a Round Table Conference between Arabs and Jews to reach "an amicable and constructive agreement," Weizmann added that it might harm current negotiations with "certain Arab personalities" and "play directly into the hands of our extremists." The WZO had accepted the Council idea in 1922 because of foolishness and "no real experience" with the Arabs, genuinely thinking that "it might be possible to come to some arrangement with them within the framework of an ordinary parliamentary assembly. But now we have learnt our lesson." Relating the visit of Ben-Gurion and Namier to MacDonald in 1931, about which Cunliffe-Lister had never heard, Weizmann proceed to laud the virtues of parity. It would prevent both Jew and Arab from dominating the other, and give "practical expression" to HMG's insistence on the "dual character" of its obligations under the mandate. Cunliffe-Lister made no promises for postponement until the next October, but added: "As you know, I'm in no hurry!" Five days later, Ben-Gurion and Brodetsky received a very sympathetic hearing for delay from Jan Christian Smuts, former Prime Minister of the Union of South Africa, who had strongly supported the Balfour Declaration when serving on Lloyd George's war cabinet.[70]

The following week, the Agency's memorandum was warmly approved by all present at a two-day meeting of the Zionists' Political Study Commission in London, held in the office at 77 Great Russell St. Ben-Gurion observed that the Executive and the mandatory were "completely at odds" regarding Jewish participation in government work; explained that unreasonable speculation and strong Arab measures against those who sold land to Jews had resulted in the Agency's purchase of only 90,000 dunams (about 40 square miles) in the last three years; and noted that it would be best for the Zionists to "gain time" with expanded immigration and development before the Legislative Council became a reality. Discussing the future of Jewish-Arab relations, a situation different from that of two years before, he asserted that they must weaken Arab opposition in order to be able to achieve more by themselves and more from the government. Kurt Blumenfeld warned against the consequences of non-cooperation with the administration, and urged the need for a strong party and press discipline. The one startling contribution was Goldmann's preference for a neutralized international status on the Swiss model, rather than an association with an Arab Federation or with the British Empire forever. His argument that a Jewish state's siding with any particular group in world politics would "involve a catastrophe to the Jews of certain countries" produced, Kohn wrote to Shertok, "smiles of incredulity."[71]

The Agency Executive in Jerusalem was divided in its members' responses to the Legislative Council. Werner Senator wished to "sell" the Agency's participation at as high a price as possible on the basic questions of immigration, land, settlement in Transjordan, and tariff policy. Rejecting parity as a chimera, Yitzhak Gruenbaum insisted on a negative attitude for the time being, but agreed that government should be presented with "a bill of claims," particularly regarding immigration and land purchase in the next five years, as the terms for the Agency's participation. Hexter thought boycott inevitable in light of the publicity already given to the Executive's attitude, although he regarded noncooperation as "a calamity." Shertok agreed that if the Council proved a success, then the Agency would have to join. He did not think that the administration would grant any concessions in advance, but the possibility existed that the Council would prove "a bad failure" soon after its creation. In any case, the Agency should do everything in its power to prevent its coming into being, including the declaration and execution of a boycott. Ruppin and Kaplan arrived at much the same conclusion, although they did not dwell much on the inevitability of joining in the future, while they stressed the import of "the factor of time" in connection with the yishuv's present growth and urged the need for delay as much as possible.[72]

Shertok particularly found fault with the London Executive's proposal of a Round Table Conference. To again suggest this past "clever tactical move," he wrote to Brodetsky, "means doing mere lip service and not talking serious politics." Coming out with the principle of parity would have been "a positive definition of our attitude," although he still preferred the original draft, which stated the Agency's negative attitude and cautioned HMG against taking "the fateful step." Replying on October 29, Brodetsky agreed with Shertok's "uncompromising opposition" to the Council, but not as a means for testing "the full force of a non-cooperationist attitude." The Agency's memorandum had acknowledged that no indication of "a spirit of goodwill and cooperation" could yet be seen on the Arab side, but, because of that very fact, a Round Table Conference had been advanced for the purpose of achieving "a genuine and sincere acceptance" by the Arabs of the Jewish National Home policy on the understanding that their interests would be safeguarded, as provided for in the Balfour Declaration and the mandate. "Our best friends in Government circles here" had advised that the memorandum not end on a negative note. In any event, Brodetsky concluded, the London Executive lacked the constitutional authority from the movement to put forward the parity proposal.[73]

Wauchope and Hall, the two mandatory officials most responsible for Palestine's welfare, kept to their views. Told by Ben-Zvi that the Va'ad HaLeumi unanimously feared the Legislative Council's impeding the yishuv's growth and noted that no basis had yet been created for co-operation between the Jews and the Arabs, as shown in the Jerusalem municipality under Nashashibi's tenure, Wauchope rejoined that the Government had given pledges to the Arabs to establish a Council of this kind. The High Commissioner reiterated this point to Ben-Gurion and Brodetsky on October 25 while assuring the pair that there would be no Council for the next six months. The cooperation of all sections of Palestine's population was needed, he declared at a dinner that evening, since neither he nor his officials were "omniscient archangels." Hall went further, asking Ruppin what really was the difference between the "Aryan" legislation in Germany and the refusal by the Jews in Palestine to employ Arab laborers? In reply, Ruppin answered that while German Jewry had legally acquired economic positions for a century or more, the yishuv sought an adequate share in public works and employment in private enterprises owned by Jews so long as Jewish workers were available. The Chief Secretary warned that such methods as picketing to achieve that end were "provocative" and "absolutely unjustifiable." Inevitably, he believed, it must create "a very strong enmity" among the Arabs and also alienate European public opinion from Zionism.[74]

The local Arab press kept up its drumbeat of invective against the yishuv. The pro-Istiqlal *Al Difa'a* wondered if it was not the mandatory's obligation to suspend Jewish immigration so as to convince the Arabs that it was taking effective means for preparing a Legislative Council. Such a body, the newspaper argued, could only be created with Arab approval, and "only Arab opinion would be decisive in the political fate of Palestine." The Hebrew press's report that 1,100 Polish Jews had recently departed for Palestine at a time when the total Jewish population in the country reached 400,000 (*sic*) was certainly not reassuring to Palestine's Arabs. They could only appeal to God in the hope that their holy places and the remnants of their holy religion would not be ruled over by strangers. *Al-Jama Al-Arabia* charged that Weizmann publicly opposed the Council because he wished to wait until, with increased immigration "in another few years," the Jews "would be able to meet the Arabs on equal ground." Did not the Arab national institutions, this paper concluded, have the duty to organize and "declare war" against Zionist designs toward colonization in Transjordan that "were endangering the life of the Arab people in the country?" On October 20 Abd al-Hadi, the one prominent leader who balked at the Legislative Council, drew up a memorandum to the League against Jewish immigration into "Arabian Palestine" and Jewish settlement in Transjordan. The Istiqlal chieftain charged that this would bring "ruin and poverty" to the Arabs and destroy "the independence and freedom of the Arab State." He concluded that the League should reconsider, "in light of international justice," the Balfour Declaration—"the most harmful and illegal" pronouncement in recent political history.[75]

One week later, Ben-Gurion and Jabotinsky signed a first agreement. It forbade within the Zionist parties all "acts of terror or violence" and outlawed "libel, slander, insult" with the penalty of expulsion from the WZO, as well as proposing a labor accord between the Histadrut and the Revisionists' National Workers' Organization. Ben-Gurion, optimistic about a negotiated Arab-Jewish peace from without, sought domestic harmony within and hoped to reform many Revisionists. For Jabotinsky, an accord would boost his influence in Palestine and in Europe and possibly enable him to influence future policy. The two had been at loggerheads for several years over tactics, but both were committed to Zionism's realization. The intercession of Rutenberg secretly brought them together in London on October 10.

Initially, Ben-Gurion's emphasis on "massive settlement" clashed with Jabotinsky's on "a petition," and their debate over deeds vs. slogans brought them to a deadlock. At their next tête-à-tête, Jabotinsky accepted the idea of an Arab Federation and Ben-Gurion accepted the petition; both disparaged Weizmann's leadership.

Jabotinsky could not support labor's right to strike, however, or give up his party's independent political action, while Ben-Gurion refused his suggestion that "both sides consider the Stavsky trial over and done with." After three more meetings, their joint declaration on October 26, seeking a modus vivendi between their respective labor organizations and endorsing a provisional non-aggression pact, left open "the big agreement," especially a plan of action and acceptance of discipline. Ben-Gurion wrote in his diary that he did not know if everyone in Palestine would accept the agreement. He still found it difficult to believe that it would go through: "It's too good to be true," Within a short time they shared letters of friendship and looked forward, in Jabotinsky's phrase, to "mutual goodwill."[76]

Jabotinsky's acolytes, except for Ahimeir's circle, accepted the agreement on November 22. Brodetsky hailed the step as "a new era for Zionism," including the stipulation, after Ben-Gurion and Jabotinsky talked further, that Betar would again receive certificates when it suspended directive "No. 60." However, many in Mapai's ranks were furious upon hearing of its contents. Katznelson cabled Ben-Gurion on November 8: "The movement is wounded and the danger is great. What good is a miracle if the main tool to carry it through breaks? More negotiations will push the public to anarchy and destructiveness." Poalei Zion Left and HaShomer HaTsa'ir attacked the pact, and workers' meetings insisted that Ben-Gurion resign from Mapai's Central Committee. Katznelson stood by Ben-Gurion, but Tabenkin and his associates pilloried the attempt at a political alliance. Not prepared to sacrifice Labor's singularity for the sake of peace, Tabenkin, who resigned from the Central Committee, demanded a Histadrut referendum. This would be scheduled for four months hence, giving both sides ample time to campaign.[77]

Ben-Gurion relayed this decision to Rutenberg on November 25. He noted that many in Mapai were not prepared to relinquish the right to strike, and that the opponents did not believe the Revisionists "would be able to change their path" even if Jabotinsky demanded it from them. *HaYarden*'s recent accusation that the Histadrut was only aiding the Communists raised great worry, Ben-Gurion added. Moreover, if Jabotinsky intended to travel to the United States in early 1935, he did not see anyone who could negotiate the essential "big agreement" from the Revisionist side. Jabotinsky continued to support the agreement, but publicly proposed a round table conference of all Zionist factions in order to settle the major problems of Zionism.[78]

The Legislative Council presented a more immediate threat for the Zionists. Ben-Gurion heard from Wauchope on November 8 that he intended in the near future to make a statement to the effect that the pledge which he had given last year when addressing the League would be carried out. He would conduct negotiations with Arabs and Jews, but the actual realization of the Council would not be put into operation until the next World Zionist Congress in September 1935. Three days later, Cunliffe-Lister wrote to Wauchope that the Jewish claim to parity (which Weizmann had pressed on October 4) "should be rejected"; the Agency's claim to be consulted before any bill is introduced into the Council "should be refuted"; and "there should be no departure from the present practice in the matter of consultation between the H[igh] C[ommissioner] and that body." The Colonial Secretary proposed that the Council be composed of 12 unofficial elected members—8 Muslims, 3 Jews, and 1 Christian; 11 unofficial members—2 Muslims, 1 of the Bedouin tribes, 5 Jews, 2 Christians and 1 representing commercial interests; and 5 unofficial members in addition to the High Commissioner, who would serve as chairman and have the right of veto. Under pressure from Secretary of State for India Samuel Hoare, the Cabinet directed Cunliffe-Lister to increase the number of Arab members and to state that religious matters would be excluded from the Council's scope—"this no doubt," writes historian Yehoshua Porath, "to appease" the Mufti. The last matter was finally dropped owing to Wauchope's opposition.[79]

Soon after returning to Palestine, Wauchope conveyed to Shertok on November 16 that the Legislative Council would go forward, though put off "for some time," without parity, which both the Cabinet and he considered "inequitable." Shertok countered by speaking of the need to deal with "qualitative, not with quantitative values," and that permanent equality alone would prevent "domination of one race by another." Minority status was enough to make the Council "utterly unacceptable to the Jews." Even before 1929, the yishuv's opposition to the Council had hardened and become uncompromising. Wauchope's tenure to date had brought about "a vast improvement" in the Agency's relations with the mandatory, but the bad experience of 1929 and its political aftermath still strongly influenced the yishuv's attitude. Their current opposition was so strong just because the growth of Jewish numbers was relatively rapid, Shertok observed. They hoped that the latter would continue at the rate of at least 50,000 a year, so that in a decade they might become 40 percent of the population. The new, moderately increased labor schedule of 9,700 was greatly appreciated, but far from their request of 18,600 certificates. They particularly regretted the very heavy deduction from this total of 2,200 certificates (including 1,800 tourists, compared with 800 six months earlier) on account of unauthorized entry. "You could either fling the gates of the country open without restriction," Wauchope rejoined, or have a regulated immigration with penalties "in order to force the law." He chose the latter course while seeking to increase the proportion of labor to the total figure.[80]

The Agency's failure to receive, in Shertok's words, "once and for all a big schedule that would provide a radical solution for the problem of labour shortage" remained rooted in British concerns about illicit Jewish immigration. Hall had made this clear to Shertok one week earlier when urging that the Agency declare itself openly against the practice and "do something really effective to stop it." The efficacy of whatever measures the Agency might adopt in this direction depended on the measure in which labor requirements could be satisfied in "an honourable and legal manner," Shertok replied. Further, the Agency "hated to see Jews coming in surreptitiously," but had no control over "these people who were falling as easy pray to all sorts of private speculation." (He said nothing about the novel phenomenon of "fictitious marriages," often dissolved at the end of six months, which allowed a young couple to arrive and to remain lawfully in Palestine as one family.) Earlier the same day, Mills intimated to Shertok that the mandatory's "extracting the full pound of flesh from us on account of the tourists was because illegal immigration had of late assumed such considerable proportions."[81]

Two months earlier, Hall had suggested to Cunliffe-Lister that one of HMG's ships patrol off Palestine's northern coast in order to discourage organized attempts at illegal Jewish entry. The Secretary of the Admiralty turned this down in October as "uneconomic" and interfering with "proper functions," but did endorse the use of small craft, assisted by airplanes, which belonged to the Palestine authorities. Buttressed by a C.I.D. estimate that 50,000 Jews had entered the country unlawfully in the last three years, and that 15,000-20,000 had come from Hauran and Syria, 100 additional policemen for coast and frontier control, along with evening and night reconnaissance by the Royal Air Force, began to operate as of mid-August. Additional attempts by 350 from aboard the *Velos* to land were thwarted as a result, and its passengers had to wander from port to port until Poland agreed to receive them in November. They later entered Palestine legally in small groups, but this failure and the financial drain involved put an end to HehHalutz's effort. The sinking of the *Vanda* near the port of Danzig with 50 Polish Betarim aboard (they were rescued), coupled with the subsequent failures of Stavsky and Betar commander in Latvia Eliyahu Glazer (later Galezer) to bring 30 Jewish students from Latvia and Lithuania to Palestine via Lebanon, also contributed to halting the Revisionist endeavor.[82]

A report on November 1 to HMG's Third Cruiser Squadron discussed these efforts, including the arrests of a sizeable number of Jews in the past month. Some were deported and others imprisoned. Upon passing sentence, the Chief Magistrate declared in a Haifa court that no one was sorrier "for the suffering of these immigrants than he." If he allowed himself to be swayed by sentiment, however, "he would have to permit nearly all the Jews from Germany and Eastern Europe to enter Palestine." The judge concluded: "A stop must be put to illegal entry."[83]

Ben-Gurion's return to Palestine on November 19 brought him another disappointment, when he found an account by Jabri in that month's issue of *La Nation arabe* (clearly with co-editor Arslan's approval) about their September conversation. Jabri's version ended with the statement that Ben-Gurion's "childish and illogical proposals" revealed "the true aim of the Zionists, which can be explained by their faith that their dream will soon be realized. It is a warning not only to the Arabs, but also to the British, who ought to ponder the consequences of Jewish expansion of this scope." Ben-Gurion immediately wrote a rejoinder (which was never sent), claiming that he had not promised that "all the Arabs who did not wish to emigrate or leave the country would be free to remain," but that the Zionists had neither the intention nor the power "to push the Arabs out" and that they were "intentionally and unintentionally" improving the Arabs' condition. Rather than allegedly stating that "we will mobilize the Jewish forces to help the Arabs in Syria," he had spoken of Jewish aid in economic and cultural activities, which alone would lead to the Arabs' "true national freedom."

Alami, according to Ben-Gurion, remarked that "he was filled with shame and humiliation" at Jabri's public account. The Zionist leader would later claim that this breach of secrecy halted the negotiations, but he had earlier divulged to the London *Jewish Chronicle*, without providing details, that his talks with "the leaders of the pan-Arab movement" in Geneva had been "very satisfactory and interesting." Ben-Gurion "could no longer delude himself," biographer Shabtai Teveth aptly concludes: "The quickest route to the mufti had proved a dead end, and there was no other way."[84]

The Hagana entertained no such illusions. One agent had reported in September that some of the Arab leaders "wished to arouse riots at any price." Information arrived the next month about the intention of the Arab Scouts and the Youth Congress to organize according to the framework of the European Fascist para-military organizations in order to combat Jewish immigration, land sales, and the embargo on Arab labor. Another source spoke of training, preparing bombs, and smuggling weapons and ammunition into the country. All of the parties within the Palestinian Arab movement "were our foes almost to the same degree," concluded Shaul Meirov in an outline on November 30 for a lecture to Hagana commanders. In his assessment, the yishuv could not hope "for one trustworthy ally in all of next season, which will be decisive in the realization of Zionism." Signs of "true democratic intelligence" with whom "a shared language could be found" were still hard to discern. The entire Arab movement in the country "is entirely trained on the use of violence and believes in fact only in that approach." "Great admiration for Fascism and Hitlerism existed in the movement," Meirov ended, and terror "shut up the mouths of those who wished to rebel here and there."[85]

On December 1, writing as Acting President of the Arab Executive Committee, Muslim Vice-Mayor of Jerusalem and National Defense Party vice-president Ya'qub Farraj informed Wauchope that the mandatory's present policy with regard to Jewish immigration and land "means, if it has any meaning at all, the extermination [*sic*] of the Arabs and the establishment of any entity for the Jews in their place." This "serious danger" threatened the Arabs' "political, economical and social future," as evinced in Passfield's 1930 White Paper, the Hope-Simpson and the French reports. At the present rate, the Jews would outnumber the Arabs within six to seven years. If the government continued to propose a policy which ran "contrary to the principles of humanity and justice and inconsistent with the terms of the Mandate," Farraj closed, then the Executive "will have recourse to the [Arab] nation which is concerned in this case and will acquaint it with this fearful position."[86]

Joined by Executive members Abd al-Hadi, Husseini, and lawyer Mughannam al-Mughannam, Farraj brought the case before Wauchope that same afternoon. Abd al-Hadi presented the essence of Farraj's letter, stressing that the official Land Registry figures showed, for the years 1930-1933 inclusive, that 118,000 dunams of Arab land had been transferred to Jewish possession, and the group had no doubt that a large number of unregistered transfers had also taken place. This affected both the fellah farmers and the town dwellers. HMG had to give "first consideration" to the Arabs' civil and religious rights, protection obligated by the mandate.

Wauchope responded that the administration was seeking to increase land productivity and safeguard the welfare of the fellahin by the Protection of Cultivators Ordinance and its amendments. Rapid development in the last two years had increased Palestine's absorptive capacity and led to a labor shortage; legal Jewish immigration had reached 36,000 during the first ten months of this year. Government had taken measures to check the "still serious" problem of unauthorized immigration, including "considerable deductions" from the last two labor schedules, and he was "glad to say" that the mandatory estimated that the numbers in 1934 would be reduced by at least half and "again be much reduced" in 1935. The welcome drainage and development of the 40,000-dunam marshy Huleh concession, just approved, would include setting apart as much as 15,000 dunams for local Arab cultivators. Finally, the Legislative Council would proceed after "a reasonable period," first seeing into the working of the new Municipal Councils and discussing proposals with "leaders of various parties."[87]

Wauchope's stand, which he made public, hardly satisfied a rising militancy within the Arab camp. In telling Akram Zu'aitir of the talk with Ben-Gurion, Arslan warned the young Istiqlalist that England, "if she wanted to stop" Zionist objectives, "doesn't have the power to do so." Moreover, Ben-Gurion's proposals reflected "the degree of impertinence" that "these groups have reached this year, especially while the Arabs of Palestine are concerned only with municipal elections and nonsense which you are familiar with. Our misfortune with the Jews is not as [bad as] our misfortune with ourselves." On December 16, the Arab Executive passed the usual resolutions, urged the convening "in the near future" of the eighth Arab Congress, and insisted on a Legislative Council. (Jabotinsky had presciently observed two months earlier that the Council would be used by "the Arab Nationalists" as "a sounding board for virulent propaganda not only of anti-Zionist but also of anti-European views.") The Istiqlal and Husseini leadership met separately to strengthen their factions at that Congress, while the Nashashibis formed the National Defense Party. The Arabs of the village of Maalul and the Bedouins of the Mezarib tribe disturbed the ploughing by kibbutz Nahalal residents of Jewish National Fund land on December 20. Three days later, the Arab Youth Organization met in Jaffa to organize a boycott of Jewish produce, set up pickets against Jewish labor, and launch anti-Jewish propaganda in Europe. Rumors circulated that some of the group also directed clandestine terrorist groups, especially in the north of Palestine, aiming to "indulge in some concrete acts" within the next few months.[88]

The Palestinian Arab press sounded a sharper note throughout the month. The Arabs had to alert the world to Britain's breaking the mandate's provision and "to insist on their rights," editorialized the *Tzavach Alshab* on December 15. It was "time for the Arabs to wake up from their apathy," it charged, for if they had "mobilized all their forces and [done] their duty to the nation," the Jews would not have had the impertinence" to "dream of a Jewish State in Palestine and of a Jewish majority in the country." Reporting the "painful sight" that Muslim women were removing their veils when entering Jewish shops in Haifa, "an offense to Arab nationalism and to Muslim tradition," *Al-Difa'a* urged three days later that "those who were keen on their manly honour and held dear their religions had to take care of their wives." Unless the government stopped Jewish picketing against Arab labor, *Al-Zart Almoustakam* averred on December 20, "the Arabs would not take responsibility for any untoward happenings. They had already suffered enough, and could not remain silent onlookers while the Arab worker was being deprived of his livelihood." A leading article eight days later in *Al-Jamia Al-Islamia* noted that the Jews, having "put their talons into Syria" by purchasing land from wealthy Arabs of Lebanon and Syria, were "squeezing out the Arabs," and who knew whether the same fate did not also await the Arabs in Iraq? To avert the Zionist danger, the writer advised that a general Arab Congress should be convened to take "united measures" against Jews' "getting a footing" in Iraq, Syria, and Palestine.[89]

Shertok thanked Wauchope on December 10 for his "straightforward reply" to the Arab Executive, especially regarding immigration and the Huleh Concession. He also provided some information about the Jewish National Fund's success in getting a new loan from Lloyd's Bank for £500,000 (then about $2.5 million) with interest at 4 percent, thereby allowing the Agency to pay off its debts by annual installments, and to make fresh funds available to assist settlement on land bought by the Fund. The Agency, he added, had decided to renew its option on Abdullah's Ghore al-Kibd lands for another 33 years, with the possibility of renewing this for two further periods of the same duration. He would "gladly renew the undertaking" made not to have Jews in "any agricultural settlement" in Transjordan without Wauchope's approval. The High Commissioner, however, feared that renewal of the lease would lead to "a very serious flare-up which would be bound to make the Emir's position most precarious" in light of the Istiqlal and other adversarial parties, and repeated his certainty that settlement "would eventually take place." Although Minister Resident Cox had proposed that the British help "extricate" the financially-strapped Emir so that he could end the option, Wauchope advised Shertok that if the lease could not be surrendered entirely, then the Agency should renew it "and await events."[90]

The Agency could hardly await developments in Germany, where, as Martin Rosenblüth, now heading the German Department at the Zionist Federation's offices in London, told the ZOA Executive on December 16, "there was no ground for believing that the Hitler regime will end in the near future." Lloyd George still had a "profound conviction" that the Jews would "gradually persuade the very practical German people that persecution is not a paying policy," and that "the Germans, while having "outbursts of ferocity," "are too sane and good-tempered a people to keep it up." Yet Dodd's diary provided ample examples of that same people enthusiastically viewing Hitler as their Messiah; of signs reading "*Juden sind unser Unglück*" (Jews are our misfortune) plastered across small towns; of maps, documents, and speeches indicating expectations for annexing nearby countries; of Göring telling the Academy for German Justice that "heads will simply be chopped off if men do not obey the inspired Hitler and submit to his decrees." Hitler "remains the unblemished one," McDonald told Cecil and d'Avigdor-Goldsmid on November 17: "We cannot expect any really effective cooperation from the Reich." By mid-December, the Nazi party's *Völkischer Beobachter* had resumed its echo of the *Protocols of the Learned Elders of Zion*, while other German newspapers harped on Jewish profiteering and racial "pollution."[91]

In a private conversation with McDonald on December 17, Roosevelt again expressed "vigorously" his opposition to the Third Reich's antisemitic policy and his "fundamental opposition" to its principles. FDR further remarked that he would do his best to get $10,000 of U.S. government funds contributed towards McDonald's budget. Western European Affairs chief Moffat had ruled out use of the State Department's emergency fund. McDonald's sense of great discouragement at this juncture was understandable.[92]

Nahum Goldmann's crusade, with Wise's strong support, for a World Jewish Congress to defend Jewish rights in the public arena had not the slightest chance of stemming the tide. Delegates from twenty countries at a third and final preparatory conference in August to set up the Congress embraced his vision. So did the late French Foreign Minister Louis Barthou, Spanish diplomat Salvador de Madariaga and his Greek counterpart Nicolas Politis, Beneš, and some Jewish luminaries including Brandeis, Socialist statesman Léon Blum, and philosopher Henri Bergson. (Although wishing to convert to Catholicism, Bergson would hold off in view of the travails inflicted on the Jewish people by the Nazis and by their French collaborators.)Yet Weizmannites in the ZOA quashed an endorsement of Goldmann's objective, concerned that it would "militate against the effectiveness" of the 1935 World Zionist Congress. The American Jewish Committee's executive joined Warburg in greatly fearing that such a body would endanger the political and civil status of Jews, confirming for many the propaganda by Hitler and others of an international Jewish conspiracy to attain power. President Leonard Montefiore of the Anglo-Jewish Association, Laski, and most of the Board of Deputies of British Jews thought the idea "damned nonsense" for the same reason, as did Jewish establishment organizations in France, Holland, and Belgium.[93]

Goldmann scored a rare triumph when meeting Mussolini on November 13. On that occasion he obtained the Duce's pledge to work towards enabling Jews in the Saar Basin to emigrate with all their assets after an impending plebiscite, pursuant to a provision of the Versailles Treaty, which would clearly return that territory from France to Germany. The Fascist leader could not fulfill Goldmann's primary request to gain full equality for Jews under the swastika, however much Mussolini declared then that "Herr Hitler is a joke which will last a few years."[94]

Of the 20,000 Jewish refugees coming out of Germany annually, McDonald told Phillips on December 18, half were being absorbed in Palestine. In his November report to the Governing Body, the High Commissioner had declared that the prosperity of that country, one of the few such regions in the world, was due "in no small part" to "the steady inflow of industrious and capable emigrants from Central Europe, bringing with them material and physical resources, and, what may be even more important, moral and spiritual resources—the creative force of an ideal." At the same time, 10,000 had to be taken care of elsewhere each year, but "the European countries had exhausted their willingness to receive these émigrés, and when they did receive them the émigrés had the utmost difficulty in receiving permission to work." Moreover, McDonald's tally did not include other hotbeds of rising antisemitism across the Continent. As for the sliver of land hugging the eastern rim of the Mediterranean, ever more contested between two peoples, Ruppin's recent study of The Jews in the Modern World had concluded that "sooner or later, both sides will have to realize that they are destined to live and work together in Palestine. Then negotiations for a delimitation of their respective rights and reciprocal duties will have better prospect of success than at present."[95] Yet as 1935 dawned, with Arab and Jew both racing against time to achieve their opposing objectives, this eventuality appeared an ideal not visible even on the distant horizon.

Endnotes

1   Armstrong speech, Jan. 30, 1934, Box 99, Armstrong MSS; Joint Foreign Committee report, Jan. 22, 1934, microfilm #1925, Warburg MSS; George Bernhard, "The Via Dolorosa of German Jewry," *JTA*, Jan. 29, 1934; *Ambassador Dodd's Diary 1933-1938*, ed. W. E. Dodd, Jr. and M. Dodd (London, 1941), 91; Berlin 1934 memorandum, Box 99, Armstrong MSS. For Eckhart's impact on Hitler, see Saul Friedländer, *Nazi German and the Jews*, 1, *The Years of Persecution, 1933-1939* (New York, 1997), 97-98. In November 2010 the German Deputy Defense Minister, Christian Schmidt, officially acknowledged the sacrifice of this number of German-Jewish soldiers who died in World War I, speaking at Frankfurt's Jewish cemetery, where some 50 are buried. The Nazis had denied this fact. Associated Press wire, reported in the *Jerusalem Post*, November 7, 2010.

2   Weizmann to Sidebotham, Jan. 2, 1934; Weizmann address, Jan. 14, 1934; both in WA. His reference to "Jerusalem of the upper regions" (a Divine sphere) reflected Weizmann's abhorrence of spocalyptic speculation, a feeling which he soon shared with a Tel Aviv audience. *HaAretz*, Mar. 29, 1934.

3   Ben-Gurion to Brandeis, Jan. 5, 1934, file 20, Mack MSS.

4   David Ben-Gurion, *Zikhronot* 2 (Tel Aviv, 1972), 4-6; London *Times*, Jan. 6, 1934; *Palestine Post*, Feb. 7, 1934; Joseph B. Schechtman, *Fighter and Prophet: The Vladimir Jabotinsky Story; The Last Years* (New York, 1961), 212-214; "World Petition," May 1934, file R4070/6A/8882/668, LNA; Esther Stein-Ashkenazi, *Betar B'Eretz Yisrael, 1925-1947* (Jerusalem, 1998), 71-72. By the end of the year, the Revisionist petition had been signed by more than 600,000 Jews in twenty-four countries.

5   *World Jewry*, July 6, 1934; Rosenstein-Y. Ahimeir interview, Apr. 29, 1973, file P-7126/2, ISA; *BaMa'aleh*, Jan. 31, 1934; *BaSha'ar*, Jan. 27, 1934; *Mishpatim*, Jan. 30, 1934; both in F30/256, CZA; *HaAretz*, Nov. 15 and 16, 1931; Jabotinsky to Yeivin, Feb. 21, 1934, letters file 1/24/2/1A, JA; Schechtman, *Fighter and Prophet*, 200. Samuel had been denied access to the police investigations, including that of Medjid. Samuel to Attorney General, Feb. 4, 1934, file M-703/23, ISA. Asked by an Arab why he had denied his confession afterwards if it was true, Medjid replied: "What can I do? They want it so—let it be so" (Atieh statement, July 2, 1934, file 30.10, G-8007/9, ISA). For Jabotinsky's memorandum about the trial, see Aide-Memoire, May 1934, A330/40, CZA.

6   Wauchope to d'Avigdor-Goldsmid, Jan. 12, 1934, microfilm #1924, Warburg MSS; Shertok-Wauchope interview, Jan. 18, 1934, ZOA files, ZA.

7   Shertok to Jacobson, Jan. 15, 1934, A180/61, CZA; King-Crane Report, July 8, 1919; Crane to House, Oct. 21, 1933; Crane to Twitchell, Aug. 24, 1931; Crane to Ibn Saud, Sept. 1, 1931; Crane to Ibn Saud, Sept. 9, 1932; all in Crane MSS; *New York Times*, Jan. 24, 1933; Ambassador *Dodd's Diary*, 24-25,

55-56; Crane to J. Crane, Sept. 10, 1933; Crane to Roosevelt, Sept. 13, 1933; Crane to Houston, Jan. 31, 1934; all in Crane MSS.

8   Haj Amin to Crane, Apr. 2, 1929; Antonius memorandum of Crane 1931 talks in Jerusalem; Crane-Haj Amin meeting, Mar. 16, 1933; Crane to Young, May 5, 1933; Crane to J. Crane, May 13, 1933; Crane to House, May 19, 1933; all in Crane MSS. R. Breitman, B.M. Stewart, and S. Hochberg, eds., *Advocate for the Doomed: The Diaries and Papers of James G. McDonald, 1932-1935* (Bloomington, 2007), 90-91; Antonius to J. Crane, Nov. 24, 1933, Crane MSS. The Concordat guaranteed the freedom of Catholicism in Germany, in return for which Catholics abandoned political activity there. Pacelli would become the next Pope in February 1939, taking the title Pius XII.

9   Antonius to J. Crane, Nov. 24, 1933; Antonius annual report, Sept. 15, 1933; Antonius to Rogers, Apr. 18, 1933; Antonius to Crane, May 15, 1933; Antonius to Crane, June 12, 1933; Antonius to Crane, Oct. 28, 1933; all in Crane MSS. Louis Fischer, *Men and Politics: Europe between the Two World Wars* (New York, 1946 ed.), 245. For the first Palestinian Arab Congress in 1919, see Ann Mosely Lesch, *Arab Politics in Palestine, 1917-1939: The Frustration of a Nationalist Movement* (Ithaca, 1979), 87-88.

10   Kohn-Antonius interview, Jan. 31, 1934, file P580/51, Leo Kohn MSS, ISA; Leo Kohn, *The Constitution of the Irish Free State* (London, 1932). Kohn would serve in this capacity until 1947, and subsequently was political advisor to Israel's Foreign Ministry, taught international relations at the Hebrew University, and drafted a constitution for the State of Israel. The Knesset, however, decided to legislate a series of Basic Laws that would eventually be consolidated into a written constitution. That document has still to see the light of day.

11   Kohn-Antonius interview, Jan. 31, 1934, file p580/51, Kohn MSS; Shertok and Ben-Zvi interview with Wauchope, Feb. 9, 1934, file XIV/1-Jewish Agency, ZA; Shertok-Wauchope interview, Feb. 22, 1934, J1/6334/I, CZA; Szold to sisters, Sept. 28, 1934, file 1, H. Szold MSS; Lourie memorandum, Jan. 3, 1934, A185/86/1, CZA; Jewish Agency Political Department report, Oct. 1933-Mar. 15, 1934, microfilm #23, Louis D. Brandeis MSS, University of Louisville, Louisville, KY.

12   Henrietta Szold, "German Youth Immigration into Palestine," Feb. 25, 1944, Box 10A, Youth Aliya MSS, HA; Rose Jacobs, "Palestine Gathers in the Exiles," *Hadassah Newsletter*, Apr. 1934, 7, 9, 20.

13   Chaim Weizmann, *Trial and Error* (New York, 1949), 369-372; Weizmann-Mussolini interview, Feb. 17, 1934, microfilm #23, Brandeis MSS; Weizmann to Ormsby-Gore, July 19, 1936; Weizmann to Mussolini, June 17, 1933; both in WA.

14   Drummond to Simon, Feb. 27, 1934, FO 371/17876, PRO; Catastini to Secrétaire Général, Nov. 13, 1933, and Minutes, Nov. 22, 1933, and Dec. 1, 1933; all in FO 371/16927, PRO; "When Mussolini Urged a Jewish state but Weizmann said: No," *Jerusalem Post*, Feb. 14, 1973. In addressing the Zionist

Actions Committee (Va'ad HaPoel HaTsiyoni), which met for the first time in Jerusalem and had the sessions conducted in Hebrew, Weizmann would repeat his critique that the "middle class Jews of ripe years" who came under the "capitalist" category constituted a "grave problem" for the yishuv. Excerpts of Weizmann address (in Yiddish), April 1934, Weizmann files, ZA.

15   David Ben-Gurion, "HaPoalim BaHanhala," *MiMa'amad L'Am* (Tel Aviv, 1955 ed.), 475; David Ben-Gurion, *My Talks With Arab Leaders*, ed. M. Louvish (New York, 1973), 22-24; Ben-Gurion, *Zikhronot*, 41-44; David Ben-Gurion, *Anahnu U'Sh'kheneinu* (Tel Aviv, 1931).

16   Ben-Gurion, *My Talks With Arab Leaders*, 15-17; Ben-Gurion, *Zikhronot*, 163-165; Geoffrey Furlonge, *Palestine is My Country, The Story of Musa Alami* (New York, 1969), 102-103, 231.

17   Lesch, *Arab Politics in Palestine*, 109; Porath, *The Palestinian Arab National Momvement*, 131.

18   Arabs to Wauchope, Feb. 5, 1934, file M-293/3, ISA; C.I.D. report, Jan. 1934, FO 371/17880, PRO; Shertok visit to Abdullah, Apr. 24, 1934, J1/6334/I, CZA; C.I. D. report, Apr. 3, 1934, FO 371/17878, PRO. Haj Amin had stifled further protests in January 1934. Matthews, *Constructing an Empire*, 221.

19   Weizmann to Sieff, Mar. 9, 1933, Israel Sieff MSS, London; Wauchope to Cunliffe-Lister, Mar. 12, 1934, CO 733/257/37356, PRO; Cohen memorandum on visit to Abdullah, Jan. 12, 1934, file P-1056/7, ISA. My thanks to the family for enabling me to see the Sieff papers.

20   Newmann to Brandeis, Mar. 20, 1933, microfilm #23, Brandeis MSS; Rosenberg to Baerwald and Warburg, July 24, 1933, General and Emergency-Germany, JDC; Rosenberg to Warburg, Mar. 19, 1934, file 111, Mack MSS; Rosenberg to Flexner, Mar. 22, 1934, Box 69, Strauss MSS; McDonald to Rosenberg, Apr. 6, 1934, file 111, Mack MSS. Mack found McDonald's letter "extremely dogmatic," contradicting Neumann as to things on which he could have no personal knowledge, and not saying on what information he based his statements. Mack to Rosenberg, Apr. 23, 1934, file 111, Mack MSS.

21   Shertok-Wauchope interview, Feb. 22, 1934, J1/6334/I, CZA; Shertok-Hall interview, Mar. 15, 1934, file XIV/1–Jewish Agency, ZA. For examples of the persistent Arab immigration from the Hauran and other areas neighboring Palestine, see Mohl to Rothschild, Apr. 5, 1934, A264/46, CZA.

22   Lloyd George to Guedalla, Mar. 6, 1934; Guedalla to Lloyd George, Mar. 7, 1934; both in file G8/12/8, David Lloyd George MSS, House of Lords Record Office, London; Laski to Adler, Mar. 21, 1934, Correspondence files, Adler MSS; G. Warburg report, July 4, 1934, file 76, Mowshowitz MSS; "Report from Nürnberg," Easter 1934, microfilm #1925, Warburg MSS. Sultan Abdul Hamid II of Turkey carried out a slaughter of Armenians in the years 1894-1896.

23   Cunliffe-Lister memorandum, Mar. 28, 1934, CO 733/257/37356/II, PRO; Karsh, *Palestine Betrayed*, 19. For the official British report on the

"disturbances," published in the *Palestine Gazette* on February 7, 1934, see file R4071/6A/10084/668, LNA.

24 *Advocate for the Doomed*, 346; McDonald to Warburg, Apr. 10, 1934, microfilm #1923, Warburg MSS; Cabinet conclusions, Apr. 11, 1934, CAB 23/78, PRO.

25 Ben-Zion Katz, "Hakirat Retsah Arlosorov—Perek ShehTsarikh L'Saimo," *HaBoker*, Jun. 24, 1955; Abba Ahimeir, *HaMisphat*, 242-246; Ben-Zion Katz, *Al Itonim V'Anashim*, 160-161; *HaZeman*, Feb. 25, 1934; Ben-Zion Katz, "Al Nezayef Et HaHistoria," *HaBoker*, Sept. 9, 1950; *Do'ar HaYom*, June 10, 1931, L59/72, CZA; *HaTsofeh*, Jan. 8, 1965; Moshe Segal, *Dor VaDor* (Jerusalem, 1985), 91-93; M. Z. Nerya, ed. *Lekutei HaRa'aya*, 2 (Jerusalem, 1991), 368; Kook statement on Aug. 18, 1929 interview, L59/71, CZA; M. Z. Nerya, ed. *Lekutei HaRa'aya*, 1 (Tel Aviv, 1990), 259-260; Kook declaration on the 1930 White Paper, file P-193, JA; Kook to Fishman (Maimon), Dec. 12, 1933, Yehuda L. Maimon MSS, Mosad HaRav Kook, Jerusalem; M. Z. Nerya, ed. *Lekutei HaRa'aya*, 3 (Tel Aviv, 1995), 115-116. At the early stage of the trial, Kook informed his yeshiva student Haim Cohen, later Chief Justice of the Israeli Supreme Court, that he did not think a Jew had it in his soul to commit such a murder. *Yerushalayim*, Mar. 3, 1989. For aspects of Kook's unique ideology, see Zvi Yaron, *Mishnato Shel HaRav Kook* (Jerusalem, 1975); Tsvi Zinger, "HaSovlanut B'Mishnato Shel HaRav Kook," *Molad* 5-6 (Apr.-May 1968), 665-686.

26 B.K., *HaAretz*, July 3, 1935; David Tidhar, *Encylopedia L'Halutzei HaYishuv*, 1 (Tel Aviv, 1947), 186-187; Kook letter, Jan. 30, 1924, KKL 5/728, CZA; Shalom Ra'anan Kook reminiscences, n.d., file P-193, JA; Ben-Zion Netanyahu interview with the author, Aug. 7, 2004; Abba Ahimeir, *HaMishpat*, 146-147, 228-229; Meeting of Mar. 13, 1934, file 8/311, Tel Aviv Municipal Archives (hereafter TAMA), Tel Aviv. Milikovsky's powerful speeches in Yiddish can be sampled in his *Folk un Land* (New York, 1928), later translated in Hebrew as *Am U'Medina* (Tel Aviv, 1994).

27 Yosef Ahimeir, ed., *HaNasikh HaShahor* (Tel Aviv, 1983), 35-36; Shalom Ra'anan Kook reminiscences, n.d., file P-193, JA; Netanyahu to Klausner, Feb. 6, 1935, file 4-1086/396, Joseph Klausner MSS, National Library of Israel, Jerusalem; Netanyahu interview with the author, Aug. 7, 2004.

28 Ben-Zion Katz, "Ma'aseh ShehLo Ye'aseh," *Hadashot*, July 16, 1939; Ahimeir, *HaMishpat*, 153, 180; *HaYarden*, Apr. 24, 1934; *HaHed*, May 1934. For the continued silence of Bialik, who had expressed himself at length during the March 13 meeting in Tel Aviv, see Monty Noam Penkower, *Twentieth Century Jews: Forging Identity in the Land of Promise and in the Promised Land* (Brighton, MA, 2010), chap. 6.

29 Ben-Gurion, *Zikhronot*, 88-96. The British expert Sir Andrew McFadyean, after studying Palestine's economy, endorsed much of the Agency's position; W. J. Johnson, Treasurer in the mandatory government, did not. McFadyean lecture, Feb. 22, 1934, file 8/317, Chatham House Archives, Royal Institute

of International Affairs, London; Johnson-Frankfurter interview, Apr. 13, 1934, A264/46, CZA.

30   *Advocate for the Doomed*, 356-376; Laski to A. de Rothschild, Mar. 19, 1934, Joint Foreign Committee, Adler-Laski files, AJCA; McDonald to Warburg, Apr. 13, 1934, microfilm #1923, Warburg MSS.

31   Weizmann to A. Cohen, Apr. 30, 1934, WA; A. Ruppin, *Memoirs, Diaries, Letters*, 265.

32   Laski and Montefiore to Foreign Office Under Secretary, May 17, 1934, microfilm #23, Brandeis MSS; Birchall to Sulzberger, Mar. 27, 1934, file Grmany-11, Sulzberger MSS; Joint Foreign Committee Report, June 7, 1934, Executive Minutes, BDA. At the same time, Goebbels's *Der Angriff* would publish a series of 12 strongly pro-Zionist articles in September-October by Baron Leopold Itz Edler von Mildenstein, written after Mildenstein had visited Jewish settlements in Eretz Yisrael. Mildenstein, chief of the Jewish Desk of the SS security service (SD) as of that August, enlisted fellow Austrian Adolf Eichmann into the Gestapo's Jewish Division. Mildenstein was removed after a dispute with SD head Reinhard Heydrich in June 1936, and joined the Foreign Ministry's Press Department. Jacob Boas, "A Nazi Travels to Palestine," *History Today*, 30:1 (1980): 33-38.

33   McDonald to Warburg, May 5, 1934, microfilm #1923, Warburg MSS; excerpts of McDonald's statement, May 2, 1934, F38/537, CZA. Wurfbain to Dieckhoff, February 21, 1934, Bentwich-Barandon correspondence, April-June 1934, both in file C1609/60, LNA. A. J. Sherman, *Island Refuge, Britain and Refugees from the Third Reich, 1933-1939* (London, 1973), 46; *Advocate for the Doomed*, 387-399.

34   Ben-Gurion, *Zikhronot*, 94-96; Brodetsky remarks, Jewish Agency British section, May 17, 1934, BDA; *Palestine, A Study of Jewish, Arab, and British Policies*, 2, 772; *Do'ar HaYom*, May 15, 1934; *Palestine Post*, May 4 and 15, 1934.

35   Urofsky and Levy, eds., "*Half Brother, Half Son*," 546-547. For Frankfurter's enthusiasm after a visit to Palestine of the yishuv's accomplishments and his extolling the Laborites, see Penkower, *Twentieth Century Jews*, chap. 3.

36   Wauchope-Va'ad Leumi-Aseifat HaNivharim interview, May 23, 1934, CO 733/257/37356, PRO.

37   Shalom Ra'anan Kook reminiscences, n.d., file P-193, JA; Milikovsky to Kook, n.d., and Kook to Ahimeir, May 17, 1934, Abba Ahimeir Archives, Ramat Gan, Israel (courtesy of Yosef Ahimeir); *Davar*, May 26, 1934, and June 9, 10, 1934; *BaMa'aleh*, May 1, 1934, and June 5, 1934; *HaPo'el HaTsa'ir*, May 25, 1934; file H-1/35/8, JA; *HaOlam*, June 7, 1934; Shmuel Avidor, *HaIsh K'Neged HaZerem* (Jerusalem, 1962), 279; *Netivot*, June 1934. For Ahimeir's heartfelt response to Kook's personal appeal, see Ahimeir, *HaMishpat*, 235.

38   Ben-Gurion, *Zikhronot*, 97-102.

39   Magnes speech, May 24, 1934, ZOA files, ZA.

40   Hall testimony, May 31, 1934, and June 1, 1934, *League of Nations: Permanent*

Mandates Commission; Minutes of the Twenty-Fifth Session, 19-30, 135-137.

41 Valero's statement, A330/38, CZA; Court sentences, June 19, 1934, CO 733/278/75146/2, PRO; Avidor, *HaIsh K'Neged HaZerem*, 277, 279; Netanyahu interview with the author, Aug. 7, 2004; proclamations, files P-193 and 5/8-H; both in JA; *Davar* editorial, June 10, 1934; *HaPo'el HaTsa'ir*, June 15 and 22, 1934; broadsides, in files 1/35/8-H, 5/8-H, 40/8-H, and Ben-Zion Katz, "Kit'ei Reshamim V'Zikhronot" (1936), file 193-P, all in JA; Eliash statement, June 25, 1934, A493/99, CZA; *HaHed*, June and July 1934; *World Jewry*, July 6, 1934; Jacobi to Jabotinsky, June 12, 1934, Abrahamov to Jabotinsky-Jacobi, July 5, 1934, both in file 22/3/1-A, JA; Kook to High Commissioner (marked "not sent"), June 29, 1934, Kook to Campbell, July 2, 1934, both in A340/21, CZA. Uri Zvi Greenberg described his caustic feelings about the trial, and specifically the leftist attacks upon him after he returned to Eretz Yisrael, in the poem "Shnatayim VaHetsi HaYiti Goleh." See Hever, *Moledet HaMavet Yafah*, 9-11. For Uziel's thoughts, see his letter to Margalit, June 21, 1934, file 38/8-H, JA. For Jabotinsky's reaction, see *Jewish Telegraphic Agency* (hereafter *JTA*), June 10, 1934.

42 Mapai Central Committee, June 13 and 27, 1934, Labor Archives. Four days later, by a vote of four (Ben-Gurion, Shertok, Gruenbaum, and Hexter) to two (A. Berkson and Senator), the Jewish Agency Executive turned down a suggestion from Berl Locker in London, interested in "calming the waters," that the Executive issue a statement supporting clemency for Stavsky. JAEJ, July 1, 1934, CZA. Also see Moshe Beilinson's critical essay, "Limno'a Tishtush," against Kook's intervention. *Davar*, July 2, 1934.

43 Weizmann to Mussolini, June 13, 1934, WA; Locker to Gillies, June 14, 1934, A263/28, CZA; Berl Locker, "The Present Position in Palestine," June 1934, Imperial Advisory Committee memos-/2, Labour Party Archives, Transport House, London; Shertok-Wauchope interview, June 20, 1934, ZOA assorted files, and Wauchope to ?, June 1934, Lipsky files, both in ZA. That Committee recommended in Novemeber that the Labour Party oppose the Legislative Council as "inopportune" at the present time. Imperial Advisory Committee Memorandum, Nov. 1934, Labour Party Archives.

44 Hexter to Warburg, June 2, 1934, file 3/6, Hexter MSS; Cohen memorandum, June 5, 1934, file XIV/1-Jewish Agency, ZA; Mr. Shahla, "Jews and Arabs in Palestine," Imperial Advisory Committee memos-/2, Labour Party Archives. At the end of the year, Oliver informed Antonius of the Quakers' interest, "owing to the pacifist nature of their tenets," to actively take steps in the conviction that Palestine represented "an ever-increasing menace to peace." Oliver asked Antonius to come to London and assist his committee, but Antonius made a "guarded reply" and said that he could not accept new commitments at the present time. Antonius to Rogers, Dec. 15, 1934, Crane MSS. For this Quaker's later praise of Arab insurgents at the height of their revolt in Palestine, see Oliver memorandum, Aug. 6, 1938, file 361/5-P, ISA.

45 William L. Shirer, *The Rise and Fall of the Third Reich*, 301-314; Messersmith

to Armstrong, July 6, 1934, Box 44, Armstrong MSS; *The Letters of Sigmund Freud and Arnold Zweig*, ed. E. Freud, trans. Prof. and Mrs. W. D. Robson Scott (London, 1970), 83; Austrian Relief Committee for German Jews to McDonald, June 26, 1934, file C1604/2, LNA; Shirer, *Rise and Fall of the Third Reich*, 385-387.

46   Shertok-Wauchope interview, July 3, 1934, A264/46, CZA; Wauchope to Shertok, July 3, 1934, microfilm #23, Brandeis MSS; Ben-Gurion, *Zikhronot*, 122-132, 137-138; *Davar*, July 25, 1934.

47   London *Times*, July 4, 1934; *Palestine Post*, July 12, 1934; *JTA*, May 20, 1934; Khalidi to Magnes, July 23, 1934, file P-1056/7, ISA.

48   Ben-Gurion, *My Talks with Arab Leaders*, 18-21; Ben-Gurion, *Zikhronot*, 165-167; Neil Caplan, *Futile Democracy*, 2 (London, 1986), 195-196.

49   McDonald to Cunliffe-Lister, May 5, 1934, microfilm #1923, Warburg MSS; Statement on Board of Deputies–Cunliffe-Lister interview, June 29, 1934, Palestine Commission minutes, BDA; Frankfurter–Cunliffe-Lister interview, June 14, 1934, A264/19, CZA; Shertok–Cunliffe-Lister interview, July 19, 1934, S25/7562, CZA; CO 733/257/37356, PRO.

50   Schechtman, *Fighter and Prophet*, 202-203; *Palestine Post*, July 22 and 23, 1934; *HaYarden*, July 25, 1934; *Davar*, July 20 and 22, 1934; Mapai manifesto, July 20, 1934, file 1/35/8-H, JA; Mapai Central Committee, July 20, 1934, Labor Archives. Palestine's Attorney General declared to the Colonial Office's chief legal advisor: "Politically, the result may be satisfactory but from a legal point of view nothing could be more unsatisfactory" (Trusted to Bushe, Aug. 9, 1934, CO 733/266/37524/II, PRO). Confessing to Alami that he was greatly surprised at the verdict, the Jewish Agency's Bernard Joseph observed that the Court of Appeals had confirmed judgments before this on less corroborative evidence. "I know from Rice," he concluded, "that you put up a splendid show, and I suppose the result was just Stavsky's good luck" (Joseph to Alami, Sept. 12, 1934, RG 30.10, file G-8007/9, ISA). "Many thanks for your kind letter" was the reply (Alami to Joseph, Sept. 16, 1934, file P-772/10, ISA).

51   Ben-Zion Katz, *HaEmet Kodemet LaShalom* (Jerusalem, 1934); newspapers quoted in the *Palestine Post*, July 22 and 23, 1934; *HaTor*, July 27, 1934.

52   Ben-Gurion, *Zikhronot*, 138-151; N. A. Rose, *The Gentile Zionists: A Study in Anglo-Zionist Diplomacy, 1929-1939* (London, 1973), 51-52. For Weizmann's later recollection of MacDonald's meeting with Ben-Gurion and Namier, as well as the Prime Minister's agreeing with his definition of parity ("we do not wish to dominate them, but we refuse to be dominated by them"), see Weizmann to Melchett, Jan. 17, 1936, WA. For the yishuv's past response to a Legislative Council, see Halperin to Hadassah, Jan. 13, 1936, Rose Jacobs MSS; Norman Rose, "HaVikuah Al HaMoetsa HaMehokeket BaShanim 1919-1936," in B. Oded, A. Rapaport, and Y. Shatzmiller, eds. *Mehkarim B'Toldot Am-Yisrael V'Eretz-Yisrael*, 2 (Haifa, 1972), 217-245.

53   Ben-Gurion, *My Talks*, 24-29.

54   Ben-Gurion–Wauchope interview, Aug. 15, 1934, A264/19, CZA.

55   A.S. memorandum, "The Arabs and the Legislative Council," July 17, 1935, file C14/9/5, BDA; *Palestine Post*, Aug. 6, 1934.

56   Lesch, *Arab Politics in Palestine*, 106-110; *Palestine Post*, July 28 and Aug. 6, 1934; C.I.D. report, Aug. 6, 1934, FO 371/17878, PRO; Uri Milstein, *Kadmon V'Havurato* (Tel Aviv, 1974), chap. 1; Yehuda Braginski, *Am Hoter El Hof* (Kibbutz Be'eri, 1965), 19-26; *JTA*, Aug. 14, 1934; Palestine *Post*, Aug. 15, 1934; Haim Lazar-Lita'i, *Af-Al-Pi, Sefer Aliya Bet* (Tel Aviv, 1957), 65-66.

57   Antonius March 1932 draft; Antonius report of Wauchope interview, Aug. 20, 1934; Antonius to Rogers, Aug. 28, 1934; all in Antonius Reports, Crane MSS.

58   Ben-Gurion, *Zikhronot*, 151-157.

59   Ben-Gurion, *My Talks With Arab Leaders*, 29-34. The Mosque of Omar, more commonly known as the Dome of the Rock, was built by Caliph Abd-el-Malik (687-705) on the site of the Holy Temple built by King Solomon. It is revered by Muslims as the traditional site from which the prophet Muhammad ascended to heaven, and by Jews as the place where the biblical patriarch Abraham brought his son Isaac as a sacrifice.

60   *Palestine Post*, Sept. 3, 1934; Lazar-Lita'i, *Af-Al-Pi*, 63-64; Ze'ev Jabotinsky, *BaDerekh LaMedina* (Jerusalem, 1950), 21-30; Schechtman, *Fighter and Prophet*, 423; Lazar-Lita'I, *Af-Al-Pi*, 64-65.

61   *Davar*, Sept. 1 and 2, 1934; Aryeh L. Avneri, *MehVelos Ad Taurus: Asor Rishon L'Ha'apala, 1934-1944* (Tel Aviv, 1985), 26-28; JAEJ, Oct. 21, 1934, CZA. Alterman's phrase "*Hayinu KeHolmim*" was taken from *Psalms* 126.

62   Shertok-Hall interview, Sept. 7, 1934, ZOA assorted files, ZA.

63   Ibid.; Shertok-Hall interviews, Sept. 14 and 18, 1934, both in J1/6334/I, CZA; Szold to sisters, Sept. 28, 1934, file 1, Szold MSS, HA.

64   Caplan, *Futile Diplomacy*, 199-202. Chamberlain's offer of an area in East Africa for a large Jewish haven was brought by Herzl to the Sixth Zionist Congress as an answer to the Kishinev pogrom. Herzl gained a Pyrrhic victory, however, when a majority voted to send a study commission to the area; a large number of delegates, mainly from Eastern Europe and including the Kishinev delegation, vehemently opposed. By the spring of 1904, the British backed down.

65   Schechtman, *Fighter and Prophet*, 246; Jabotinsky to Sirkis, Sept. 8, 1934, A340/8, CZA; Yosef Klausner, "Tsa'ad Bilti Medini U'Vilti-Leumi," *HaYarden*, Sept. 26, 1934; Mapai Central Committee, July 28, 1934, Aug. 30, 1934, both in Labor Archives; Menahem Sarid, *LaShilton Behartanu: HaMa'avak Al HaHegmonia BaYishuv U'VaTsiyonut* (Herzliya, 2004), 395-397, 400-408. Jacob Frank (1726-1791) founded a sect in Eastern Europe which proclaimed him the Jewish messiah.

66   Netanyahu interview with the author, Aug. 7, 2004; Avraham Yitzhak Kook, "*Lo L'Olam Muaka...*," ed. D. Schlesinger (Tel Aviv, 2005); Avidor, *HaIsh K'Neged HaZerem*, 285-291, 295; Avraham Yitzhak Kook, "Repentance and

Peace," Sept. 2, 1934, file 193-Peh, JA; *HaHed*, Oct. 1934; Mapai Central Committee, Aug. 20 and 29, 1934, Sept. 22, 1934, all in Labor Archives; Ya'akov Goldstein, *B'Derekh L'Hegmonia*, 202-204. Katznelson drafted a statement for Mapai which, while censuring Revisionist and Brit HaBiryonim tactics, called for unity. See "To the Yishuv and the Entire Zionist Movment," n.d., file 4-6-1934-237, Labor Archives. For Katznelson's cynical response against the Histadrut majority vote, see Histadrut Va'ad HaPo'el, Oct. 21, 1934, Makhon Lavon.

67   Brodetsky report of visit, Aug. 29-Sept. 2, 1934, Germany files, AJCA; McDonald to Fuld, Sept. 16, 1934, Box 1, AR 7162, Box 1, Leo Baeck Institute (hereafter LBI), CJH.

68   *Advocate for the Doomed*, chap. 17; McDonald to Warburg, Sept. 18, 1934; microfilm #1923, Warburg MSS; McDonald to Fuld, Sept. 15, 1934, Box 1, AR 7162, LBI; Laski memorandum, Sept. 1934, file 76, Mowshowitz MSS; *New York Times*, Oct. 20, 1934.

69   *Advocate for the Doomed*, 457-458 and chap. 18; Laski to Adler, Oct. 2, 1934, Adler-Laski, JFC files, AJCA; Sept. 1934-Aug. 1935 "Strictly Confidential Report," file 215A, WJCA; Schmolke to American Joint Distribution Committee, Oct. 13, 1934, file C1610/67; McDonald to d'Avigdor-Goldsmid, Nov. 17, 1944, file C1609/62; both in LNA.

70   McDonald to Fuld, Sept. 16, 1934, Box 1, AR 7162, LBI; Weizmann–Cunliffe-Lister interview, Oct. 4, 1934, WA; Jewish Agency Executive Memorandum, Oct. 4, 1934, file 154, Central Agudas Israel Archives, Jerusalem; Kohn-Graves interview, Sept. 13, 1934, A185/86/1; Kohn to Shertok, Oct. 17, 1934, J1/6334/I; both in CZA. Speaking to the English Zionist Federation, Weizmann added that the WZO had agreed to the Legislative Council proposal in 1921 "under pressure" because it was "threatened with the refusal to ratify the Mandate unless that provision was included" (Oct. 7, 1934 meeting, PAC files, James G. McDonald MSS, Herbert Lehman School of International Affairs, Columbia University, New York City).

71   Political Study Commission, Oct. 15-16, 1934, ZOA files, ZA; Kohn to Shertok, Oct. 17, 1934, J1/6334/I, CZA.

72   Shertok diary, Oct. 7, 1934, A245/1, CZA.

73   Shertok to Brodetsky, Oct. 11, 1934, microfilm #1923, Warburg MSS; Brodetsky to Shertok, Oct. 29, 1934, ZOA files, ZA. The suggestion for the Round Table Conference had been urged by London *Times* foreign editor Philip Graves and Minister of Agriculture Walter Elliot, who both argued that it would be "most unwise" for the Agency to send a purely negative statement. Kohn to Shertok, Oct. 9, 1934, microfilm #1923, Warburg MSS. William Rappard of the Permanent Mandates Commission also advised that "the Zionist element would be putting itself in an invidious position if they opposed, without any alternative suggestion," the establishment of some such legislative body (Rappard to Brodetsky, Oct. 27, 1934, A508/9, CZA; and Brodetsky's reply, Nov. 1, 1934, file C14/10, BDA).

74   Ben-Zvi to Brodetsky, Oct. 14, 1934, file C14/10, BDA; Kohn to Shertok, Oct. 26, 1934, A223/26A, Hall-Ruppin conversation, Oct. 16, 1934, A107/100, both in CZA.

75   *Al Difa'a*, Oct. 12, 1934, *Al-Jama Al-Arabia*, Oct. 12, 1934, both cited in Jacobs circulated material, Rose Jacobs MSS; Abd al-Hadi memorandum, Oct. 20, 1934, file R4071/6A/15553/668, LNA.

76   Sarid, *LaShilton Behartanu*, 425-431; Ben-Gurion, *Zikhronot*, 182-199. When word of the "small agreement" got out, Katz implored Jabotinsky to press for a neutral, public investigation of Arlosoroff's murder. Without the final revelation of the truth and the "moral punlishment" of the guilty, he claimed, the matter would remain as "a tragedy for generations, like the Protocols of the Elders of Zion" (*HaYarden*, Nov. 28, 1934).

77   Schechtman, *Fighter and Prophet*, 251; Ben-Gurion, *Zikhonot*, 215-243; Sarid, *LaShilton Behartanu*, 432-480. JAEL, Nov. 10, 1934, Z4/20443; JAEJ, Nov. 20, 1934; HaKibbutz HaMeuhad–HaVa'ad HaPoel, Nov. 22, 1934, A116/66; all in CZA.

78   Ben-Gurion, *Zikronot*, 243-244; *JTA*, Dec. 16, 1934.

79   Ben-Gurion, *Zikhronot*, 225-228; Nov. 11, 1934, CAB 24/251, PRO; Porath, *The Palestinian Arab National Movement*, 149-150. Shortly thereafter, Cunliffe-Lister told the Cabinet that he did not intend to establish the Council or even publishing the Order-in-Council constituting it until after the Zionist Congress two years hence. Cabinet Conclusions, Nov. 28, 1934, CO 733/265/37502/II, PRO.

80   Shertok-Wauchope interview, Nov. 16, 1934, file XIV/1-Jewish Agency, ZA; ZOA Executive, Dec. 16, 1934, ZA.

81   Hall-Shertok interview, Nov. 9, 1934; Mills-Shertok interview, Nov. 9, 1934; both in file XIV/1-Jewish Agency, ZA. Writing about this marriage ruse, Henrietta Szold decried the evils growing out of the practice, noting that the Agency's Yitzhak Gruenbaum justified "any device" that enabled these men and women, including his own son, to escape "from the hell" in Poland (Szold to sisters, Nov. 16, 1934, H. Szold MSS).

82   Secretary of the Admiralty to Cunliffe-Lister, Oct. 5, 1934, FO 371/16932; Avneri, *MehVelos Ad Taurus*, 26-32; Lazar-Lita'i, *Af-Al-Pi*, 67-69; Eliyahu Galezer, *B'Terem Zarha HaShemesh, B'Sheirut Tenuat Jabotinsky* (Jerusalem, 1984), 65-70.

83   Enclosure to Third Cruiser Squadron, Nov. 1, 1934, FO 371/17876, PRO; *Palestine Post*, Oct. 31, 1934.

84   Caplan, *Futile Diplomacy*, 199-200; Ben-Gurion, *My Talks With Arab Leaders*, 39-40; London *Jewish Chronicle*, Oct. 26, 1934; Shabtai Teveth, *Ben-Gurion: The Burning Ground, 1886-1948* (Boston, 1987), 490.

85   Yoav Gelber, *Shorashei HaHavatselet: HaModi'in BaYishuv, 1918-1947*, 1 (Tel Aviv, 1992), 131.

86   Farraj to Wauchope, Dec. 1, 1934, S25/22789, CZA.

87   Wauchope-Arab Executive Committee interview, Dec. 1, 1934, CO

733/257.37356, PRO.

88   Caplan, *Futile Diplomacy*, 201-202; Jabotinsky to Rappard, Oct. 6, 1934,
      A508/10, CZA; Review, Dec. 9, 1934-Jan. 5, 1935, file C14/9/4; A.S., "The
      Arabs and the Legislative Council," July 19, 1935, file C14/9/5; both in BDA.

89   "The Arab Press," Internal Press Review by the London Zionist Organization,
      Jan. 11, 1935, Rose Jacobs materials, Jacobs MSS.

90   Shertok-Wauchope interview, Dec. 10, 1934, file XIV/1-Jewish Agency, ZA;
      Wauchope to Cunliffe-Lister, Dec. 1934; Cox to Wauchope, Dec. 1, 1934;
      both in S25/22774, CZA.

91   Dec. 16, 1934, ZOA Executive, ZA; Lloyd George to Guedalla, Nov. 6, 1934,
      file G8/12/8, Lloyd George MSS; *Ambassador Dodd's Diary*, 164, 170-171,
      174, 181, 191-192, 199, 201; McDonald to Cecil, Nov. 17, 1934, A255/539,
      CZA; McDonald to d'Avigdor-Goldsmid, Nov. 17, 1934, file C1609/62, LNA;
      Joint Foreign Committee, Dec. 11, 1934, file Adler-Laski, JFC files, AJCA.
      After meeting Hitler in 1936, Lloyd George most admiringly compared *Mein
      Kampf* to England's Magna Carta and called Hitler "the resurrection and the
      way" (Andrew Roberts, *The Holy Fox: A Life of Lord Halifax* [London, 1991],
      69). Also see Martin Gilbert, *The Roots of Appeasement* (New York, 1970
      ed.), 197-211. Not long after Poland fell to the *Wehrmacht*, he said openly
      in Parliament in October 1939 that Hitler's peace offer must be considered
      seriously, thinking that Britain had no chance of winning the war against the
      Third Reich.

92   *Advocate for the Doomed*, 577-579, 581n. To Ruppin, who hoped that
      McDonald would make plans for the annual evacuation of some 20,000
      younger Jews from Germany in the next decade, McDonald opined that
      the High Commission should be, if possible, wound up by October 1, 1935
      (McDonald to d'Avigdor-Goldsmid, September 28, 1934, AR7162, LBI).

93   *Unity in Dispersion: A History of the World Jewish Congress* (New York, 1948),
      37-39; Statements of Barthou and others, file 405; Wise to Goldmann, May
      29, 1934, file 403; both in Kallen MSS; Oct. 14, 1934, National Board, HA;
      Oct. 30, 1934, Executive Committee, AJCA; Rosenberg to Warburg, Oct.
      31, 1934; Warburg to Rosenberg, Nov. 2, 1934; both in microfilm #1924,
      Warburg MSS; Laski to Adler, Nov. 18, 1934, Adler Correspondence file,
      AJCA; Laski to Kux, Dec. 17, 1934, file 76, Mowshowitz MSS.

94   Mussolini-Goldmann interview, Nov. 13, 1934, Z5/365A, CZA. For the pre-
      war efforts of the World Jewish Congress, which was created in August 1936,
      see my essay "Nahum Goldmann and Jewish Statesmanship, 1919-39," in
      Monty Noam Penkower, *The Holocaust and Israel Reborn: From Catastrophe to
      Sovereignty* (Urbana, 1994), 3-16.

95   Diary, Dec. 18, 1934, William Phillips MSS, Houghton Library; Norman
      Bentwich, *The Refugees from Germany* (London, 1936), 156; Arthur Ruppin,
      The Jews in the Modern World (New York, 1934), 399.

3. Test Cases for Zionism

New Year's Day 1935 began on a promising note for the World Zionist Organization. For the first time, the Administrative Committee of the Jewish Agency met in New York City, with several non-Zionists taking part. Hexter pointed to the tremendous rise in Jewish immigration to Palestine, the potash works at the Dead Sea, approval of the Huleh concession, self-supporting agricultural colonies, and various prospects for future growth. Mack's assertion that Transjordan "ought always to be aimed by us as a part of Palestine" drew applause. Locker declared that "it is impossible for us to have even the slightest shadow of a war" with the British government, and extolled Wauchope as "really a friend of ours and of our cause." There certainly existed "a very serious and a very sincere national movement" among Palestinian Arab youth, he observed, but Arab-Jewish cooperation also was "much bigger than anybody realizes," and the Arabs "have learned that the Jewish immigration is a very serious thing, and it has come to stay." While differences arose at the two-day gathering over unauthorized immigration, unity and "a great deal of goodwill" reigned. Non-Zionists Laski, Warburg, and American Jewish Committee president Cyrus Adler joined hands with Wise, Mack, and *Jewish Frontier* editor and Labor Zionist Chaim Greenberg in approving the Agency Executive's stand during the past year with regard to the grant of immigration certificates and the Legislative Council, emphasizing that the latter's implementation "at this time would prove menacing to the interests of the Jewish National Home as well as the larger interests of Palestine."[1]

At the same time, Laski, together with Adler, Judge Joseph Proskauer, and others of the American Jewish Committee executive, continued to take a firm stand against the preparations for a World Jewish Congress. From their perspective, it provided a base for the people who were spreading the *Protocols of the Learned Elders of Zion* and encouraged accusations of dual loyalty. To the philosopher and Congress supporter Horace Kallen, "the fear of *ma yomru hagoyim* [what will the Gentiles

say]" dominated all these groups. Since much of the effect of the opposition had been secured by attributing to the Congress planning
committee's 1932 resolution "a racial Hitlerist intent and ideology"
because of its expression "*volksorganismus*," and especially by blasting
Goldmann's use of the term "sovereign," Kallen sought clarification.
Goldmann quickly replied that "sovereign" meant an organization entitled to determine its program and tasks for itself, in no way to "collide
with the duties of Jews of different lands to their respective countries."
While pleased with this reply, Kallen regretfully reported that, owing to
inadequate finances and organization, the Congress could not be held
before the summer of 1936. Brandeis had agreed with this assessment,
made imperative after Kallen's swing around the United States revealed
that "the ignorance of Jewry concerning its own problem is appalling"
and "elementary spade work," which could be accomplished in a year,
was essential.[2]

Goldmann gained support for the Congress's creation from the
Va'ad HaLeumi on January 9, but far more urgent concerns exercised
some within the Zionist leadership. Colonial Office Under-Secretary
Parkinson told Brodetsky and Lourie that the Agency Executive's effort to turn the option on Abdullah's lands into a long-term lease was
unwise. In full agreement, Wauchope repeated to Shertok on January
11 his conviction that "with a proper pace of progress the time would
come for a Jewish settlement in Transjordan," and declared that he
was seriously considering taking away from Ahimeir and his jailed Brit
HaBiryonim associates their Palestinian citizenship. (Shertok strongly
objected to this step on principle.) In public speeches in Nahalal and
Tel Aviv before returning to London, Weizmann assailed the dangers
of internecine conflict within the yishuv, and pointed to the problems
arising from a large non-selective immigration. He called for more
agricultural settlement, as well as "reorganization and profound read-
justment" in the educational system for the yishuv's youth. "The real
people in the movement must become aware that our very idea is in
danger," he wrote from Port Said to an ally in Johannesburg on January
17, "that we are undoing everything which we have created at such a
cost, that we are destroying the third temple before it has been fully
erected. What it will mean to the position of the Jews in the world at
this terrible time of stress, I dread to think!"[3]

Little could be as stressful as the Nazis' ever-tightening grip, which had become more evident four days earlier, when the residents of the Saar voted overwhelmingly (by 91 percent) to return their coal-rich territory to the Reich. By an agreement the previous month between Germany and the League of Nations Council, during a year-long period the Saar inhabitants would not be "subjected to any discrimination on account of their language, race or religion," and would be "given every facility" to retain or sell their property if they wished to leave that territory. Some 7,000 refugees, including 2,000 Jews, fled to France, which called on the League to have them protected under the Nansen International Office for Refugees. The Council approved the extension of "Nansen passports" to the group, entrusted their protection to that office, and approved of a special grant for settling them in France and Paraguay. When Hitler proclaimed that he had no further territorial claims on France, Anglo-French proposals were advanced pledging an equality of armaments and mutual guarantees of borders between Germany and her eastern neighbors along the lines of the 1924 Locarno Treaties for western Europe. The Führer welcomed the first offer, which would leave his regime free to accelerate publicly an already intensive rearming program, but dodged on the other because it would tie his hands for expanding eastward into the main area where, as *Mein Kampf* had first made clear, German *Lebensraum* lay.[4]

The League representatives involved told McDonald "categorically" that the question of the Saar refugees should not be "confused" with the general problem of Jewish refugees from Germany. They wished to do everything possible to "reduce the chances" of a large refugee problem. Since Berlin had never liked the setting up of his office, and his activities had not "endeared" him to the Reich and Party authorities, League officials in Geneva advised that it would be best if neither he nor his colleagues intervened in the Saar question. The prompt and effective action accorded the Saar refugees contrasted sharply with McDonald's own efforts, further leading him to explain to Cecil why it appeared necessary to envisage a procedure whereby the High Commissioner's office would be closed by the year's end, and some of its remaining duties transferred to another organization, preferably with the League. Acknowledging that the Governing Body was "useless" at present, Cecil in turn revealed that the Foreign Office had rejected his own request to move the office in Lausanne nearer the League on the grounds that it would irritate Germany and might imply that London was prepared to assume a financial obligation. (Cecil did not relay Simon's additional point to him that HMG had already "more than played our part in the settlement of the refugees," including 17,000 out of 27,000 in Palestine alone.) Washington also decided not to make a $10,000 contribution to the High Commission, despite McDonald's direct intervention with Roosevelt and an associate's press of the State Department.[5]

Palestinian Arab increased activity to prevent land sales to Jews, and especially Haj Amin's assigning the matter religious overtones, gave the yishuv still another cause for concern. Columnists for _Al-Jama Al-Arabiya_ and other newspapers praised Sheikh al-Muzaffar on his release from prison for taking part in the October riots: he was the only one arrested who had refused to sign bonds promising not to undertake any illegal acts for three years, and criticized Arab sellers of land. The journalists traveled to villagers in an effort, at times successful, to persuade them not to engage in such transactions. Some newspaper editors and the Mufti himself took part in these visits. In addition, according to Jewish Agency sources, the Arab Bank and Haj Amin were behind a group to buy Abdullah's Ghore al-Kibd territory in order to end the Agency's option there. [6]

On January 25, under the direction of Haj Amin and his Supreme Moslem Council, a Congress of the country's 'Ulama (arbiters of Islamic law) and Muslim religious heads declared that the massive Jewish immigration and land purchases "could not be tolerated or ignored from a _Shari'a_ [Islamic law] point of view." Every Muslim in the world and particularly those in Palestine and their spiritual leaders had to "resist this danger with all possible means in order to safeguard their existence, their religion and their religious places in the Holy Land." Their _fatwa_ (religious ruling), backed by counterparts whom Haj Amin had contacted in Iraq and India, excommunicated those who refused to obey. The Congress resolutions, conveyed by Haj Amin to Wauchope the following week, included the "absolute prohibition" of further Jewish entry; the admission without limit of all Arabs who wished to return from abroad; legislation against land sales and for the protection of small Arab owners and cultivators; and permission enabling Muslims who desired to make their private land a family possession or a charitable Waqf (an inalienable Islamic religious endowment) to do so.[7]

As early as 1923, Jabotinsky had respectfully analyzed adamant Arab opposition, his essay "The Iron Wall" advocating the only solution to be a Jewish majority with a formidable army in an independent Jewish state on both sides of the Jordan. Now his attention was focused on securing approval at the Sixth Revisionist World Conference in Cracow of his agreement with Ben-Gurion. Determined opposition arose, mainly from the majority of the Palestinian delegation. Menahem Begin, a Betar commander in Poland, joined this attack and pointed out that Ben-Gurion had once called the Revisionist chief "Vladimir Hitler." Jabotinsky replied that Ben-Gurion, Ben-Zvi, and Golomb had worn the uniform of the Jewish Legion in the Great War, and would fight again if the Zionist cause demanded it. Moreover, he had signed "a provisional *modus vivendi*," with final results to be obtained only through a Round Table Conference which might produce a coalition executive on the basis of equal partnership. The World Conference overwhelmingly ratified the agreement while upholding separate political action, as did the Second Betar World Conference that same January. At the latter Jabotinsky paid tribute to the imprisoned Ahimeir, "who teaches us the truthful patriotism," and presented a codified text of that youth movement's ideology called *"HaNeder"* (The Oath). Its first paragraph stipulated devoting one's life to Revisionist ideals and a monistic creed that rejected any fusion with "alien" creeds (primarily socialism), and urged a mode of thought and deed termed "hadar." Jabotinsky, designated "Rosh Betar" as of 1929, defined that term broadly as "beauty, respect, self-esteem, politeness, and faithfulness."[8]

Jabotinsky set off for a trip to the United States soon thereafter, meant to gain adherents for the World Union of Zionist-Revisionists. His inaugural speech, delivered on January 26 at New York City's Mecca Temple, draw an enthusiastic audience of 4,000 which heard his warning of catastrophe in Palestine if Transjordan settlement, immigration, and export of the yishuv's products were limited by the mandatory. Zionist publications and spokesmen, especially Wise, pilloried Jabotinsky's militarist philosophy as close to Fascism, however; he received a cool, at times hostile, reception when speaking to the National Board of Hadassah. Speaking engagements in other major cities did not draw large crowds and some potential allies sat "on the fence." America, Jabotinsky came to realize, was probably the hardest field to conquer for his movement: "Revisionism is 'dead earnest' because it was born in that European and Palestinian milieu where national ideals mean the actual salvaging of the nation, not the erection of flower-shops."

American Jews, under the spell of Roosevelt's New Deal domestic reform program, were drawn to what he called "salon Socialism." Finally, the Revisionist-Zionists in the United States lacked a hardcore group of supporters, one member admitting that no work had been done to build up an organization, even to create a central office with salaried staff. Jabotinsky's voyage having accomplished little, he discounted the United States as a political factor which could pressure Britain against retreating from its obligations under the mandate.[9]

Jabotinsky's initial hopes and those of Ben-Gurion for a final agreement unraveled quickly. On February 1, Jabotinsky charged the Agency Executive with "deliberate infringement, both in the spirit and in the letter" of that preliminary accord, and thought that "any further peace negotiations with the present Zionist Executive alone would be futile." Insisting that only a Round Table Conference could adjudicate the issue, Jabotinsky particularly found fault with the question of certificates for Betarim, the Executive's statement attacking the World Union's Tel Hai Fund (its main financial instrument), and the announcement that a "discipline clause" would be introduced as part of the shekel payment required to participate in the World Zionist Congress elections. Ben-Gurion, by contrast, considered that the Revisionists' insistence at the Cracow Conference on independent political action had ended the negotiations. He had already told the Mapai Central Committee that the next Congress would have to resolve the main issue of discipline within the movement. While the Agency Executive had already decided that the Revisionists must be read out of the WZO, some within Mapai's Political Committee and the General Zionists did not wish to pursue this path. The question of workers and the Histadrut, "one and the same," lay at the heart of the conflict. Mapai, Ben-Gurion concluded, had to worry now about the forthcoming Zionist elections in order to achieve a majority coalition at the next Congress, starting with the dispatch of emissaries to the Diaspora.[10]

Jabotinsky also lost a rare voice among the few in the yishuv who had sought an end to remorseless enmity between Left and Right. The trial regarding Arlosoroff's murder took a relentless toll on Milikovsky. Seven months after Stavsky's release, he died at the age of fifty-five. Despite severe weather, Kook came to eulogize his "precious" friend, whose heart was "filled with strength and life," and whose "sublime effort" to save a Jew "in the days of wrath" was carried out with "such faith and dedication." At the close of the initial thirty-day mourning period, he further lauded Milikovsky as an exceptional orator, dedicated to Torah, to the Jewish people, and to its national renaissance. That same month, Dizengoff and the Tel Aviv municipal council voted to grant Kook honorary citizenship. The vote, with Mapai representatives abstaining, elicited the Chief Rabbi's warm gratitude.[11]

At this point, the land question occupied the Agency Executive's main sphere of activity. On February 1, Wauchope threw out to Shertok a suggestion that any transfer of land should require the High Commissioner's consent, with approval not given unless the owner retained a certain area of land for himself. He wished to protect small owners thereby but, as Shertok replied, the proposal represented "a very serious departure" from past practice. Coming hard on the heels of Haj Amin's attempt to halt land sales to Jews, this legislation could further stifle the yishuv's growth. Without land, Shertok emphasized on February 12 at their next meeting, accompanied by Ruppin and Ben-Gurion, "there was no foundation or future for the Jewish National Home." Ruppin urged that the administration set up a joint development plan with the Agency, the results of which would benefit the Arabs as well. Scientific research, he added, might well discover subterranean deposits of water in the Negev and the possibility of collecting rain deposits there, a region where archeological remnants showed that ancient cities had maintained large populations. (This would "solve the last question for us for decades," Ruppin wrote in his diary a half-year earlier.) The Agency wished to form a balance in Palestine between urban and rural life, observed Ben-Gurion, not "a new Jewish Carthage." For "moral and political reasons," they were also obligated to improve the Arabs' lot, and not create two different standards of living for the peoples of Palestine. The Agency would submit a development plan to the next Congress, he declared, but it required the administration's cooperation in order to achieve success.[12]

The same day, McDonald presented to the Governing Body in London his views for a permanent settling of the German refugees. In the past two years since Hitler's advent to power, he began, 20,000 had been absorbed in Palestine, 2,500 in South American countries, 200 in South Africa, and approximately 500 elsewhere overseas. To facilitate the placing of the 25,000 still in temporary homes, McDonald planned on a three-month tour in the spring to South America. The High

Commissioner's survey of various countries led him to the realization that a process of individual placement for the larger numbers of refugees, with a limited group emigration for the balance, offered the only method of resolving this problem. Unfortunately, the newly created U.S. Refugee Economic Corporation, financed by private Jewish organizations at his urging, had raised only a bit more than $1 million of the several millions that were announced by its founders in early 1934. The funds were to be targeted for various productive enterprises, operated on an investment basis, and could include loan banks in certain European and South American countries for the purchase of equipment so that "in all probability" the refugees could become self-supporting. None of these funds, in any event, had yet been made available.[13]

Foreign Secretary Simon's projected journey to Berlin, in search of an agreement aiming at "peace and security in Europe for at least the next five years," prompted Jewish organizations in Britain to have him intercede on behalf of their German co-religionists during that visit. Writing to Whitehall, Laski and Montefiore requested Simon to "bear in mind" certain facts: Jewish origin disqualified citizens for German public service "from Judge in the Supreme Court to instructor at a municipal swimming bath"; the Ministry of Education recommended for use in schools the *Protocols of the Learned Elders of Zion* and similar publications; all government departments, except for the *Reichswehr* Ministry, rigidly ignored tenders from Jewish firms or even those of limited companies whose directors might include some Jews. Owing to difficulties of finding employment, German Jewish youth would likely join the scores of thousands who had already emigrated. All these circumstances, Laski and Montefiore observed, had produced "a feeling of anger and disgust" amidst the Anglo-Jewish community, sentiments shared by "a large number of our fellow citizens." Kurt Battsek, the German-Jewish Central Bureau's representative on the Jewish Refugees Committee in London, went further, asking that Simon explain to his German counterparts that unless the "Jewish question [was] not entirely dispensed with by the German government," thus relieving rising unemployment elsewhere by the influx of refugees beyond its borders, neighboring countries could not "arrive at internal peace."[14]

These appeals fell on deaf ears. In May 1934, Simon had proposed equality of arms to Germany, which the French had then sharply rejected. At the end of January he turned aside Cecil's strong endorsement that McDonald's High Commission and its Governing Body be reorganized as a constituent organ of the League, noting among other arguments that this "might just be the sort of last straw that might frighten Germany away from Geneva for good." Characterizing the Germans as "a stupid people, generally speaking, and very backward in intellectual and spiritual civilization," Cecil rejoined that "sweet reasonableness, I am certain, is quite thrown away upon them." He suggested, in a debate at the House of Lords on February 6, that all related organizations be "amalgamated into one organization directly" under the League because the refugee question constituted "a serious danger" threatening the preservation of world peace. With instructions received from the Foreign Office not to indicate that HMG was prepared "to abandon this somewhat passive attitude" toward the High Commission or to "agree to any alterations" in its "existing status," Under-Secretary of War Lord Strathcona and Mount Royal expressed in reply the government's continued "sympathy" for McDonald's endeavors, then added that only the Assembly could consider any alteration in the status of that office.[15]

The influential Lord Lothian, a wartime assistant to Lloyd George who had later aided the former Prime Minister considerably in drafting the Treaty of Versailles, shared Simon's inability to comprehend Hitler's mind. Following an interview with the Führer, Lothian pronounced in the London *Times* that Germany sought not war but "real equality." Most importantly, Hitler told him that "he will pledge Germany not to interfere in his beloved Austria by force." Not having the "slightest doubt" that Hitler was "sincere," Lothian believed that the cruelty and "merciless oppression of weak minorities" characteristic of the Nazi regime were due, in large measure, to the fact that Germany had not enjoyed these rights "at any time in the last sixteen years." Urging his fellow countrymen to treat the Third Reich "as a friend," Lothian asserted that Germany "is not imperialist in the old sense of the word.... Its very devotion to race precludes it from trying to annex other nationalities." Reading this and a similar expression of view by Lord Allen of Hurtwood after his meeting with Hitler, the Joint Foreign Committee observed that it had pursued "precisely the same object"—equality for all Germany's citizens. "Unfortunately," the Anglo-Jewish establishment body concluded, "there is no sign that the spirit which Germany so ardently desires should prevail in international relations is likely to govern her own treatment of the Jews. So far as they are concerned, equality of treatment remains in Nazi eyes an outworn relic of an age that is past."[16]

In Shertok's mind, growing Arab hostility in the region to Zionist aspiration and achievement crowded out the German reality. On February 18 he told Wauchope that the Istiqlalists, no longer restrained after Feisal's death, had spurred on the present Iraqi government to take the lead in working for an "all-round" Arab independence by following "the line of least resistance" with attacks on Zionism. The Mufti's activities, including propaganda about Jewish designs on the Mosque of Omar, had "no doubt been a contributing factor." Contacts with Jews abroad, and the yishuv in particular, had been outlawed, Baghdad not realizing that Palestinian Jewry's progress opened prospects of cooperation and mutual economic advantage for both countries. The Jewish brothers Kalai, both educators and Palestinian subjects, had been arrested and brutally compelled to leave Iraq at an hour's notice. In Palestine itself, the particularly daring attack four nights earlier on the new kibbutz Ramat HaKovesh, seriously wounding one guard, was reminiscent of the murderous attack on Nahalal two years earlier. This newest incident, in Shertok's judgment, indicated an attempt to start in the south "the same kind of outrages" which had so far been committed by Arabs in the north of the country. "Visibly impressed" by the account, of which he said he had not heard, Wauchope took down the essential details.[17]

After this interview, Wauchope sent the Agency a confidential, written document reformulating his views of the land question. Reaffirming his opinion that it was necessary, by means of a special ordinance, to secure a "subsistence area" for the Arab cultivator, he noted that this area could be "reassessed from time to time according to its varying productivity." At the same time, Wauchope conceded that "it is essential for the good of the National Homeland that a high proportion of the Zionist settlers should work on the land in Palestine." Birkat Ramadan (near Netanya) and the Huleh offered examples where, through improved drainage, fresh land could be made available for Jewish settlement and the lands of existing Arab fellaheen improved. "It is hoped," the High Commissioner went on, "that by water-boring in the Negev further lands, on an even larger scale, may be made available for the same double purpose." Finally, with a reference to Transjordan, he declared: "Later—other lands, elsewhere—may become available."[18]

Haj Amin's efforts expanded in March with his creation of the

Palestine Arab Party, its central office located in Jerusalem's Sheikh Jarrah Quarter. So as not to jeopardize his posts of Grand Mufti and president of the Supreme Moslem Council, Jamal al-Husseini became president. Vice-president Alfred Rock (Roche) attracted considerable support in the Roman Catholic community, in which this wealthy Jaffa citrus grower was a prominent fixture. The new party's prestige largely derived from being identified with Haj Amin, and it became the most powerful in the Arab community. Its platform called for a repudiation of the Balfour Declaration, a full halt to Jewish immigration, and the immediate establishment of Palestine as an independent Arab state. While competing political groups equally advocated this program, Haj Amin could claim independent success in rousing popular interest over the land issue, which he had first championed with the creation in 1931 of the Arab National Fund in order to check Jewish purchase of Arab realty. He also assumed personal command of Abd al-Qadir's secret terrorist group, of which he had been informed by its young leader one year earlier.[19]

Arab illegal immigration into the country went on unabated as well, E. N. Mohl, director of the Palestine Economic Corporation, informed Brandeis on March 8. A study by Mohl's experts and an Agency representative had just completed the section dealing with the southern part of the plain up to and including Jaffa and Tel-Aviv. The number of permanently settled Arab immigrants with their wives and children was very high. The foreign Arabs came from French Syria, Hauran, Transjordan, Yemen, Mecca, Egypt, and the Sudan, with considerable numbers of Druses and Circassians from Syria. About 8,000 Syrians and 1,000 tents of Egyptian Bedouin, each tent containing 4-5 individuals and a high percentage with their families, centered in Nebi Rubin near Rishon LeTsiyon. A few thousands lived near Abu Kishk; about 2,000 in Rehovot; 3,000-4,000 in Wadi Chanin-Nes Ziona; over 2,000 in Rishon LeTsiyon—Beit Dajan; and at least 4,000-5,000 in Petah Tikva. Ben-Gurion and Shertok, apprised of these figures by Mohl, had consequently been aroused to what Mohl called the "aggravated danger to security arising from the incoming hordes, especially in view of their scattered abodes, concentrating in small groups around all the centres." In response to his repeated remarks that the Agency Executive's day-to-day administrative problems seemed to preclude thought on important matters "of a longer distance," Shertok had recently said that the

Agency was setting up a committee to deal with those matters.[20]

Harold F. Downie, head of the Colonial Office's Middle East Department, still believed that Palestine was developing too rapidly, and that the economic boom which had attracted so many illegal Arab immigrants "could not last very much longer." In an interview on March 5 with A.L. Fellman, former economic and political secretary to the Jewish Agency, he expressed the thought that "an undercurrent of disgruntled Arabs" stirred beneath the "peaceful atmosphere." Downie noted the Zionist ideal of purely Jewish labor, brought up the charge of numerous "landless Arabs," and questioned what would occur if Jewish land purchases continued. Fellman pondered afterwards why the Colonial Office's Palestine policy was based on presumptions of what might happen in fifty years' time, rather than adopting its generally empirical policy, which led to a line of action determined by actual circumstances. Two days later, Downie wondered if Jewish immigration was "rather moving too fast." He also gave the impression to Fellman of being prejudiced against the yishuv's communal settlements, specifically the scarce intimate connections between parent and child, "and that if this was going to be the type of the New Jerusalem, he for one would vote for the good old Jewish tradition of family life."[21]

Hitler experienced no hesitation in moving quickly, decreeing on March 16 a law which established compulsory military service and provided for an army of roughly half a million men. Germans rejoiced, considering this startling move on the Führer's part a restoration of their nation's honor. The generals, also taken by surprise, were "immensely pleased," recalled William L. Shirer about his attending the Heroes' Memorial Day ceremony in Berlin's State Opera House the next day. Contemplating the "hair-raising" war scare that soon followed, New York Times foreign correspondent Frederick Kuhn in Berlin sent a brief note to his father: "I think most people are really convinced for the first time that they've got to go through another terrible time in a few years." Britain and France did protest this end to the military restrictions of Versailles, but Simon kept to his scheduled visit to Berlin. Owing to the further deterioration of Germany's foreign exchange situation, Dodd later informed Hull, the Reichsbank also began to allot capital from month to month to Palestine emigrants only in proportion to the monthly currency inflow from German exports to Palestine, assigning capital to only twelve to fifteen emigrants each month.[22]

None of this prevented a Histadrut referendum from rejecting the tentative agreement which had been signed by Ben-Gurion and Jabotinsky five months earlier. On March 24, by a vote of 15,227 to 10,187, an impressive majority turned down the proposal. One week earlier, Ben-Gurion had failed to win over his own comrades in support of ratification at Mapai's third conference in Hadera; Labor was not prepared to follow his sudden *volte-face* toward the Revisionists and their charismatic leader. Tabenkin's impressive victory in the referendum could not be denied. The result did not cancel the newly established friendship which had developed between Ben-Gurion and Jabotinsky, who exchanged private letters of mutual respect. "If we must battle each other," Ben-Gurion wrote, "remember that among your 'enemies' is a man who esteems you and feels your pain as his own." Jabotinsky replied: "Go in peace. If you can, get your aides not to make the 'war' any more bitter than it has to be.... I wish you success. In any event, as you wrote so shall it be: a scene the likes of which Israel has never encountered, war with two hands outstretched over the battlefield." A singular opportunity for compromise and consensus between their two movements had been lost, this rejection, in Shabtai Teveth's apt phrase, to be "the determining factor in Zionism's fateful factionalizing and ongoing internal strife."[23]

The week-long sessions of the Zionist Va'ad HaPo'el (Actions Committee), which opened on March 27 in Jerusalem, reflected this break. Rejecting Jabotinsky's demand for a Round Table Conference as "the last chance to save Zionism and the Yishuv from utter disruption," the conferees also condemned the Revisionists' international petition campaign. The text of the shekel (membership dues in the World Zionist Organization) underwent change, obliging every voter for the next Zionist Congress to observe discipline, thereby precluding any Revisionist political action. The rigid proposal passed by a majority of 36 to 13, the latter voters including the Revisionists and part of the Mizrachi faction. This minority abstained on a unanimously passed resolution to strengthen the Histadrut and its authority, with punishments to be meted out to anyone who violated discipline in political matters, in some cases even expulsion from the WZO. Jabotinsky warned from the United States that if his idea of a Round Table Conference were turned down, the World Union of Zionist-Revisionists would arrange a worldwide plebiscite, which "will affect the future of the entire Zionist movement." After consulting with him, the World Union's headquarters in Paris announced on April 7 that the Revisionists would not take part in the elections for the nineteenth Zionist Congress, and ordered its seven representatives to leave the Va'ad HaPo'el conclave.[24]

Weizmann remained above the fray, "deeply shattered by the happenings in this country." Writing to Ruppin on April 5, he asserted that he had "worked all these years anonymously, and cooperated loyally, in the hope that there will come a time when we shall accomplish a great deal. This time could be now, yet I do not observe our rising above the usual commonplace dissensions and petty quarrels. Rather, we are deeper in them." Out of the WZO presidency for the last four years, he was happily rid of these points of strife, and shuddered at the thought of "incurring the risk of again getting into this soulless affair." Weizmann did not see in "the decayed organization" those forces which could and would influence the reconstruction needed. Ensconced in his chemistry laboratory at the Daniel Sieff Research Institute in Rehovot, he could peacefully continue in his sixty-first year in a field of work which could be valuable for the country one day. His effort to draw the yishuv's attention to the bad conditions had failed, and would also fail in the future, "because one cannot fight against avalanches." "Therefore, I cannot be a leader. I lack the courage, force and the ... loving devotion that helps one to overcome difficulties." He would leave for London and return in October to his home in Rehovot. He did not propose to come to the Zionist Congress, Weizmann's private *cri de coeur* ended, "because there I have nothing to seek, nothing to say and nothing to do."[25]

Political rifts also plagued the Palestinian Arab community, giving Jamal al-Husseini an opportunity, soon after his party's creation, to take the lead in protesting HMG's policy. The actions of the mandatory, he wrote to Wauchope four days later, were "unjust, inequitable and will lead to the extinction of Arab nationalism and Islam in this country, and is even inconsistent with the terms of the detestable mandate." The High Commissioner, a "gallant soldier" of "independent means," by refusing to enforce the recommendations of the Hope-Simpson and French Reports, had not lived up to their expectations. "Thousands" of Arabs were being evicted daily from their homes because of Jewish land purchase, while Jewish immigration, including illicit entry, was "over-flooding Palestine and sweeping the Arab people away." The Legislative Council idea had been abandoned through pressure from

Zionist "promoters of despotism." Arab government officers, threatened with loss of their appointments through Zionist influence, could not "discharge the responsibilities legally imposed upon them by giving you just and loyal advice." The present form of government, Husseini declared, "is defective, imperfect, loose and unstable." Since it lay beyond Wauchope's powers to establish an "independent parliamentary, national Government" and abrogate the mandate, the Palestine Arab Party asked for effective measures against land sales and "detrimental" immigration, as well as the establishment of self-government in the country.[26]

Haj Amin followed up with a long speech on April 16 at a reception in Jaffa. He began with thoughts about "the distresses and difficulties which have overcome this country." Their fathers and grand-fathers made their "historic awe-inspiring stand" at this coast, shedding blood and spending treasure in order to save Palestine and to ward off invaders. The lands sold in our time contained "the corpses of your fathers and forefathers, the martyrs and the friends of the Prophet and the true warriors." Forty days after Musa Kazim's death, the Mufti went on, a poem by Sheikh Fuad Pasha al-Khatib with these lines had been read in Jerusalem: "You have found a land to bury him in. Will you have land for your dead tomorrow?" The duty of every Arab was to see that the land not be lost to "the foreigners." "Artificial false propaganda," claiming that the country was "divided against itself" and that all its inhabitants were traitors, sought to deprive Palestine of the sympathy of the Arab and Muslim worlds. "Your enemies the Zionists" spread this "in a devilish manner" here, but the majority of the country's inhabitants belonged to "an honorable element" who were really "sons of those conquerors, the friends of the Prophet, may God bless them." Those who feel "like the rock" in the Al-Aqsa Mosque in Jerusalem, and who sing like the Scouts today, "This is my hand, if ever the world raises a hand, it will never submit. I hope to fight today and tomorrow with my heart and will. We do not tire or weaken," deserved to defend this country. Our difficulties will disappear, a confident Haj Amin closed, drawing on a quotation from the Koran: "Do not be weak or depressed and you shall gain the upper hand if you are true believers."[27]

The Nashashibi forces, Haj Amin's primary competition for leadership, soon counterattacked. *Falastin* and *Al-Jamiah Al-Islamiya*, then supporters of the moderate National Defense Party, published on April

19 a photostat of a letter dated Geneva, February 20, 1935, from Arslan to Haj Amin. Therein the Druse nationalist attempted to persuade the Mufti, currently accused in Arab newspapers of failing to show "a hostile attitude towards England," to commence pro-Italian propaganda in the Arab countries as soon as possible. Haj Amin's "attachment to the friendship" of the British, Arslan wrote, would make him "lose not only your influence on your fellow Palestinians, but also that on other peoples." London's opposition to Italy's encroachment on Abyssinia (Ethiopia) afforded an excellent opportunity to "expose the wrongs" of the Abyssinians against the Muslims. Mussolini had personally given Arslan assurances that Italy "will not treat us as England and France have treated us." A visit to Geneva by Husseini could obtain more details of these assurances. Arslan had told the Duce that Abdullah was "a creature of the British" and that we could not expect anything good from him, especially as he had "turned to the circle" of Ragheb Nashashibi and his supporters. "God's peace and His Mercy be with you," the letter closed.[28]

The Nashashibi newspapers charged that only on this basis could recent articles in praise of Italy, appearing in Haj Amin's newsapaper *Al-Jama al-Arabiya*, be understood. The Mufti's backers claimed that the letter was a forgery, but these denials had little effect. Italy's ties with Haj Amin and the Istiqlalists were known to British intelligence and the Jewish Agency. Italian radio broadcasts in Arabic from Bari and articles in Palestinian Arab newspapers under Italian influence became more and more anti-British in tone. Before long, C.I.D. and other reports noted the activity of Italian agents in Palestine. Mussolini, like Hitler, openly wished to rectify what he considered to be the injustice of the Paris Peace Conference at Versailles. The Fascist leader regarded the Mediterranean as *mare nostrum* (our sea, recalling the most glorious days of the Roman Empire), a dream that could be fulfilled by aggression against Ethiopia, Eritrea, and Somaliland, these countries to be subsequently contemplated as bases for attacking Tunisia, Egypt, and the Levant. The Duce had already completed his conquest of Libya by 1930. German propaganda shrewdly aided Mussolini's designs by subsidizing "educational" activities in Iraq and encouraging the openly Nazi-styled "Green Shirts" of Ahmed Hussein in Egypt. In Palestine, the Istiqlal newspaper *Al-Difa'a* took a transparently pro-Nazi line, editor Ibrahim Shanti making extensive use of material supplied by

Goebbels's ministry, while Fritz Reichert served as the Gestapo's agent there.[29]

This latest example of internal Arab strife found Ben-Gurion far off on a four-day journey from Jerusalem to Akaba and back, intent on familiarizing himself and his companions, Katznelson and Agency Arabist Eliyahu Epstein (later Eilat), with the west bank of the Jordan and the Negev. On the night of April 17, after identifying places and sights by their biblical names and visiting Petra, the trio held a make-shift Passover Seder in an Arab hotel in Ma'an. On the second day of Passover, they left Akaba for Um-Rashrash (to become Israel's Eilat in March 1949, millennia after it had been rebuilt by the Judean king Azarya in the late eighth century B.C.E.), reached a place which they identified as the biblical Kadesh Barnea, and then made for Beersheba, a small Bedouin enclave of 3,000-4,000 with not one Jew. The trip convinced Ben-Gurion that across this vast, empty space Zionists could make the desert bloom without friction with the Arab inhabitants, and that "a great future lay in store if we succeed, before anything else, to become established in the gulf of the Red Sea." "There is a place," he later told Hadassah's National Board, "to build up a real Jewish state." Reporting to the Agency Executive on April 21, he emphasized the territory's great strategic value, especially for British Imperial interests à la Singapore. "Extraordinary pioneering" was called for now in this regard, Ben-Gurion felt, and the yishuv did not require much money to start. Three days later, he sailed from the port of Haifa for a brief stay in Europe and from there to the United States.[30]

In the same period of time, the Jews' parlous situation under the swastika had markedly deteriorated. "The utter hopelessness" of every Jew within the Reich, wrote the Joint Distribution Committee's Jonah Wise after a visit abroad, "makes it impossible to draw a picture other than one of the blackest despair." "Cold brutal terror" confronted the Jews there, Rabbi Morris Lazaron of Baltimore informed U.S. General Douglas MacArthur, adding the assessment of authoritative sources in Germany that "unless prevented, Europeans will wake some fine morning to find their capitals bombed and the German colossus reaching out and taking what it wants in a short, sharp air war backed by a rapidly moved mechanized army." To Warburg, Lazaron sent from Berlin the first account, written by an Amsterdam committee, of the brutal treatment in "reeducation camps" meted out by Himmler's SS to returned refugees, which included 45 Jews out of the 1,200 there. The peril had been recently aggravated by a violent agitation in the German press, noted the Joint Foreign Committee, which also found increasing dangers to Jews in Austria, Poland, Rumania, and Czechoslovakia. "Starvation or suicide is the only alternative left for these unfortunates of Europe," wrote Josiah Wedgwood M.P. to the Zionist Pro-Palestine Federation of America. He continued: "Yet we allow this horror to go on without protest. It is not Germany; it is England and America committing the crime and washing hands like Pilate. England could open the doors of Palestine at once, and both open their own front door. Instead we send them to prison and deport them to Hell."[31]

Jabotinsky moved forward with his personal crusade as soon as he returned to Paris, convincing his eight-man party executive to take the initiative in creating "an independent new Zionist Organization." It also accepted his proposal on April 25, precisely a decade after the World Union's establishment, to submit to a plebiscite of the Revisionist movement a motion to convene in December the constituent congress of that body. The assembly would be based upon the "Jewish State principle" of Herzl's "pure and old shekel," without the new WZO "discipline clause." In this way, their statement soon read in *HaYarden*, they stood ready to fulfill the historic mission of the World Union: "The Kingdom of Israel means the redemption of Israel, and we will not tread another path!" Jabotinsky wished for "a clean and clear-cut *basta*," with no more equivocation that had "caused us endless friction within, and a reputation for insincerity without." In case the plebiscite did not give a positive answer, he informed a long-time friend, "I will at last become a writer. I have a real craving to write, I have a hundred books in my head!" On the last day of the month, his confidence renewed, Jabotinsky shared with William E. Rappard the conviction that for 99 percent of the Zionists "it is a firm and stubborn assurance," indeed coming to be something of "a certainty," that Palestine will ultimately become a Jewish Commonwealth with a Jewish majority. "I quite understand that conception as a hope," promptly replied the director of the League's Mandate Department and Rector of Geneva University, "but certainly not as a rational certainty."[32]

George Antonius, in the meantime, had made significant inroads for his own cause. A lecture tour across the United States, arranged by Crane's Institute for Current World Affairs, brought the Palestinian Arab case to influential quarters for the first time. Isaiah Bowman, the U.S. specialist on territorial matters at the Paris Peace Conference who had just become president of Johns Hopkins University, recommended that President Wilson's papers be opened for Antonius's study of the Arab nationalist movement. Ray Stannard Baker, Wilson's private secretary at the Versailles conclave, had heard from other sources of "the high opinion" in which Antonius was held, and agreed to get together with him privately. Antonius also obtained a half-hour meeting at the White House on May 1, during which Roosevelt expressed his own admiration of Feisal, noting that in view of the late king's powers of statesmanship having developed on "an ever-broadening basis" since their meeting in 1919, he might have "rendered still greater services to his nation than the very eminent services that he had already rendered." Wallace Murray, chief of the State Department's Division of Near Eastern Affairs, later told Antonius that FDR had even added laudatory text to the Department's very complimentary tribute to Feisal on the occasion of a memorial ceremony held by an Arab committee in New York. The gist of these conversations, Antonius subsequently informed a sympathetic Murray, was featured in *Al-Muqattam*, Cairo's largest daily that was owned by his father-in-law.[33]

The following day, Antonius discussed the Legislative Council before the influential Council on Foreign Relations, publisher of *Foreign Affairs*. Reviewing its history since HMG's first proposal in 1922, he explained the reasons for past Arab rejection, and charged that Britain ruled Palestine "as she does her most backward territorial outpost." The Arabs began now to consider the Council as "a real means of cooperation between the two peoples," he noted, but until all classes were willing to collaborate, "there can be no real peace or tranquility in Palestine." Julian Mack promptly observed that this "quite moderate" presentation neglected the basic truth that so long as the leading Arabs would not admit the validity of the Balfour Declaration and of the mandate, there was no point in talking about a Council. Jew and Arab first had to gain experience in the simpler unit of town government, the U.S. Circuit Court judge stressed. Noting that he had tried many times to get Jew and Arab to cooperate on non-political issues, Warburg added that the

Arab leaders were "intransigent" and refused cooperation even on these matters. Antonius countered that "until Britain publicly states that she will not make of Palestine a new Zion—only then will the Muslims be reassured, only then will they participate in the general national life." Crane went much further, asserting that the tension could be lessened by stopping Jewish entry into Palestine "until the new elements can be assimilated."[34]

The on-going "civil war" amongst Palestine's Arabs, Hexter observed to Warburg, tended to make "all of the parties extreme; that is their battle cry." Antonius and his charming wife, Kitty, trumpeted an un-compromising anti-Zionist line when cultivating all the consulates' younger men and especially the wife of the German consul-general, herself a Jewess who successfully hid this fact, at lavish and constant dinners in their beautiful Jerusalem home. Meeting in Haifa on May 10, the 400 participants at the second general conference of the Arab Youth Congress agreed with leader Ya'qub al-Ghusayn, who attacked "British and Jewish" imperialism and especially warned of the "gather-ing of the Jewish forces," claiming that "undoubtedly the day will come when we will fight for life or death." Some of the Supreme Muslim Council tried to have a telegram of thanks dispatched to Arslan for his activities, but the conferees overwhelmingly voted this down. If the mandatory government persisted in its lenient policy regarding Jewish entry and purchase of land, their resolutions concluded, the party would return to demonstrations like the ones that took place at the end of October. The Istiqlalists' *Al-Difa'a* strongly criticized the Youth Congress, however, for not advocating the obstruction of boats disem-barking Jewish immigrants and direct action against Arabs engaged in land sales; the Nashashibis' *Falastin* joined in strong protest of the conference as well.[35]

By contrast, Ben-Gurion found the Zionist movement in the United States hampered by "inertia and self-complacency." Always a tower of strength, Brandeis championed an active struggle against the Legislative Council, and provided him with the first substantial monetary contri-bution ($20,000) to Akaba's development if he could secure the remain-ing $80,000 in cash. The richest Jewish center worldwide of 4 million members had "ceased to be a factor in Zionism," however. It lacked a powerful, united front, Ben-Gurion noted to the ZOA Administrative Committee on May 19, amounting to only 80,000-90,000 payers of the shekel. In light of our people's current extraordinary needs, including the fact that Jewish youth in Poland "is being ruined" and "nothing can be expected" from Russian Jewry, this situation was "most deplorable." Viewing the tremendous gap between what should be done and what the yishuv had thus far accomplished, "a new yardstick" was required in order to raise vast funds and to bring pressure upon the British government for a larger immigration schedule and other advances. Only thus, Ben-Gurion asserted, could the entire question of Arab-Jewish understanding be resolved satisfactorily on the basis of "a majority in Palestine of the entire Jewish people, and then Palestine will truly be 'Eretz Yisrael.'"[36]

Non-Zionist participation in the Jewish Agency raised another pressing difficulty. Warburg expressed interest in Ben-Gurion's argument that an outlet should be prepared for the yishuv in the Negev and the harbor of Akaba, developing a fishing industry in the Red Sea region, as well as exporting towards the East, and thus obviating reliance on the Suez Canal. Considering the shortage of land in Palestine, an associate on the U.S. Refugee Economic Corporation agreed that a study of that area ought to be undertaken. Warburg balked, however, at Ben-Gurion's insistence that the 1929 agreement of 50-50 percent representation between Zionists and non-Zionists in the Agency Executive be altered because non-Zionist effort was nil other than from Great Britain and the United States, and "he did not believe in constitutional forms or logic; he believed in realities." Any attempt to change this percentage, Warburg cautioned, could only be accomplished by dissolving the Agency, which he considered "a most dangerous thing for the Zionists to undertake." Maurice Karpf and others within the American Jewish Committee executive, joined by d'Avigdor-Goldsmid and his non-Zionist circle, would likewise deny their consent to this alteration. Ben-Gurion's plans for a wide program to meet increased immigration evinced "a lack of patience," Warburg declared. Ben-Gurion shot back: "Masses of Jews were impatient because they could not remain where they were," and impatient Gentiles were also insisting on the exodus of the Jews from Europe.[37]

Ben-Gurion and Warburg did agree that Weizmann must return to the Jewish Agency presidency at the next Zionist Congress. Far more than anyone else in the movement, he held HMG's trust and respect. In addition, having failed to achieve an agreement with Jabotinsky,

Ben-Gurion also needed the older statesman to create the broadest Zionist consensus possible. Seized with many doubts, however, Weizmann frankly confided in Locker that, after the "deep suffering" which the Congress of 1931 had inflicted upon him, he had finally found real happiness in the absence of official responsibility. He now hesitated to return to "a stuffy and airless prison," and doubted if he could satisfactorily serve his scientific "master" concurrently. He understood the need of uniting as many Zionist factions as possible, especially now that the Revisionists were threatening to set up a competitive organization, but still believed that it would be very difficult for him to work with people from the extreme Right. At the same time, he considered it his duty to offer his help at a juncture when the yishuv faced both great opportunities and grave dangers. In view of this "very complex situation," he felt obligated to hold off on giving any definite decision.[38]

The condition of the Jews still in Germany also perturbed Weizmann greatly, and he turned on May 20 to Col. Richard Meinertzhagen, Britain's former Chief Political Officer in Syria and Palestine (1919-1920) and a staunch pro-Zionist, for help. With Hitler not allowing Jews equal rights or exit with more than £1,000 and 20,000 marks in goods, he wished the Führer's acquaintance to try and get Berlin to free all emigration to Palestine and give Jews local facilities, such as schools for the children to learn Hebrew, to prepare themselves to this end. Their position, Weizmann asserted, "is a living death"; as time went on, it "approximates more and more closely to that of rats in a trap. There is no escape for them." At Meinertzhagen's request, the Agency Executive's London office prepared an *aide-memoire* which noted that almost nine-tenths of those wishing to move to Palestine as "capitalists" could not do so because of the Reichsbank's recent refusal to grant more than a very small percentage of the funds needed to satisfy British immigration law. The memorandum also requested freedom in economic activity and the community's organizing itself "on the basis of its own culture," with the leadership recognized by the National-Socialist government as a legal institution, so that a program of planned emigration could be achieved.[39]

The Nazi anti-Jewish campaign, commented on by diverse observers, unmistakably increased in ferocity. On April 27, Interior Minister Frick publicly stated that Jews would be excluded from German citizenship, as well as the holding of any public office. On May 10 British Ambassador

Sir Eric Phipps reported to Simon from Berlin that the individual Jew's outlook today "is blacker than ever before"; Passport Control Officer Foley dubbed it "desperate," even for those possessing capital. Speaking because "I am pro-human, pro-Christian, and pro-civilized," popular columnist Dorothy Thompson warned the Jewish Relief Fund in Philadelphia that "the avowed purpose of the Nazi government is *not* to limit and define the status of the Jew but to *eliminate* him." "I expect Jews to be put in prison and maltreated if not killed," recorded Dodd in his diary for May 25. The same day, Baeck hailed Youth Aliya's efforts in Germany as "the great proof of our will to live, of our confidence, and our belief in the future," as well as of the feeling that "the will to live shall grow stronger in us, that we remain young in all our suffering, our pains, and burdens." How much longer could such faith be sustained by an increasingly beleaguered community? Less debatable was the observation of U.S. Consul to Vienna, George Messersmith, who advised the Council on Foreign Relations after Simon's visit to Berlin that the Nazis would triumph over the Reichswehr in the end, and "this of course will result in war."[40]

Hitler's designs did not deter Wauchope from proceeding towards a Legislative Council. Receiving frantic cables in this respect from Shertok in early May, the Executive in London sided with Lewis Namier's idea of parity on the basis of two chambers (one each for Arabs and Jews, both inside and outside Palestine), but agreed that putting forward such a suggestion now would probably merely obscure the issue. Accordingly, it advised that the Agency's attitude for the present remain one of "unconditional opposition." The Agency could not, on the other hand, refuse to enter into conversations (as Brandeis had told Ben-Gurion), but it would be "highly desirable" to postpone even these informal discussions until after the Zionist Congress lest they dominate the election campaign. On May 22, Shertok conveyed this stand to Wauchope, who "hit the nail on the head" by concluding that the Agency did not want the Zionist "extremists" to be able to argue that since HMG wished to establish a Legislative Council there was no point cooperating with it altogether. When Shertok expressed doubt that a new Executive would change its attitude vis-à-vis the Council, the High Commissioner insisted that his promise to Cunliffe-Lister about starting discussions on the topic was "already overdue." The Council itself would probably come into being only a year from now, but the preparatory steps had to be taken without delay. The main features of the scheme had already been agreed upon by the Cabinet last summer, and this he now intended to communicate to both sides.[41]

Why the hurry? Weizmann asked Cunliffe-Lister on June 4. Apart from a few "professional politicians," there was no urgent demand for the Legislative Council at all, and no real interest in it. Confirming rumors that he was leaving office, the Colonial Secretary noted that undertakings had been given before the League and elsewhere. Indicating that the initiative was coming from Palestine, he thought that a further postponement, which Weizmann had urged, would be difficult. "Definite steps," even though taken in private, had been pursued in Jerusalem. This did not commit HGM irrevocably, Weizmann replied, and he urged Cunliffe-Lister to bring about a delay as his last official act. The Colonial Secretary smiled but did not commit himself.[42]

Wauchope stood his ground in his next meeting with Shertok on June 12. Rather than have certain "reserved subjects" excluded from the Council's deliberations, he had decided in favor of leaving any measure "repugnant to the mandate" up to the High Commissioner's judgment. This was not done to secure Arab cooperation, he insisted, but to make certain that the Chief Justice not apply a "too strictly legalistic view." Shertok considered this a very wise decision, and they agreed to follow up the matter the following Sunday. He awaited Shertok's further views, but could not delay the communication about the Council to "the other side" for too much longer. Wauchope made not the slightest allusion to the appointment of Cunliffe-Lister's successor four days earlier, and Shertok judged it better not to refer to the matter.[43]

The Zionists had very good reason to be pleased with the appointment of Malcolm MacDonald, the new Colonial Secretary, who had served as the Parliamentary Undersecretary of State for Dominion Affairs during the past four years. The thirty-four year old bachelor had played an important role in helping to defer some of HMG's legislative proposals to restrict Jewish land purchases, and to have his father, then Prime Minister, effectively cancel the immigration strictures laid down in the 1930 Passfield White Paper. Not surprisingly, soon after receiving a cable about Shertok's impression that Wauchope wished to carry out his plan for the Council during his first term, so as to have it ready in the spring of 1936, Weizmann sent MacDonald a letter urging the Council's postponement. It may have reached the young man in the first hour of his assuming office. MacDonald promptly requested Wauchope to delay for a week in order to enable him to study the papers involved. Wanting to help Weizmann gain re-election as WZO president at the next Zionist Congress, he proposed to the High Commissioner on June 14 and in additional telegrams that the principle of parity between Arabs and Jews be adopted for the Council.[44]

Wauchope, caught unawares by this sudden turn, felt committed by now. Although Shertok had expressed doubt about whether the High Commissioner could obtain any clear definition from the Arabs of their attitude regarding the Legislative Council in "the present state of internal strife and confusion" among their various political parties, Wauchope had just informed Nashashibi that since the Jerusalem municipal elections were over, the mandatory intended to take the Council matter in hand. He had not provided any further details, he assured Shertok on June 16, but the Agency's political director feared that the Zionists were "on the threshold" of a new crisis in their relations with the government. Following the crises of 1922 and 1930, he noted, Arlosoroff and Wauchope had worked successfully together to restore "the devastated areas of mutual trust" between the yishuv and the administration. Given the High Commissioner's advocacy at present of a scheme which they "could not possibly accept and which made a new crisis inevitable," the Zionists were therefore "doubly depressed." Taking a very serious tone in reply, Wauchope declared that the Council was necessary because HMG had given its pledge. Perhaps it may have been a mistake to promise the Council, but, as it stated "somewhere in the Bible," a promise, once given, had to be carried out. This ended their conversation.[45]

Wauchope had also informed some Arab leaders of the Cabinet's decision, he wired MacDonald on June 28, and he could not go back on his word. In discussing the Council now with Husseini, he discounted rumors that Nashashibi had been promised the presidency, and suggested that he might fill that office himself. Receiving this information from a source code-named "Oved," the Agency's Arab Office heard, too, that the Mufti's cohorts wished general elections based on only two lists—Jewish and Arabic, whereas the Nashashibis demanded elections based on the party system. The Istiqlalists would not recognize the Council since they did not recognize the mandate, Abd al-Hadi told Wauchope, but party members would participate as private individuals and give the Council a chance. The creation by Mayor Khalidi on June 22 of the Reform Party, wishing to avoid domination by the Husseinis and adopting a moderate line in practice, despite its initial pan-Arab nationalist manifesto, presented yet another faction that accepted the Council as an intermediate step towards majority rule. Hearing of Khalidi's views from Vice-Mayor Daniel Auster, the Agency also had obtained copies of some of the Wauchope-MacDonald correspondence, which corroborated Ben-Gurion's view that young MacDonald would not challenge "the old man" on the Council's creation.[46]

On a number of counts, anxiety gripped Weizmann and other knowledgeable Jewish leaders. At most, Wauchope informed Shertok on June 27, preliminary discussions on the Legislative Council would be postponed until mid-July. Having won what historian Norman Rose characterizes as "a minor tactical victory," Weizmann begged Shertok "most urgently" to see that the matter "should not receive the slightest publicity, should not even be talked about among our friends, and ... above all, exploited as a triumph." As for German Jewry, Lothian, whom Weizmann also recruited to intercede with the Reich authorities, got nowhere when telling German Ambassador Joachim von Ribbentrop that it was "essential" that "the persecution of individuals [sic] by an omnipotent government should be ended" if Hitler wished to establish friendly relations with England. A Berlin-London agreement on June 18, giving Germany the right to extend her navy up to 35 percent of that of the British, resulted in a cooling of the Anglo-French Entente. It also signaled a new pro-German tone which could be found among such leading voices as the London *Times*, Lord Rothemere, the Archbishop of Canterbury, and the Prince of Wales. The same day, an American Jewish Committee conference with representatives of Jewish organizations abroad noted that Marshal Pilsudki's death augured ominously for Polish Jewry; antisemitism was on the rise in France and widespread in Argentina thanks to Nazi propaganda; the situation in Rumania and Latvia was "also very bad." "As time goes on," wrote Weizmann to Lady Reading after the death of gifted Zionist orator and author Shmaryahu Levin, "one feels the loneliness of a Jew in this cold, selfish world, one feels the utter necessity of relying on the few."[47]

Wauchope's insistence on establishing the Council became clear in his interview with *Palestine Post* founder and publisher Gershon Agronsky (later Agron) on July 3. He intended to postpone its announcement so as to help Shertok and colleagues at the Congress elections, the High Commissioner declared. HMG had definitely decided against parity, a proposal which had first been suggested in 1930 by Wauchope's "great and good friend" Arlosoroff. Agronsky argued that the Council would "destroy the fruits" of the Agency's confidence in him; give "a new lease of life" to the Revisionist-Zionist movement; create "turmoil and possibility for exploitation" by the Zionist leadership's opponents; create "a mill grinding out poisonous Arab propaganda"; have a "shattering effect" on the Zionist movement; and, finally, make better relations with the Arabs "a hopeless task." He did not know if the Council would satisfy the Arabs, Wauchope responded, but "he had to keep the pledge." He was not afraid of another Arab outbreak like the one in October 1933, but feared that the "moral effect" ten years later of a broken pledge would be greater than any immediate harm from the Council. If the evil must come, Agronsky asked, what were the prospects of his remaining as "a safeguard"? "I love this country," Wauchope answered, and "if I'm asked to stay, I'll stay."[48]

In Abdullah's opinion, the Jews were making "a big mistake" in negating the value of a Legislative Council. Palestine's Arabs were difficult, the Jews were obdurate, and the British "were more stubborn than both of them," he told Shertok in Amman on July 11. Palestine's Jews had reached a high level of development because of their "stubborn stand" and "great perseverance," but the Arabs were "the natives of this country and they had natural rights over it." He was prepared to bring the parties together; the Council would be a first step toward mutual understanding. Shertok responded that the Jews had no place but Palestine, "which could serve as a tiny foothold," becoming a majority in their haven. Only then would the Arabs respect them. Nondomination of either party could alone come about by the granting of equal representation on the Council. Why not let the Arabs rule today, "and if tomorrow fate grants you a majority, then you should rule"? the Emir asked. Shertok replied: "We did not come here as conquerors, but as a nation which regards this country as its only homeland, and which recognizes that there is enough room in it for the Arabs." The Council might lead to the uniting of Palestine and Transjordan, and would open new horizons for Jewish settlement, Abdullah suggested. (Two months earlier, the Emir's newspaper had called for uniting Syria, Palestine, and Transjordan under Abdullah.) Parity was not yet the

Zionist movement's policy, Shertok remarked, but if he found "an attentive ear" among the Arabs, many within the movement would fight for its realization.[49]

Shertok's clarification to Wauchope five days later that the Agency had never formally agreed even to a parity basis for the Council strengthened the High Commissioner's hand. Approving the High Commissioner's position, the Cabinet authorized him to open unofficial discussions with both sides. MacDonald informed Weizmann the next day that Wauchope was doing all he could to "meet his difficulties" about the Council in connection with the coming World Zionist Congress. Gloomy, regretting that the discussions should have been started at this time at all and that HMG had not first taken the Agency into its confidence, Weizmann could only suggest that a Round Table Conference consisting of an equal number of Jews and Arabs meet to seek agreement on the matter. This was out of the question, McDonald remarked, as it could only result in disagreement and consequent delay. "None of this was helpful," the Colonial Secretary informed Wauchope, and he told Weizmann that he still hoped that the Congress could be persuaded to leave the matter open and not force the Executive to resist the setting up of the Council.[50]

Wauchope discussed the details of the scheme with Shertok and Ben-Gurion on July 19 and 21. The Council would consist of 8 elected and 3 nominated Muslims; 1 elected and 2 nominated Christians; 3 elected and 4-5 nominated Jews; and 5 British officials and 1-2 commercial members. The High Commissioner had an unrestricted veto; powers of legislation when the Council was not in session; exclusive financial initiative; and powers of dissolution. If the administration concluded that the Council served "only agitation without useful work," it would dissolve the Council and consider its pledge fulfilled. In reply, Ben-Gurion stated that the Agency was "fundamentally and categorically" opposed to the entire proposal, even if based upon parity, in light of Jewry's present position in the Diaspora and the possibility of Palestine's rapid development. For Jewry, "it was a question of life and death whether they should be able to save their people and save Palestine for the Jewish people." As long as the Arabs opposed the "central idea" of the mandate and there was no Arab-Jewish understanding, "there was no place" for a Legislative Council in Palestine. The root of their opposition, Shertok pointed out, was that the Council's practical effect would be to make more difficult free Jewish growth through im-migration and land settlement. Acknowledging that their stance was "perfectly honourable" and that they had not been a party to HMG's pledge, Wauchope concluded that "it would be dishonourable" for the government not to carry out its given word.[51]

Haj Amin and Husseini raised some objections when informed by Wauchope on July 22 of the mandatory's plan. Those that appeared "insuperable" were election based on the population, rather than citizenship (many Jews had not yet been naturalized); the number of Jewish nominated members; and the broad powers given to the High Commissioner. Jews, they argued, were protected by the power of veto. The pair preferred the communal system of election and direct elections, as indirect ones tended "to lead to corruption." They had no objection to women voters in the Jewish constituencies, but strongly opposed Jewish women sitting as members of the Assembly. The phrase "sub-jects liable to promote ill-feeling between the communities," inserted to rule out Council discussion on such matters, they deemed was so wide as to include any subject touching the Jews. They proposed the nomina-tion of 8 Muslims, 1 Christian, and 3 Jews, along with 3 Muslims, 1 Christian, 2 Jews, and one foreign commerce representative as official appointees. The fact that the Jews would choose not to take part in the Council, Wauchope reported to Parkinson, "makes them all the more eager to do so."[52]

Wauchope found Ragheb Nashashibi far more amendable than the Husseinis during their meeting the next day. The head of the National Defense Party thought the number of five nominated Jewish members too large, but the two for Christian members just and fair. Unlike Haj Amin, far more popular with the Palestinian Arab masses, he preferred a purely nominated Council. Nashashibi favored an outsider as a chairman (Wauchope thought the Chief Secretary a better choice), and agreed with Wauchope that the High Commissioner should not intervene in debates. Like the Husseinis, he thought strongly that only Palestinian citizenship should entitle one to the right to vote. He would prefer indirect elections and that government should choose the council members, explaining that "Muslims will never agree among themselves." Like Wauchope, Nashashibi felt that Palestine's Muslims were "quite unprepared" for a Jewish woman to sit in the Assembly. Unlike Haj Amin, he agreed with the High Commissioner's veto; his exclusive right to decide matters of finance and customs; and the right of suspension. As to dissolving the Council, Nashashibi preferred a fixed date, say one year, for re-assembly, and thought that Arab leaders could not accept a condition which would prevent discussion by the Council members.[53]

Throughout that same month, a few warned that no diminution of brutality could be seen in the Nazi regime. Writing to the editor of the *Manchester Guardian*, Harold Laski regretted that Lords Lothian and Allen, among others, had failed to see the true nature of Hitlerism— the speeches of Goebbels, the atrocities against Jews, the vast rearmament, the murder and kidnapping of German anti-Nazis living abroad, Berlin's encouragement of Japanese imperialism against China. When Meinertzhagen, acceding to Weizmann's request, broached the subject of the Jews in Germany to Hitler on July 15, his host "changed from sanity to insanity, the face changed from normal to ferocity, the voice from an almost whisper to a shout, even the hair became untidy, fists hammering the table and eyes aflame with hatred." The editor of the *Kansas City Star* reported to Billikopf the anti-Jewish excesses in Frankfurt and Munich and the "Jews Not Wanted" signs that were a common sight throughout Franconia. On July 16, scattered attacks on Jews and Jewish premises broke out even in Berlin. Eminent public figures, Montefiore observed to the Joint Foreign Committee, had urged British public opinion to suspend judgment on Nazi Germany, "to think tolerantly, to make allowances," but "surely we must not wait for yet more terrible occurrences for that judgment to be decided and publicly recorded?"[54]

James McDonald entertained no illusions. His travels that spring in Brazil, Argentina, and Uruguay, together with the extensive trips of a friend across South America, revealed growing antisemitism and little promise for any large refugee settlements. On July 17, while hailing Palestine as "the chief country of refuge" for having absorbed 27,000 out of the estimated 80,500 German Jewish refugees, he recommended at the Governing Body's public meeting that the League assume direct responsibility for the pressing refugee question, and that his office be terminated so that the refugees might be served more effectively. Cecil had privately agreed with this plan, but advised that liquidation by the year's end might have to be considered anew if the Assembly failed to take any action. He also approved in principle James Rosenberg's idea that McDonald's final statement speak to the rights of religious and racial minorities, focusing the reader's attention not only on the persecution of Jews, but on the Third Reich threat of world war. A brief on German anti-Jewish legislation and on past international intervention for persecuted minorities, the research to be done by Oscar Janowsky and Melvin Fagen at the recommendation of Rosenberg and Mack, would be appended.[55]

One week later, McDonald sent a long communication, to which Cecil did not object, to Eleanor Roosevelt. Harboring a deep "sense of impending doom" about Nazi intentions, he forecast a program to force Jews out of Germany gradually by creating conditions that would make life "unbearable," as well as the party's determination to establish a State church that would assume priority over loyalty to any of the country's established religions. With this "extreme form of statism" bound to have repercussions far beyond the German frontier, McDonald questioned if the time had not come, in harmony with other precedents in American history, for Washington to take the initiative in protesting against the "prevailing violations of elementary and religious rights in Germany." The First Lady informed him on August 1 that she was sending the document at once to the President. She did so, adding the handwritten notation "important." There is no indication that Roosevelt replied to McDonald's letter, which came to final rest in FDR's Official Files. A similar request on July 26 from the American Jewish Committee, American Jewish Congress, B'nai Brith, and the Jewish Labor Committee, a rare joint effort, elicited Undersecretary of State Phillips's bland reply that "the American people are always sympathetic" to the maintenance of "the concepts of religious freedom and liberty of conscience for all" in the United States "as well as in other nations."[56]

The Husseinis returned on July 30 for a further discussion of the Council with Wauchope. Haj Amin observed that since neighboring countries had fuller powers of legislation than those which HMG now offered to Palestine and a wider representation of the people, the Palestinian Arab leadership might be divided over its support. He and Husseini urged that non-Palestinian citizens should not vote or sit as members, and that all members should be directly elected: nominated members would be looked on as government servants. While they would try to fulfill Wauchope's request for a representative Arab committee before November to decide whether to accept or reject the proposals, "the difficulties were great." They wanted some power in the High Commissioner's Executive Council, and feared that a foreign commercial member might be a Jew. Finally, they wished to show the people that the Council was a real step in advance of the proposals of 1922, so that "moderates like themselves" would unite in carrying out the mandatory's final proposals. Otherwise, the "extremists would become violent, would make everything difficult for the government, and disturb the peace of the country." These reservations notwithstanding, and in light of Nashashibi's virtual approval, Wauchope felt sufficiently confident to wire MacDonald on August 5 that he would secure the Arabs' cooperation and that the Colonial Secretary should not yield to Jewish pressure.[57]

Two days later, Ben-Gurion and Shertok took leave of Wauchope before departing for the Zionist Congress on the banks of the Vierwaldstattersee in Lucerne. Since Labor represented about half the delegates, Ben-Gurion observed, it would have to bear the major share of the responsibility for the Agency's future policy. While crediting the High Commissioner's great contribution to Palestine's security and to the yishuv's growth, he felt duty bound to explain to the Congress why the Agency opposed the Legislative Council, and to set out its complaints about not obtaining a fair share in public services and adequate funding from the substantial Treasury surplus for colonization activities. The Agency continued to have its "most serious grievance" over curtailed immigration, he went on, particularly given the Jewish people's situation in Germany and in Poland. During this same week, truckloads of S.A. cruised through different cities, chanting repeatedly "Jewry Perish" and "Let us kill the Jew off."

Speaking confidentially, Wauchope expressed his belief that the Italian-Abyssinian conflict would not affect the country's present stability, and could not say when the turn of the region around Akaba would come for land settlement. Nor had he changed his mind regarding Jewish movement to Transjordan, although he would discuss the subject further in London with MacDonald. He was impressed with the yishuv's strides towards industrialization, but the administration's Treasurer, W. J. Johnson, appeared to think that the manufacturers' request for setting up a separate Trade and Industry department was premature. Ben-Gurion ended the interview by saying that while he and Shertok had been very happy in their personal association with Wauchope, they "regretted deeply" the very serious controversy in which they now found themselves on account of the Council.[58]

Wauchope's chief advisors raised serious doubts both with regard to Transjordan and to Akaba. Hall entirely agreed with the High Commissioner that any scheme for "transplanting" Palestinian Arabs to the former was "evil," quite impractical, and, as Wauchope put it, probably "a veil to screen some even dirtier work"—acquiring a large tract of land for Jewish settlement there. Transfer would be contrary to the mandate, which required HMG to "ensure that the rights and position of other sections of the population are not prejudiced," and be politically dangerous for the Jews and for HMG. Incidentally, Hall observed, "religion in Palestine seems to be becoming increasingly an expression of nationalism, and the more the Arabs realize their gradual defeat materially, the more intensely do they cling to their religion." On August 16, the Air Officer Commanding recommended against a fishing concession at Akaba to the yishuv, which his staff argued "bears a definite complexion" of Jewish colonization and penetration into Transjordan, and which the Arabs would not fail to recognize. That area had long been regarded as an important strategic spot, where two Royal Air Force landing grounds and a Transjordan Frontier Force camping area were situated. Its location within at least six miles of the Saudi Arabian frontier might precipitate a successful raid from across that border. In addition, such a concession would stimulate "hostile feeling," and Arab agitators in Palestine and Transjordan would quickly enlarge upon this in order to create public unrest. In sum, he concluded, the grant of a concession for Jewish settlement was, at best, premature.[59]

To Ben-Gurion, the question of "implementing" Zionism had to be brought before the Congress as comprehensively as possible. No need existed any longer to discuss the necessity of Zionism, since it had never been "so obvious" both to the Jewish people and the entire world that the existence of Jews in the Diaspora "has become impossible." The Congress's main task, he had told the Hadassah National Board in June, was to create a new spirit of Zionism as "the greatest reality in Jewish life," and to unite Jewry in the belief that "Palestine can save the Jewish people and can absorb great masses." A broad coalition of all the parties under Labor's hegemony, he subsequently wrote at length to his children Geula and Amos, had to be formed to "accelerate" the work, avert possible internal dangers, and meet the real threat of "a global conflagration."

In Ben-Gurion's view, Weizmann—a *"great man"* with "a holy flame in him," a magnificent record, and an enormous reputation in the English-speaking world, and who was trusted by HMG—should return to the presidency. At the same time, he believed that Weizmann ought to be given limited powers. He changed mood rapidly, was "accustomed to people taking his word as gospel," yielded on crucial issues like immigration, and did not understand the internal problems of the movement. In two meetings with non-Zionists Hexter, Karpf, Laski, Waldman, Senator, and Julius Simon, Ben-Gurion refused to even discuss the 50-50 principle of Agency Executive membership: "it cannot ever again be put into practice." ("He is the Stalin of the movement," a deeply offended Laski wrote to d'Avigdor-Goldsmid four days later.) Finally, Ben-Gurion wished for a new organizational structure enabling non-party Jews to belong to the movement as individuals, thereby weakening the parties and reducing the influence of the Revisionists in particular.[60]

The Nineteenth Zionist Congress, which Sokolow opened on the evening of August 20, represented for the first time in the movement's history nearly one million Zionists from almost 50 countries. With the Revisionists out, Labor, including a respectable delegation of 26 supporters from the United States, now commanded the largest faction: 48.8 percent of the 467 representatives. Sokolow asserted that the Hitler government's discrimination challenged the rights of all Jews, and asserted that Palestine was for Polish Jewry "the embodiment of economic and cultural salvation." Lloyd George, sending a message of praise for the yishuv's accomplishments, found it heartening to see that "when Israel is again facing cruel persecution ... its sons and daughters" were finding refuge "in the land of their ancestors of immortal fame." McDonald remarked that our daily Grace for meals had to include "Thank God for Palestine!" especially when the doors of nearly all the countries were almost entirely closed against immigration; it provided a hope for thousands of Jews in Germany, Poland, and elsewhere, inspiring the Jewish people "in their resolve" and serving as "a force making for their solidarity." The next morning, delivering a long address in Yiddish, Ben-Gurion discussed Zionism's major responsibilities within the context of settling 1 million Jewish families during the next quarter century. He also took the mandatory authorities to task while stressing that the need for cooperation remained "the immutable basis of Zionist politics."[61]

During the following eight days, speakers analyzed finance, immigration, colonization, land purchase, and culture. To sustained applause, Weizmann was elected president of the Congress at the third session. To mark Henrietta Szold's seventy-fifth birthday, all groups rose to pay tribute and resolved to found a colony in her honor. As "a silent protest" against the persecution of the Jews in Germany, a half-day of mourning was declared on August 28 with blue-white flags draped in black hung at half-mast, Mizrachi delegates observed a fast, and all activities were suspended. Mizrachi delegates took no active part in the proceedings on the ground that their demands had not been satisfied as regards Sabbath observance in agricultural settlements financed by Zionist funds. The one tumultuous moment in the general debate, which stretched over nine sessions, came when a motion to question the ha'avara agreement was overwhelmingly rejected, leading the small Jewish State Party faction, which had seceded from the Revisionist-Zionists, to shout "Heil Hitler"—a cry whose full significance only the German Jewish delegation could grasp. Katznelson vigorously denied the opposition's allegation that labor was "strangling" industry, and said that Mapai favored parity on the Legislative Council.

Shertok answered for the Agency Executive, supporting ha'avara—now placed under the Executive's control—and championing the yishuv's right to free development in every sphere while benefiting the Arabs of Palestine. The crisis of German Jewry did not receive serious discussion, with Wise's the only speech devoted to the issue. This was due to the presence of Gestapo agents, who caused Siegfried Moses, heading the German-Jewish delegation, to avoid any provocative stance. Choosing to avoid talk about a "Jewish state," Weizmann posited that the yishuv's security and only answer to the "Jewish tragedy" lay in the upbuilding of a normal social structure, reflected in the "harmonious synthesis" of the Histadrut. [62]

Yet, as the month closed, the office of WZO president remained vacant. Ben-Gurion lobbied hard for Weizmann's candidacy, aware along with many others that Sokolow, a gifted writer with an encyclopedic knowledge, was not suitable to be Zionism's political representative. Representing Mapai and the Histadrut, Ben-Gurion had asked Weizmann to return to the post some time ago, but the older statesman vacillated. On August 30, Weizmann announced that he would agree to head the Agency's Political Department if Ben-Gurion became president. When Ben-Gurion replied that this was out of the question, Weizmann then proposed that Sokolow continue in the office and he would enter the Executive in charge of political affairs. The Labor faction was pleased by this suggestion, and the Congress delegates rejoiced at this news; even Weizmann's detractors were "astonished, and conceded that he had acted bravely." Vera Weizmann, however, still smarting from her husband's fate at the 1931 Congress, refused to have him serve under Sokolow. That same evening, Israel Sieff came from London to inform Ben-Gurion that he now favored Weizmann's return to the presidency—but to be elected outside the Executive and to direct Zionist politics. British cabinet members had told Sieff that the Abyssinian dispute might lead to war in the eastern Mediterranean, the days of 1914-1918 would return, and only Weizmann could play a pivotal role in these circumstances. Ben-Gurion's closest associates agreed with his immediate rejection: Weizmann could not possibly become a kind of "political dictator." The next day, Wise, Mack, and the General Zionists' Group A concurred with Ben-Gurion's stand. Ben-Gurion advised Weizmann on behalf of both groups that he had to be either president or a member of the Executive. Weizmann asked for more time to think it over, and there the matter stood.[63]

On the afternoon of September 1, after Locker and Kaplan went to see Weizmann, he reluctantly agreed to be nominated for the presidency. Late the same evening, Weizmann announced this officially at a small "coronation" party of the leaders of Labor and the General Zionists Group A. Wise, trusting Labor's judgment after an inspiring visit to Palestine and following the majority, now promised firm assistance; Locker praised Weizmann's service over the past four years as a loyal soldier. Ben-Gurion declared that both the movement and Weizmann realized that they needed one another: Mapai was poised to lead with "a will and a path," while Weizmann's immense prestige and authority could unite Zionist ranks and "quite possibly add new conquests to his already remarkable record." The Congress, deeply saddened over the news received earlier of Chief Rabbi Kook's death in Jerusalem, rejoiced at this *dénouement*. Ben-Gurion declared to the assembled that the WZO was "entering a new era, when new conditions are opening for Zionism," and "the great genius of the Jewish people has now been restored to the leadership of the Zionist Organization." "Profoundly touched" by what old friends and old opponents had said, Weizmann responded that Vera's faith, Mapai's support, and the cooperation of British Zionists had encouraged him during the four years of his absence from leadership, and he thanked the Zionists of South Africa and others who had stood by him since 1931. On September 3, Weizmann was unanimously elected (with six abstentions from the Jewish State Party and the pro-binationalist HaShomer HaTsa'ir of the Left) as President of the WZO and the Agency. The Congress ended with the singing of the Zionist national anthem, HaTikva.[64]

Labor's political coming of age had arrived. Now the decisive force in Zionism, its triumph was crowned with Ben-Gurion's election as chairman of the Jewish Agency Executive. Having engineered Weizmann's return to the presidency, he was able to achieve a broad coalition, but a small Executive, composed of Labor (3), the reunited General Zionists (3), and Mizrachi (1). Jerusalem's primacy was recognized over the London Executive, the latter represented by Weizmann and by Locker as the third member of the General Zionists—sent to be a watchdog over the new president. The fourth meeting of the Jewish Agency Council endorsed this governing coalition, with three non-Zionists (Hexter and Simon in Jerusalem and Karpf in London) added to the Executive. The 50-50 percentage formula of representation would never return. Ben-Gurion's one failure came with Hadassah, which he would deem "the greatest [Zionist] force in America." That women's organization chose not to join the Labor faction at Lucerne but the General Zionists Group A. Its National Board also decided, with Brandeis's hearty approval, to withdraw gradually from the general medical field in Palestine and to concentrate its energies and financial support on Youth Aliya independently of the protesting ZOA. Yet, even as the difficult task of winning Hadassah over to his side lay ahead, Ben-Gurion had forged a Mapai-Weizmann alliance rooted in self-interest and a unity of purpose. So long as Ben-Gurion and Weizmann could overcome their clear differences in political style and temperament, that new bond could dominate Zionist politics and lead the movement, ultimately, to statehood.[65]

With Palestine "today the only country where Jewish immigrants are being absorbed on a large scale," the Agency Council called on public opinion to assist the Jews in their efforts "to re-establish the National Home in peace and freedom in the historic land of their origin." Reaffirming the Jewish people's determination to live in harmony with the Arabs in Palestine and throughout the region, the Agency Council appealed to Britain to fulfill its mandatory obligations by initiating an "active and systematic" policy of furthering the yishuv's development on a scale which Jewry's position in many lands demanded and which Palestine's free development could make possible. It "reluctantly" expressed a "categorical rejection" of the projected Legislative Council since, relegating the Jews of Palestine to minority status, that proposed body violated the mandate's recognition that Palestine's future was the concern of "the Jewish people as a whole." Further, the grant of legislative power to those "who openly repudiate the mandate and oppose the Jewish National Home" could not but be regarded as an "infringement" of the mandate, and would likely become "a source of dissension and strife between the two sections of the population" and "jeopardize the chances of cooperation between the population and the government." Since "the root of the Jewish tragedy" lay in the "landlessness of the Jewish people" and Jewry's return to Palestine "is in its essence a return to the soil," the Agency Council also called on the Jewish people to make possible a large increase of the yishuv's agricultural population, and requested the government to assist this form of settlement. Finally, the Council urged that HMG accord far greater scope to Jewish immigration and to industrial growth.[66]

A few days later, Jabotinsky's proposal to establish a New Zionist Organization (NZO) came to fruition when 310 delegates, representing 750,000 Revisionist voters in 34 countries, convened in Vienna's Concert Hall on September 7. Jacob de Haas, Herzl's English secretary and, as editor in Boston of the *Jewish Advocate*, the individual who had first introduced Brandeis to Zionism, presided. Pledging a "war to the bitter end" against the Third Reich as a measure of Jewish self-defense, Jabotinsky declared that the NZO would seek "not only to build Palestine, but to liquidate the Diaspora." To this end, he suggested a ten-year plan in order to secure a Jewish majority on both sides of the Jordan, providing for the settlement of 1.5 million Jews in the next decade, and a bank capitalized at $500,000 to further Palestine's development.

While attacking the government's policies and branding the proposed Legislative Council, about which Jabotinsky had already protested to Wauchope, "treachery to the Jewish people," he expressed a belief in England's "chivalry" in helping to create the Jewish State. That achievement, he now emphasized, was to be followed by *Shivat Zion* ("the return of Jewry to its Homeland"), with the third step to be the establishment of "a national center of culture radiating its influence over the whole world—*"MIZion Tezeh Torah"* (from out of Zion shall come Torah). Jabotinsky called for appreciation of the work of private capital; said that religion remained a private affair but Zionist youth should be educated under a religious influence—the latter reflecting his great admiration for Kook's defense of Stavsky and Rosenblatt; and asserted that labor questions should be decided by the courts. His program and choices for the NZO Executive were accepted. The delegates enthusiastically elected Jabotinsky president, and the movement's headquarters were transferred from Paris to London.[67]

From the mandatory's perspective, Arab concerns impinged on Zionist hopes. A C.I.D. report revealed that Emir Saud had recently met with Arab politicians in Palestine and Syria, in which Abd al-Hadi and Haj Amin both took part. These leaders agreed that if war broke out between Italy and Abyssinia and other European powers became involved, Istiqlal delegations would try to insure that Yemen, the Hejaz, and Iraq should remain neutral; that an all-Arab Congress be held to seek an alliance between the Arab rulers; that Ibn Saud should seek to have the Emir, his oldest son, succeed to the Syrian throne; and that relations be reestablished between Abdullah and the Istiqlal—all to "exploit the situation" and force HMG to grant them independence. On September 10, a National Defense Party delegation protested to Hall over the killing of an Arab by Jews over a land dispute at Kuskus Taboun, the wounding of another at Netanya, and acts of "hooliganism" committed by Jews against Arabs in Tel Aviv and Jaffa. Arguing that these crimes were the result of the "excessive" immigration of Jews into Palestine, Nashashibi called for shutting the door to further entry and giving those Jews who had been allowed to enter the country, "whether justly or unjustly," an opportunity "to adapt themselves to their surroundings." In return for his party's continued policy to cooperate with the mandatory, Nashashibi hoped that the government would "find a solvent for the present troubled situation."[68]

Amidst this growing state of tension, the Reichstag's enactment of the Nuremberg Laws on September 15 irrevocably separated Jews from the rest of the German population. As Hitler ordered at the end of a speech blaming the Jews for the volatile international situation, these measures (supplemented in November) were intended to protect German "blood and honor" and to distinguish between *Reichsbürger*, persons of "German or related blood," and *Staatsbürger*, at best guests of the state. Depriving Jews of political equality, the new legislation also prohibited marriages and sexual relations between Jews and Germans, the employment of German maids under the age of forty-five in Jewish households, and the raising by Jews of the German flag. "Aryanization" of German Jewish property, purchased at highly favorable terms by Gentile competitors, would soon increase considerably, as did the number of applicants to the Jewish *Hilfsverein* for emigration. Shortly after the annual Nuremberg congress, Hitler spoke to a small circle of Party members about the Jews' consequent isolation within Germany, but also declared ominously to the head of the Racial Policy Office that "in case of a war on all fronts, he would be ready [regarding the Jews] for all the consequences." A London *Times* editorial poignantly captured the Third Reich regime's "tormenting of a people in a cage": "After being denied the rights of citizenship, they are coming to be denied the right to live."[69]

Five days after the Nuremberg party gathering, Weizmann requested Warburg to place at his disposal a special sum to "ward off the anti-Jewish propaganda" in Palestine itself and in the Near East generally. "Terribly disappointed in the crudeness and incredible bestiality of the Nuremberg performance" and unable to see "how my people can stick it out in that country any longer," so he informed McDonald, Warburg replied to Weizmann that he required the money for anti-Nazi activities in America. (He also considered the Council's treatment of the non-Zionists, reported to him by a bitter Laski, "unnecessarily humiliating and unfriendly.") Waldman proposed to his American Jewish Committee associates that they, unlike German Jews' approach of "increasingly adopting the nationalist Jewish philosophy that life for the Jew outside of Palestine is a *Galuth* (life of exile) with all its abnormalities and disabilities," concentrate on uniting "substantial elements throughout the country in our common undertaking" of emancipation.[70]

Additional Jewish responses emerged. Wise appealed to Beneš, then president of the sixteenth League Assembly, that the member states stand by the Jewish people "in its defense of the fundamental principles of humanity." The Union of Orthodox Rabbis of the United States and Canada called for prayers and a half-day fast on September 22, the first day of *selihot* (penitential prayers), in preparation for the Jewish New Year. The Joint Foreign Committee recorded its "indignant protest," and pledged itself to pursue every lawful means against this "deliberate act of the German State." Weizmann kept a focus on Palestine, adding to Warburg his sense that "our shares now stand rather higher, particularly in view of the international situation, than they did." As his first official contact after returning to the WZO presidency, he would see MacDonald.[71]

On the morning of September 25, after consultation with Ben-Gurion, Weizmann asked the Colonial Secretary for "favorable action" on immigration, land, and a government surplus that represented money due primarily to Jewish efforts in Palestine. MacDonald noted his colleagues' opinion that a severe economic setback would occur in the next two or three years, to which Weizmann replied that Palestine suffered currently from the disadvantages of being part of the British Empire, and had none of the advantages of an independent country. Despite the money, knowledge, and skill present in Palestine, he observed, no normal development of industry existed. MacDonald finally said that he, Wauchope, and a government economic advisor should sit down with Agency representatives and discuss these matters over dinner in two weeks' time. He also gave his personal opinion that Italy would almost certainly attack Abyssinia, leading Weizmann to remark that, in these circumstances, HMG had to decide whether it wanted a strong Palestine or a weak Palestine. "A strong Palestine from the British point of view," he added, "must mean a strong Jewish National Home."[72]

Weizmann's last argument carried less weight for British officialdom than the uncertainty of how the Arabs would respond to war in the eastern Mediterranean. According to a report which reached the Foreign Office at the end of the month, the majority of the Syrian pan-Arab leaders favored Great Britain, particularly if France sided with

Italy, and wished to secure an understanding with London supporting an Arab Federation. Hassan Sidki Dajani, secretary of the National Defense Party, met in Damascus with such Syrian leaders as Jamal Mardam and Rida Pasha Rakabi in his effort to oppose the Istiqlalists. Haj Amin, on the other hand, had concurred with certain points in the agreement between the Italian authorities and Arlsan and Jabri, but was loathe to commit himself. While in Lebanon, he was reported to have asked Milham Kasem, a rebel leader who gave the French much trouble, to settle the feud in Tripoli between two warring Arab families; as he did not confine himself to this, the French forbade him to visit Damascus.

Yemen's Imam Yehia declared his neutrality regarding the Abyssinian question, and rumors swirled about Ibn Saud's contemplating the same path. Fuad Hamzeh, the Saudi Foreign Minister who was well connected with some Istiqlal members in Palestine, endeavored to obtain a decision in favor of Ibn Saud's speaking in the name of Syria and Palestine. The receptions for Emir Saud in Palestine, particularly since they indicated Haj Amin's leanings, did not have Abdullah's approval. Yet another rumor had Haj Amin, with French knowledge and at the inspiration of the Italian authorities through the Syrian-Palestine delegation of Arslan and Jabri in Geneva, travel to assist in effecting an understanding between the French government and the Syrian nationalists.[73]

Intriguingly, Shertok informed the London Executive on October 3, side by side with the Arabs' general preparedness to become "an active thorn" in HMG's position went a strengthening of the pro-British orientation among the Arab countries. Egyptian nationalists understood the menace involved in the Italian threat, through a conquest of Abysinnia, to Anglo-Egyptian domination of the Sudan, while the Yemeni king realized that Italian ascendance spelled for him the yoke of foreign hegemony. Ibn Saud feared to antagonize Italy completely, but understood that his flank would be permanently threatened if Yemen fell to Italian control. Iraq certainly sided with the British camp, while in Syria Britain's stock was rising among the Syrian nationalists, a fact that Hall and a prominent Syrian nationalist leader had recently confirmed to Shertok. In addition, Iraq and Syria feared the prospect of Turkish imperialism, backed by the Soviet Union, to the northern frontiers of both countries, to which only Britain could prove an effective bulwark. Consequently, Shertok wished the Executive to stress in talks with HMG, Britain had little to fear for the future as far as the Arab attitude was concerned. There may be "temporary aberrations from this main course," he noted, leading to British efforts at pacifying Palestine's Arabs like the Legislative Council and a restrictive land law. At the bottom, however, fundamental interests existed to compel Arabs to take a long view, which "dictates a course of loyalty."[74]

Italy's invasion of Abyssinia that same day, taking Adua on October 6, worried Ben-Gurion far less than Weizmann. Writing from London to his wife, Paula, the new chairman of the Agency Executive did not fear a war between Britain and Italy. Most of public opinion and the three major political parties in England favored economic and financial sanctions against Italy (the application for which the League Council began arranging after declaring Italy the aggressor on October 7). However, few Britons, Ben-Gurion explained, were prepared to oppose Italy by force, because that could transform into a world war, which they did not want. They also knew that France, afraid of Germany, wished to maintain its friendship with Italy, and Britain would not fight unless France did. For the WZO president, however, the Jewish New Year had begun "catastrophically." He wondered where this "bloody war," unleashed by the action of "a single individual" (Mussolini), would yet lead. Zionist work in Palestine, "almost the only bright point in our sky," would be gravely affected by the conflict in the East. "We are, after all," he added to his close friend and banker Walter J. Baer of Zurich, "a plaything of the fates over which we have no power at all." In the twenty years since 1914, our hope that the World War "would give birth to a better world—a war to end wars!" had been shattered. Weizmann ended "until better days": "We did our work in a cold and rigid world based on selfishness, with a Jewry that was hardly able or willing to reflect on itself. We have accomplished something, and I hope it is strong enough to withstand this tempest too. But who knows!"[75]

Shertok found little comfort in an interview three days later with Hall, administering the government in Wauchope's absence. While measures were being taken to prepare Haifa against any sudden Italian bombardment, the Chief Secretary considered that inevitable sanctions would immediately cause "a dislocation" in Palestine, cutting off some supplies and canceling transports. This, along with a probable slump in the building trade, adding to the loss of confidence already evidenced by a run on Palestine's banks in early September, precluded the Agency Executive's request for an advance of 2,000 immigration certificates. Shertok pointed to the "new high tide" of applications for Palestine since the Nuremberg Laws, and stressed the need to clear out the halutz training centers lest they be closed due to an impression that the Agency was using them as a pretext to find new economic opportunities for Jewish youth remaining in Germany. When Hall quoted Antonius's assertion that the moderate faction of German industrialists and financiers was gaining the upper hand, Shertok noted that some of Antonius's friends firmly believed, or at least said they believed, that the Zionists had put Hitler "in the saddle" with the deliberate intention of using the anti-Jewish legislation in Germany as a lever for increased Jewish immigration into Palestine. According to the Agency's information, the position of Reichsbank head Hjalmar Schacht, representing the more moderate faction, was "tottering," and his removal appeared likely in the near future. With Hull remaining obdurate, Shertok urged that Weizmann raise the difficulty in London of getting Jewish funds out of Germany, a very serious matter inasmuch as capitalist immigration helped finance the absorption of halutz immigration.[76]

Immigration Commissioner Eric Mills had no doubts that the Nazis sought to "eliminate the Jew from German life.... Mortality and emigration provide the means." Reporting this on October 6 to the Foreign Office after a ten-day visit to Germany, he hoped that a number of governments could be induced to informally ask Berlin to expedite Jewish emigration. Hearing this from Mills, James McDonald again asked Whitehall that Phipps and Dodd together seek Berlin's approval for the orderly transfer of refugee property. Foreign Office officials feared, however, that such an initiative would either be rebuffed or force HMG to consider taking more German Jews into the United Kingdom. At a meeting on October 9 with Lionel and Anthony de Rothschild at their New Court headquarters in the City, Mills added that "there was a determined and scientific policy of exterminating [sic] the Jews who could not be eliminated."[77]

"Really touched" and spurred by Mills's information that German-Jewish leaders (Max Warburg of the *Hilfsverein*) had a far-reaching plan for evacuating the young generation and salvaging Jewish assets, Anthony de Rothschild now took the lead to see if ways could be found to rescue at least some of his co-religionists and a substantial part of their property. Informing Felix Warburg of these developments, McDonald urged that a joint Anglo-American Jewish appeal be made to evacuate about 200,000 from the Reich over a decade: 10,000 annually to Palestine, 5,000 to the United States, and 5,000 elsewhere. He soon repeated this call to the League of Nations' Permanent Committee as well. From his talks with leaders of threatened East European Jewry, McDonald got the feeling that they realized the Nuremberg Laws and general Nazi assault were "an attack on all Jews," and would therefore be prepared "to make large sacrifices" in order to give German Jews priority in rescue.[78]

Weizmann opted to concentrate on the Legislative Council, pressing Wauchope on October 10 to consider the undesirability, and indeed the dangers, of proceeding in the "present unsettled state of affairs." The High Commissioner said that he was obliged nevertheless to go ahead, and would be very sorry to have a Council without Jews. Perhaps in the end, he added, the Arabs would refuse it, "which might after all be the best way out." Weizmann concluded that Wauchope was "by no means enamoured of the Council idea, and would not be sorry to see it fall through, provided he could say that the government had kept its word." Wauchope chose not to reply as to his intentions regarding Akaba, but did ask Weizmann about granting Jabotinsky's "violent applications" that HMG reverse its 1930 decision and permit him to return to Palestine; Weizmann replied that it was not for him to reply on this matter. A few days later Cunliffe-Lister, now Secretary for Air, suggested the accuracy of Weizmann's assumption about Wauchope's views when expressing regret that the Zionist Congress had erred greatly in passing an uncompromisingly negative resolution on the Council: "If we had only shown some signs of wavering, the chances of an Arab refusal would have been very greatly increased." Weizmann replied that this showed the Zionists were "honest people and not tac-ticians," to which Cunliffe-Lister stated that the Council "had to come" but that Wauchope "was not really keen on it."[79]

On October 15, Weizmann, Ben-Gurion, and Brodetsky sat down with MacDonald, Wauchope, Mills, and Parkinson. Talk of the Council, as Weizmann had suggested earlier in a memorandum to MacDonald, was purposely postponed for another occasion. The British agreed to investigate the possibilities with regard to Eilat, Ben-Gurion strongly putting the case for developing the Negev and digging wells, as biblical patriarchs Abraham and Isaac had done in the area of Beersheva, and Weizmann indicating interest in helping the Arab fellahin there, as had been done in the Huleh. MacDonald agreed to begin investigation of land ownership and water availability in the south. He also consented to Weizmann's appeal that the authorities examine every industrial possibility. Expenditures from the surplus for the coming year were already spoken for, Wauchope observed, which brought up the question of immigration. Acknowledging that some 60,000 Jews had entered in 1935 to date, Ben-Gurion recalled that the Colonial Office had seen the Agency's request two years earlier of 24,000 as "an astronomical figure" and then cut it to 5,000. Mills thought Palestine's position "unhealthy," however, and Wauchope interjected: "What will all the masses brought now to Palestine do when a depression breaks out, when a war occurs?" Any Jewish unemployment did not harm Arabs, Ben-Gurion replied, and, in any event, conjectures of economic depression should not hamper Jewish entry into Palestine. Weizmann: "Whatever the Jew does will not be justified in Gentile eyes," so "when then will we receive immigration?" The group broke up after three hours without any definite resolutions, but Ben-Gurion felt that the meeting appeared to remove his worry of getting no schedule at all in light of the Italian conflict.[80]

The accidental discovery of a large weapons delivery at Jaffa port the next day threatened to staunch Wauchope's effort for the Council. Within a consignment of 537 drums marked "Belgian White Star Cement," shipped from Antwerp aboard the SS Leopold II, police found a large quantity of rifles, ammunition, revolvers, automatic pistols, and related items. All traces of consignee "J. Katin" of Tel Aviv, in actuality Asher Peled of the Hagana, vanished. The discovery united the National Defense Party, the Youth Party, and Abd al-Latif Salah's new National Bloc Party, which met daily to formulate a Palestinian Arab response. Nashashibi cabled to Wauchope, still on holiday in England, that this smuggling of illicit arms gave credence to the Arabs' belief that the Jews were preparing a general attack "as if the British Bayonets and the unjust imperialistic policy are insufficient to protect them and to realize their unlawful ambitions." Haj Amin, continuing in office despite having instigated past Arab riots, urged Hall to search all Jewish settlements, especially Tel-Aviv, in order to confiscate any weapons found.[81]

Different Arab factions, meeting in Jaffa on October 21, worked together on a program of action. Even Husseini dropped his independent stand. A general strike was called for Saturday, five days later, when the Jews would not benefit in view of their desisting from work on the Jewish Sabbath. A memorandum to the government called for the collection of weapons from Jews, a systematic search should Jews fail to surrender their weapons, and the Arabs to arm themselves if HMG decided not to conduct the inspection. It also requested the replacement of Jewish port customs officials by Britons and Arabs, as well as more effective customs examinations. An umbrella committee of all the parties but Istiqlal was appointed to execute these decisions: Nashashibi, Dajani, Husseini, Ghusayn, Salah, and Issa Bandak of the Reform Party. A deputation to Hall of the Arab Women's Federation went further, demanding that if the Jewish population did not surrender thousands of weapons and ammunition within ten days, Jewish leaders should be deported or else the Federation would call on Palestine's Arabs to arm and protect themselves. All Arab areas in Palestine observed the general strike, with shops reopening that evening.[82]

Tensions did not subside easily. Hall assured a Palestinian Arab party delegation on October 23 that their people had no cause for fear, and that the mandatory had "ample forces" at its disposal "to protect any section of the community in all circumstances and would not hesitate to use them." This carried scant balm, however, particularly after a large Jewish gathering in London's Anglo-Palestine Club heard MacDonald and Wauchope laud the achievements of the emerging "Jewish National Home." While declaring that "there is no question of the establishment of a Jewish State" in Palestine, thereby echoing a government memorandum which responded to a cable and letter from Arslan, the Colonial Secretary expressed his certainty that the Arabs' standard of life would be raised by the Jewish National Home. In the most forthright speech of the evening, Lady Eva Reading called for HMG to adopt a Palestine policy corresponding to the desperate German-Jewish situation, insisted that it was unfair to wait indefinitely for permission to cross the Jordan, and argued that the Abyssinian problem required the development of a strong Jewish hinterland beyond Haifa and the Jordan that could always be counted on to be loyal to Britain. *Per contra*, Palestinian Arab newspapers hailed the general strike for its show of unity, and went on to assert that if their rights were not conceded, the Arabs were prepared for "maximum sacrifices." The Jewish press countered that the Belgian cement consignee had not been found; that the Arabs had regularly been the aggressors and carried on weapon trading across the open Transjordan frontier; and that the provocation of Arab agitators poisoning the minds of the people was more important than a seizure of arms.[83]

The eighteenth anniversary of the Balfour Declaration brought Arab and Jewish differences in Palestine to the fore. For the yishuv English daily *Palestine Post*, the occasion served as "another milestone" in world Jewry's "long and torturous climb towards the dignity and status made possible of attainment by the National Home." That some Arabs saw in the day "a cause or culmination of their grievances and a peg on which to hang their expression of supposed betrayal" reflected "a painful manifestation of a lingering misunderstanding" of the very causes which had moved the nations to recognize the Jewish rights to Palestine, and "of a persistent and deliberate ignoring of the benefits this recognition has brought to the Holy Land and its Arab inhabitants." In sharp contrast, *Falastin's* front page featured a black border, and prodded Arab party leaders to use "all means" to end the Balfour Declaration in the strong faith that the country would be made independent. In Nablus, encouraged by Istiqlalist Akram Zu'aiter, a crowd of about 1,000 protested that Arabs should arm themselves against the Jews—said to be already prepared for attack, and it denounced the recent addresses by MacDonald and Wauchope at the pro-Zionist banquet. The speakers also made an appeal to "plant the hatred of England in every Arab heart," and called on Muslims and Arabs everywhere to cooperate with the Palestinian Arab cause.[84]

A battle between British police and an Arab terrorist group on November 20 stirred Palestinian Arab public opinion to storm pitch. The murder on November 7 of Sergeant Moshe Rosenfeld, who sought thieves of citrus fruit from Ein Harod orchards, was discovered to have been committed by a guerilla band (The Black Hand) led by sixty-four year old Sheikh Iz al-Din al-Qassam. A charismatic Syrian native who, having fought the French there fled to Palestine in 1921 to fight the British, preached in one of the Haifa mosques and in local villages for a *jihad* (holy war) as the only means of liberating Palestine from infidel Britons and Jews and transforming it into an Islamic state, Qassam and some members of his *Ikhwan* (Brotherhood) *al-Qassam* had killed and wounded individual halutzim from Yagur, Nahalal, Kfar Yehoshua, Balfouria, and Kfar Hasidim during 1931 and 1932. Haj Amin approved of his activities, but had declined Qassam's proposal in 1933 for an open rebellion on the pretext that he still sought a political solution. Tracing the terrorists to the village of Ya'abad west of Jenin, a strong force of police killed four of the gang, including their leader. His funeral in the village of Balad ash Sheikh, southeast of Haifa, turned into a mass nationalist demonstration. The Arab press immediately labeled them "martyrs" who had died for the Arab nation and its faith. Arab party heads sent telegrams of sympathy to the mourning families. Qassam was proclaimed a national hero; Arab leaders and the community's various newspapers completely identified themselves with the deeds of the group.[85]

Qassam's death caught the Palestinian Arab leaders in a fierce struggle for hegemony and stoked the fires of militancy. According to Agency Arab Department intelligence, Ghusayn decided to shift his ties from the Mufti's circle to the Nashashibis in order to attain greater political influence, leading Haj Amin and Husseini to contact Zu'aiter, who felt that Abd al-Hadi's leadership did not suit the hour, to organize a new youth organization. When Haj Amin defended the latter as one of the most popular personalities in the pan-Arab movement, Zu'aiter invited a number of young men to Nablus for a meeting on future action. Salah, a relative of Zu'aiter, was increasingly shifting his forces from the Nashashibi to the Husseini camp. Wauchope's delay in establishing the Legislative Council, disappointing all the Arab political parties, increased anti-British sentiment and raised the possibility of partisan terrorist warfare along the Irish model. Italian funds, funneled through Jabri to Istiqlalist Rashid al-Haj Ibrahim, manager of the Arab Bank branch in Haifa, were used both to purchase the Husseini newspaper *Al-Jama Al-Arabiya* and to arm the *Qassam* band. The terrorists themselves were divided in regard to attacking only the Jews (the Husseinis always favored this approach) or both Englishmen and Jews. Nashashibi had no hand in these deliberations and opposed a memorandum to Wauchope that included threatening language, but he was forced to join in order to avoid breaking up the parties' coalition. Arab youth, for their part, spread dangerous rumors that Jews planned attacks, including bombs on Al-Aqsa during Friday mid-day prayers. The Supreme Moslem Council remained in the fray, ordering the Imams in the Jaffa, Haifa, Nablus, Jenin, and Jerusalem mosques to recall the Qassam martyrs and pray for their souls.[86]

On November 25, a delegation of five out of the six Palestinian Arab parties (the Istiqlal abstaining) met with Wauchope in a common front for the first time and submitted a memorandum on their demands. Nashashibi charged that the High Commissioner's policies had benefited "a foreign people who are invading the country," endangering the language and religion of the native Arab inhabitants, obtaining the best lands, and importing arms that would be used either against the Arabs or the British. Aside from a search for Jewish weapons, their memorandum called for three fundamental demands: creating a democratic government in Palestine; putting a complete end to Jewish immigration; and stopping all land purchases by Jews. A negative reply from the administration would lead to the resignation of the Arab leaders, who could "no longer restrain the population." Convinced that HMG's current policy would "eliminate them from Palestine," Husseini warned that every Palestinian Arab might one day emulate the path of Qassam and his fallen comrades. Claiming that the National Home promised by Great Britain to the Jews had been fulfilled, Salah and Ghusayn urged that a new pro-Arab policy should be adopted in keeping with the Balfour Declaration's other pledge that the creation of that home not "prejudice" the rights of "the non-Jewish inhabitants."

Halting immigration and land sales constituted matters of major policy, Wauchope replied, which HMG would have to consider. Greater demands for labor had led to increased Jewish immigration in recent years, but, as MacDonald had said publicly, "there could be no question of a Jewish national state." A Legislative Council, which London had now decided to confer, would benefit the country and have its people associated with the government. Every effort was being made to uncover the identities of the criminals behind the previous month's arms discovery in Jaffa port. A new rural property tax, improved village water supplies, and closer connection between the authorities and the rural population would improve the welfare of Arab village fellahin. Husseini insisted upon one month in order to reply to the delegation's demands, but the High Commissioner emphasized that HMG required more time to deal with this difficult issue.[87]

The sharp rise in Palestinian Arab militancy impressed Ben-Gurion. The "cement barrels incident" had united the Arabs, he informed the Mapai Central Committee on December 2, while Qassam's death provided the Arab youth and many others with "moral strength" and pride. For the first time, the country's Arabs possessed a leader who sacrificed his life for an ideal, just as Joseph Trumpeldor and five other halutzim slain at Tel-Hai in 1920 had inspired the yishuv. This iconic example would also awaken more Arab guerilla efforts, he warned, in turn leading the English to think of Palestine as "a new Ireland," a land of anarchy. With the country no longer symbolizing development and prosperity, an image which the Zionists had cultivated successfully, continued large funding worldwide for the yishuv enterprise was in imminent jeopardy. HMG would likely reduce the immigration quota for Jews, whose unparalleled entry of more than 60,000 in 1935 alone had understandably worried the Arab community. Palestinian Arab leaders could not but be encouraged by Britain's ending its League of Nations Mandate over Iraq in 1932. All these circumstances, coupled with the Arab parties' "well-grounded" presentation to Wauchope, suggested that the Jewish *risorgimento* faced "a new political atmosphere" which had turned from bad to worse. In the final analysis, Ben-Gurion ended, "we could only rely on ourselves."[88]

On December 18, Wauchope presented the Jewish Agency with more reason for worry. Meeting with Ben-Gurion and Shertok, the High Commissioner declared that he had fixed the number of additional workers that Palestine could absorb during the coming half year at 4,400. The Agency had requested 10,900 certificates for this first schedule to come after the Nuremberg Laws. Its detailed memorandum also noted that although Prime Minister MacDonald had pledged to Weizmann in 1931 that one-third of the country's public works would be assigned to the Jews, no part had been received in the last few years even though the Jewish share in the mandatory's revenue had grown continuously. In addition, Wauchope intended to subtract 1,200 certificates from the total on account of Jewish tourists remaining in Palestine and entering the labor market without official sanction, reckoning these illegal immigrants on the basis of 200 per month. Hearing Ben-Gurion's request that he take "the long view" into account, Wauchope noted the worrisome Abyssinian situation, and insisted that another High Commissioner would not have granted any schedule at this vexing time. Their protests against the drastic reduction failed to shake his resolve.[89]

The appointment of a new Colonial Secretary, J. H. Thomas, selected by Prime Minister Stanley Baldwin after an unexpected Conservative victory in the mid-November elections, did not alter HMG's fundamental stance on the Legislative Council. To Wedgwood, Thomas indicated on December 6 that although "doubtful about the expediency" of the step, it was too late to stop the process directly. He told Simon Marks, Sieff's brother-in-law and another Weizmann loyalist, the same day (so Ben-Gurion heard from Marks) that "much water would flow under the bridge until the Council had been established." A Parliamentary Committee delegation chaired by Wedgwood on December 18 was likewise informed by Thomas that the Council would go forward, although the group came away thinking that its actual setting up was "far from accomplished." The following day, Brodetsky and Simon Marks heard the same tidings. When the pair raised Shertok's concern that issues relating to land and immigration would be included in the Council's purview, Thomas promised that he would throw his support in opposition. Further, the Colonial Secretary offered the assurance that he would do his utmost to secure from the Arabs, at the Council's establishment, their acceptance of the mandate.[90]

On December 21, receiving the mandatory Executive Council's support and London's approval, Wauchope presented his version of a Council to an Arab delegation and, one day later, to a Jewish representative group. Reflecting the yishuv's dramatic expansion to nearly 400,000, a doubling in the last four years thanks to sizeable immigration from Germany and the consequent growth of capitalist enterprise, the projected ratio on the Council of Arab to Jew now stood at 2:1. Determination of the labor immigration schedule remained in the High Commissioner's hands. The Council would be in session for three months of the year, its president an Englishman from outside the country. That officer could preclude any action which he thought ran counter to the mandate, or might be "offensive" to either neighboring rulers or foreign states in "friendly relations" with the British government. The High Commissioner would have the fullest veto power, initiate all financial matters, and could enact any of his proposals into law even if the Council voted otherwise. He possessed the authority to disband the Council for twelve months, and longer if the Colonial Office considered it desirable or necessary. If any community refused to take part in the Council elections, the High Commissioner had the power to nominate either British officials, or such individuals in their place as he thought suitable. Wauchope's radio address that same evening publicized his intentions.[91]

At the time, the Arab delegates limited themselves to a few technical questions, but their Jewish counterparts immediately expressed sharp objection. Weizmann took the lead, charging that the Council represented a "grave departure" from the underlying conceptions of the mandate, giving such a high level of legislative power to those who "openly reject and defy" the establishment of the Jewish National Home. The Zionists had "time and again" stretched out "a hand of peace" to the Arabs, he observed, but these offers had been rejected; the Council could only help the Arabs to hinder Jewish progress, which had been particularly "remarkable" under Wauchope's leadership. Va'ad HaLeumi chairman Ben-Zvi and Sephardic Jewry's representative Avraham Elmalah concurred. The ultra-Orthodox Agudas Israel's Rabbi Moshe Blau decried the fact that HMG, chosen by Providence to bring back a dispersed people to their home after "a terrible exile" of 2,000 years, should transfer that trust to a Council whose majority would "certainly not be loyal" to its execution, and just when Diaspora Jewry was suffering almost unparalleled persecution. In response, Wauchope repeated that HMG had pledged itself to establishing a Council, and he hoped that the Jews would see their way to taking part in the scheme before very long.[92]

In reporting to Thomas, Wauchope realized that not all the Arab parties would accept the Council. A C.I.D. report on December 4 had trenchantly observed that "party leaders will find themselves forced to adopt an extremist policy" in order "to restore their prestige and prevent the leadership of the nationalist movement from passing out of their hands." While the National Defense and Reform parties continued to support the Council's creation, with one pro-Nashashibi sheikh saying that Nashashibi would regain thereby public office that he had lost to Khalidi in the election for Jerusalem's mayoralty, the Palestinian Arab Party's newspapers continually published articles from late December on showing the disadvantages of the proposal. Agency Arabist head Eliyahu Sasson heard from an editorial board member of Al-Liwa that the Palestinian Arab Party's executive had decided on December 19 not to accept the Council proposals in their present form, and certainly that it would approve no Council that, directly or indirectly, acknowledged the mandate. The success on December 12 of militant Egyptian nationalists, rioting fomented by the Wafd Party, to restore the 1923 parliamentary constitution and resume negotiations for their country's independence from HMG reinforced the Husseinis' stand to pressure Britain "with all their strength so that the Palestinian question will be solved in a manner suitable to Arab aspirations." The young Istiqlalists persisted in their staunch rejection, while Abd al-Hadi told Wauchope on December 30 that he would take no part in the scheduled meeting of the Arab parties two weeks hence. He hoped that the restrictions could be modified, but Wauchope said that this would be difficult as London had approved of the main points.[93]

Weizmann did not fear any serious Arab disturbances so long as the economic situation remained "fairly steady." He suggested to Marks that, "merely to render" the Council's imposition "as innocuous as possible," London should insist on an unqualified Oath of Allegiance to "the Government of Palestine as by mandate established." On the occasion of planting a first tree in the George V Jubilee Forest at the hills of Nazareth, Weizmann expressed the yishuv's gratitude "for the great things that have come to pass" during the current monarch's reign, noting that the pace, "if slower than we might have wished," had been "well and truly laid" and augured well for solid achievement "in which all sections of the population of Palestine will share." However, writing to Lord Luggard and to Rappard on December 22, he confessed to true depression over the administration's "generally indifferent and negative attitude" toward the Zionists' efforts, ranging from the Legislative Council, to inadequate grants—despite a surplus of £6 million—for public health services and education, to lack of an equitable share in public works, to delays in settling land ownership disputes. Since returning to Palestine, Weizmann also realized that as many opportunities for absorption of refugees as possible had to be created, and quickly. With agricultural colonization, "the rock of our work," by nature "a slow business," he therefore asked Lord Melchett in London to press for sound industrial development, and chemical projects in particular.[94]

Weizmann found more worrisome the "increasingly difficult" position of Germany's Jews, he informed Marks on December 15, and particularly reports that some prominent non-Zionists were considering princely sums for refugee settlement outside of Palestine. A recent Berlin conference of the *Hilfsverein*, of which Max Warburg was president, sharply criticized the WZO's ha'avara activities and expressed support for Jewish colonization in South America, South Africa and the Far East. Weizmann had also just heard that, at a meeting in New Court of the Central British Fund one month earlier with Marks and McDonald in attendance, the Rothschilds had advanced Warburg's plan (which Warburg discussed with Schacht) to create a bank capitalized at £3 million for liquidating German-Jewish property and granting loans to Jewish émigrés for Palestine and other countries, leaving property behind. While Marks had proposed a fund for settling 30,000 Jewish youngsters over three years in Palestine and another 30,000 in Palestine or elsewhere, Weizmann warned him not to lend a hand to any of the non-Zionists' "hare-brained schemes," "which can only serve to weaken our position." "The Warburgs and the Rothschilds and their methods have gone forever," he declared, and "it is not for us to bolster up their failure, and render their policy, which was historically unjustified and ineffective, and which has brought Jewry to its present plight, more apparently effective than it deserves to be."[95]

Since November, Agency leaders had been discussing with German Zionist representatives in Palestine their own plan to create a central bank in London for liquidating Jewish capital and investing it in Palestine. Ben-Gurion spoke for them all when asserting, at the Va'ad HaLeumi on December 11, that German Jews were "doomed to destruction" if they did not come to Eretz Yisrael. After Weizmann pleaded at a public meeting in Jerusalem of the German Settlers' Association that Jewry cooperate with the WZO in saving in Palestine as many as possible "from destruction," Kurt Blumenfeld, former head of the Zionist Organization in Germany, noted that over the past two years 60 percent of the country's total industry had been brought into being by immigrants with capital from Germany, with 10 percent of this mostly middle-class element having settled on the soil. On December 31, Ben-Gurion cautioned the Agency Executive that a prospective delegation to the United States of Samuel, Marks, and Lord Bearsted, chairman of Shell Oil, on behalf of the Warburg scheme, in which Palestine would only receive 20 percent of the funds, "could ruin our work. The Jewish nation, for whose fate we are responsible, is not to be forfeited.... The flag of Eretz Yisrael is the only flag of rescue." He closed: "The house that will stand at the forefront of activity will be this house—because this is the house of the Jewish Nation—and not the House of the Jewish Lords in England."[96]

That same day, not long after McDonald submitted his Letter of Resignation with an accompanying memorandum, his withdrawal as High Commissioner took effect. The lengthy Letter, published in its entirety by the London *Times* and the *New York Times*, described the "catastrophic" conditions that threatened "the pauperization or exile" of hundreds of thousands of Germans not considered "Nordic" by the Third Reich. More than half of the Jews remaining in Germany had already been deprived of their livelihood, he observed, the Jewish people used as "the scapegoat for political and partisan purposes." The Nazi concepts of "blood, race, and soil," propagated with "fanatical enthusiasm," menaced not only Jews, but "all those who remain defiantly loyal to the old ideals of religious and individual freedom." Noting that "the doors of most countries are closed against impoverished fugitives," he called on members of the League and other nations to resort to "friendly but firm intercession" with Berlin for a modification of policies "which constitute a source of unrest and perplexity in the world, a challenge to the conscience of mankind, and a menace to the legitimate interests of the States affected by the immigration of German refugees." During the last three centuries, the Letter continued, the principle of respect for the rights of minorities had been "hardening into an obligation of the public law of Europe," the League Assembly itself championing this cause. McDonald emphasized that "protection of the individual from racial and religious intolerance is a vital condition of international peace and security," and closed with a personal plea that public opinion "move to avert the existing and impending tragedies."[97]

Filled with a good deal of anxiety, Weizmann asked Rappard to help get the League to assist the WZO in absorbing the largest possible number of Jews in Palestine. Certain anti-Zionist Jewish "die-hards" were proposing "fantastic projects" for settling refugees in South America or Africa, he wrote, while the mandatory, fearing the international situation and also bending to Arab pressure, would try to dole out immigration certificates in "a more parsimonious fashion" than they had in the last few years. Yet Palestine, extolled in McDonald's Letter of Resignation for absorbing more than half of the German refugees who had found new homes, could continue to take 50,000-60,000 a year, enabling the Agency to allot to German Jewry a proportion of from 25 to 30 percent in immigration certificates. Weizmann also heard from Rosenblüth that the present situation of Jewish refugees in France,

Belgium, Luxemburg, Yugoslavia, Austria, and Poland was "catastroph-ic"; the Jews of Poland and Rumania especially demanded the Agency's attention. He appealed to Herbert Samuel on December 31 to support funds to bring emigrants only to Palestine, as did Ben-Gurion to Marks, Ben-Gurion seeing Max Warburg's plan as a reflection of the tug of war between "philanthropic assimilationism" and Zionism, between the select rich and the large masses of the Jewish people.[98]

On the same, final day of 1935, the *Palestine Post* editorialized that McDonald had been able to extend some help and influence to 80,000 German Jewish refugees, although their remaining 350,000 co-reli-gionists in the Third Reich were being tortured to "the limits of endur-ance." The ex-High Commissioner had also witnessed "a corresponding growth of indifference, apathy, and insensitivity of the world outside." It concluded: The Nuremberg Laws, utilized as "progressive measures" for "eliminating" Jews "it might almost seem from human life alto-gether," signaled that "the new ghetto in Germany is to be finished off even to the most humiliating detail."[99]

Fully aware of this deepening crisis, Ben-Gurion viewed the German-Jewish question as "an historical test case for Zionism." Concurring, Weizmann put it thus to Marks: "The disaster is so overwhelming that unless some radical measures are taken fairly soon, we Zionists may stand charged, when history comes to be written, with criminal indif-ference in the face of the greatest trial to which Jewry has been sub-jected in modern times."[100] With eyes fixed both on the international arena and on the Promised Land, they and associates, whatever their differences, realized that the sands in the hourglass were descending, inexorably, with ever greater speed.

Endnotes

1   Dec. 31, 1934-Jan. 1, 1935, Jewish Agency Administrative Committee meeting, ZA; Warburg to Weizmann, Jan. 4, 1935, microfilm #1930, Warburg MSS; Laski at Joint Foreign Committee, Jan. 29, 1935, Minutes, BDA. For Adler's remarks at the Washington Conference soon thereafter, see Jan. 20, 1935, address, Box 2, Cyrus Adler MSS, Jewish Theological Seminary (JTS) Archives, New York City.

2   Kallen to Goldmann, Jan. 10, 1935; Goldmann to Kallen, Jan. 28, 1935; Kallen to Goldmann, Feb. 14, 1935; all in file 405, Kallen MSS. Laski to Adler, Feb. 5, 1935, Adler files-1935 correspondence, AJCA.

3   Va'ad HaLeumi, Jan. 9, 1935, J1/7236, CZA; Parkinson talk with Brodetsky-Lourie, Jan. 10, 1935, file C14/10, BDA; Wauchope-Shertok interview, Jan. 11, 1935, ZOA assorted files, ZA; JAEJ, Jan. 13, 1935, CZA; HaAretz, Jan. 17, 1935; Weizmann to Greenberg, Jan. 17, 1935, WA. For the proposed deportations in 1935 of Ahimeir and his jailed associates as "undesirables," see CO 733/278/75146/2, PRO.

4   "Strictly Confidential Report," Sept. 1934-Aug. 1935, file 215A, WJCA; Sherman, *Island Refuge*, 52n; Shirer, *The Rise and Fall of the Third Reich*, 387-390. In 1921 the League had appointed the famous Arctic explorer Fridtjof Nansen to focus on dealing with refugees from Russia, then those from Greece, Armenia and Assyria. With his death nine years later, the legal and political protection of refugees carrying special "Nansen passports" had been transferred to this office, a body directly responsible to, and receiving administrative funds from, the League Assembly.

5   McDonald to Warburg, Jan. 21, 1935, McDonald MSS; McDonald to Cecil, Jan. 22, 1935, file C1609/62, LNA; *Advocate for the Doomed*, 617-618; Simon to Cecil, Jan. 28, 1935, FO 371/18861, PRO; Chamberlain to McDonald, Jan. 23, 1935, file C1611/76, LNA.

6   Jewish Agency review, Dec. 9, 1934-Jan. 5, 1935, file C14/9/4, BDA; Kabha, *Itonut B'Ein HaSe'ara*, 126-128; JAEJ, Jan. 23 and 27, 1935.

7   Tazsir Jbara, *Palestinian Leader Hajj Amin al-Hussayni, Mufti of Jerusalem* (Princeton, 1985), 134-135; Haj Amin to Wauchope, Feb. 4, 1935, file N-295/6, ISA.

8   Schechtman, *Fighter and Prophet*, 251-252; HaYarden, Jan. 15, 1935. Jabotinsky's "The Iron Wall" first appeared in Russian in *Rasvyet* (Paris) on November 4, 1923, with a related essay on November 11. *HaAretz* published "The Iron Wall" in Hebrew translation on July 21, 1925, under the title "Parliament." Ahimeir would be released in early August after an eighteen-month imprisonment. He proceeded with Revisionist comrades to the Wailing Wall, where he offered up prayers for the well-being of Kook, Jabotinsky, and Horace Samuel (*JTA*, Aug. 5, 1935).

9   Schechtman, *Fighter and Prophet*, chap. 14; National Board, Jan. 30, 1935, HA; U.S. Zionist-Revisionists meeting, Feb. 7, 1935, HaTsahar-U.S. files, Box 2, JA; Hanokh Rosenblum, "Artsot-HaBrit V'Yehudeha B'Hashkafato Shel Ze'ev Jabotinsky," in *Ish BaSa'ar: Masot U'Mehkarim Al Ze'ev Jabotinsky*, ed. A. Bareli and P. Genossar (Sdeh Boker, 2004), 427-432. For Jabotinsky's address to the American Economic Committee on Palestine, see Minutes, Feb. 6, 1935, microfilm #24, Brandeis MSS. His response to Wise, where he emphatically championed "old-fashioned parliamentarism" over any "totalitarian State" and repeated the Revisionist contention that "in Palestine there is room for all the Jews who will ever need it and for all the Arabs with their progeny," is in *JTA*, Mar. 17, 1935.

10   Schechtman, *Fighter and Prophet*, 252, 275; *JTA*, Feb. 13, 1935; David Ben-Gurion, *Zikhronot* 2, 277-279.

11   Sa'adya Milikovsky Netanyahu, ed., *HaArakhot V'Tai'urim Shel Ishiyuto U'Peulotav Shel HaRav Natan Milikovsky Al Yedei Ishim Yedu'im B'nai Zemano* (n.p., n.d.); *HaTur*, Feb. 20, 1935; Kook to Dizengoff, Feb. 22, 1935, file 4-3737A, TAMA.

12   Wauchope-Shertok interview, Feb. 1, 1935, J1/6334/1, CZA; Ben-Gurion, *Zikhronot*, 279-284; A. Ruppin, *Memoirs, Diaries, Letters*, 267. Carthage, an ancient city-state on the northern shore of Africa, was tightly built under an aristocracy of nobles and wealthy merchants. Its greatest weakness lay in the rivalry of the leading families, who traditionally backed opposing policies.

13   McDonald memorandum, Feb. 12, 1935, A255/381, CZA.

14   Laski and Montefiore to Foreign Affairs Under-Secretary, Feb. 26, 1935, file C11/6/4/2, BDA; Battsek to Schiff, Feb. 27, 1935, file C1606/6, LNA.

15   Simon to Cecil, Jan. 28, 1935; Cecil to Simon, Jan. 29, 1935; and minutes; all in FO 371/18861, PRO; *Parliamentary Debates, House of Lords*, Feb. 6, 1935, vol. 95, 822-846.

16   London *Times*, Jan. 31, 1935, and Feb. 1, 1935; Joint Foreign Committee, Feb. 1935 report, Executive Minutes, BDA. Also see Lothian's lecture, Mar. 5, 1935, file 8/371, Chatham House Archives.

17   Wauchope-Shertok interview, Feb. 18, 1935, J1/6334/I, CZA.

18   David Ben-Gurion, "The Land Problem With Special Regard to Negev and Akaba," June 4, 1935, file 118, Mack MSS. British Minister-Resident Cox continued to oppose Jewish settlement in Transjordan. See Cox note, Apr. 4, 1935, S25/22774, CZA.

19   *Palestine Post*, Mar. 28, 1935; J. C. Hurewitz, *The Struggle for Palestine* (New York, 1950), 61; Porath, *The Palestinian Arab National Movement*, 131.

20   Mohl to Brandeis, Mar. 8, 1935, microfilm #24, Brandeis MSS. The Palestine Economic Corporation (connected to the American Economic Committee for Palestine), created by the Brandeis-Mack group in 1926 to provide financial aid to the yishuv's agricultural and industrial growth, had also enabled an increasing number of Jewish immigrants to become self-supporting

citizens. See *Palestine: A Study of Jewish, Arab and British Policies*, 345-347.

21 Downie-Fellman interviews, Mar. 5 and 7, 1935, microfilm #24, Brandeis MSS. To Colonial Office colleague John Martin, Downie declared that "the Zionists will never succeed in Palestine because they killed Jesus Christ" (Martin interview with the author, June 20, 1976).

22 Shirer, *The Rise and Fall of the Third Reich*, 391-392; Kuhn to Pop, Mar. 22, 1935, Frederick Kuhn MSS, Special Collections, Butler Library, Columbia University; Hull to Dodd, Nov. 8, 1935, 867N.5562/11, U.S. State Department Archives, Suitland, MD.

23 Ben-Gurion, *Zikhronot*, 290-299; Schechtman, *Fighter and Prophet*, 253-254; Teveth, *Ben-Gurion*, 492-493.

24 *Moshav HaPoel HaTsiyoni B'Yerushalayim, 27 Adar 2–5 Nisan 5695* (Jerusalem, 1935); Schechtman, *Fighter and Prophet*, 276. Jabotinsky also contributed a three-part series of articles adumbrating his views for the *Jewish Daily Bulletin* (*JTA*, Apr. 10-12, 1935).

25 Weizmann to Ruppin, Apr. 5, 1935, WA. Weizmann's warnings a few days earlier at the Va'ad HaPoel were reprinted in *Do'ar HaYom*, Apr. 2, 1935.

26 Al-Husseini to Wauchope, Apr. 9, 1935, S25/22789, CZA.

27 Grand Mufti's speech, published in *Al-Jami'a Al-Arabiya*, April 16, 1935, file N-295/6, ISA.

28 *Palestine*, 774-775; *Palestine Post*, Apr. 19, 1935.

29 *Palestine*, 775, 778; Gelber, *Shoroshei HaHavatselet*, 133; Lukasz Hirszowicz, *The Third Reich and the Arab East* (London, 1966), 13. The British expelled Reichert in June 1939.

30 Teveth, *Ben-Gurion*, 494-495; National Board, June 5, 1935, HA; Ben-Gurion, "Hazona Shel Eilat," *Eilat, HaKinus HaArtsi HaShoma-Asar L'Yediat HaAretz* (Jerusalem, 1963), 1-2; JAEJ, Apr. 21, 1935, CZA. The first biblical reference to Eilat is in *Deuteronomy* 2:8. Later ones refer to King Solomon (*Kings* 1, 9:26, as "Eilot") and Azarya (*Kings* 2, 14:22). The Edomites later reconquered Eilat (*Kings* 2, 16:6). Also see *Chronicles* 2, 8:17. The first biblical mentions of Kadesh Barnea and of Beersheva are in *Numbers* 32:8 and *Genesis* 21:14. The most famous photograph of Israel's 1948 War of Independence is known as the "hanging of the ink flag." The picture was snapped in March 1949, just as the war came to an end. It shows a young man shimmying up a pole to hang a homemade flag of Israel in the barren desert outpost of Um Rash-Rash. The actual hanger of the ink flag was a twenty year-old soldier named Avraham "Bren" Aden. Aden went on to become one of Israel's legendary commanders, including commanding the tanks that crossed the Suez Canal over the bridge that Ariel Sharon laid in the 1973 Yom Kippur War. Operating on the west bank of the canal in the Egyptian heartland, Aden's forces encircled half the Egyptian Army in less than a week.

31 J. Wise to S. Wise, Apr. 8, 1935, microfilm #24, Brandeis MSS; Lazaron to MacArthur, Apr. 10, 1935, with attached April report, microfilm #1928,

Warburg MSS; Joint Foreign Committee report, Apr. 10, 1935, Joint Foreign Committee files, AJCA; Wedgwood to Elias, Apr. 12, 1935, Pro-Palestine Federation of America files, Box 2, ZA. For the activities of the Pro-Palestine Federation of America since its founding in 1930, see Elias to Wise, June 24, 1937, file 87, Robert Szold MSS, ZA.

32 Schechtman, *Fighter and Prophet*, 276-278; *HaYarden*, Apr. 28, 1935; Rappard to Jabotinsky, May 1, 1935, A508/10, CZA.

33 Baker to Bowman, Apr. 30, 1935; Antonius to Murray, Sept. 20, 1935; both in Crane MSS. Four months earlier, following the State Department's advice to reiterate its stand that the Balfour Declaration intended the Jews to have no more than a home in Palestine, Roosevelt emphasized to the Zionist Organization of America's president his "deep and abiding interest" in all that pertains to the development "of the great conception of creating in Palestine a home of happiness and prosperity for those of the people of the Jewish race who turn to the land of their fathers" (Moore to McIntyre, Dec. 28, 1934; Roosevelt to Rothenberg, Jan. 10, 1935; both in PPF 601, FDRL).

34 Meeting, May 2, 1935, Records of Meetings, Box 3, Council on Foreign Relations Archives (hereafter CFRA), New York City; Mack to Frankfurter, May 3, 1935, microfilm #266, Brandeis MSS.

35 Hexter to Warburg, May 27, 1935, microfilm #1926, Warburg MSS; A.S. (Sasson) memorandum, May 15, 1935, S25/3457, CZA.

36 Ben-Gurion, *Zikhronot*, 305-314, 341; ZOA Administrative Committee, May 19, 1935, ZA. For Ben-Gurion's memorandum to Brandeis about the Negev and Akaba, see Ben-Gurion, *Zikhronot*, 321-326. According to Robert Szold, treasurer of the Palestine Endowment Fund, Brandeis gave about $750,000 to the Fund during his lifetime (Szold interview, Nov. 13, 1961, file SC-12240, AJA).

37 Ben-Gurion, *Zikhronot*, 314-315, 317-318, 320-321; Warburg to Hexter, June 4, 1935, file 3/7, Hexter MSS; Kahn memorandum, June 5, 1935, microfilm #1931, and Ben-Gurion–Laski-Hexter interview, June 28, 1935, microfilm #1929; both in Warburg MSS; Laski to Brandeis, June 12, 1935, file C14/9/10, BDA; Conversation, June 16, 1935, file 88, Mowshowitz MSS.

38 Ben-Gurion, *Zikhronot*, 320; Locker-Weizmann conversation, May 26, 1935, WA.

39 Richard Meinertzhagen, *Middle East Diary, 1917*-1956 (London, 1959), 152-153; "The Position in Germany," June 3, 1935, WA; Memorandum, June 10, 1935; Weizmann to Meinertzhagen, June 11, 1935; both in L13/165, CZA.

40 Phipps to Simon, May 10, 1935, FO 371/18861, PRO; Speech, May 12, 1935, VII, Box 6, Dorothy Thompson MSS, Syracuse University, Syracuse, NY; *Ambassador Dodd's Diary*, 256; Baeck speech, May 25, 1935, file 325, Box 44, Youth Aliya MSS, HA; George Messersmith, "The Situation in Central Europe," May 7, 1935, Records of Meetings, Box 3, CFRA.

41 Ben-Gurion, *Zikhronot*, 300; Lourie to Kohn, May 14, 1935, Z4/17122, CZA;

Shertok–Wauchope interview, May 22, 1935, microfilm #1927, Warburg MSS. For Namier's earlier articulation of principal arguments against a Legislative Council and in favor of parity, see Draft, Feb. 5, 1935, Z4/17122, CZA.

42   Weizmann–Cunliffe-Lister interview, June 4, 1935, microfilm #1929, Warburg MSS.

43   Wauchope–Shertok interview, June 12, 1935, microfilm #1929, Warburg MSS.

44   Rose, *Chaim Weizmann*, 279-285; Shertok to Weizmann, June 9, 1935, Weizmann to Shertok, June 17, 1935, both in Z4/17122, CZA. MacDonald to Wauchope, June 14, 19, and 22, 1935, CO 733/275/75102/I; Parkinson minute, Sept. 20, 1936, CO 733/314/75528/II; all in PRO.

45   Shertok–Wauchope interview, May 22, 1935; Shertok–Wauchope interview, June 16, 1935; both in microfilm #1927, Warburg MSS. Ben-Gurion, *Zikhronot*, 329-331. Wauchope most probably had in mind the biblical text in *Numbers* 30:3. Shertok still hoped that Wauchope would continue as High Commissioner "for a number of years to come," eliciting Wauchope's gratitude and sense that their mutual feeling of "trust and friendship" was based "on the sure knowledge that each is working for principle" (Shertok to Wauchope, June 28, 1935; Wauchope to Shertok, June 29, 1935; both in microfilm #24, Brandeis MSS).

46   Wauchope to MacDonald, June 28, 1935, CO 733/275/75102/I, PRO; "Oved" report, June 21, 1935, ZOA assorted files, ZA; Auster report, June 24, 1935, A297/25, CZA; Ben Gurion, *Zikhronot*, 329-330, 335, 338-340.

47   Rose, *The Gentile Zionists*, 58; Lothian to Weizmann, June 18, 1935, L13/165, CZA; Diary, June 4, 1935, Armstrong MSS; Laski to Adler, June 17, 1935, microfilm #1929, Warburg MSS; Conference, June 18, 1935, and Adler to Laski, June 26, 1935, both in file P13/2/13, CAHJP; Eva Reading, *For the Record: The Memoirs of Eva, Marchioness of Reading* (London, 1972), 170.

48   Agronsky-Wauchope interview, July 3, 1935, A209/2, CZA.

49   Shertok-Abdullah talk, July 11, 1935, S25/10122, CZA; Aaron S. Klieman, "The Arab States and Palestine," in E. Kedourie and S. G. Haim, eds., *Zionism and Arabism in Palestine and Israel* (London, 1982), 125.

50   Shertok–Wauchope interview, July 16, 1935, microfilm #1928, Warburg MSS; MacDonald to Wauchope, July 22, 1935, S25/22724, CZA.

51   Ben-Gurion, *Zikhronot*, 348-353, 355-360.

52   Wauchope interview with Haj Amin and Jamal Husseini, July 22, 1935, S25/22724, CZA; Wauchope to Parkinson, July 22, 1935, CO 733/275/75102/I, PRO.

53   Wauchope-Nashahsibi interview, July 3, 1935, S25/22724, CZA.

54   *Manchester Guardian*, July 7, 1935; Meinertzhagen, *Middle East Diary*, 154; Harry to Billie, July 15, 1935, microfilm #1931, Warburg MSS; Montefiore statement, July 21, 1935, Minutes of meetings, BDA.

55   Monty Noam Penkower, "Honorable Failures against Nazi Germany," 256-262.
56   Ibid., 262.
57   Husseinis–Wauchope interview, July 30, 1935, S25/22724, CZA; Wauchope to MacDonald, Aug. 5, 1935, CO 733/275/75102/I, PRO.
58   Ben-Gurion–Shertok-Wauchope interview, Aug. 7, 1935, microfilm #1928, Warburg MSS. For a contemporary report on attacks on Jews in Germany, see Hoffman, "German Non-Aryans," Sept. 1, 1935, Presbyterian Historical Association, Philadelphia.
59   O.A.G. (Hall) to Wauchope, extract, attached to Air Staff memorandum, Aug. 16, 1935, and Air Officer Commanding letter, Aug. 19, 1935, all in S25/22774, CZA.
60   Ben-Gurion, Zikhronot, 381, 384-395, 411-417; National Board, June 5, 1935, HA; Ben-Gurion to Zuckerman, July 2, 1935, A180/129, CZA; Meetings, Aug. 15, 1935, microfilm #1929; Laski to d'Avigdor-Goldsmid, Aug. 19, 1935, microfilm #1926; both in Warburg MSS.
61   HaKongres HaTsiyoni HaYud Tet V'HaMoshav HaRevi'i Shel Moetset HaSokhnut HaYehudit (Tel Aviv, 1937), xxxiv-xlii, 1-8, 11-12, 14-35,43-56.
62   Ibid., 57-356; Dan Omer, B'Ikvot Amud HaEsh (Tel Aviv, 1981), 92. For Ussishkin and Ben-Gurion's speeches at the Political Committee on August 29, see S25/10140, CZA.
63   Ben-Gurion, Zikhronot, 408-410, 417-419. Wise, who had opposed Weizmann in 1931, already had concluded on the eve of the Congress that Weizmann would probably become president, "though if so with limited power and restricted rights to do mischief." Warburg wished for Weizmann's return to the office, thinking that views like Ben-Gurion's on the Agency Executive would subsequently not prevail, and that Weizmann would work for unity with the non-Zionists and the original 50-50 principle could be preserved. Wise to Levine, Aug. 18, 1935, Box 1671, Joseph Levine MSS, AJA; Warburg to Karpf, Aug. 28, 1935, microfilm #1926, Warburg MSS.
64   Ben-Gurion, Zikhronot, 419-420; Wise to Newman, Sept. 27, 1935, Box 117, Wise MSS; HaKongres HaTsiyoni HaYud Tet, 382-385, 486-488, 495-502.
65   Ben-Gurion, Zikhronot, 423-437; HaKongres HaTsiyoni HaYud Tet, part 2, 3-79; Ben-Gurion, Zikhronot 3 (Tel Aviv, 1973), 77; National Board, June 26, 1935, HA; Landauer to Jacobs, Aug. 27, 1935, in Zena Harman, "History of Youth Aliya," vol. 2, Box 2, Youth Aliya MSS; National Board, Nov. 6, 27-28, 1935; Jacobs address, "The History of Hadassah's Assocation with Youth Aliya," May 7, 1957, file 286, Box 39, Youth Aliya; all in HA.
66   HaKongres HaTsiyoni HaYudTet, part 2, 66-69.
67   JTA, Sept. 9, 1935; Wauchope to Jabotinsky, Aug. 5, 1935, file 2/23/3/1A, JA; Schechtman, Fighter and Prophet, 282-290; de Haas to Brandeis, Sept. 23 and 25, 1935, microfilm #39, Jacob de Haas MSS, ZA. The phrase regarding Torah from Zion, found in Isaiah 2:3, is used in the Jewish prayer service when a Torah is taken from the Holy Ark for reading from the scroll. Two

3. Test Cases for Zionism

months after this final break with the WZO, the Agency's aliya department informed all Palestine offices abroad that no more certificate privileges would be given to Betar as a movement, but that all must apply henceforth as individuals. Gruenbaum and Barlas letter, Nov. 10, 1935, published on page one of *HaYarden*, Nov. 20, 1935.

68 C.I.D. report, Aug. 24, 1935, FO 371/18957, PRO; Hall-National Defense Party interview, Sept. 10, 1935, S25/22789, CZA.

69 Friedländer, *Nazi Germany and the Jews*, 141-165; Sherman, *Island Refuge*, 58-61; *Palestine Post*, Nov. 15, 1935.

70 Weizmann to Warburg, Sept. 20, 1935, WA; Warburg to McDonald, Sept. 18, 1935, microfilm #1927, Warburg MSS.; Warburg to Weizmann, Oct. 10, 1935, Z4/17026A, CZA; Waldman to Laski, Oct. 1, 1935, microfilm #1926, Warburg MSS; Waldman memorandum on his sojourn abroad, June 29–Sept. 17, 1935, Chronos file, AJCA.

71 Wise to Beneš, Sept. 18, 1935, file 214A, WJCA; Press release, Sept. 22, 1935, Va'ad HaHatsala files, Agudas HaRabbonim Archives, New York City; Special meeting, Sept. 24, 1935, Joint Foreign Committee files, AJCA.

72 Ben-Gurion, *Zikhronot*, 440-442; Weizmann–MacDonald interview, Sept. 25, 1935, WA.

73 Report, Sept. 28, 1935, FO 371/18957, PRO. Arslan was then engaged in convening a European Muslim Congress, held that October in Geneva (Martin Kramer, *Islam Assembled* [New York, 1986], Chap. 12). For continuing Italian efforts to court Arab support with a strong anti-Zionist stand, see Epstein memorandum on his visit to Rome, Nov. 1935, S25/22648, CZA.

74 Shertok to London Executive, Oct. 3, 1935, Jewish Agency files, ZA.

75 Ben-Gurion, *Zikhronot*, 445; Weizmann to Baer, Oct. 6, 1935, in Chaim Weizmann, *The Letters and Papers of Chaim Weizmann*, vol. 17, ed. Y. Rosenthal (Jerusalem, 1979), 24-25. For the response of the Mapai Political Committee, see Ben-Gurion, *Zikhronot*, 446-453.

76 Shertok-Hall interview, Oct. 9, 1935, Shertok to London, Oct. 10, 1935, both in microfilm #1926, Warburg MSS; Shertok to Hall, Oct. 14, 1935, A24/194, CZA.

77 Mills to Foreign Office, Oct. 6, 1935, FO 371/18859; Baxter minute, Oct. 18, 1935, FO 371/18862; both in PRO. Meeting at New Court, Oct. 9, 1935, microfilm #1927, Warburg MSS.

78 *Refugees and Rescue*, 42, 45; McDonald to Warburg, Oct. 10, 1935, Warburg files, McDonald MSS; McDonald statement to Permanent Committee, Oct. 16, 1935, A306/59, CZA. McDonald's letter to Warburg reached Roosevelt via Herbert Lehman. For FDR's response, see *Refugees and Rescue*, 71-72.

79 Weizmann–Wauchope interview, Oct. 20, 1935; Weizmann–Cunliffe-Lister interview, Oct. 14, 1935; both in microfilm #1931, Warburg MSS; Ben-Gurion, *Zikhronot*, 455-456

80 Weizmann to MacDonald, Oct. 13, 1935, microfilm #1931, Warburg MSS;

Ben-Gurion, *Zikhronot*, 466-475. For Abraham and Isaac digging wells at Beersheva, see *Genesis* 21:25-31, 26:32-33.

81   Peled testimony, June 1951, file P28/27, Dinur MSS; Yosef Avidan, *BaDerekh L'Tsahal, Zikhronot* (Tel-Aviv, 1977 ed.), 70-74; Nashashibi to Wauchope, October 16, 1935, S25/27789, and Hall (O.A.G.)–Supreme Moslem Council interview, Oct. 18, 1935, S25/22737, both in CZA. For Salah's National Bloc Party, see Lesch, *Arab Politics in Palestine*, 112-113. The Arab riots of March and April 1920 focused on Jerusalem and the Upper Galilee settlements. The May 1921 riots began in Jerusalem and were followed by large-scale attacks elsewhere, killing 47 Jews and wounding 140 more. The August 1929 riots included the killing of 67 Jews in Hebron, 34 in Jerusalem, 17 in Safed; a total of 133 Jews were murdered and more than 300 wounded. The settlements of Be'er Tuvia and Hulda were destroyed. These riots led the then High Commissioners to suspend Jewish immigration. Haj Amin emerged as an uncompromising opponent of the yishuv and the mandatory government. Although he had been tried and convicted in absentia by a British court to 15 years for his role in inflaming the murderous 1920 riots, he was appointed by High Commissioner Herbert Samuel, seeking to placate Arab nationalist opinion, as Grand Mufti of Jerusalem. In 1922, he was elected president of the Supreme Moslem Council, but continued in the office on a permanent basis. For Haj Amin's role in instigating these riots, see chap. 1, n21.

82   Air Headquarters Intelligence report, Nov. 1, 1935, S25/22735, CZA; *Palestine Post*, Oct. 25, 1935.

83   Hall–Arab party leaders interview, Oct. 23, 1935, S25/22737, CZA; Ben-Gurion, *Zikhronot*, 486-490; Government memorandum on Arslan cable and letter, Sept. 24, 1935, S25/22713, CZA; *Manchester Guardian*, Oct. 22, 1935; McDonald to Warburg, Oct. 23, 1935, AR 7/62, Box 1, LBI; Air Headquarters Intelligence report, Nov. 1, 1935, S25/22735, CZA.

84   Matthews, *Constructing an Empire*, 238-239; *Palestine Post*, Nov. 3, 1935.

85   Ben-Gurion to Mack, Jan. 6, 1936, file 20, Mack MSS; Yehoshua Porat, *MiMehumot L'Merida, HaTenua HaLeumit HaAravit HaPalestina'it, 1929-1939* (Tel-Aviv, 1978), 163-165; Shai Lachman, "Arab Rebellion and Terrorism in Palestine, 1929-1939: The Case of Sheikh Izz al-Din al-Qassam and His Movement," in E. Kedourie and S.G. Haim, eds., *Zionism and Arabism in Palestine and Israel* (London, 1982), 52-99. Qassam would later be considered the founding father of the Palestinian Arab *jihad*, linking the Islamic concept of a holy war to the struggle for national liberation, as well as the pioneer of Palestinian Arab armed revolutionary thought (Joseph Nevo, "Palestinian-Arab Violent Activity during the 1930's," in Michael J. Cohen and Martin Kolinsky, eds.. *Britain and the Middle East in the 1930s: Security Problems, 1935-39* [London, 1992], 173-175). Since October 2001, the armed branch of Hamas, the Iz al-Din al-Qassam brigades, has fired thousands of Qassams, steel rockets filled with explosives, from Gaza against

Israeli civilians.

86 A.A. (Epstein) report from "P.D.," Nov. 20, 1935; A.S. (Sasson) report from "Oved," Nov. 21, 1935; both in A24/194, CZA.

87 Wauchope-Arab leaders interview, Nov. 25, 1935, CO 733/278/75156/II, PRO; Cohen report, Nov. 26, 1935, A24/194, CZA.

88 Ben-Gurion, *Zikhronot*, 529-533. Joseph Trumpeldor and five other men under his command were killed in a Bedouin attack on March 1, 1920, against the Upper Galilee settlement Tel-Hai. His last words, "Never mind, it is worthwhile to die for the country" (better known in the formulation by the Hebrew writer Yosef Hayim Brenner, "it is good to die for our country"), achieved legendary status within Zionist ranks. The Right, particularly through the Betar (Brit Trumpeldor) Revisionist-Zionist youth movement, stressed the defenders' armed resistance, while the Left emphasized their settling of the land. See Yael Zerubavel, *Recovered Roots, Collective Memory and the Making of Israeli National Tradition* (Chicago, 1995), 148-157.

89 Ben-Gurion, *Zikhronot*, 548-549; Ben-Gurion to Mack, Jan. 6, 1936, file 20, Mack MSS.

90 Thomas-Wedgwood interview, Dec. 6, 1935, CO 733/275/75102/III, PRO; Lourie to Kohn, Dec. 9, 1935, S25/6298, CZA; Ben-Gurion, *Zikhronot* 3, 2; Lourie to Shertok, Dec. 20, 1935, S25/1378, CZA.

91 Executive Council, Dec. 16, 1935, file M-4754/31, ISA; Wauchope–Arab representatives interview, Dec. 21, 1935, S25/22724, CZA; Wauchope–Jewish representatives interview, Dec. 22, 1935, file 154, Central Agudas Israel Archives; Ben-Gurion, *Zikhronot* 2, 552-558. By the end of 1935, the Fifth Aliya (1929-1939) had witnessed an entry of 30,000 Jews from Germany, about one-fifth of the total immigration that was successfully absorbed into Palestine.

92 Wauchope-Arab representatives interview, Dec. 21, 1935, S25/22724; Dec. 23, 1935 report, A158/31; both in CZA.

93 Wauchope to Thomas, Dec. 23, 1935, CO 733/275/75102/II, and C.I.D. report, Dec. 4, 1935, FO 371/20018, both in PRO. Talk with Ragheb Nashashibi, Dec. 8, 1935, S25/3051; Joint Bureau News, July 2, 1935, S25/3139; Joint Bureau News, Dec. 15, 1935, and Talk with Jamal al-Husseini, Dec. 3, 1935, both in S25/3051; A.S. (Sasson) report, Dec. 22, 1935, A24/194; Auni Bey to Wauchope, Dec. 23, 1935, and Auni Bey- Wauchope interview, Dec. 30, 1935, both in S25/22789; all in CZA. Charging that the Jews "are a source of weakness to any Power contracting the enmity of others for their sake," and that the Arabs were frightened at the Jews' great increase in number and the Jewish declaration of intending to "build a Jewish Kingdom in Palestine," Abdullah sought to have his delegate explore the situation in Egypt. In reply, Wauchope thought that this "might well be very seriously misrepresented" (Dec. 1935 correspondence, S25/22774, CZA).

94 Weizmann to Marks, Dec. 1, 1935, Z4/17098, CZA; Weizmann to Marks,

Dec. 15, 1935, WA; Weizmann remarks, Dec. 19, 1935, A203/187, CZA; Weizmann to Lugard and to Rappard, Dec. 22, 1935, and Weizmann to Melchett, Dec. 23, 1935; both in WA.

95   Weizmann to Marks, Dec. 15, 1935, WA; *Jewish Telegraphic Agency*, Dec. 5-7, 1935; McDonald to Warburg, Nov. 7, 1935, microfilm #1927, Warburg MSS; Rosenblüth to Landauer, Nov. 13, 1935, S25/9809, CZA; Adler-Rudel to Marks, Nov. 26, 1935, McDonald to Warburg, Nov. 15, 1935, and M. Warburg-McDonald conversation, Dec. 28, 1935, all in High Commissioner files, McDonald MSS. Max Warburg had earlier contemplated refugee settlement in Cyprus and in Syria (Kahn to F. Warburg, May 11, 1935, microfilm #1930, Warburg MSS). Sieff, like Marks, supported the idea that the WZO should "encourage and welcome" the assistance of groups outside the Zionist movement, such as Bearsted's "aggressive initiative" (Sieff to Weizmann, Dec. 30, 1935, Israel Sieff MSS).

96   JAEJ, Nov. 23, 1935; Landauer to Ruppin, Dec. 27, 1935, S7/256; Ben-Gurion at Va'ad Leumi, Dec. 11, 1935, J1/7236; all in CZA; Weizmann to Sieff, Dec. 25, 1935, WA; *Palestine Post*, Dec. 22, 1935; JAEJ, Dec. 31, 1935, CZA. Lord Bearsted first hosted the group on November 20, and eventually agreed to join on a mission to the United States the next month (McDonald to Warburg, Nov. 21, 1935, Box 1, AR7162, LBI).

97   London *Times* and *New York Times*, Dec. 30, 1935. For the drafting of this letter and its annex, see Penkower, "Honorable Failures," 265-275.

98   Weizmann to Rappard, Dec. 29, 1935, WA. Rosenblüth to Weizmann, Dec. 11, 1935, L13/105; Weizmann to Samuel, Dec. 31, 1935, Z4/17025; DBG (Ben-Gurion) to Marks, Dec. 31, 1935, S25/9756; all in CZA.

99   *Palestine Post*, Dec, 31, 1835.

100   Ben-Gurion, *Zikhronot* 2, 570; Weizmann to Marks, Dec. 15, 1935, WA.

4. Enveloping Shadows

Ben-Gurion could not imagine a better celebration of the New Year 1936 than the news that His Majesty's Government had just extended Wauchope's term for another five years. The official announcement, he wrote to the High Commissioner on January 1, signaled a year of peace, stability, and development, which every Palestinian resident would welcome "with a full heart." The record admission into the country of more than 60,000 Jews in 1935, an achievement which reflected Jewry's combined "tragic fate and creative ability," would not have been possible without Wauchope's goodwill and wise leadership. "Serious disputes" remained over the Legislative Council and the administration's obligations as regards Jewish immigration and settlement, Ben-Gurion acknowledged. Yet Wauchope's awareness of all of Palestine's general needs and those of Jewry in particular, his success to date, and his willingness to hear and understand the Zionists' perspective—all offered "the best guarantee" that the Jewish Agency could bridge its outlook and that of the mandate government.[1]

Privately, the chairman of the Agency Executive harbored considerable worries regarding that gap. Aside from Wauchope's insistence on establishing the Council, the government had just proposed raising the entry requirement for "capitalists" from £1,000, which had been the standard for the past ten years, to £2,000. Not since the Passfield White Paper had the question of "non-cooperation" with the mandatory assumed such importance, Ben-Gurion warned a special meeting of the yishuv's political parties and organizations. Immigration Commissioner Eric Mills, claiming not to be antisemitic but an objective judge, did not believe in a great Jewish national power or ascribe importance to a large Palestinian Jewish settlement. Ben-Gurion concluded (as did Shertok) that the complex international situation, sparking England's fear of war and a desire to appease the Arabs, explained Wauchope's stand.

The Zionist movement must switch to a strong political offensive, Ben-Gurion argued, using the German Jewish crisis as "a lever" in order to press for large immigration to Palestine. McDonald had done "almost nothing" for the good of German Jewry—he could not, but he performed "a historic service" to the Jewish nation with his Letter of Resignation. The public and newspaper response in Great Britain to that document demonstrated interest and sympathy for the plight of the Jews in Germany. The Agency had to shift its attention from the Colonial Office to Baldwin and Anthony Eden, the new Foreign Secretary; Great Britain remained the center for decision. Additional efforts, Ben-Gurion posited, should be made in France, Germany's main protagonist, as well as in Geneva, in countries like Poland and Rumania that wished their Jews to leave, and with Prime Minister Smuts of South Africa.[2]

Indeed, warmly endorsing McDonald's Letter and annex as a "damning indictment" of Germany, a number of the world's leading newspapers called on Berlin to restore full equality to Jews and others oppressed by the Nazi government. The London *Times* thought it "scarcely credible" that Germany's leaders could remain much longer insensitive to public opinion abroad and to the injury being done to German interests internationally; the *Prager Presse* of Czechoslovakia characterized the German attempt to refute McDonald's accusations and shift the blame to the League as "far from convincing." A *New York Times* editorial judged that the accused in this case were bound "to answer at the bar of moral justice"; the *Boston Globe* considered McDonald's final statement "a service to the human conscience to which he appeals." Regarding the document as a parallel to the Lytton report on the Japanese invasion of Manchuria in 1931, the *Nation* wrote that McDonald's departure "may well prove to be the most effective action of his two years' service." The British Foreign Office thought otherwise, considering the Letter "an unwise document, which did a disservice to the real interests of the Jews in Germany," and in which "the guiding hand of Zionism was apparent."[3]

After two days of silence, the Third Reich news agency commented that the nations of the world had no right to criticize Germany's treatment of her Jewish population while Germans were being persecuted in other countries. The *Völkischer Beobachter* laid the blame for McDonald's action on "the countless complaints from all countries of Europe about the German refugees," who were seen as "human garbage." This official organ of the Nazi party resented the League's "insolence" in supposing that it could deal with domestic German conditions, and advised the League to occupy itself with the Jewish persecution of Christians in various countries outside of Germany. A number of other German newspapers attributed the Letter of Resignation to "Bolshevik circles," which had made Geneva "an instrument of their policy." After reports from foreign countries showed a strong positive reaction to the Letter, the *Völkischer Beobachter* charged that the real cause of the resignation was lack of funds, and that Soviet Russia, as well as the Freemasons, had inspired McDonald's action to hide this fact.[4]

Eric Mills and Frank Foley both agreed with McDonald's assertion that the exodus of Germany's remaining 430,000 Jews was an international responsibility, but they differed over Palestine as the principal haven. Palestine's Immigration Commissioner hoped that the Samuel-Bearsted-Marks venture would lay "no emphasis" on the possibilities of the Holy Land. Mills foresaw the need for "clear sighted prudence" on his part, he wrote on January 11 to Bentwich, who was about to head the Emigration Department of the newly created Council on German Jewry, since "a difficult time" likely lay ahead in the Holy Land and "the highest degree of diplomacy is essential." Rejecting Bentwich's appeal to try to "stretch" again Palestine's absorptive capacity by transferring the property of German Jews there, he recommended Jewish refugee movement to the British Dominions. This would allow the Empire to "enrich itself," Mills added, since no "reservoir" existed in the United Kingdom from which to "renew supplies of British population" in Canada and Australia. HMG's main passport officer in Berlin, on the other hand, urged that the bulk of emigrating Jews be sent to Palestine, that a larger labor schedule be allowed, and that the Ha'avara scheme be enlarged. The Third Reich's antisemitic persecution, Foley's memorandum to Whitehall advised, "was as relentless as ever though perhaps more subtle in method," and he noted a "definite disposition on the part of the Economics Ministry to do everything possible to facilitate emigration of Jews, that is to say, to find a solution of the transfer problem."[5]

Mills's colleagues shared his perspective. On January 2, Wauchope assembled top advisors in order to discuss the current situation in Palestine, including how to check the incitement to violence by Arab youth under the direction of Zu'aiter in Nablus. Although police investigation did not corroborate reports that some sheikhs around Jerusalem and Hebron intended to resume the terrorist activity Qassam had initiated, the group decided to reinvigorate internal security programs and to check further on the possibility of new "disturbances." (The Agency's

Arab Department heard concurrently of efforts by Zu'aiter, Rashid al-Haj Ibrahim, and other extremists at recruiting members to emulate the methods of Qassam's band.) The administration also insisted that the Jewish State Party, when legally registering as a new political entity once it broke away from the Revisionists' World Union, change its formulation from "the re-establishment of a Jewish State in Palestine based on the Jewish majority" to "the re-establishment of a Jewish National Home." As for Agency lobbying in League corridors, the British insisted to the Mandates Section that Nahum Goldmann, recognized by the last WZO Congress as the Jewish Agency's representative there, substitute "à Geneve" for "auprès de la Societé des Nations" in his official title.[6]

Non-Zionist initiatives to aid German Jewry, and particularly the Samuel-Bearsted-Marks trip to America, also exercised the Zionist leadership. Writing to Marks on January 7, Weizmann emphasized that "we should be the guiding spirit in their work." New organizations, "springing up like mushrooms," weakened the Agency just when the high percentage of hired Arab labor was creating Jewish unemployment. It was the WZO's duty to keep "a very tight grip" on the Ha'avara, which might "canalize" German-Jewish money into Palestine. The "philanthropic colonization" of a non-Zionist body like PICA had no place in Palestine. Weizmann did not trust Max Warburg's judgment as regards a projected Liquidation Bank, or the results of his negotiations with the German authorities. Since Marks turned down the request from the Agency Executive in Jerusalem that he visit Palestine for a discussion before departing for the United States, Weizmann urgently asked his long-time friend not to commit himself to any scheme "before we have had full opportunity of thrashing it out." He considered the Agency Executive's decision that Kaplan attempt to reach an agreement in London with the non-Zionists to be "a fatal error": in the best circumstance, it would only be a discussion, in the worst, an argument.[7]

In Weizmann's opinion, the Agency especially had to take an intransigent attitude regarding the Legislative Council. Any attempt to divide Jewish opinion on this proposal, he told Wauchope on January 10, would meet with the Zionists' "vigorous opposition." To Melchett, Weizmann observed that HMG had reneged on Ramsay MacDonald's original agreement, from 1931, to parity. Malcolm MacDonald, the former Prime Minister's son, although originally "an ardent advocate" of equality in representation on the Council, had proven to be "a weak man and broken reed" as Colonial Secretary by accepting Wauchope's argument that the Arabs would never accept that principle. Thus the project in its present form was adopted. Former Colonial Secretary and currently Conservative MP Leopold Amery agreed with the Agency's objections, Weizmann noted, and even Samuel, "the worst offender in this case," had "unbent."[8]

The Council's fundamental defect, Weizmann wrote to Rappard, was that the Jews were to be reduced to the status of a "national minority," rather than the mandate's "basic inspiration" that the Jews were "to enjoy in Palestine a status of national freedom." Worse, they would be faced by a solid Arab majority "which maintains complete hostility to all our efforts and achievements—however much the Arabs may have benefited from them." Further, the Council was hardly likely to make for interracial peace, since vital questions such as immigration and land would be up for discussion, and the administration inevitably would seek compromise and make concessions to the yishuv's detriment. Word had also been received recently that the government was about to impose further restrictions on Jewish land purchase, just as it appeared determined to double the amount required of immigrants of the capitalist class. "We now seem to be faced with an iron wall in every direction," Weizmann concluded.[9]

Three mass meetings in Vienna on January 9 protested against the proposed creation of a Legislative Council in Palestine. The majority of the speakers, who represented various Zionist movements, were outspoken in their criticism of British policy. Gruenbaum, for example, charged that Palestine ought not to be used as "an object of barter" in the interests in British policy, while Dr. Sokal of the Jewish workers declared that England was sacrificing Palestine to her Imperial interests. Revisionists had such a large crowd on the same evening that the police had to control the entrances to that hall. Two leading articles in the pro-Catholic Viennese newspaper *Reichspost*, asserting that Catholics in Palestine were being "swamped" by Jewish emigration, called on the mandatory power to issue a declaration in which "the traditional rights of the Palestinian Catholics are officially recognized," a declaration that would become part of international law with the League's approval. One week later, Cardinal Theodor Innitzer, Archbishop of the Austrian capital, returned to that theme, demanding that which has been sealed with the "blood of Christians throughout centuries should not be surrendered to party caprice."[10]

The Jewish Agency had some knowledge of London's intentions. Its "authentic information" about legislation aimed to further limit land sales, which Weizmann also shared with Sieff, Namier, and Melchett, emanated from a Cabinet meeting of January 15 that approved this law in principle. The Agency did not know that Thomas, who continued to dislike the present Council plan, had put forward two suggestions to the Cabinet five days earlier that he hoped would lead to the Arabs' rejection. The first insisted on the participation of women, the second on limiting the Council's Jurisdiction. At that same meeting, the Cabinet agreed to Wauchope's suggestion that the Council's proceedings and authority be so limited as to deprive its members of any decisive power. Unaware of the latter decision, a very anxious Weizmann was convinced that "they are making our life here a misery," and he concluded that HMG was making a "studied attempt to crystallize the National Home."[11]

The Colonial Office had its own concerns, which surfaced on January 15 during an interdepartmental discussion on German refugees and McDonald's successor. All present agreed that a new High Commissioner for these refugees should be appointed, but the Colonial Office spokesman made it clear that his associates were worried about any additional attempts to increase Jewish immigration to Palestine. The "uncertainty of the economic future of the territory" could not be overlooked, he remarked. Moreover, "it would be quite inadmissible that the High Commissioner should himself conduct an examination of the capacity of any particular territory to absorb emigrants." At most, the new appointee could ask governments about the possible admission of refugees. The Foreign Office counterpart at this meeting took issue with a proposal that the Commissioner should negotiate with Berlin or directly aid the Jews before they were forced to leave their country of origin, but the Home Office representative noted that the crucial transfer of emigrant funds could not be avoided.[12]

The nod for High Commissioner for German refugees eventually went to Britain's retired Major-General Sir Neill Malcolm, who reiterated Secretary-General Avenol's insistence that the League "has nothing to do with the domestic policy of Germany," and that his office dealt "with persons when they become refugees and not before." Malcolm was not to concern himself with settlement and relief. In addition, this 66-year-old Scot refused to have the High Commission act as an unofficial clearing house on behalf of refugees as McDonald had done, and would form an International Liaison Committee only a year later, and then strictly for organizational purposes. Nor did he wish to receive funds from private sources. The secretary of the liaison committee subsequently wrote to Felix Warburg that Malcolm, who had a total budget of $16,000 for the year, appeared "devoid of initiative and ideas." Bentwich lamented that it was "sad to see what a comatose affair" the High Commission had become.[13]

The Agency Executive in Jerusalem was divided within its counsels on what to do next. For Shertok, as he put it at length to his colleagues on January 19, Wauchope's dramatic hike of the capital requirement presented the greatest danger, since it threatened the yishuv politically, economically, and psychologically. Ben-Gurion considered the question of immigration far more serious than that of the Council, presenting the movement as it did with a difficult position which possibly had no equal since 1930. HMG's "change of course," he thought, was probably connected to the "very complex" international situation, aggravated by Italy's invasion of Ethiopia. Pointing to rising Arab pressure, Senator proposed that his associates review their "defective" Arab policy and the decision not to enter the Council. Gruenbaum disagreed, and urged that Zionist action be undertaken not only in England, but also in Poland and Rumania, whose Jews would in a short time be in the position of their fellows in Germany. Ussishkin reminded Senator that the Agency had spoken of compromise with the Arabs over the last seventeen years, but this had failed because "the Arabs do not want to cooperate with us in Eretz Yisrael." He, Kaplan, and Mizrachi's Jacob Fishman (later Maimon) posited that a concentrated effort should be made with the Foreign Office, which sought friendship with the Arab countries in view of the international scene, an objective that would be purchased at the Zionists' expense. At the close of the meeting, all agreed that the Agency should prepare a comprehensive development plan that would be presented to the British authorities in Palestine and in London.[14]

Jewry's worsening plight in Germany especially occupied Senator, who headed the Agency's Immigration Department. As deeply as he had "resented" the entry of illegal immigration into Palestine when it first started, Senator wrote to Hyamson, mandate officials continued to deduct severely from the schedules even though that movement had very much decreased. "You [can] imagine what every certificate means for us now, at a time of the German tragedy," he added. In a memorandum of January 17, Senator despaired that no solution of the German-Jewish problem could take place within a short period of time. Only an estimated half of the remaining Jews there were candidates for emigration during the next ten years. The others "must be left out of consideration—at any rate for the time being." The German-Jewish arrivals, he informed Warburg two days later, numbering 30,000 during the last two-and-a-half years, had invested an estimated £10 million in Palestine. Further programs for emigration were dependent on a certain stability of conditions in Palestine, as well as in Germany. That future was uncertain.[15]

Perhaps no Zionist moderate felt this more keenly than Henrietta Szold. Addressing the Survey Graphic Associates in New York City, she bemoaned the fact that most people read only the headlines about German Jewry's catastrophe, and therefore their consciences were not stirred. The Promised Land's gates had once been wide open at a time when Zionists did not think only of refuge. They deplored, she went on, the "hastened tempo" forced on them by the situation in Hitler's Third Reich: "We cannot now, for instance, sit down as we had always planned and think how we are going to solve the Arab question, which I consider, and many others consider, the acid test of our right to form a community in Palestine. We cannot do it now with the same energy and the same hope as before." Speaking as the director of Youth Aliya, Szold hailed the achievements of the 950 Jewish adolescents who had arrived in the last thirty-six months. At least another 10,000 between the ages of 15-17 were waiting in Germany to be brought out, and she did not know if Palestine could harbor them all. The "remarkable dignity" of the German Jews, expressed first and foremost in their attitude towards their children's education and future, could not be denied. The funds would be forthcoming, she was sure, but "not a single Jew may remain in Germany, certainly not a single boy or girl who can still be made to participate in a life of joy, of creativeness, of constructive work of promise, of hope and of fulfillment."[16]

Wauchope clarified his own intentions to Shertok on January 19. Based on the replies he had just received from the Arab political parties, he concluded that they would accept the Council, "although with wry faces." Yet the press reported that the Palestine Arab Party insisted on a wholly selected (not elected) Council membership and a "national government" elected by the Council, Shertok responded, together with scraping the High Commissioner's veto, regularizing his status by a treaty to be concluded between HMG and "the National Government of Palestine," and having the Council choose its own president. The National Defense and Reform Parties were, for the most part, positive, but the Arab Youth Party's position ran along the lines of Haj Amin's stance; the National Bloc of Nablus had not yet shown its hand. Unmoved, Wauchope then declared that he would definitely forbid any land sale lower than a "lot viable" (land sufficient) for the fellah class's subsistence, excluding urban or citrus land and the entire Beersheba sub-district. The Zionists would "fight for every inch of land," Shertok declared, this and other anti-Jewish legislation proving to Jewish opinion worldwide that "a new, cold wind was blowing from this hill on which Government House stood." Shrugging his shoulders, Wauchope replied that he had already told the Arabs that no change had occurred in the administration's polity. "Did he have to tell the same thing to the Jews?"

The doubling of the capital entry requirement, Shertok next observed, would be "a mortal blow" to Jewish immigration from Germany. Samuel, Bearsted, and Marks had just left for America to seek aid for German Jews who wished to emigrate, and all these efforts would likely fail if the mandatory, at the very same moment, adopted laws that went in "the opposite direction." Raising that requirement was not "practical and immediate," Wauchope replied, and he still had time to think this over. "In the end it looks as if the ghosts of the White Paper of 1930 had been revived," Shertok remarked. Indeed, Wauchope shot back, but he had personally blocked the demand—"a peril that still existed"—to prohibit altogether the sale of land to Jews. Was his real motivation governed by benefiting the fellahin, or by a concern to do something "which might calm the spirits" in light of the general political unrest and the fears that were agitating the Arab minds? Shertok queried. Hearing that it was just the former, he expressed even greater regret. He could have understood the logic of the second argument in order to relieve the tension, although such concessions would "only invite further pressure." With the first he had to disagree entirely, convinced that the proposed new land law would harm the Arab peasant class. Nor was Wauchope prepared to register some Jewish illegal residents as Palestinian citizens, although he was greatly distressed at their fate and "his heart went out to them." As long as the unauthorized residence of these tourists continued, he declared, nothing could be done for them in his duty as High Commissioner.[17]

Two days later, the Samuel-Bearsted-Marks delegation arrived in New York City harbor aboard the SS Majestic. As spokesman for the trio, Samuel issued a statement to the press that "they had not come with any specific proposals," but rather to discuss various plans, and to agree upon methods for aiding "the Jews who are forced to leave a country in which their lives have been made intolerable." Large numbers of them had gone or would go to Palestine, others in smaller numbers to other countries. The three Englishmen hoped to engage in discussions with the American organizations which had already done so much for the Jews of Germany. They realized that funds on a much larger scale than hitherto would be needed for whatever proposals would be adopted. They hoped, finally, to agree on plans, both administrative and financial, which would effectively help "in the rescue of as large a number as possible of the Jewish population of Germany from the tragic position, in which they have been placed."[18]

Behind Samuel's public release lay a dramatic turn in the group's original intentions. Max Warburg had initially broached the idea to Minister of the Economy Hjalmar Schacht of having Jews overseas pay for a large-scale exodus of German Jews, this accomplished through buying German goods with an enormous loan that would be collateralized by Jewish property left behind in Germany. The Rothschilds had converted Samuel, a past champion in Parliament of an anti-German boycott, to this scheme. Sensing correctly, at the same time, that American Jews and trade unionists would never accept a plan based on increased German exports, Samuel discussed the matter with the Foreign Office without mentioning the Zionists' opposition to what was now renamed the "Bearsted plan." British Ambassador Phipps in Berlin advised that if foreign countries agreed, through the League, to import additional German goods, the Third Reich government would probably cooperate "if it were made clear to them that the object of the scheme was not to cast reflections on their treatment of Jews but to help them to get rid of unwelcome population." Assistant Under-Secretary Orme Sargent cautiously advised that this might work if the Jewish organizations handled the affair privately.

Samuel, Bearsted, and Marks prepared to sail with two plans. The Warburg-Bearsted scheme required an initial £500,000 from the

Americans. Marks's alternative called for creating a £3 million fund (two-thirds of it from the Americans) in order to enable 100,000 young German Jews to leave within four years, half to Palestine and half elsewhere. On January 3, the delegation secretary, Joseph L. Cohen of the Marks and Spencer department store chain, informed Felix Warburg of the second plan. He also suggested that personal interviews be arranged with leading Jews who could make large contributions.[19]

On January 6, however, secrecy was breached when the *New York Times* ran a front-page article headlined "World Jewry to Be Asked to Finance Great Exodus of German Co-Religionists." Naming the three Britons, it went on to state that the project to allow the exit of 100,000-250,000 Jews with their capital was based on "conditions designed to restore economic and financial prosperity to the German Reich." Correspondent Frederick T. Birchall had corroborated rumors in London that circulated around the city about Max Warburg's plan, a contact named Poliakoff having heard this from Samuel, and decided to send the story as "the background of a situation" which was taking Samuel *et al.* to the United States. The story did not say that the emissaries had a plan or had accepted the Nazi plan, but that the plan and the threat backing it had been presented to British Jewry through "media which could be repudiated." Writing to publisher Sulzberger, Birchall added that "the medium we understand was Max Warburg." Birchall sent the piece unsigned from Paris, since he dared not to have it attributed to him in Germany. Weizmann subsequently corroborated its essence in an interview with the *JTA*.

Asking Poliakoff if he should deny the story, Samuel said "All I care about is that I don't want anybody to think I am backing a scheme to sell German goods." Birchall stood by every word in his dispatch as written, which stated that the trio was merely going over to the United States to find out what to do about the plan. He considered it "a good thing to bring the matter into daylight," so Sulzberger was informed, noting that German economic regulations against Jews were being held in reserve "in case a further club is needed to extract the funds which Germany sorely needs." The best Samuel could do upon arrival in New York was to declare, with the "vigorous corroboration" of Bearsted and Marks, that the delegation had not come with "any specific proposals."[20]

The "unfortunate publicity" in the *New York Times* created "an unfavorable impression," Felix Warburg cabled Samuel, necessitating a conference at his home the same evening of the group's arrival before undertaking any campaign. American Zionist leaders telephoned Marks, who said that "it was rot," but Wise feared that Marks might be "beguiled by Sir Herbert, who neither knows nor cares, and by the multi-millionaire Bearsted, into taking action that may be harmful." Albert Einstein, who left Germany upon Hitler's ascension to power and ultimately accepted a professorship at the Institute for Advanced Studies in Princeton, New Jersey, wrote to a sympathetic Brandeis against a transfer of Jews through the "dumping" of German goods on world markets, and suggested that a public declaration in condemnation of the plan be issued. The Agency wired Marks, insisting that "BULK LIQUIDATED JEWISH CAPITAL GERMANY SHOULD GO PALESTINE." In a memorandum to his staff, Sulzberger declared that he "would not bargain with a dictator, even if he could be trusted to keep his word." He continued: "Democracy is closer to me than are German Jews, and bitterly as I fear for them, I would do nothing that may help to sustain fascism in the world. The German Jew is unhappily in the front line of this world battle."[21]

At Warburg's Fifth Avenue residence, the delegation insisted that the newly created Council for German Jewry would "not take any action likely to involve it in serious controversy, either in relation to Palestine, or in relation to the export of German goods as a means of securing the transfer abroad of the capital of German Jewish emigrants." Warburg assured the British visitors that everything would be done to aid their effort, but the greatest need existed for specific plans and programs. The following evening, with JDC and United Palestine Appeal (UPA) representatives present, a sub-committee was formed that would meet at Bearsted's apartment at the Waldorf Astoria. It was pointed out that the separate JDC and UPA appeals would have to continue, but all sums beyond their minimum budgets could be made available for a coordinated effort for the German Jews. How to raise $10 million in America over a period of four years for the Marks plan was also discussed. Eventually, a large meeting of Zionists and non-Zionists suggested to the delegation that the full details not be announced publicly in view of the possible repercussions that might occur in countries like Poland and Rumania, but perhaps use a figure of 20,000-25,000 a year instead of the four-year total. During the next week, Warburg and the three foreign guests spoke at meetings in different cities on behalf of the cause.[22]

On January 24, Shertok urged Wauchope not to commit himself on the land sale law until he spoke to Weizmann, who felt strongly that the measure was in "complete contradiction" to Ramsay MacDonald's letter to him of February 1931. Shertok added that, on those grounds, the Agency could not accept the entire program. In reply, the High Commissioner planned to announce his scheme to the Arabs three days later and send an official letter to the Agency, but he was prepared to receive the WZO president before this, on January 26. Confidentially, Wauchope disclosed that he had no formal authorization to do so from Thomas, whom he had never met. Wauchope feared that the press would leak the story, but Shertok requested permission to share the information with his colleagues on the Executive after Weizmann's interview with the High Commissioner. Wauchope ultimately agreed to this condition, with the Arabs to be informed on January 28. It was agreed that Shertok, Ben-Gurion, and Ruppin would take part in the Weizmann–Wauchope confrontation.[23]

The Zionists' interview with Wauchope on January 26 was a heated one. Citing MacDonald's 1931 letter at length, Weizmann blasted the land policy as "a breach of faith," and said that while he felt "distressed" as a Jew, he felt "simply humiliated" as a British subject by what was proposed to be done in the name of HMG. At a time when "the Jews were simply drowning in their own blood," the Cabinet's measures for a Legislative Council, immigration restrictions, and land legislation were bound to "strangle" them. He, who had devoted the past fifteen years or so to cooperation with the mandatory government as "his lifework," could not go on. Their whole future might be lost, and they would "fight to the last ditch"; Jewish immigrants would swim to Palestine if the government closed its gates. King George V, who had died six days earlier, had told the WZO president of his faith in the return of the Jews to Palestine. Weizmann had tried to be reasonable with the government all these years, very often to his personal disadvantage, but "for the sake of Zion he could not keep quiet!" Wauchope countered that while the details of the land measure had not been fixed, "it would mean nothing approaching strangulation," but Weizmann noted the Zionist benefits to the Arab population and complained that they had not been consulted prior to the drafting of the legislation.[24]

"How grieved I am," Wauchope wrote to Shertok one day later, that Dr. Weizmann and members of the Agency should view the government proposals "in so unfavorable a light." The High Commissioner concluded: "I truly believe that certain fears and anticipations as to the results of our proposals, though at present perfectly genuine, will not be realized." Shertok, who had praised Weizmann to the Mapai Political Committee as "a great warrior" engaged in a "majestic" fight "for life and death" during the interview with Wauchope, did not reply. His meeting with Wauchope soon thereafter elicited no change in the His Excellency's fundamental position.[25]

Weizmann immediately cabled Namier about the interview and urged the Agency's London headquarters to try to stop the British announcement. Upon reading the deciphered telegram at 10 a.m. on January 27, Blanche Dugdale, Balfour's niece and a Weizmann confidante, told Buck de la Warr, chairman of the Labour Party, that Thomas was "playing the fool" over Palestine, and that he should press Ramsay MacDonald to have the proposed legislation halted. A few days earlier, she had confided to her diary that Thomas would be a very bad Colonial Secretary from the Zionist point of view: "weak, ignorant, blustering, insolent and indiscreet." Namier tracked down Malcolm MacDonald, his former student at the University of Manchester and now Dominions Secretary, and warned "how serious and dangerous" the position was. Namier first discussed the threatened land law and the restrictions on immigration. Next, emphasizing that the Zionists required parity of numbers on the Council and would never "give up the justified claims in the Galuth [Diaspora] to be considered as a voice in such an assembly," the renowned History professor advised that Malcolm see his father. He had come to Malcolm because the pledges given by his father to Weizmann, originally agreed between Malcolm and Namier, were being "flagrantly broken."

Malcolm did talk to his father. Ramsay "proved very stiff," however, took a negative attitude, and said that the matter had already been discussed in the Cabinet in full. His son advised de la Warr that "rich Jews should bombard Thomas" with visits and telephone calls. This would be difficult, since all Cabinet ministers were preparing for the King's funeral the next day at Windsor Castle. Sieff, joined by Weizmann's associate Harry Sacher, set out to talk to Thomas as soon as possible.[26]

As scheduled, Wauchope met with the Arab party leaders on January 29 and read a statement from Thomas in reply to their memorandum of November 25, 1935. Ishaq Budeiri of the Reform Party noted that the proposed Council did not provide for a majority of elected members; Husseini was concerned that nominated British businessmen would be under Jewish influence. Ghusayn focused on deciding the country's economic absorptive capacity and the protection of the fellahin; Nashashibi and Salah wondered why Beersheba should be excluded from the land sale measure. Husseini considered the proposals to protect the small Arab owners to show "a little good will" on the government's part, but suggested that "a general rush" by Jews to purchase land before the ordinance was enacted would occur, particularly in the Beersheba area. Examining Wauchope's statement in general, he thought that the various proposals would not be sufficient to satisfy Arab public opinion in regard to their demands of the previous November.

"In this world we cannot get all that we want," the High Commissioner responded, and he put a question forward: would not the position of the Arabs be better if the Council were set up? The majority of the Arabs feared that the Council might have "regrettable consequences," Husseini answered. The Arabs were weak, and any agreement with the government in this regard would weaken the Arab case in the eyes of the British and the Muslim worlds. Yet a unanimous Arab resolution in the Council would "carry more weight than any propaganda," Wauchope rejoined. In addition, the discussion of immigration and the sale of land would definitely be permitted. HMG contemplated no departure, however, from the principle first enunciated in the 1922 White Paper of allowing future Jewish immigration based on the country's economic absorptive capacity. Salah still considered that, with more than 400,000 Jewish immigrants having entered Palestine, a neutral commission would find that that capacity had been reached. Wauchope concluded by asking the leaders not to think of "an ideal world" but to consider whether or not Palestine's Arabs would benefit from the proposals which he had made.[27]

Having secretly obtained a copy of this interview and of Wauchope's full statement to the Arabs, Ben-Gurion sent off a detailed report on both to Brandeis the next day. After reviewing the land sale proposal ever since it had been first raised by the High Commissioner to Shertok one year earlier, Ben-Gurion summarized the gist of the interview of January 26. He also referred to Wauchope's letter to the Agency Executive before the High Commissioner's meeting with the Arab leaders, which stated that the annual total of Jewish land purchase had increased fourfold during the last five years, and that any setback in the economic situation, bringing unemployment in its wake, would make the position of the Arab small land owner very difficult unless he was able to obtain a livelihood from his land. The yishuv's National Companies had seen to it that the fellahin and tenants retained adequate subsistence areas, but private land purchasers had not done so—hence the need to exercise "a limited measure of control" over land transfer within the areas specified. The High Commissioner reserved the right to permit the sale of "subsistence areas" in certain circumstances, which Ben-Gurion claimed was due to "our desperate struggle" against the very principle. "The first encounter has been lost," he concluded, since the administration would not likely retreat once the Arabs had received Wauchope's statement. The Agency, with help from world Jewry, now had to fight over "the second encounter," which turned on the interpretation of the principle and the terms of the law.[28]

At noon on January 31, a united delegation of Anglo-Jewry met with Thomas, Shuckburgh, and Parkinson to express its opposition to the Council. As the primary speaker, Melchett observed that some of the Arabs had agreed to join the Council with the avowed intention of obstructing the mandate's implementation, and their lack of goodwill precluded that legislative body's making for harmony and better understanding between the Jews and the Arabs. Second, no provision had been made for the Jewish Agency, representing Jewry worldwide according to the mandate, to be represented on the Council. Third, the Jews were a minority elsewhere, and the imposition of that status in Palestine ran counter to the spirit of the mandate. Fourth, it was always understood that a Council was dependant on the development of local government, which had not yet proved successful in the country, and the present proposal seemed to constitute "too great an advance" in regard to the experience of the Arab population with democracy.

Melchett then turned to the larger world arena. In view of the grave tension in the eastern Mediterranean, he thought it "a most unfortunate moment" in which to initiate a step of this kind, and which would undoubtedly result in "a good deal of unnecessary trouble." He also hoped that the unparalleled crisis through which Jewry was now passing would be also taken into consideration. Laski came back to Melchett's first argument, remarking that the desideratum of "mutual appreciation" between Arab and Jew, a "fundamental essential" in contemplating the creation of self-governing institutions, had not been attained "in anything like full measure." A Council which the Arabs would use for "destructive purposes," he added, constituted "the worst possible auspices" for the inauguration of representative government in Palestine.

In reply, Thomas acknowledged the representative nature of the delegation, congratulated them for presenting their case "devoid of any personal bitterness," and assured the group that its "genuine expressions of misgiving" would be given his "very careful and full consideration." The High Commissioner was carrying out a decision of the government, he went on. No task was more difficult than that of the High Commissioner in Palestine, and no one had discharged those "onerous duties" with "greater capacity and distinction" than Wauchope. Thomas reminded them that he was one of the few public men in Great Britain who had never hesitated to denounce the outrages which were being committed against the Jewish people. If he could, in their "time of tribulation," do anything to help he would most willingly do so, because he felt that "the soul of a people was being destroyed, and there was no greater calamity that he could think of." He was the first minister in the Labour Government to reaffirm the Balfour Declaration, an attitude which he had never regretted; indeed, that was his view today. As for the Council, the matter had been fully discussed and adopted, as well as declared at Geneva, and he found it as a fait accompli when he entered office. The Cabinet intended, clearly and unanimously, that nothing in the Council should allow the Arabs to interfere in any way or harm the mandate.[29]

That same day, the Agency Executive publicly registered its "profound disappointment" over the projected land legislation. It pointed out that besides the mandatory's obligation to actively promote Jewish settlement, the government's own survey of 1932-1933 showed that only 656 Arabs had been displaced by Jewish land purchases over the past decade. Shertok had reminded Wauchope on January 30 that the Agency had pleaded a year earlier for a program of constructive assistance to Jewish settlement work, which would also safeguard the fellah's necessary retention of land, and that many delays had occurred in court disputes, cases "pounced on" by the Waqf Administration under Haj Amin, where the lands clearly belonged to Jews. "Germs of agrarian anarchy" were in the air, he noted, with continued serious land trespass leading to "all respect for law and order gone." The High Commissioner still intended to go forward, however, certain that it would be better for the yishuv to have Arab fears of their lands passing into Jewish hands, particularly among the fellahin, assuaged by the proposed law.[30]

Sieff reported to Weizmann on January 31 that he and Sacher had received Thomas's private assurance that the powers of the Council would not be "greater than a Parish Council." The Arabs would probably reject the scheme because of his insistence on the eligibility of women. The Colonial Secretary also made light of the land sale restriction and the increased entry requirement for capitalists. Since these three matters were well advanced before Thomas assumed office, Sieff continued, it appeared obvious that Wauchope and Parkinson, "the permanent people," were most responsible. Their influence upon policy "is steady and persistent." Thomas had spoken very strongly and sympathetically to them about the position of the German Jews, and warned about Zionist propaganda against him, as he was their friend. "Our agitations," Sieff concluded, should be directed against the policy, and not against persons or HMG. The present government, he added, differed markedly from the late Labour government, which, as a minority, was "very much more at the mercy of an agitation."[31] The Agency's next campaign against HMG on behalf of the Jewish National Home was about to begin.

"The times are becoming even more difficult and the questions ever more complex," Weizmann wrote from Rehovot on February 1 to his friend Walter Baer. For two reasons, the WZO president confided, he might pay a brief visit to Europe in a fortnight or so. The Marks-Samuel-Bearsted delegation wished to see him upon their impending return to London. Perhaps they were "bringing the large bag of money," and Weizmann would see how much of it would fall to Palestine. Second, "I am again fighting the Government here; they *want* to make us great *tzores* ["troubles" in Yiddish], and I must be in London." Actually, he ought to be in Palestine and in London at the same time. Depression reigned in Palestine, particularly of an economic nature, but principally due to politics. The Italian-Abyssinian war and disturbances by nationalists in Egypt and in Syria greatly frightened the mandatory government, which was prepared to make concessions to the Arabs at the Zionists' expense. Weizmann concluded: "Immigration is reduced, land laws are to be harsher; there is unemployment—*tout comme chez nous!*"[32]

The Anglo-Jewish delegation had a busy schedule that same Saturday in Washington, D.C. Samuel came to the White House, where Roosevelt assured him of a sympathetic attitude on the part of the American consulates in Germany in the case of "all suitable applications" for emigration visas to the United States. He, Marks, and Bearsted later met with Brandeis. That evening, Samuel and Marks attended the opening session of the UPA's National Conference for Palestine, where Marks spoke. Among other matters, he pointed out that the new Central Committee, which was to concern itself with the planning of emigration projects, would, of course, cooperate and work with the Jewish Agency. He pointed out, at the same time, that other organizations in Palestine were prepared to cooperate with the emigration of German Jews to Palestine, and the Central Committee would work with them as well. This statement aroused considerable opposition. Marks then summarized the gist of his talk in a radio broadcast later that evening.[33]

The UPA National Conference deemed it imperative to insist that any future activities affecting Palestine that would be initiated through the delegation's efforts had to be planned jointly with and executed by the Jewish Agency. While appreciating the "high sense of public responsibility" displayed by the distinguished British visitors, its resolution on February 2 also reiterated the conviction regarding "the primacy and uniqueness of Palestine as the place for the rehabilitation of Jewish life by settlers from Germany and all other lands." Wise, who accepted the UPA chairmanship, was particularly concerned that the trio really wished to create a "super-agency" that would result in "the substitution of live anti-Zionists, such as Bearsted, for dead non-Zionists, such as obtain in America and elsewhere." Marks's lavish praise of Hexter and his work in Jerusalem, which drew a "blistering reply" at the conference from the Histadrut executive's Goldie Meyerson (later Golda Meir), convinced Wise that Weizmann might have to break with Marks. Warburg's "quite unfriendly" attitude to Weizmann over Magnes presented another difficulty, Wise observed to Goldmann. As for the World Jewish Congress, he thought that the Zionist forces would have to rally to their banner because Wise was now "so deeply implicated" in the UPA.[34]

Indeed, Warburg had become increasingly critical of the Agency Executive. A letter in October to Weizmann was tinged with bitterness against the WZO's act of negating the 50-50 Executive principle; its opposition to the Legislative Council and the various non-Zionist colonizing bodies in Palestine; its insistence on Palestine for refugees; and its crowing of phrases like "Jewish State" and "National Land," which hampered Jewish-Arab understanding. Weizmann attempted to mollify him with a long reply, but Warburg, responding to Hexter's reports from Jerusalem, agreed with Hexter that the "new regime" was "working for political agrandisement." In his view, Samuel properly sought to bring about cooperation without superimposing his views over others who may have had more experience, "and without special greed in getting as large a money power into his hands as possible." Bearsted, on the other hand, wanted to get large amounts from Christians where Warburg and associates had failed, aiming to dispose of these funds in a manner his small committee in London would deem wise. Marks had made some good speeches, Warburg admitted, but he was "very limited in his viewpoint" and "has been playing entirely into the hands" of the Zionists.[35]

Having stayed away from the UPA National Conference because he did not wish to be a party to an anti-Legislative Council resolution or to endorse the JNF as part of the UPA appeal, Warburg soon made clear his strong objections to the final resolution about the Agency's involvement in all Central Committee activities regarding Palestine. At a final meeting of all the American representatives with the delegation at Bearsted's apartment on the morning of February 4, he pointed out that the formula in that resolution was unacceptable to many present. Wise vigorously defended the Agency as representing Zionists and non-Zionists alike, with its authority stemming from the mandate and not likely "to be superseded by a fund-raising group." Since the Central Committee would discuss the question of cooperation with the Agency, Wise and his colleagues were prepared to abide by any decision which would be reached in London with Weizmann. Warburg responded that in view of the resolution, no written agreement could come to be, but he wished to assure the delegation of the full cooperation on the part of the organizations with which he was associated. Samuel declared that the Committee was not intended to pool all JDC and UPA funds collected, but to serve as an advisory body to coordinate various projects; the execution of agreed upon projects would be left to existing agencies. A small executive of six members, composed of the delegation and three Americans, would undertake this task.[36]

Opinion divided as to the delegation's accomplishments. Marks felt that the group was returning to England with empty hands, and that they had accomplished very little. The JDC's Paul Baerwald thought the visit very valuable, as it had "stimulated greatly" interest in and sympathy toward the problem of Germany's Jews, and renewed JDC efforts would collect larger amounts of funds which would be used for the purposes for which the delegation had come. His colleague Moses Leavitt soon observed that Bearsted's promised list of individuals to whom he had talked regarding substantial contributions toward the $10 million effort had not yet been received, and "a good deal of confusion" appeared in the minds of many Jewish leaders throughout the country as to the methods whereby that sum would be raised over the next four years. "The visit of the three Englishmen was very pleasant," Warburg wrote Weizmann, "and although they were not able to achieve all they wanted to accomplish, I think it has been very useful for us to meet and to look in each other's eyes and understand not so much what is being said as what the aims are." "They came without any agreed plan," the Palestine Economic Corporation's Bernard Flexner informed Frankfurter, and they only "made the confusion worse confounded." Their public statement upon returning home, that the visit had been justified because they believed that they had aroused the American Jews as to the real situation, he considered "both arrogant and impertinent."[37]

Addressing the Council on Foreign Relations, Samuel had linked German Jewry's plight with Palestine's future. The Nuremberg Laws made it obvious that the Jew would not only be deprived of economic opportunities, but "be subject to moral and spiritual indignities," he declared. The younger generation, whose growth would be stunted by the new laws, had to be given permanent assistance. Great Britain finally came to realize that the Jewish persecutions were not "a temporary outburst," and McDonald's Letter of Resignation and accompanying memorandum to the League convinced them of this fact. The 100,000 Jews between the ages of 17 and 37 must be sent to other countries, half to Palestine and half elsewhere during the next four years. Realizing that "migrations must be planned in advance," Samuel explained that his organization intended to investigate how this could be achieved. Palestine's population, 600,000 when he was High Commissioner, now stood at 1.3 million. The Palestine government "has been obliged to limit immigration, otherwise every Jew in Eastern Europe would have trekked to the new Zion." Still, the country could easily support an influx of 12,000-15,000 German Jews in any one year. The Arabs, though profiting greatly by the post-war development, resented the Jewish infiltration. They did not need to fear that "Mohammedan culture" would be extirpated, however, for Palestine west of the Jordan could support a population of 3 million. "As long as the Arab and Jewish elements continue to balance one another," Samuel emphasized, "neither side has anything to fear."[38]

In a remarkable show of unity, American Jewish organizations had just closed ranks in also joining German Jewry and Palestine. Meeting at New York City's Hotel Astor on January 26, twenty-five Zionist and non-Zionist bodies "unqualifiedly" protested the proposed Legislative Council. They declared it "in essence undemocratic and contrary to the spirit and intent of the mandate and of the Balfour Declaration," and asserted that "it is repugnant to elementary principles of Government and fair play" that legislative government be entrusted to "hostile elements" in Palestine, who sought to defeat the mandate's provisions for the establishment of the Jewish National Home. The Council would "provoke racial strife" and eventually undermine the mandatory power's authority. Determined to give "the maximum of its moral and financial support to the rebuilding of the National Home," those in attendance trusted that the Palestine authorities would give "the fullest effect" to the idealism which prompted the issuance of the Balfour Declaration and the granting of the mandate to Great Britain. In the face of the "disaster" which had befallen Germany's Jews and the tragic position "in which so large a part of the Jewish people finds itself in other lands," the resolution ended, "there is greater urgency that the foundations of the National Home be made secure and that any attempt to weaken Jewish rights under the mandate be resisted."[39]

Wise and other Zionists were also greatly encouraged by Roosevelt's statement to the UPA National Conference on February 1. Acknowledging that the participants were meeting in Washington to "mobilize American Jewry behind a constructive effort to further the rebuilding of the Jewish homeland in Palestine," the president's letter to Dr. Wise continued:

> Every American knows of the love of Jews for the land associated with the great beginnings of their history and every Jew must rejoice that this undying loyalty has been crowned by the establishment of a Jewish National

Home resting upon the sure foundations of Justice and well-being for all the residents thereof.

The American people which has, by the action of Presidents and a joint resolution of Congress, attested its sympathy with the great purpose of a national Jewish home in Palestine will, I am persuaded, be ready to cooperate generously with the United Palestine Appeal which aims to provide a home for homeless Jews. I confidently hope that the cooperation of the American people will contribute to the further progress of the Holy Land, which, I am sure, will continue to give light and leading to all the world.[40]

This letter reflected the reconciliation that had taken place between Roosevelt and Wise on January 11, 1936. The two former friends had clashed over Wise's campaign in 1931-1932 with the Rev. John Haynes Holmes against the corrupt mayor of New York City, James J. Walker, whom Roosevelt, then New York State Governor, had supported; Wise backed the Socialist Norman Thomas for the presidency in 1932. According to Wise's confidential reports to Brandeis, Einstein, and the American Jewish Congress right after the White House meeting, FDR's first words were "Max Warburg wrote to me lately that things were so bad in Germany ... there was nothing that could be done," and then the President remarked that "it would be intolerable to permit goods to be dumped in America in order to get Jews out of Germany." "FDR and Wise Bury the Hatchet," announced the *American Jewish World*. The Yiddish daily *Morgen Journal* noted that Wise discussed the situation of the Jews of Germany and invited the president to the UPA National Conference. Wise soon told Frankfurter, who confirmed Roosevelt's feeling of "warm affectionate pleasure" over his "renewal of old ties" with Wise, that he would put aside as much as possible all of September and October in order to campaign for Roosevelt's re-election against "the Tories of 1936." "The friendliest of relations have been restored between the President and myself," Wise subsequently wrote to Weizmann, "and as in old days I have direct and immediate access to Roosevelt. Any reasonable and feasible plan which we might present to Roosevelt regarding pressure on Downing Street would be presented with every hope of effectiveness."[41]

Wise's euphoric tone appeared premature. Roosevelt had dropped from Wise's draft for his statement to the UPA conference a hope that the "notable" record of 61,000 Jews admitted to Palestine "would be surpassed in the present year," and a request urging Jews to "make this effort the means of opening wide the doors of Palestine to the largest number of homeless Jews, especially from lands of religious persecution and racial oppression." Nor did FDR accept Wise's suggestion during their meeting to write a word of appreciation of McDonald's work and his proposals. A brief message from Roosevelt to the American Mizrachi convention soon thereafter praised religion's important role in civilization, with the caveat having first been given to the Commissioner of Education that his draft and another presidential message to the United Synagogue of America "not be misunderstood" if "the Nazi question" came up for discussion.[42]

McDonald also failed when seeking one more time to obtain some intercession from Washington. A twenty-minute talk at the White House on February 6 with Roosevelt, who "was as cordial as ever," did not result in a statement denouncing Nazi persecution. McDonald tried another tack. He had made an appeal to the Foreign Office the previous month about its making informal representations in Berlin, preferably in cooperation with the U.S. government, to support the evacuation (similar to Marks's plan) of 100,000-150,000 German Jewish youngsters within 4-5 years. He raised the same subject with Undersecretary Phillips on February 7, repeating the point he had made earlier to Whitehall that Jewish groups would undertake the financing. Unbeknownst to McDonald, the British had already decided not to intercede. The State Department concluded soon thereafter that it could not do so for a non-American group, and that the immigration laws did not permit the extension of any preferential treatment.[43]

Instructive, too, was Roosevelt's reply to an anxious Crane, who had written him from Palm Springs on January 28 about an effort (as publicized by the Samuel-Bearsted-Marks delegation) to bring "something like" 100,000 Jews out of Germany. While this was "a perfectly proper movement" because he doubted that Berlin would change her attitude toward the Jews "for a long time," Crane asserted that the real problem was that of "disposing of them" in such a way as not to increase further "the anti-Semitic feeling which has grown so much since the War." The feeling against the Jews was "rising all the time" in Palestine, he observed, where there were "a hundred thousand too many people" already and where the Jews now owned most of the valuable land. Crane recommended that the German Jews go to Russia, where large blocks of rich land had been entirely set aside for Jews, and where they could "have their Republic and their national home with infinitely less molestation than they could anywhere else in the world." On February 10, FDR responded thus: "I do not think the movement you speak of will affect this country much for everything is still on a quota basis."[44]

The limits of Wise's influence could readily be seen in the appointment of the anti-Zionist George Wadsworth to succeed the antisemitic Paul Knabenshue as U.S. Consul General in Jerusalem. Writing as UPA chairman to Roosevelt on February 13 against this step, Wise repeated Mack's admonishment to Phillips that the American representative there should have "an understanding and a real sympathy" for the Jewish National Homeland. Phillips's "poor buttery words," in Frankfurter's characterization, had promised that "the fullest possible consideration to us" would be given in this regard, yet Wadsworth got the nod. Wadsworth's long State Department service in Beirut, Teheran, and Bucharest was likely to be "a bad experience" for understanding "the wholly different aims and endeavors in Jewish Palestine," Frankfurter agreed, while pointing out to Wise that the president acted "pro forma" on State's recommendations, and this was probably the first that FDR knew about Wadsworth. He is a career service officer, Roosevelt replied to Wise with a draft from Secretary Cordell Hull on February 21, and had the Department's "full confidence." Further, Wadsworth had served during 1924-1928 mostly in the Near East Division, where he was charged with prime responsibility on matters concerning Palestine, and State records indicated that he possessed "to an unusual degree" the knowledge and understanding necessary for the successful administration of that consulate. Unless Wise was prepared to give "fullest detail" against Wadsworth's suitability for the post, FDR was inclined to believe that the appointment should stand. It did.[45]

Wauchope tried to assuage Weizmann's fears, writing to him frankly on February 2 during a week's trip to Cairo "as man to man, I hope I may say as friend to friend." It was not intended that the Legislative Council, the entry requirement for capitalists, and the land sale law should appear "to come to a head" at the same time, the High Commissioner began. He still disagreed with the Agency on all three measures, and greatly regretted the Agency's refusal to take part in the Council. He had the highest regard for Weizmann, Ben-Gurion and Shertok, who believed in his "honesty of purpose," and the "highest admiration" for the spirit that animated the making of the National Home; remained confident in that Home's "permanence and lasting success"; and desired "very deeply that it should avoid evil days." He agreed with Weizmann's statement that the hostile anti-Jewish frontier had extended westward from the Vistula to the Rhine, and that the chief support of the Jews rested on England. If so, "the first and essential business" was to make the yishuv's foundations secure. Risks could not be undertaken when there was but one Palestine and but one National Home. The unstable economic situation, the "state of unrest" between Arab and Jew, and the genuine—even if groundless—Arab fear that Jews were "eating up the land" all threatened the Zionist enterprise. He now sought to remove one or two of the "weak spots" which he saw or imagined he saw in "the solid foundations of the Jewish National Home."[46]

Additional concerns preyed on Weizmann, just then attending a closed meeting of the Va'ad HaLeumi and some community leaders on February 2 in Jerusalem. Perhaps he would not see the day when the yishuv became the majority in Palestine, mused the WZO president, but the continuing arrival of unauthorized Jewish immigrants now brought a criminal element. It brought to his mind the Jewish "underworld" of Warsaw, and it weakened the movement's political strength. Heretofore, world opinion had admired Zionism's "holy ideal" of bringing Jews to Eretz Yisrael who were prepared for every sacrifice. Unity, rather than the largely *"eirev rav"* ("mixed multitude") of Jews in Palestine today, must be achieved above all. "You must sweep out the evil from your midst," Weizmann quoted from the Bible, arriving also at some modus vivendi between Jewish farm owners and workers and improving civil relations in general.

Others who were present focused on different issues. Ussishkin thought that Jewish Communists, who supported the Arab demonstrations of October 1933, and especially a large Arab intelligentsia posed a graver threat. Katznelson emphasized the need to maintain the yishuv's united political stand against the proposed British measures, since it faced a difficult period after some years of calm, and to present constructive demands to the mandatory. Ben-Zion Mossinsohn doubted that the Arab progression could be halted, but he wished that Weizmann had put forward details on what to do now. He suggested that just as the Arabs mounted protests almost daily, the Agency should organize demonstrations and appeal to other nations and to the League. Moshe Podhorzer (later Pedhatzur) warned that the Jews of Safed, where only two Jewish policemen served, found themselves in the heart of "a stormy sea"; militant Arab Scouts paraded regularly and even were setting up an orchestra. If Safed were destroyed, he asserted, the entire Upper Galilee would follow. Ben-Zvi ended the gathering with a call for discipline, since anarchy in private land sales and unclear settlement plans, for example, sparked speculation and other ills. The Va'ad HaLeumi chairman also thought it imperative to raise the level of Hebrew culture to match the tempo of immigration, and to make an effort to get 150,000 Jews registered for Palestinian citizenship and so strengthen the yishuv.[47]

Ben-Gurion advised Melchett of his own priorities on February 4, correctly sensing that HMG's changing policy evolved from the international scene and from fears of "entanglements" in the Mediterranean region. Enlisting British public opinion, which had been aroused by McDonald's resignation letter, to concentrate on the "terrible distress" of German Jewry and press for a larger Jewish immigration from there and elsewhere could alter that policy. He had unsuccessfully urged Weizmann during the last few weeks to travel to London without delay for this purpose; the Zionists had to "strike while the iron was hot." At present, 5,000-6,000 Jewish unemployed workers in Palestine did not present a danger when 80,000-90,000 had jobs, but a halt in building construction and industrial development would question the Agency's call for increased immigration. The success of "the German campaign" depended on improving the general situation in Palestine, calling in turn for a joint political-economic Zionist program. The Prime Minister should be seen by a strong, influential delegation, which ought to focus on German Jewry, but also on the Jews of Poland and Rumania, who lived in conditions that could be termed "a constant pogrom." It should ask Baldwin for increased immigration, Ben-Gurion closed, which also meant HMG's systematic, active help for developing the yishuv's industry and agricultural settlement.[48]

Ben-Gurion also understood that developments in Egypt and Syria since the autumn of 1935, coming a few yeas after Iraq's road to achieving independence, had sharpened Palestinian Arab nationalism. The restoration of the Egyptian constitution of 1923 following a week of anti-British riots led by students in Cairo, together with a general strike against the French authorities for more radical demands, including independence and the unification of all parts of Syria, could not but influence events in the Holy Land. The Pan-Syrian Istiqlalists took the lead in sending money to the Syrian Strike Committee, and held a major solidarity meeting in Nablus at the end of January. Husseini's declaration to Wauchope on January 29, that accepting the Legislative Council might be interpreted as weakening the Arab case in British eyes and throughout the Muslim world, had to be viewed in this setting. Parties, organizations, and newspapers called on Palestine's Arabs to follow the lead of the "older sister" Syria and to fight for sovereignty and unification. "Ties of blood and religion" and "an instructive example" existed, Ben-Gurion would later remind a Va'ad HaLeumi conference, and the Arabs of Palestine did not have to wait for instruction and direction from the mandatory government. They were "capable of operating from their own will."[49]

Antonius's report to Crane on February 8 reflected this turn of events. In Egypt, the king had appointed a delegation of all the parties to open negotiations with High Commissioner Miles Lampson. A more serious political crisis was currently developing in Syria, following a sudden French raid in early January on the offices of the Nationalist Party Executive, the seizure of its archives, and the arrest of two of its leaders. The raid had been carried out because that party had begun organizing systematic opposition to a new French scheme for consecrating the existing division of Syria into separate political units. Shops closed, clashes erupted against the authorities, and labor and student strikes broke out. The disturbances in Damascus impacted on Aleppo, Homs, Homa, and other centers. A large number of people, including members of the police, were killed or wounded, and more leaders were arrested. The "effervescence" spread to Palestine, where several large Arab meetings condemned French methods and expressed solidarity with the Syrian protesters. Telegrams of protest that were dispatched spoke of "the people of Southern Syria," and not "the people of Palestine." Antonius thought that the French armed forces would prove too strong for this wave of popular resentment. If the military authorities took charge, he wrote, they would undoubtedly use their "customary measures of repression and nip the insurrection in the bud."[50]

Competing Arab and Jewish nationalism in Palestine also threatened Ben-Gurion's fervent hopes that the Negev, a large region still not on the Land Register, would contribute mightily to the yishuv's progress. He, Ruppin, and Hexter discussed the issue in early February. Wanting to discover water sources and oil in the south of Palestine, Ruppin in the meantime had asked the mandatory's geologist for government maps and surveys of the area. The desired documents could not be given without the administration's approval, but this expert expressed his preparedness to conduct diggings if the Agency assumed the expenses. Concurrently, Agency intelligence obtained a copy of Wauchope's letter to Thomas on February 8, which indicated the interest of an English group in soon acquiring and developing 50,000 dunams of land in the vicinity of Akaba, with a lawyer named Wadi Bustani to be their agent. Bustani informed the Assistant Chief Secretary of his agreements for the sale of land within Palestine at that location. A Christian Arab "with strong nationalist opinions," in Wauchope's words, Bustani referred to the area's strategic importance and to the desirability from the British point of view of developing the overland communications between Haifa and Akaba as an alternative to the Suez Canal. His memorandum also brought up possible economic developments there in connection with the transport by railway of potash from the Dead Sea and the transport of fish from Akaba to the Palestine markets. Bustani suggested the desirability of the development of the area around Akaba by British and Arab capital—"to the exclusion of any other sort of capital."[51]

Given this confluence of circumstances, Ben-Gurion advised during a meeting with Shertok and Kaplan that Weizmann arrange an interview with Wauchope before departing for London. At that occasion, the WZO president should seek clarification of the administration's plan for the coming five years, informing the High Commissioner that everything which had transpired recently "shook our faith and trust in England." The Zionists did not know HMG's intentions, and Jewry was filled with "great doubts." If the government felt a need to calm the Arabs, it also had to calm the Jews. A new declaration of policy was not necessary, but the Agency must know if it would only face restrictions while the Arabs received active help. Since Wauchope's term had been extended for another five years, the Zionists would prepare a five-year plan in four specific areas. These included land (the Jordan Valley, the Negev, a change in land policy, and Transjordan); Jewish employment in government services and public works; encouraging industry and export (duties and Imperial preference); and immigration, which also meant an active effort from the authorities to increase the country's absorptive capacity.[52]

The night before Weizmann's interview with Wauchope, Shertok met at Magnes's home to hear the Hebrew University president's complaints against the Agency's stand on the Legislative Council. Hexter, Senator, Smilansky, Daniel Auster, Yisrael Rokah, Yosef Luria, Ya'akov Thon, Gad Makhnes, and Oved Ben-Ami also attended, all invited by Magnes because their views resembled his own. In the course of five hours, Magnes presented the subject within the broader context of the "Arab question," which he believed had been "criminally neglected" by the Jewish community. In his view, the Council offered perhaps the last chance to meet the Arabs, and much could be achieved through explanation, even obtaining Arab approval for such vital matters as Jewish immigration. The other invitees argued that inasmuch as the Council would arise, the Agency had to participate. Only Luria, head of the Va'ad HaLeumi's Education Department and of the defunct pro-binationalist Brit Shalom organization, opposed the Council while agreeing with Magnes on the Arab issue.

Shertok charged that Magnes was insufficiently apprehensive about Zionist growth in Palestine, as if the entire issue was only a matter of a settlement between the present Arab and Jewish populations. Smilansky remarked that he insulted Magnes with this characterization, but Magnes rejoined that he was, indeed, prepared for a limitation on Jewish entry in order to arrive at a peaceful settlement with the Arabs. After detailing the Agency's efforts with regard to the Arabs, Shertok explained its stand regarding the Legislative Council. The Council had not yet been established; it was not even known if the Arabs would consent to it, and the council's existence was not certain even if it would arise. There was therefore no need to surrender in advance and support an institution that all agreed harms the Zionists and "does not confirm our right of existence." After a while, if the Council did come into being and influenced Palestine's development, then the Agency would discuss our situation. Shertok got those assembled to agree not to publicize the meeting or to take any action without first turning to the Agency. Shertok informed the Executive of the meeting, prompting Ben-Gurion to note that Magnes and the other participants represented only themselves and that elections would prove this to be the case.[53]

With Zionism needing "all the friends it could muster" at this hour,

Ben-Gurion was particularly concerned over Warburg's current attitude towards the Agency leadership. Ben-Gurion felt "very much aggrieved," Hexter was informed, that Warburg had written to Weizmann that "it is no use treating the Executive like gentlemen," and thought it a calamity that Warburg's name would not be associated with the UPA campaign. Hexter pointed, in turn, to Warburg's great disappointment at the Zionists' insistence on a separate campaign from the JDC and the Federation of Jewish Philanthropies; the slights suffered by non-Zionists at the Lucerne Conference, including the exclusion of Laski and Karpf from the Agency Executive; and the "constant negative approach" which he had personally experienced as a non-Zionist member of the Executive. This frank exchange ended with Hexter's remark that Zionism's friends need not necessarily work under the aegis of the Agency, "and that in general he knew our point of view on the totalitarian state."[54]

Warburg and others in his circle stood firm. He advised Marks to tell Weizmann to cooperate with organizations outside of the Agency's control that were interested in Palestine's development. Echoing Hexter, he also urged that the Agency should also not "lightheartedly" declare the Agency's non-cooperation with the Council if its execution could not be postponed. Karpf reminded Lipsky that the non-Zionists at Lucerne had not opposed the Zionists' stand against the Council only because they were told that to do so would break up the Agency. He considered the Agency's position "dangerous," and warned Senator that a boycott by the Executive would cause many non-Zionists either to withdraw from the Agency or fight such a procedure within it.[55]

Similar sentiments could be heard within the American Jewish Committee and JDC leadership. The annual meeting of the Committee heard Executive Secretary Waldman warn of "a cleavage between the view that regards Jews as essentially different from their neighbors and seeks the solution of their problems in a resurgent nationalism, and the view that it is the destiny of the Jews to live in the world at large as members of the nations in which they live." Fundamental differences in *weltanschuung*, he stressed, precluded united action. His colleague and JDC board member David Bressler advised Warburg against inaugurating a large publicity campaign speaking of Jewish mass migration from Germany. This he considered not only questionable in practical terms but, even more important, would be "tantamount to admission by the Jewries of the world that the Nazi program has triumphed and Jewish wealth is engaged in finding new homes for its persecuted Jewish citizens."[56]

Their British counterparts shared related views. Laski, Bentwich, Lionel Cohen, and Leonard Stein agreed with Warburg about the Council, but joined a conference which resulted in Anglo-Jewry's deputation to Thomas on January 31 as "a sop to the masses." They feared that this Jewish public would otherwise have "run out of control" in its great indignation against the proposed legislative body. Replying to Karpf, who cabled that any protest meeting might lead to "crystallization [of] differences" among non-Zionists, d'Avigdor-Goldsmid observed that a representative gathering was meant to "avoid the possibility of noisy, mass demonstration" by the Zionist Federation of Great Britain and Ireland. Criticizing the Agency's "disastrous policy," Sir Robert Waley Cohen objected strenuously even to this rationale, thinking discussion in the Council the way for Jews, for the first time, to "show up" Arab "mis-statements" and "bring out publicly in detail the identity of Jewish aspirations in Palestine with every ideal of good government and civilized advance." Fundamentally in agreement, Laski considered the resulting conference "à faute de mieux" which avoided an open statement of hostility against HMG. At the same time, he reminded Waldman of their mutual concern that the Zionist leaders definitely sought to "capture the direction of Jewish affairs the world over [a reference to the World Jewish Congress], not only inside and outside Palestine."[57]

Weizmann, accompanied by Shertok, presented the Zionist case to Wauchope on February 16. He sought government assurances that irrigation facilities which might be discovered in the Negev would be used in the interests of Jewish settlement, all the while retaining sufficient land of the Arab holders, as was done by giving them 15,000 dunams when the Agency received the Huleh concession. The Agency also wanted to examine what use it could make of certain areas that were termed "waste lands," such as its success in Kiryat Anavim. Shertok called for a Jewish share in all the essential public services and works at least equivalent to their nearing 30 percent of the population, especially in the police force to counter the influence of incitement on Arab policemen. It was dangerous, he remarked, to leave the railways and ports entirely in the hands of Arab workers; wherever Arabs and Jews worked together, "both sections were exercising a mutually restraining influence."

Weizmann supported the Va'ad HaLeumi's claim for a direct share in the administration budget, including grants-in-aid to Jewish health and education services. More systematic efforts by the mandatory should also be made to encourage Jewish industry, and he would take this up with Treasury officials in London. Immigration, Shertok emphasized, was "the underlying and over-riding consideration of all their representations," and they therefore very much appreciated Wauchope's statement on January 29 to the Arab leaders that Palestine's economic absorptive capacity was the only principle determining admission policy. Finally, Weizmann said that he intended to present to Eden what part he thought Jewish settlement was destined to play in this country, "through which the jugular vein of the British Empire ran."[58]

Six days later, Weizmann replied to Wauchope's letter of February 2 as "friend to friend," reiterating the reasons for his opposition to the Council, limits on Jewish immigration, and restrictions on land purchase. Hoping for parity on the Council, he feared that otherwise that body would become "but a sounding-board for the dissemination of Arab nationalist propaganda directed as much against the Mandatory Power as against the National Home." He hoped that, taking into consideration "the extraordinary intensity of Jewish family ties—the natural result of our history of dispersion," Wauchope would appreciate that no additional restrictions should be set on the number of dependent relatives, while doubling the capitalist entry requirement would be "a mortal blow" to Jewish immigration from Germany. In the matter of land sales and all other spheres of official policy, Weizmann urged that the administration should "at last give up the part of a mere umpire as between Jew and Arab and should administer the country on positive and constructive lines." This function was essential for the maintenance of peace, but the Jews had not received the full "positive assistance" due them under the terms of the mandate.

Convinced that the yishuv was "laying here the foundations of a new civilization which will not merely bring salvation to our long-suffering race but will bridge the gulf between East and West," Weizmann asserted, too, that those who continued to put obstacles in its way would not be able to stop its progress. It was, however, in the hands of Wauchope's government "to smooth our path or to render it more stony." Weizmann's lengthy, concluding sentence summed up his credo on the convergence of British and Zionist interests:

As one who has devoted his political life work to the

task of cementing the union between the British Empire and the renascent Jewish people I pray, not merely in the interests of our work but no less so in that of the greater Pax Britannica, that the policy of His Majesty's Government in this country may be such that those who will ultimately be the guardians of peace in this part of the world shall be inspired by feelings of real loyalty and affectionate attachment to the nation and the Empire which first opened to them the way of return to their ancient home.[59]

One Englishman, thinking that he could offer a new plan for Palestine that would satisfy both HMG and the warring parties, publicized his thoughts in the *Spectator* on February 21. Archer Cust, Assistant Secretary of the Royal Empire Society, knew that Prime Minister MacDonald had "solemnly assured" an Arab delegation, a pledge that was repeated in the Passfield White Paper, that the government intended to take immediate steps to set up a Legislative Council. With the Jews and the Arabs now objecting to the proposal as it stood, Cust suggested a "Cantonization" scheme, whereby the whole mandated area inclusive of Transjordan would be divided into autonomous Jewish and Arab cantons. A Federal Government, controlled by the mandatory, would be at the center. Jerusalem and Bethelem, both religious "world possessions," would be reserved to direct administration by the government, as would Haifa's port and oil area, which had become a vital element in the communications and naval strategy of the Empire. The Arab canton would consist of Transjordan and the hill country of Galilee, Samaria, and Judea, with Nablus to be its capital. The Jewish canton, with Tel Aviv its capital, would embrace the four plains of Sharon, Emek (Esdraelon), Acre, and Huleh. A detached area in the south, terminating north of the Muslim center of Gaza, would allow for an Arab corridor through the essentially Arab areas of Ramleh and Lydda to the sea at Jaffa.

Elected representatives from each canton would sit on the Federal Council, over which the High Commissioner would preside, with some of his subordinates also serving as members. The President of the Jewish canton would acquire a status of independence such as Abdullah now enjoyed. This evolution would not mean the forcible transfer of any persons or their property. Jew and Arab could live and own property in the other's canton, where their respective language and law would prevail. The new arrangement would be "an extension" of the "natural processes," as seen in Arab Jaffa and Jewish Tel Aviv, by which Palestine was in effect "cantonized" at present. Once the fundamental political issue was solved and all "the hatred, suspicion and deception that now sully the Holy Land" were cleared away, it could be expected that a minority of Jews would be welcomed as settlers in the rich, undeveloped lands of Transjordan. This scheme, Cust concluded, would be "a just and reasonable interpretation" of HMG's obligations under the mandate, and conflict with none of them. It would establish in Palestine a Jewish National Home that would go much further along "the road of Nationhood" than was possible today; preserve the rights of the Arabs, for which the mandatory was "equally responsible"; introduce the self-governing institutions that Article 2 of the mandate required; and secure the interests of the British Empire in this vital corner of the world.[60]

The hard-pressed Zionists were hardly in a frame of mind at this juncture to consider Cust's radical solution of provincial autonomy, but Weizmann did not foresee the full-scale debate on the Council scheme that took place in the House of Lords on February 26. The WZO president's earlier letter to Namier concerning parliamentary strategy, which dealt at length with the proposed land legislation, had envisaged the medium of questions "ranging over the whole" of McDonald's 1931 letter. Even Namier's briefing of Lord Eustace Percy for the debate did not mention the Council. The Gentile Zionists, particularly those on the Labour benches, took the initiative. That party's Advisory Committee on Imperial Questions had recently called for continuing the mandate "until such time as Arabs and Jews can live together in tolerable harmony politically and economically," and opposed the immediate establishment of a Council, which would "probably promote irresponsibility and discord, without satisfying Jews or Arabs, or facilitating good government." Some ten peers from all the three parties spoke in favor of Lord Snell's motion, which asked whether HMG had considered the "widespread objections" and requested deferring the proposal "until greater experience in local government" had been obtained. Only the Earl of Plymouth, the Colonial Under-Secretary, defended the government's policy along the lines of Thomas's letter to Melchett a few days earlier.

"Marvelous result," Dugdale recorded in her diary. She added: "We now hope for a further Debate in both Houses." In a letter to Wise, Melchett described the debate as "the greatest castigation I have ever seen of a government on any question." Indeed, he judged it "a tremendous step," for the possible formation of "an emasculated Arab council sitting in conjunction with a few British officials" would inevitably be "a trouble and burden" to the administrators, thus fully justifying the Zionists' "having no part in it."[61]

On the morrow of this remarkable parliamentary triumph, Weizmann disclosed to Wise his changing perspective as to Zionism's next steps. He would depart on March 1 for London to see Thomas and others in order to explain the points that had been recently raised with Wauchope, who "realizes that we mean business." More was needed, however, in view of the terrible situation in Germany and particularly in Poland, where people were "used to make pogroms" and whose "half starved" Jewish community was more numerous than the German one. The time had come to "reopen the whole of our problem with much more force, because of our achievement in Palestine and because of the critical situation of our people, than we did in 1916."

The thoughts that came next, not yet fully formed, showed a revolutionary adjustment to changed circumstances. Weizmann believed that some solution to the Arab-Jewish problem along the lines of the League's transfer of Greek-Turkish populations was urgently required, which he felt "could make a powerful appeal to civilized humanity." As a necessary corollary, the WZO president considered the opening of Transjordan and "the establishment of some sort of organization which may be less than a state, but certainly more than what the Jewish Agency is now." Only if the Zionists "possessed a certain amount of executive power [would] we be able to conduct our business properly." They had grown too large for "a merely voluntary organization." It was becoming "increasingly untenable" that the British controlled the executive power and income, while "the difficulties and responsibilities rest on us." Although politically a moderate, Weizmann decided that the moment had come now "for a very serious attempt on the lines adumbrated." This, he concluded, offered "the only possibility of finding a partial solution of our troubles now."[62]

The debate in the House of Lords, and its unexpected victory for the Zionists, fell as a bitter blow on the Palestinian Arab leaders. According to a C.I.D. report, they had assumed that at least a few influential peers could be relied upon for support, and were shocked at the lack of any real knowledge of the Arab case. Some comfort came with the news of the resumption on March 2 of negotiations for signing a treaty between Egypt and Great Britain. (Italy's threat to the Mediterranean weighed strongly in HMG's decision to regularize relations with Egypt and reinforce the regional fleet, now based in Alexandria, Port Said, and Haifa.) In Syria, too, after a strike that lasted fifty days, a delegation was invited to Paris to discuss a treaty along the lines of England's treaty of 1930 with Iraq, which had confirmed that country's complete independence and sovereignty. *Al-Liwa* exhorted the Mufti's supporters that "vanquished Palestine should follow in Syria's footsteps." It appeared logical, the paper's editor told Eliyahu Sasson, head of the Agency's Arab Department, that the same tactics of riots and a general strike should be adopted in Palestine in order to gain political concessions from the mandatory administration.[63]

Al-Ahram, the oldest Arabic newspaper in Egypt (1875) and largest in the Near East, linked these developments to the Palestine question. Britain's imperialist designs in Palestine, a lead article asserted on March 2, sought to deprive Arabs, Christians, and Jews of their rights. Palestine was an inseparable part of Syria, it charged, and the Syrian demand for independence also included Palestine. The Jewish right to own property should have been limited to those already living there, but HMG had "flooded" the land with "strangers," who now numbered about 400,000. Jabotinsky's claim to settle 2 million Jews on both sides of the Jordan, as well as Samuel's statement that Palestine's population could be doubled and there was no possibility to halt Jewish immigration after they had invested millions to create the National Home, mirrored Jewish aspirations. England had not paid attention until now, the newspaper warned, either to the feelings of the peoples under her rule or to the views of some "enlightened Jews" who oppose the concentration of Jews in Palestine. Perhaps the last disturbances would awaken the British conscience to realize that the creation of a National Home for the Jews "is not suitable to the attachment of the Arabs to the land of their fathers." The London *Sunday Times* had recently declared that Palestine had significance, above all, as a transportation crossroads in the East today, just as it had importance in the last war when Turkey threatened the Suez Canal. From this, concluded the article, one could see that England did not care about the fighting between Jews and Arabs "so long as her interests suffered no harm."[64]

In an interview with Wauchope, Nashashibi pointed out the influence on the Palestinian Arab street of France's concessions to the Syrians. The pro-Jewish statements that had just been made in House of Lords debate, he observed, greatly angered the Arabs, who "deeply resented" that England did not listen to their nationalist demands. The Syrian achievements pleased them, and the radicals in Palestine were consulting how to pressure England in the manner of the Egyptians and the Syrians. In this "frenzied time," HMG had to appease the Arabs by widening the authority of the Council, enact the restriction of land purchase, and cut Jewish immigration. These measures would "quiet somewhat" the Arabs, who feared for their fate when compared with the progress of their brothers in Egypt, Iraq, Syria, and Saudi Arabia, and help the Arab moderates in Palestine to advocate for the Council. He would be ready to launch "open propaganda" for the good of the Council if its power would be enlarged. Wauchope promised, in turn, that he would convey Nashashibi's appeal to London and explain the "true situation" to the Colonial Secretary.[65]

Fully cognizant of the impact of the Syrian situation on Palestine's affairs, Ben-Gurion urged a Zionist political offensive in Great Britain of "scope and long-range direction." He observed to Wauchope on March 2 that the Syrian strike, the negotiation with the French on a treaty, and the possibility of soon abolishing the mandate undoubtedly would strengthen the Palestinian Arab war against the Zionists and the administration. For this reason, in addition to others, the building of the National Home had to be expedited. Only a quick reinforcement of the yishuv could put an end to all possible "confusions and disturbances." If the Syrians got their way, he wrote to Kaplan two days later, Palestine would remain the one "A"-category mandate, the Jewish National Home then the only hindrance to the Arab countries receiving independence of some sort. That, added to the "anticipated hurban [destruction] for the Jews of Germany and Poland and the rest of the East European countries," augmented the need to hasten the yishuv's development and increasing strength. The British government and public opinion had to be aroused to champion an "activist" Zionist program of immigration and wide settlement. He suspected that Weizmann, impressed more by personal contacts than by realistic results, lacked the "diligence, patience, and enthusiasm" for this systematic, relentless campaign. Weizmann intended to spend only a few weeks in London, and even then he would be involved in discussions with Samuel and Marks. "I cannot restrain myself from a bitter and depressing feeling," Ben-Gurion confided, "that we do not now have a supreme political leadership."[66]

Zionism's weak standing in the United States, he wrote to Barukh Zuckerman, Rubashov, and Meyerson the same day, gave the Agency Executive chairman additional grounds for concern. Aside from the uncertainty of Palestine's share in the Samuel-Bearsted-Marks plan, he sensed that the hatred for Zionism and the WZO among "our friends the non-Zionists" was intensifying and growing. In his view, the JDC and "the philanthropic assimilationists" exhibited a clear tendency to take control of the Jewish community and the Jewish people in the Diaspora and Eretz Yisrael, and conditions for this effort were more propitious than they had been in a long time. In almost all the eastern countries and the Balkans, the Jews lacked the political possibility of sounding their voices, and the despair and increased poverty there created "a convenient atmosphere" for outside "men of good" to rule; economic difficulties in Palestine enhanced their appeal as well. The non-Zionists also backed the Jewish Telegraphic Agency in its fight against the WZO's Palcor (Palestine Correspondence) news agency. Only the organized American Zionist movement could stand in the JDC's way, but it lacked significance in this largest and richest Jewish community, which had the greatest political and economic possibilities. The Jewries of Eastern and Western Europe could not provide strength to Zionism, certainly not in the measure demanded at this hour. A fundamental reorganization of the party could prepare the ground for recovery, with Hadassah "the center of gravity." He was ready to travel to the United States for this, and only this, objective, if grounds for hope existed to carry out the task.[67]

The growing divide between the Zionists and non-Zionists could not be denied. In a letter to Weizmann on March 3, Warburg expressed the hope that Bressler would be available to go to London and study the German material available. The JDC had established "promising connections" in Argentina, and their expert on Jewish settlements in Soviet Russia had just returned from examining the possibilities in Costa Rica and Guatemala. He and other friends in America, England, and Palestine believed that if the Legislative Council were set up, the Jews ought not to abstain. Compared with the 1922 proposal, which was acceptable to the Jews when Samuel served as High Commissioner, it seemed that there was "more profit" in the present set-up. In addition, Warburg observed, the individuals "about whom you now talk so disparagingly" were to a great extent connected with organizations in Palestine that Weizmann had once helped create, and they should be treated in the same way "as the people who vote Zionistic tickets regularly." Privately, he warned Hexter, who informed Ben-Gurion of his own wish to resign from the Executive, that Weizmann "certainly wants the heavens and the earth and what is beneath the earth in his control, and he is a good fighter!" A few days later, Jonah Wise, chairing the JDC's Fund-Raising Committee, publicly advocated the evacuation of 100,000-150,000 Jews to "liquidate the German question," and thus "abate international Jew-baiting in the public press, and what is more important, in the public mind." His statement, which asserted in closing that "the next ten years [would] tell the tale of the position of the Jews in the civilized world," carried nary a mention of Palestine.[68]

Sponsorship of a Petition to the League in support of McDonald's Letter of Resignation reflected a wider ideological rift as well. The pro-Zionist, liberal, and militant American Jewish Congress wanted it undertaken by Jewish organizations alone, claiming that "self-respect" and "dignity" demanded that the case be presented to the governments of the world as the "Jewish people." The non-Zionist, conservative, and assimilationist American Jewish Committee and B'nai B'rith, on the other hand, pointed out that the inclusion of non-Jewish organizations and groups would carry more weight at the League. Waldman particularly feared that Wise, the philosopher Horace Kallen, and other Congress spokesmen sought thereby to "manouevre [sic] the enterprise from the angle of Jewish nationalism and within its framework," much as they were "going ahead full speed" on establishing a World Jewish Congress that summer. Goldmann's activities as the Agency's political representative in Geneva filled the Committee with "profound disgust," as he had reneged on an earlier promise not to be active in "Diaspora" politics by working assiduously for the World Jewish Congress's creation. Reluctant to confess it to himself, Waldman warned colleague Alan Stroock that against the Zionist "nationalist juggernaut," the AJC had been "almost completely unavailing."[69]

Thomas actually began to retreat on the Legislative Council at this very moment. The debate in the House of Lords and a probable repeat of this scenario in the Commons had made its mark. In addition, Thomas, together with his major subordinates Shuckburgh and Parkinson, all preferred the parity principle. On March 6, Thomas suggested in a "private and secret" cable to Wauchope that the Order-in-Council providing for the creation of the Council be postponed until after the Colonial Office's budget vote in July. Wauchope could come to London in the meantime for further consultation. The High Commissioner attempted to have Thomas stand steadfast, warning in reply three days later that any such move would lead to unfortunate results and to the loss of the Arabs' faith in his goodwill and power. A personal threat to resign followed: "If His Majesty's Government were however to withdraw the present proposals under adverse criticism in Parliament, then beyond acting as an official mouthpiece the less I am identified with such withdrawal the better for this county and my influence in it." Wauchope concluded that unless Britain's proposals were adhered to, "civil disobedience and disturbances are almost certain to result and particularly so in view of the apparent success achieved by disorder in Syria and student rioting in Egypt."[70]

All this was placed on the back burner when Hitler sent in the Reichswehr suddenly on March 7 to occupy the demilitarized zone of the Rhineland. The Reichstag greeted this news from their "new god, the Messiah" with slavish salutes and hysterical cheers, although correspondent William L. Shirer immediately grasped that Hitler could not survive if the French humiliated him by occupying the west bank of the Rhine. The acute danger of war between Germany and France hovered over the continent, yet, faced with this open violation of the Versailles and the 1925 Locarno Treaties, the French army took no action. The British stood by as well, Dugdale recording that most of the nation, "the horror of war" upon them, accepted Hitler's placing the blame on the French-Soviet pact. Hearing about the German troops' march onto the left bank of the Rhine, Roosevelt asked British visitor Arthur Willert: "Does not the avoidance of war now merely mean its postponement?" Although telling Sulzberger days earlier that "Germany wanted war, it was a question of when and with whom," FDR felt that the American public's preference for isolationism made it impossible for the United States to do anything on behalf of peace and collective security. Hitler's victorious gamble, with "no army worth mentioning" and a "ridiculous" air force, as the Führer admitted to Albert Speer, confirmed his belief that the Western governments had again proven themselves "weak and indecisive." A new phase in European history, with appeasement of the Nazi dictator evident to everyone, had ominously begun.[71]

Without referring at all to Hitler's triumph, Ben-Gurion urged the Mapai Political Committee on March 9 to inaugurate "a policy of creating a Jewish state." Wauchope's intended legislative actions, dramatic changes in Egypt and especially Syria, and, most importantly, the plight of European Jewry combined to force "a turning point" in their political work. Expanding upon his letter to Kaplan and other letters to Melchett, Ben-Gurion wished to launch a public campaign demanding that HMG assist in the immigration and absorption in Palestine of 1 million Jews from Germany and Poland within five to ten years. It was true that, before departing for London, Weizmann had said that now is the time to demand a Jewish state, but he did not weigh matters objectively and preferred personal diplomacy. "One does not simply approach Thomas and say 'Give me a Jewish state,'" Ben-Gurion jeered. Weizmann was essential to begin the drive, but a major effort was required, covering politicians, journalists, and the public at large, using the disaster facing Jewry abroad as "a lever for our political work." This required a revised outline of the stages leading to the Zionist goal, he emphasized. A Jewish state, the axis on which all else turned, would allow for mass immigration, thus creating a majority which, in turn, would solve the Arab question and bring about the realization of Zionism. Skeptical colleagues, including Katznelson, Yosef Sprinzak, and David Remez, concluded that Ben-Gurion should work out the details of his proposal for their next meeting.[72]

In a further letter to Kaplan, Ben-Gurion suspected that the recent debate in the House of Lords, for all its great, positive value for the Zionist cause, would not entirely be a blessing. Melchett, who agreed fully with Ben-Gurion's future program, had just warned the Agency Executive chairman that the dispute over the Council had "hardened the Colonial Office against us, and also the Government." The Colonial Office was not prepared to "face a real row with the Arabs." The Treasury thought that Palestine was "bound to be a small country" and could never support a large population; was unsuited for industrial purposes; and should not be allowed to build up what they regarded as an "unsound position" on the basis of a tariff policy. Other than this, Ben-Gurion feared the danger that the movement would concentrate all its attention on "a negative war," and not stand on the principal point: "the desperate position of the Hebrew nation" and the necessity for immigration and settlement to a wide degree.[73]

Soon after arriving in London on March 8, Weizmann set to work in his own fashion. A formal letter to Samuel, the newly chosen chairman of the Council for German Jewry, presented the Agency's plan of bringing 12,000-15,000 German Jews to Palestine in the course of one year at a cost of £610,000, with 8,000 of these refugees to be absorbed into agriculture. Learning that non-Zionists in the United States opposed equality of membership between Zionists and non-Zionists on the Council for German Jewry, Weizmann backed Wise in a dispute with Warburg over the fourth nominee on the American half of this body. In a first meeting with Neill Malcolm, Weizmann advised McDonald's successor that he personally would run a ten-year plan in Palestine on the basis of some 30,000 Jewish agricultural settlers a year. These arrivals would provide work for twice that number in the towns, resulting in a total of about 100,000 new settlers a year for ten years, "and then we would see!" He begged Malcolm to remember that Palestine was the only place in the world where the Jew "does not fill room—he *makes* room." In a private interview with Thomas on March 12, Weizmann asserted that the Arabs would accept the Legislative Council on any terms because they wished to use it in their war against the Jewish National Home. Talking with Gentile allies, he wondered how, with Jewry's difficult situation, could the Zionists get out of "the vicious circle"? All replied that "the crooked could be straightened" through one avenue: Parliament.[74]

In early March, a meeting of Melchett, Brodetsky, Namier, Lourie, and M. David Eder, a former member of the Executive and past president of the English Zionist Federation, had bruited about the question of pressing for further parliamentary action as regards the Council. The principal matter, Lourie wrote to Weizmann, revolved around whether or not a debate in the House of Commons would be desirable. Voting on party lines presented a risk. A more serious danger was that Thomas might force the matter to a vote by "putting on the whips" and defeating the resolution. A suggestion arose that perhaps the leader of the Opposition and Thomas could agree in advance that the debate would be "moderate in tone," in which case there would be no vote. Weizmann opposed any debate taking place out of worry that it might antagonize the government, and later claimed that he had informed his parliamentary friends of his wishes, without success.[75]

The Labour Party, prodded by Wedgwood, again took the lead, an initiative made easier because firm leadership in the Cabinet went abegging. Government decisions, Weizmann heard on March 12 from Walter Elliot, Minister of Agriculture and Dugdale confidant, had become almost completely up to each department involved. Thomas confided earlier that morning to the WZO president that he had "inherited" the Council, and while introducing conditions in the hope that the proposal would fail, had not succeeded in holding it up "indefinitely." With Wauchope's threat of resignation, "he had no alternative." Malcolm MacDonald added to Weizmann that Wauchope had told the Cabinet what its decision should be regarding the Council, and then informed the Zionists that the Cabinet itself had decided. Wedgwood, Amery, and Liberal Party leader Archibald Sinclair all agreed, in separate letters to the London *Times*, against imposing the position of "a statutory minority" on the Jews, introducing into Palestine "quasi-Parliamentary institutions of the conventional type in a country still so profoundly divided," and advancing an experiment which could not "possibly succeed" without the cooperation of both Arabs and Jews. On February 17, Cecil heard from Dugdale that "it is not fit that the future of Zion should be in the hands of a drunken ex-engine driver" (Thomas). Dugdale and other opponents of the Colonial Secretary sought to have him deposed.[76]

The Foreign Office's attention was drawn to Iraqi moves in the troubled Middle East. In early March, Nuri Pasha al-Sa'id broached to Ambassador Archibald Clark Kerr the possibility of a union of Transjordan with Iraq under the latter's control. Eden quickly agreed with Kerr's reserved attitude toward this first mention of the idea from an Iraqi Foreign Minister in an official conversation, noting that the possibility of such intrigue had disappeared after King Feisal's death, and Nuri had doubtless spoken without previous consultation with his colleagues in Baghdad. Aside from the obvious geographical obstacles, no form of union would be possible unless and until Transjordan was granted full political independence. Since that country was still subject to the provision of the mandate for Palestine, the League Council's consent would have to be given in this respect. Another very serious obstacle was the fact that the Transjordanian territory was most unlikely to become financially independent in the near future. On the contrary, the administration of Transjordan was only made possible by virtue of the annual grant in aid provided by HMG's Treasury Department. George Rendel, heading the Middle Eastern department, signed this reply on behalf of the Secretary of State for Foreign Affairs on March 6.[77]

An Iraqi parliamentary delegation's visit to Palestine shortly thereafter roiled the atmosphere further. The 15-member group received a warm reception in all the various Arab towns visited. Zu'aiter, welcoming them to Nablus, referred to the six-month local insurrection in 1920 soon after the League's Supreme Council had awarded HMG the mandate over Iraq. The Istiqlal leader lauded their rebellion, during which several British garrisons were besieged for weeks before the movement could be suppressed, as the struggle "by which independence had been obtained." Sa'id Thabit, replying as head of the delegation, pledged in the name of Iraq "to assist the Palestinian Arabs in their struggle." In Jaffa, he stated unequivocally: "O Arab brethren, launch a Holy War and the Arab Nation will stand behind you." In another speech, he advised: "Don't expect us to send an expeditionary force. You have to begin and the remainder is upon us." The C.I.D. and the Palestinian Arab press both took note.[78]

Weizmann's interview with Parkinson on March 16 left little doubt of Wauchope's dominating influence with the Colonial Office. The Zionist chieftain's request for the possible admission of 1,000 Jews who had already been trained in Germany for agricultural work in Palestine, in addition to the next Labor Schedule, met with the response that it would be up to the High Commissioner. In view of Wauchope's definite statement with authority from London, the Permanent Under-Secretary declared, there must be land legislation. Together with Wauchope, Parkinson felt that Arab fears of "being swamped" by the Jews in Palestine equally applied to settlement in Transjordan. Further, the Council and land legislation should "make ultimately for goodwill between the two races which had to live together in Palestine." Weizmann rejoined that this would only come about when extremists on both sides realized that both had got to stay in the country. With the Mufti "quite irreconcilable" and Husseini hoping for "an Arab rising which would utterly destroy the Jews in Palestine," he did not think that the proposed actions of HMG would have any real effect in allaying Arab fears. He would like himself to get into closer touch with leading Arabs, but did not find this possible. A positive government scheme of development would safeguard the Arab and help the Jew, Weizmann asserted, a sense of "common citizenship" between Jew and Arab inevitably following on the nurturing of common economic interests. He would see Sir Warren Fisher of the Treasury about issuing a £2 million loan for the yishuv's growth, which Parliament had actually authorized.[79]

Three days later, Parkinson wrote an internal office minute giving his impression that "the Arab reaction is such that the Government certainly should proceed with its proposals." The Reform Party had accepted the Council scheme, and the Nashashibi was moving in that direction. (Ya'qub Farraj, a Greek-Orthodox, and Alfred Rock, a Greek-Catholic, had also crossed rival Nashashibi and Husseini lines, respectively, to tell Wauchope that Christian Arab opinion unanimously favored the scheme, although the Arab population wished to have the right to claim "wider powers" for the Council and "stronger representation".) Some of the Arab leaders will press for more power, Parkinson continued, but that was no reason why the government should not proceed now. It was "quite natural" that the Arabs should ask for more. "In present circumstances there is no question of giving more," he concluded, "but admittedly this is a step in a process (it will be a long process) of granting as H.M.G. is bound to do under the mandate, self-government institutions in Palestine."[80]

Major A. J. Kingsley-Heath, author of the British police constable's manual, shared these views. After informing the Agency's Bernard Joseph on March 16 that rumors from Haifa of an Arab proclamation in Nablus for a fifty-day strike on the Syrian model were unfounded, he remarked that if any trouble in Palestine occurred, the Jews would have themselves to blame. They had opposed Wauchope and his policy on the Legislative Council. Disturbances would have broken out if His Excellency had not announced the proposal when he did, and Kingsley-Heath felt strongly that if the Jews were successful in blocking the measure riots would certainly result, apart from the fact that Wauchope would resign. That would be the last thing that the Jews would want, Joseph replied, and it was a mistake in a place like Palestine to permit one's policy to be "actuated by fear of force." The House of Lords debate and Cecil's firm opposition showed that the Jews were not alone in considering the Council policy as unwise, he added, but for Kingsley-Heath it was surprising how "thoroughly ignorant and ill-informed the Lords seemed to be." In his view, the Council would strengthen the hands of the

Arab moderates; if it were withdrawn the "extreme element" would fix Arab policy. When Joseph argued that the risk involved in the Council's creation was too great, Kingsley-Heath responded that His Excellency had proven to be a very clever person who could handle the Arab leaders and "hold them in check."[81]

One week later, Ben-Gurion found out from Ussishkin that Abdullah was prepared to sell one million dunams of land for £1 million to Rutenberg, who had maintained secrecy up to now. While he trusted Ussishkin entirely, Rutenberg feared that word to the Agency Executive would reach Weizmann, and Weizmann would ruin the matter. Indeed, "R" (Rutenberg) had written a "highly confidential" message on March 8 to "the chief" of the Palestine Electric Corporation in London that, as further consideration for this loan of capital to develop land in Transjordan for Arab settlement, the Transjordan government was to give a Jewish company the concession for one million dunams in order to settle Jews. The Arab zone would be to the south of a river boundary agreed upon with Amman, the Jews in the north to become citizens of Transjordan, with each group developing an autonomous cultural entity. "E" (the Emir) was considering the proposal, but HMG knew nothing about it. A British company capitalized at £2 million should be set up, Rutenberg proposed, half of that amount going to the Arabs secured by the land and the other half to Jewish development and colonization. All this would be outside of the Palestine immigration schedules. The Jewish Agency would be informed when Rutenberg was ready, but he feared Weizmann. There should be no meetings or correspondence about this plan, the letter ended.[82]

Melchett was also thinking about making a start at once with Transjordan, intending to settle over 2 million Jews there and in Palestine, a scale comparable to the Greek postwar immigration. The only right solution to the "utterly intolerable" position of Jewry in Europe today, his "secret" memorandum of March 18 read, was the mass evacuation of European Jewry "to reduce it to a level more commensurate with the number of Jews which each country can reasonably absorb." German Jewry might be deemed to have a prior claim, but the Polish, Rumanian, and other Jewries must be taken into account, too. With the establishment of "this new country in the Near East," a benefit to the world and particularly an immense strategic boon to the British Empire, in turn clearing the way for a better understanding between

England and Germany, it was essential that HMG should pursue an "active and preparative" policy in this regard. While echoing Ben-Gurion's call for a great political offensive in Great Britain, Melchett advised that Weizmann appoint a small committee to act under his instructions in his absence from London, the work absorbing the whole energies of the Zionist movement. The desire for peace in Europe, likely to be intense, made the present moment favorable for the consideration of these ideas, he thought, and the solution of the European Jewish problem by Zionist methods "will appear extremely attractive to the governments all over the world."[83]

Weizmann hinted at this when informing Wise five days later that a small committee would be formed, with Melchett "a tower of strength," to keep in touch with political people in London. His earlier letter of February 27 to Wise had noted that the whole problem of Palestine and Transjordan must be placed "on a different plane," given a yishuv of 400,000 strong and the fact that Jewish needs from the Diaspora "press ever harder on us." The power of Palestine and Transjordan to absorb Jews was unlimited for all practical purposes, and if the British government did not block the Agency's direct negotiation with the Transjordan Arabs—"our minimum request for the present"—the Zionists would most likely succeed. "It will clearly be increasingly difficult to carry on in Palestine unless the congestion is relieved in some way," Weizmann continued. So far, the mandatory had limited itself to the purely negative action of imposing restrictions on Zionist work. He thought, from his short experience in London the past fortnight, that the Palestine administration's attitude did not command too much sympathy there, but it did take a long time for any idea "to percolate through the hard skull of the Palestine official." They, therefore, had "to keep plodding on in the hope that in time something will happen." When he returned in May, Weizmann hoped to have the support of friends like Amery, Sinclair, and Snell, with many other MPs and members of the Cabinet for this endeavor.[84]

The debate on March 24 in the House of Commons over the Council appeared to confirm Weizmann's optimism. Wedgwood initiated it during the second reading of the Consolidated Fund Bill, when there was no opportunity for a vote. Thomas, who had complained earlier that day to Weizmann about the Zionists' propaganda, made a poor defense of the government's policy even when arguing that the Council would have very limited powers. The Colonial Secretary drew the support of only one Conservative MP. Subsequently, Wedgwood wrote to his daughter that he had "actually slain the Palestine constitution. I got Churchill, and [Austen] Chamberlain and Amery and Sinclair to speak, and they did, leaving the Rt. Hon. J. T. Dress-shirt [Thomas] in tears." Churchill, spoken to earlier by Melchett, movingly talked of the "added emphasis upon this question of Jewish migration" at a time "when the Jewish race in a great country is being subject to ... a cold 'pogrom' as it has been called ... every form of concentrated human wickedness cast upon these people by overwhelming power, by vile tyranny." When that was the case, he emphasized, surely the Commons "will not allow the one door which is open, the one door which allows some relief, some escape from these conditions, to be summarily closed, nor even to allow it to be suggested that it may be obstructed by the course which we take now."[85]

The overwhelming setback to Baldwin's Cabinet convinced Churchill and some other parliamentarians that the Council was "dead if the two oppositions choose to pursue their advantage." Conservative MP Robert Boothby informed Dugdale that he foresaw Wauchope's resignation, and that War Secretary A. Duff Cooper already had a successor in mind. Lord Lloyd, the former High Commissioner for Egypt and Sudan who had just talked confidentially in Palestine with Wauchope, thought that Wauchope would resign because he had pinned his personal honor to the Council and feared to "lose face" with the Arabs. The next day Weizmann heard from Thomas, "*literally* lachrymose" over the position in which the Commons debate had placed him, that he was left to "carry the baby" by his previous two predecessors, and that he might have to resign. Namier found out that Lothian thought of suggesting in the House of Lords on April 2 a purely advisory Council with parity, the Council not to come into effect until discussed by both Houses of Parliament. This news prompted the Agency's London headquarters to send off a cable without delay to Ben-Gurion suggesting that the new proposal might be acceptable to Jews. The Arabs would probably not accept, and the position would thus be very advantageous for the Zionist camp.[86]

Less optimistic than Weizmann, Ben-Gurion judged this last success a "mixed blessing." Writing to the Agency Executive in London the next day, he noted that while the parliamentary debate in the Lords and the Commons proved that Zionism still had "faithful friends" in at least "one enlightened country," he thought it a mistake to have concentrated all of the movement's political forces on "an adverse fight" and a single issue—which was not the principal one. The end result only increased the opposition of Thomas and of Wauchope, and the Zionists were creating the impression that without the Council "all is well." Rather, along with an assault on the Council and other anti-Zionist legislation, the debate should have focused on HMG's "general passiveness" in furthering the establishment of the Jewish National Home and in increasing immigration and colonization given "the tragic hour" for Jews in Germany and in Poland. It was not yet known in England that the situation in Poland is "even worse" than in Germany. The question now was the immigration of hundreds of thousands entering Palestine each year and the establishment of the Jewish National Home "at a rapid tempo," as intended in the Balfour Declaration and the mandate. Weizmann's work during the last few weeks had been very important, but he had left London for Rehovot at a time when "systematic clarification and concentration of all our forces" had to continue or the ground gained would be lost. The entire Executive in Jerusalem, Ben-Gurion pointed out, shared this overall view.[87]

A pogrom in Przytyk on March 9, which claimed three Jewish lives, as well as destroying shops and homes, reflected mounting antisemitic terror in Poland. After Marshal Pilsudski's death the previous May, the virulent, semi-Fascist Endek and Nara political parties had stirred the peasant masses to violent attacks on the country's Jewish citizens. Scores of Jews were murdered and hundreds more wounded. Separate "ghetto benches" for Jewish students were installed in universities, while heavy taxes threatened the traditional practice of kosher slaughter (shehita). Individual assaults and the throwing of bombs increased. Premeditated riots after the Przytyk pogrom followed in Novo-Wilekja, Swiernik, Czestochowa, Lodz, and elsewhere, with tragic results. The Jewish Telegraphic Agency had warned in January that Polish Jewry "is living on a volcano which may erupt at any moment." One month later, Gruenbaum had urged the Va'ad HaLeumi to press for an international campaign to protest and to fight for Jewish equality of rights there. Laski headed a Joint Foreign Committee delegation on March 26 to see Col. Beck, at which time they were told that they had to "face the fact of the uprising of chauvinist Nationalism in a number of countries, one of the results of which had been increased anti-Jewish activity." The Polish

Foreign Minister expressed to the group his certainty that the disturbances were of a temporary nature, and said that there was no reason to
fear that the Warsaw government would not be able to quell them in the
future.[88]

There were two main currents of English public opinion concerning
the increasingly volatile development in European affairs, Laski pointed
out to Waldman a day after the Commons debate on Palestine. One desired to procure peace in Europe at any price, including acceptance of
Germany's invasion of the Rhineland as only going into her own territory.
The latest speeches in Commons of Austen Chamberlain, Churchill, and
others, on the other hand, showed that there existed "a strong body of
informed, responsible and representative public opinion that will never
so long as it exists cease to be mindful of the persecution of the Jews,
and will never cease to remind others of its continuance." Yet he feared
that "too much of an obtrusion of Jewish news designed to maintain a
hatred of Germany or to reduce the chances of an understanding" would
lead to accusations that the Jews were fomenting war and disturbing the
chances of peace. "Whatever we do is wrong for someone," he realized,
but Laski was certain that the "Stephen Wise technique" of protest demonstrations at that time would be "absolutely and fatally wrong."[89]

The Commons debate fully convinced Thomas, attacked by Baldwin in
Cabinet the next day over this marked opposition from all the parties to
HMG's policy, that "there is practically no support in the House for the
Government proposals." Even the London *Times*, often reflecting Cabinet
views, asserted that the Council scheme would "do more to hinder than
to promote" the development of genuine self-government. Its lead editorial concluded with a question: "Why not make haste slowly, and give understanding time to grow under the protection of an impartial authority
which can be trusted to deal justly with Jew and Arab alike?" Although
Thomas was impressed by Wauchope's March 9 cable and showed its
contents to the Cabinet, he then asked the High Commissioner in a "secret and private" cable to consider the alternative proposals made in the
debate. Those included appointing a Commission of Enquiry or inviting
Arab and Jewish delegations to London for a Round Table Conference.
The Cabinet agreed with this move on the morning of March 25.[90]

Later that day, the Colonial Secretary told Weizmann, accompanied
by Marks and Sacher, that he had instructed Wauchope to "drop all
idea" of raising qualifications for immigrants with capital *"and to open*

negotiations re Transjordan!" Dugdale, resorting to italics when recording the WZO president's report of the interview, later discovered that
Thomas had not informed the Cabinet before taking this step. Thomas
had refused to circulate the telegram in question, saying that it was
only a private wire. Weizmann, Namier, and Dugdale herself decided to
do nothing at the present in order to influence the course of events,
Namier quoting to her Lord Shelburne's saying "Inactivity may be a
political curb, when it proceeds neither from indolence nor from vice."[91]

The Agency Executive in Jerusalem was uncertain how to proceed
when hearing on March 27 of Lothian's proposal for the Legislative
Council. One telegram from Melchett spoke about a purely advisory
body, which reflected Wauchope's preference. A second gave Melchett's
opinion that the Cabinet would accept representative membership based
on parity of numbers between Jews, Arabs, and British representatives.
The Arabs would object to an advisory body, Ben-Gurion remarked, and
the key issue was authority rather than parity. Ussishkin, an opponent
of parity, argued that an advisory body would make decisions, and
Wauchope would resign if his own proposal were not adopted. Having
objected to minority status, Ben-Gurion reminded his colleagues, the
Agency could not refuse the "great achievement" of parity, first suggested by Amery, if HMG made that offer. Wauchope would not accept
this change; Thomas, attacked from all sides in Parliament, was likely
seeking a compromise.

Senator agreed with Ruppin that since the Arabs would oppose, the
Agency should accept. The Executive had to decide how far it would go if
Parliament endorsed parity, he added. If the Agency caused Wauchope's
resignation, London would not forgive us and we, too, would regret this
in light of our experience with other High Commissioners. Ben-Gurion
concluded that if the government proposed parity, the Executive would
discuss it and summon the WZO's Va'ad HaPoel (Executive Committee).
It was too early to argue about making a choice between "the High
Commissioner or the Council", although the fact could not be ignored
that the parliamentary debate had aroused anger in Wauchope's circles.
He intended to call Melchett and to cable that the mandatory administration would certainly not accept the parity proposal.[92]

Three days later, Mapai's Political Committee discussed what Ben-
Gurion should raise as Zionism's immediate objectives when meeting
next with Wauchope. Katznelson advocated immigration, more access

to government lands, a greater share in public works, and government aid in securing national capital. Moshe Beilinson added defense of the yishuv's agricultural and industrial economy, along with vigorous help for a large development program. Ben-Gurion wondered if the time was ripe to discuss a fundamental change in the administration's policy, to expand Palestine's absorptive capacity so that the yishuv could take in 100,000 immigrants per year. Katznelson doubted if something would be gained from such talk, "even in front of a friend," given the current political situation. Dov Hos thought of the mandatory's help for raising a loan; Golomb considered immigration most important.

Remarking that attacks against Jews in Poland might be followed by the same here, Sprinzak asked: "How can we walk calmly here and not pay attention to the mounting Arab strength in Palestine and its surroundings?" Locker wished to concentrate on immigration, although agreeing with Sprinzak that the Arab question was "the most important question." He expressed concern that the leadership was not "quite engaged" in this matter "out of despair, out of the recognition that we do not have a solution now." If we had focused on this problem, he added, perhaps we would have found solutions, even if partial ones. Ben-Gurion immediately responded to this point. There were only two solutions to the Arab question, he declared: a mutual agreement, which the Arabs did not want, and "reliance" on England. He would have chosen the first, but in the circumstances, we had to rely on England. Disagreeing with Locker's statement, Ben-Gurion disclosed that a few weeks previously an important Arab had suggested that he meet with Husseini. He agreed but Husseini refused, saying that an agreement would not ensue and the hour was not suitable for a mere conversation. Before us lay "a burning question," Ben-Gurion ended: the need to bring the Jews of Germany and Poland to Eretz Yisrael. Since the Arabs did not want this, there was for the moment no other option but to depend on England.[93]

Ben-Gurion knew of recent Arab activities by leading opponents of Zionism. On March 25, his diary recorded that Haj Amin had traveled to Egypt to discuss with its political leaders the Arab stance in the event of world war, along with the organizing of a pan-Arab congress. Riyad as-Sulh, a Sunni Muslim and leading Lebanese nationalist, discussed these matters with him as well. Abd al-Rahman Shahbander, a prominent Sunni politician and head of the pan-Arab movement in Syria, presided over a meeting in Cairo, where Syrians and Palestinian Arabs heard his appeal for an Arab Union. Shahbander also called on the Palestinians to act. This group agreed on joint action to be launched by the Arab Scouts, students, and youth organizations; rejection of the Legislative Council; mass meetings in Palestine similar to those which had occurred in Syria; and propaganda in Egyptian newspapers in support of the Arabs of Palestine.[94]

For the Arab leaders, the debate proved that the British would either modify Wauchope's Palestine proposals or postpone them, as MacDonald's letter to Weizmann had fundamentally nullified the Passfield White Paper. Government intelligence reported the Arabs rapidly feeling that their only hope lay in "a more militant policy." Meeting on March 29, the National Defense Party resolved to accept the Council as a first (though inadequate) step towards self-government; request Wauchope to accelerate the Council's formation; adopt "a sterner attitude" if the scheme were shelved or postponed; and protest to the League of Nations and to the Arab kings against the Parliament's "interference." Two days later, Nashashibi, Husseini, and Ghusayn decided to prepare a memorandum for their parties' approval, urging that the Council be set up without delay, a "state of civil disobedience" to be declared if they received no satisfactory answer within ten days. The Arab press went further in outspokenness, none more so than the usually moderate Christian daily *Falastin*:

> Recent events have proved that the Jews are the actual mandatory—this alone is sufficient pretext for the termination of the mandate ... the English do not understand leniency and kindness, we should therefore be most extreme and speak to them in a language they do understand. The Arabs, who are doomed to annihilation in ten or twenty years, thanks to the British and Jews, must be prepared to commence working for their salvation forthwith and must also be prepared to die on the field of honor, which is preferable to succumbing to the Anglo-Zionist policy of cunning and poison.[95]

Wauchope was keenly aware of the shadows enveloping the Promised Land and the Near East, as well as to those casting a pall over European Jewry, and he had to reply quickly to an anxious Thomas about the

Council. Two weeks earlier, in response to protest from the European Muslim Congress held in Geneva a half year ago, Wauchope had officially declared "there is no question of the establishment of a Jewish State in Palestine." On March 26, Minister Resident Cox warned him that Abdullah's messengers had put it to the National Bloc in Syria that the Emir should be king of "an amalgamation" of Transjordan and Syria, and he added that young Syrian nationalists would take "a very prominent part" in any future agitation in the region. Wauchope also realized that HMG was not in a position at present to carry out the pledge of a Council. Responding on March 28 to Thomas's request for his views, he declared his preference for a Royal Commission to determine the time for introducing the Council. The Arabs would boycott a Round Table Conference, the High Commissioner pointed out. He thought it best that Thomas invite a deputation of representatives of the major Palestinian Arab parties to visit London and state their case. The Colonial Secretary accepted this suggestion two days later, but expressed to Wauchope on March 31 that, frankly, he could give these visitors nothing.[96]

This accumulation of rising tension occurred just when the country's introduction to radio broadcasting inflicted a new insult on the yishuv. On March 31, the Palestine broadcasting service to the world was inaugurated with Wauchope's address presented in English, Hebrew, and Arabic. Arab nationalists took umbrage, however, to the official translator's using the Hebrew words "Eretz Yisrael" whenever "Palestine" occurred; in protest, Khalil al-Sakakini resigned from his post as the director of Arab broadcasts. Wauchope then ordered that only the two letters "Ai" should be pronounced on the radio, to conform with the Hebrew initials A.I. ("Aleph" and "Yod" for Eretz Yisrael), exactly as they appeared alongside the English and Arabic on mandatory coins and stamps. "Even my unpatriotic, certainly un-chauvinistic Jewish soul is hurt," Szold confessed, "though at the same time I cannot deny that the Arab agitators are consistent—if they object to the mandate and to the Jewish National Home, they are right in insisting upon Palestine, and banishing Eretz Israel [sic]."[97] The impasse between Jew and Arab appeared more insoluble than ever.

Endnotes

1. David Ben-Gurion, *Zikhronot*, 3, 1-2.
2. Ibid., 10-11, 21-24, 27-28. Before 1925, the capitalist entry requirement was £500. In 1931, Arlosoroff had requested that it return to that sum, without success (ibid., 26).
3. "Repercussions of the McDonald Letter of Resignation," n.d., Box 55, Morris R. Cohen MSS, Special Collections Research Center, University of Chicago Library, Chicago; *Nation*, January 15, 1936; Sherman, *Island Refuge*, 65. The Report of a League of Nations commission of inquiry under the Earl of Lytton, signed on September 4, 1932, found that Japanese action one year earlier was not self-defense, and that Japan's creation of the Manchukuo puppet government did not flow from "a genuine and spontaneous independence movement." It recommended the establishment in Manchuria of an autonomous administration under Chinese sovereignty with international advisors and recognition of Japanese economic interests.
4. "Repercussions," Box 55, Cohen MSS. For one pro-German response by an American citizen against "Hebrew-made Bolshevism," and Hitler "fighting the battles of all progressive men," see Ehlers to McDonald, January 3, 1935 (should be 1936), McDonald MSS.
5. Bentwich to Mills, Jan. 1, 1936, A255/325; Mills to Bentwich, Jan. 11, 1936, A255/294; both in CZA; Foley memorandum, Jan. 23, 1936, FO 371/19919, PRO. For the creation of the Council, which McDonald had encouraged before his resignation, see David Silberklang, "Jewish Politics and Rescue: The Founding of the Council for German Jewry," *Holocaust and Genocide Studies* 7.3 (Winter 1993): 333-371; *Refugees and Rescue*, 79, 99-100; McDonald to Warburg, Nov. 13, 1935, High Commissioner files, McDonald MSS.
6. Meeting, Jan. 2, 1936, and 1936 report, S25/22735; Cohen memorandum, Jan. 24, 1936, S25/10187; all in CZA; Grossman at National Board, Jan. 29, 1936, HA; Wilson to Mandates Section, Jan. 8, 1936, file R4066/6A/668/668, LNA.
7. Weizmann to Marks, Jan. 7, 1936, WA; Ben-Gurion, *Zikhronot*, 9. For Kaplan's views on this subject, see Kaplan to Brodetsky, Jan. 3, 1936, S46/50, CZA. PICA (Palestine Jewish Colonization Association) was founded by Baron Edmond de Rothschild in 1923 (date also variously given as 1912 and 1924) to renew the work of the Jewish Colonization Association (ICA). PICA was directed by James Armand de Rothschild (1878-1957). By 1930, it had acquired about 12,000 acres in different areas, setting up fifty settlements of different types, including the towns of B'nei Brak and Herzliya. It assisted rural settlements as well as developing or financing economic enterprises such as wineries, the Potash Company, the Palestine Electric Company, and Nesher Cement. PICA also drained swamps, giving the land thus redeemed to existing or newly founded rural settlements there. In 1934, PICA purchased

the Huleh valley. After May 1948, PICA made a free gift of all its lands to the Israeli government.

8   Ben-Gurion, *Zikhronot*, 14; Weizmann to Melchett, Jan. 17, 1936, WA.

9   Weizmann to Rappard, Jan. 27, 1936, WA. Also see Rappard to Weizmann, Jan. 2, 1936, A508/17, CZA. To Rappard's argument that an oath of loyalty to the mandate would meet the Agency's fears, Weizmann doubted that the government, wishing to secure Arab participation, would insist on this. In addition, "the Irish example should have taught us what value is to be attached to enforced oaths and declarations."

10   Selby to Eden, Jan. 18, 1936, FO 371/20019, PRO.

11   Cabinet conclusions, Jan. 15, 1936, CAB 23/83; Thomas memorandum, Jan. 10, 1936, CAB24/259; both in PRO; Weizmann to Sieff, and Weizmann to Namier, both Jan. 22, 1936; Weizmann to Melchett, Jan. 23, 1936; all in WA.

12   Sherman, *Island Refuge*, 67-70.

13   *League of Nations—Official Journal*, Jan. 20, 1936, file R5719/50/22122/7100, LNA; Bentwich to McDonald, Feb. 8, 1936, microfilm 1935, Warburg MSS; Barbara McDonald Stewart, *United States Government Policy on Refugees from Nazism, 1933-1940* (New York, 1982), 230-232. For a brief evaluation of the subsequent work of the High Commission, which continued to be "bound and shackled" until the office closed with the outbreak of World War II, see Michael R. Marrus, *The Unwanted: European Refugees in the Twentieth Century* (New York, 1985), 164-166.

14   JAEJ, Jan. 19, 1936, CZA.

15   Senator to Hyamson, Jan. 8, 1936, S49/88; Senator memorandum, Jan. 17, 1936; Senator to Warburg, Jan. 19, 1936; both in S7/219; all in CZA.

16   Szold talk, Jan. 1936, file 4, Szold MSS, HA. By then, Szold was rather doubtful whether Arab-Jewish reconciliation could take place. In 1935 she recalled having met young Arab teachers in Palestine fifteen years earlier, to whom she explained the Jewish "inmost wishes" for return to Palestine, where everything was sacred and precious as "the background of our Holy Scriptures." In response to her appeal that they work in peace on the "old soil," one Arab asked: "When you Jews profess so much good will, why then have you called the Britons to be our boss?" Another angrily declared: "It is impossible for us Christian Arabs to cooperate with you. You have crucified our Saviour Jesus and we never can forgive you." Very sadly, Szold responded: "If this really happened, it happened two thousand years ago, and if you want to argue about facts so far away then it is impossible to discuss the problems of the present and the future" (Herz to Bernstein, Sept. 16, 1940, H. Szold file, Philip Bernstein MSS, University of Rochester Library, Rochester, NY).

17   Moshe Sharett, *Yoman Medini, 1936* (Tel Aviv, 1976), 15-26.

18   Samuel statement, Jan. 21, 1936, Box 341, Felix Warburg MSS, AJA.

19   Shepherd, *A Refuge from Darkness*, 108-110; Bentwich to McDonald, Dec. 4, 1935, PAC files, McDonald MSS; "Summary of cable correspondence with

London Delegation," Feb. 7, 1936 memorandum, Box 341, Warburg MSS, AJA.

20 *New York Times*, Jan. 6, 1936; Birchall to Sulzberger, Jan. 29, 1936, German files, Sulzberger MSS.

21 "Summary of cable correspondence," Feb. 7, 1936 memorandum, Box 341, Warburg MSS, AJA; Wise to Goldmann, Jan. 8, 1936, file 10/20, Horace Kallen MSS, AJA; Einstein to Brandeis, Jan. 7, 1936, microfilm #145, Brandeis MSS; Governing Council minute, Jan. 10, 1936, AJC; Mack to Billikopf, Jan. 21, 1936, file 13, Billikopf MSS, AJA; Jewish Agency to Marks, Jan. 17, 1936, Jewish Agency files, ZA; Sulzberger memorandum, Jan. 6, 1936, German files, Sulzberger MSS.

22 Memorandum on Visit, Feb. 7, 1936, Box 341, Warburg MSS, AJA.

23 Sharett, *Yoman Medini*, 25-26.

24 Wauchope–Agency delegation interview, Jan. 26, 1936, A264/406, CZA.

25 Wauchope to Shertok, Jan. 27, 1936, A264/47, CZA; Sharett, *Yoman Medini*, 37, 41-47.

26 Namier memorandum, Jan. 27, 1936, A312/44, CZA; N. A. Rose, ed., *Baffy: The Diaries of Blanche Dugdale, 1936-1947* (London, 1973), 2, 4; Lourie to Shertok, Jan. 29, 1936, WA.

27 Wauchope–Arab delegation interview, Jan. 29, 1936, CO 733/297/75156/I, PRO. The Jewish Agency obtained a copy of this document (S25/22789, CZA).

28 Ben-Gurion to Brandeis, Jan. 30, 1936, microfilm #25, Brandeis MSS; Hall to Agency, Jan. 29, 1936, microfilm #1934, Warburg MSS.

29 Thomas – Anglo-Jewish delegation interview, Jan. 31, 1936, microfilm #1934, Warburg MSS.

30 Jewish Agency statement, Jan. 31, 1936, microfilm #1934, Warburg MSS; Sharett, *Yoman Medini*, 41-47. The Agency's statement about the 656 displaced Arab land owners added that only a fraction of this small total declared its readiness to avail themselves of resettlement opportunities that the administration offered, showing that the remainder had in the meantime been absorbed into Palestine's economic life. Moreover, the bulk of these 656 were not former land owners but tenant cultivators, for the benefit of which category the government had passed protective legislation in 1935.

31 Sieff to Weizmann, Jan. 31, 1936; Sieff to Thomas, Jan. 31, 1936; both in Israel Sieff MSS.

32 Weizmann to Baer, Feb. 1, 1936, in *The Letters and Papers of Chaim Weizmann*, vol. 17, 170-171.

33 Wauchope–Weizmann–Shertok interview, Feb. 16, 1936, microfilm #1934, Warburg MSS.

34 Memorandum of visit, Feb. 7, 1936, Box 341, Warburg MSS, AJA.; Wise to Goldmann, Feb. 3, 1936, file 10/20, Kallen MSS.

35 Warburg to Weizmann, Oct. 10, 1935, microfilm #1931; Weizmann to Warburg, Jan. 24, 1936, microfilm #1933; Warburg to Hexter, Feb. 3, 1936, microfilm #1935; all in Warburg MSS.

36 Warburg to Hexter, Feb. 3, 1936, microfilm #1935, Warburg MSS; Memorandum of visit, Feb. 7, 1936, Box 341, Warburg MSS, AJA; Wise to Goldmann, Feb. 4, 1936, Wise MSS, Box 49, AJA.
37 Memorandum of visit, Feb. 7, 1936, Box 341, Warburg MSS, AJA; Warburg to Weizmann, Feb. 5, 1935, microfilm #1933, Warburg MSS; Flexner to Frankfurter, Feb. 20, 1936, Robert Szold MSS, ZA.
38 Samuel remarks, Feb. 5, 1936, Box 4, Records of Meetings, CFRA.
39 Resolution, Jan. 26, 1936, National Board minutes, HA.
40 Roosevelt to Wise, Feb. 1, 1936, reprinted in *Palestine and the Destiny of the Jewish People, Harold Ickes Address, UPA Dinner, May 24, 1936* (New York, 1936). The unanimous joint Congressional resolution of 1922 favored "the establishment in Palestine of a national home for the Jewish people, it being clearly understood that nothing shall be done which may prejudice the civil and religious rights of Christian and all other non-Jewish communities in Palestine, and that the holy places and religious buildings and sites in Palestine shall be adequately protected." This was signed by President Warren Harding on September 21. Similar statements were made subsequently by Presidents Calvin Coolidge in 1924 and Herbert Hoover in 1928. *Palestine, A Study of Jewish, Arab and British Policies*, 251-252.
41 Carl Herman Voss, *Stephen S. Wise, Servant of the People* (Philadelphia, 1970), 174, 208-210; Wise to Brandeis, Jan. 12, 1936, microfilm #25, Brandeis MSS; Governing Council, Jan. 14, 1936, AJC; Fertig to McIntyre, Jan. 14, 1936, PPF 601, FDRL; Frankfurter to Wise, Jan. 30, 1936, Box 109; Wise to Weizmann, Mar. 6, 1936, Box 122; both in Wise MSS. Wise had thought Thomas, "for all his limitations and blunderings," "infinitely better" than Roosevelt, "who is an irresponsible Boy Scout with a beautiful smile and a winsome manner back of which is exactly zero. The country will have every reason to regret his election, which now seems inevitable" (Wise to Lowenthal, Oct. 27, 1932, Box 67, Wise MSS).
42 Draft to UPA convention, n.d., PPF 601, FDRL; Wise to Frankfurter, Jan 12, 1936, microfilm #155, Brandeis MSS; Message, Feb. 13, 1936, and Early to Commissioner of Education, Jan. 29, 1936, both in PPF 995, FDRL.
43 *Refugees and Rescue*, 111-112. For the view of the British ambassador in Berlin against McDonald's proposal, see Sherman, *Island Refuge*, 63-64.
44 Crane to Roosevelt, Jan. 28, 1936; Roosevelt to Crane, Feb. 10, 1936; both in PPF 462, FDRL. Crane's reference to Russia must have meant Birobidzhan, the "Jewish Autonomous Region" that was officially created in May 1934 by the Soviet leadership in order to strengthen the security of the Soviet Far East, to improve its relations with the West, and to provide a partial solution to the economic difficulties facing Soviet nationalities while offering a Communist alternative to Zionism. Jewish collective farms, Yiddish theatre and publications, and Jewish councils were created in this area of 13,900 square miles. Stalin's purges of 1936-1938 would prove a shattering setback to this development, with the Jewish settlement there not exceeding 20,000

on the eve of World War II.

45   Wise to Roosevelt, Feb. 13, 1936, OF 1978, FDRL; Frankfurter to Wise, Feb. 27, 1936, Box 68, Wise MSS; Roosevelt to Wise, Feb. 21, 1936, OF 1978, FDRL; Wise to Frankfurter, Mar. 10, 1936, Box 109, Wise MSS. For Knabenshue, see Naomi Cohen, *The Year After the Riots: American Responses to the Palestine Crisis of 1929-1930* (Detroit, 1988), 28-31.

46   Wauchope to Weizmann, Feb. 2, 1936, WA.

47   Va'ad HaLeumi, Feb. 2, 1936, J1/7236, CZA. Weizmann's biblical references to the "mixed multitude" and "sweep out the evil from your midst" were based on *Exodus* 12:38 and *Deuteronomy* 13:6.

48   Ben-Gurion, *Zikhronot*, 64-65.

49   Porath, *The Palestinian Arab National Movement*, 159-160; Ben-Gurion, *Zikhronot*, 161-162.

50   Antonius to Crane, Feb. 8, 1936, Crane MSS.

51   Ben-Gurion, *Zikhronot*, 65-66, 70; Wauchope to Thomas, Feb. 8, 1936, S25/27774, CZA.

52   Ben-Gurion, *Zikhronot*, 68-69.

53   JAEJ, Jan. 16, 1936, CZA. Thon served as the managing director of the Palestine Land Development Company, Smilansky led the Farmers' Federation, Auster served then as Deputy Mayor of Jerusalem, Rokah would soon become Mayor of Tel Aviv on Dizengoff's death, and Makhnes founded HaNoteah to purchase land in Palestine. Ben-Ami chaired the B'nai Binyamin organization, which founded some early agricultural settlements in Palestine and was named for Baron Edmond de Rothschild, and was the long-time Mayor of Netanya. For Brit Shalom, see Adi Gordon, ed., *Brit Shalom V'HaTsiyonut HaDu-Leumit: HaSh'ela HaArvait K'Sh'ela Yehudit* (Jerusalem, 2008).

54   Hexter–Ben-Gurion conversation, Feb. 3, 1936, microfilm #1935, Warburg MSS.

55   Warburg to Marks, Feb. 13, 1936 and Hexter to Warburg, Jan. 18, 1936, both in microfilm #1936, Warburg MSS; Hexter to Warburg, Feb. 1936, file 842, Hexter MSS; Karpf to Lipsky, Jan. 14, 1936, ZOA files, ZA; Karpf to Warburg, Jan. 21, 1936, Karpf to Senator, Feb. 4, 1936, both in microfilm #1933, Warburg MSS.

56   Waldman statement, Jan 5, 1936, Chronos file, AJCA; Bressler to Warburg, Jan. 23, 1936, microfilm #1935, Warburg MSS.

57   Laski to Warburg, Jan. 6, 1936, microfilm #1933, Warburg MSS; d'Avigdor-Goldsmid to Karpf, Jan. 10, 1936, Waley Cohen to Laski, Jan. 13, 1936, and Laski reply, Jan. 14, 1936, all in file E3/201, BDA; Laski to Waldman, Jan. 20, 1936, Boycott Germany-England files, AJCA; Laski to Waldman, Jan. 16, 1936, microfilm #1932, Warburg MSS.

58   Weizmann–Shertok–Wauchope, Feb. 12, 1936, WA. Weizmann cited the figure of 15,000 dunams given to the Arabs in the Huleh when addressing the Va'ad HaLeumi in early February. Va'ad HaLeumi, Feb. 2, 1936, J1/7236, CZA.

59   Weizmann to Wauchope, Feb. 22, 1936, S25/31, CZA. Weizmann sent Felix Warburg a copy of this lengthy reply.

60   Archer Cust, "A New Plan for Palestine," *The Spectator*, Feb. 21, 1936, 294.

61   Rose, *The Gentile Zionists*, 61; Weizmann to Namier, Feb. 5, 1936, WA; Thomas to Melchett, Feb. 20, 1936, Minutes, BDA; Advisory Committee on Imperial Questions, Palestine, Feb. 1936, International Subcommittee MSS, Labour Party Archives; *Baffy*, 6; Melchett to Wise, Feb. 28, 1936, Box 116, Wise MSS. In 1930, Labourite Henry Snell had submitted a dissenting report with a more pro-Zionist conclusion as a member of the Shaw Commission.

62   Weizmann to Wise, Feb. 27, 1936, WA. A savage conflict broke out between the Greeks and the Turks in 1919 over the Smyrna region and islands in the Aegean. Populated mainly by Greeks, these had been assigned to them by the Allies, but the Turks refused to give up territories that were geographically a part of the Turkish homeland. Kemal Ataturk formed a nationalist Turkish army in Anatolia, where Greeks were partly massacred and partly expelled in the course of a full-scale war. Peace was only restored in 1922. Ratified by the Treaty of Lausanne (July 24, 1923), and aided by the League and the Near-East Relief Commission, some 1,250,000 Greeks were repatriated in exchange for some 350,000 Turks until 1930.

63   C.I.D. report, Mar. 17, 1936, FO 371/20018, PRO; Porath, *The Palestinian Arab National Movement*, 160; E.S. (Sasson)-Y.F. (Fransis) talk, Mar. 3, 1936, S25/3051, CZA.

64   *Al-Ahram*, Mar. 2, 1936, J1/4139, CZA.

65   E.S. (Sasson) memorandum, Mar. 4, 1936, A24/197, CZA.

66   Ben-Gurion, *Zikhronot*, 237, 78-79.

67   Ibid., 75-77. Jacob Landau headed the Jewish Telegraphic Agency. Henry Montor, Palcor's managing editor, also served at this time as publicity director of the combined JDC-UPA appeal. Since he was working full-time on the latter, his other job had to remain a secret. He fulfilled both tasks by taking an office for Palcor in the Chainin Building, a few floors below the Allied Jewish Appeal office on 42nd St. in the Pershing Building, rushing back between both or running over to the Associated Press office (then on 383 Madison Ave.) if there was a news article that he particularly wished to call to its attention (Montor to Meltzer, Jan. 29, 1971, A371/38, CZA). Founded in 1934, Palcor was dissolved in 1948.

68   Warburg to Wise, Mar. 3, 1936, microfilm #1933, and Warburg to Hexter, Mar. 2, 1936, microfilm #1932; both in Warburg MSS; Ben-Gurion, *Zikhronot*, 89; J. Wise to Brandeis, Mar. 10, 1936, microfilm #25, Brandeis MSS.

69   Waldman to Rosenberg, March 2, 1936, file 1/33, Morris D. Waldman MSS, AJA; Waldman to Laski, Mar. 6, 1936, file P-13/2/13, CAHJP; Waldman to Stroock, Mar. 19, 1936, Foreign Countries/Palestine file, AJCA. From the same perspective, the American Jewish Committee and the Board of Deputies of British Jews, reflecting the stand of their respective governments, opposed the American Jewish Congress's endorsement of a boycott of German

goods and articles. See Naomi W. Cohen, "The Transatlantic Connection: The American Jewish Committee and the Joint Foreign Committee in Defense of German Jews, 1933-1937," *American Jewish History* 90 (December 2002): 363-365. For the ultimate fate of the Petition, see Monty Noam Penkower, "Honorable Failures Against Nazi Germany," 282-285.

70 Thomas to Wauchope, Mar. 6, 1936; Wauchope to Thomas, Mar. 9, 1936; both in CO 733/293/75102, II, PRO.

71 William L. Shirer, *Berlin Diary: The Journal of a Foreign Correspondent, 1934-1941* (New York, 1941), 48-59; *Baffy*, 6-8; Memorandum, Mar. 4, 1936, Roosevelt file, Sulzberger MSS; Memorandum, Apr. 14, 1936, Box 14, Arthur Willert MSS, Sterling Library, Yale University, New Haven, CT; *Inside the Third Reich: Memoirs by Albert Speer*, trans. R. and C. Winston (New York, 1971 ed.), 113.

72 Mapai Political Committee, Mar. 9, 1936, Labor Party Archives.

73 Melchett to Ben-Gurion Mar. 6, 1936, A180/129, Melchett memorandum, Mar. 18, 1936, A185/55, both in CZA; Ben-Gurion, *Zikhronot*, 88-89. When an Anglo-Zionist delegation complained that the dumping of Japanese goods on the Palestine market was unfair to the local population, which could not reciprocate with selling goods to Japan, a Colonial Office representative remarked that "it seemed not unlikely that the country was approaching the limits of the possible increase in agricultural production" (Clauson-Brodetsky-Lourie interview, Mar. 3, 1936, microfilm #1934, Warburg MSS).

74 Weizmann to Samuel, Mar. 11, 1936, Z5/17025; Lipsky to Wise, Mar. 10, 1936, and Weizmann to Wise, Mar. 12, 1936, both in Z4/17198; all in CZA. *Baffy*, 7; Weizmann remarks at Jewish Agency Executive Jerusalem, Apr. 10, 1936, CZA. Weizmann's use of "The crooked could be straightened" derived from *Ecclesiastes* 1:15.

75 Rose, *Gentile Zionists*, 62; *Manchester Guardian*, Aug. 9, 1937. Eder, the first practitioner of psychoanalysis in Great Britain, had earlier advocated Israel Zangwill's Jewish Territorial Organization (ITO) to acquire land in East Africa or elsewhere for Jewish refugee settlement. He embraced Zionism after visiting and then living in Palestine for some time as a member of the Zionist Commission that the Foreign Office had sent in April 1918 to serve as a liaison body between the yishuv and the British authorities there. Three years later, the WZO Congress replaced the Commission with the Palestine Zionist Executive, which then became responsible for administering all Zionist activity in Palestine.

76 Weizmann remarks at the Jewish Agency Executive Jerusalem, Apr. 10, 1936, CZA; Lourie to Shertok, Mar. 13, 1936, WA; *Palestine Post*, Feb. 19, 1936; Rose, *The Gentile Zionists*, 64.

77 Rendel to Kerr, Mar. 6, 1936, FO 371/18965, PRO. Jewish Agency intelligence obtained a copy of this letter (S25/22713, CZA).

78 Porath, *The Palestinian Arab National Movement*, 160-161.

79 Parkinson-Weizmann-Lourie interview, Mar. 16, 1936, CO 733/289/75054,

PRO and WA. Asked about the Revisionists, Weizmann indicated that whereas "they counted for very little" as a body in Palestine, their influence was strong in Poland, "where desperation had led many people to give quack remedies a trial."

80   Parkinson minute, Mar. 19, 1936, CO 733/297/75156/I; Wauchope to Thomas, Mar. 9, 1936, CO 733/293/75012/II; both in PRO.

81   Kingsley-Heath–Joseph interview, Mar. 16, 1936, microfilm #1934, Warburg MSS.

82   Ben-Gurion, *Zikhronot*, 91; R. (Rutenberg) to Chief, Mar. 8, 1936, A251/27, CZA. It is likely that Herbert Samuel, chairman of the corporation's board, was "the chief."

83   Melchett "secret" memorandum, Mar. 18, 1936, A185/55, CZA.

84   Weizmann to Wise, Mar. 23, 1936, Box 122, Wise MSS.

85   *Parliamentary Debates, House of Commons*, 310, cols. 1079-1150, 1166-1173, Mar. 24, 1936; C.V. Wedgwood, *The Last of the Radicals* (London, 1951), 191; Weizmann remarks at the Jewish Agency Executive Jerusalem, Apr. 10, 1936, CZA.

86   *Baffy*, 10-11.

87   Ben-Gurion, *Zikhronot*, 97-98.

88   *JTA*, Mar. 11, 1936; JTA "Report on the Situation of the Jews in Poland," Jan. 1, 1936, file 122, Mowshowitz MSS; Va'ad HaLeumi, Feb. 16, 1936, J1/7236, CZA; Laski–Goodman–Brotman memorandum and interview with Beck, Mar. 26, 1936, Foreign Countries-Poland, AJCA; Joint Foreign Committee minutes, Apr. 22, 1936, BDA. One report listed 118 Jews killed and 1,350 wounded between Pilsudki's death and January 1937. *New York Times*, Feb. 7, 1937. In the aftermath of the Przytyk pogrom, many people were arrested. The trial started on June 2 and involved 43 Polish and 14 Jewish defendants, the latter charged with aggressive behavior towards Polish peasants. The verdict was pronounced on June 26, with eleven of the Jews sentenced to prison terms of from 6 months to 8 years, while 39 Poles received sentences from 6 months to 1 year. The accused Jews claimed they were acting in self-defense, but the court rejected those arguments. The verdict outraged the Jewish community in Poland, leading to a number of nationwide strikes. News of this pogrom horrified the Polish Jewish population, as well as Jews around the world, and contributed to a significant emigration of Jews from Poland. The Yiddish poem *Es Brent* ("It is Burning") was written by Mordechai Gebirtig in 1938 about the Przytyk pogrom.

89   Laski to Waldman, Mar. 25, 1936, file P13/2/13, Mowshowitz MSS.

90   "A Council in Palestine?" London *Times*, Mar. 25, 1936; Cabinet Paper 87(36), Mar. 21, 1936, CO 733/293/75102, and Thomas to Wauchope, Mar. 25, 1936, CO 733/293/75102/II, both in PRO; Weizmann remarks at the Jewish Agency Executive Jerusalem, Apr. 10, 1936, CZA.

91   *Baffy*, 11.

92   JAEJ, Mar. 27, 1936, CZA.

93 Mapai Political Committee, Mar. 30, 1936, Labor Party Archives.

94 Ben-Gurion, *Zikhronot*, 99.

95 Air Headquarters Intelligence report, March 31, 1936, S25/22733, CZA.

96 Orts report, "Palestine," *League of Nations, Permanent Mandates Commission, Minutes of the Twenty-Ninth Session* (Geneva, 1936), 190; Cox to Wauchope, Mar. 26, 1936, S25/22779, CZA; Wauchope to Thomas, Mar. 28, 1936; Thomas to Wauchope, Mar. 30, 1936; Thomas to Wauchope, Mar. 31, 1936; all in CO 733/307/75438/1, PRO.

97 *Palestine Post*, Mar. 31, 1936; al-Sakakini, *KaZeh Ani, Rabotai!*, 184-185; Szold to sisters, Apr. 10, 1936, Szold MSS. The biblical connection (*Joshua*, chap. 7) particularly disturbed Szold, who concluded: "But Ail City where Joshua was defeated on account of the misdeeds of his people. Spelled Ayin not Alef, but in our imperfect pronunciation the two sound alike. That makes the insult smart still more."

5. The Arab Revolt Begins

On April 1, 1936, the British Cabinet accepted Wauchope's advice that implementation of the Legislative Council proposals be postponed pending further consultation with the Palestinian Arabs, Thomas to announce this decision in Parliament. The same day Wauchope informed Thomas in a "private and secret cable" that Haj Amin made a "spontaneous suggestion that in view of Jewish propaganda it would be necessary to send Arab representatives to London to present the Arab case and he had already suggested this to the Supreme Muslim Council." In addition, Nashashibi informed the High Commissioner by letter that the National Defense Party accepted the scheme, while repeating that the Balfour Declaration should be abrogated and the Arabs granted self-government. It appeared that these perennial rivals understood that the Council would be lost for good unless they and other leaders acted swiftly.[1]

The following afternoon, Wauchope informed five Arab party leaders of the invitation, an Istiqlal representative markedly absent. He suggested that they agree upon a deputation without delay, and that a sixth individual represent the Arab Christian community. He could not help them in the choice, but they would be free to make their own contacts in London. In reply to Husseini, Wauchope stated that the delegates would be at liberty to put forward their views on immigration and land sales, although he could hold out no hope that Thomas would modify the reply received from him on January 29. The final decision, the High Commissioner made it clear, would rest with His Majesty's Government. After a short discussion, they all accepted.[2]

Earlier that morning, Ben-Gurion met with Wauchope. Although Jewish Agency intelligence informed Ben-Gurion just before then that the Chief Secretary had approved an Arab delegation to London, Wauchope did not mention this at all. Telling the High Commissioner that Weizmann had obtained the Treasury's approval in principle to a large loan for the yishuv, Ben-Gurion then dwelt on the current dangers facing Jewish communities, particularly in Germany and Poland. With the world's doors closed to us, he asserted, the Jewish people would have "no choice but suicide" if Palestine also had no room for Jews. Confronted as well by Palestinian Arab leaders "whose orientation is pointed to a new world war," their agitation influenced by present developments in the international arena and in the Near East, the Zionists had to attain a larger immigration and a quicker tempo of development. When the Arabs saw this as an irreversible reality, he claimed, they would take it into account, just as the Agency took account of the reality of the Arabs in Palestine and the surrounding countries.

The renewal of Wauchope's appointment for another five years, Ben-Gurion went on, held the promise of future stability in the hands of an experienced High Commissioner who knew Palestine, its people, and its problems, and had accomplished great things in his first term. These five years could be critical in our people's fate. If Jewish immigration could continue annually for the next five years at last year's number, almost all of the National Home's difficulties would be solved and the political stumbling blocks removed. Told that Douglas G. Harris, the mandatory's expert on absorptive capacity, was not hopeful about Palestine, Ben-Gurion noted that Harris's past experience with Australia, Canada, and India did not suit Palestine. Despite the country's far smaller size, the Zionists had made unique progress building here "because we do not have another land." We wish to begin now with the Jordan Valley and the Negev, he noted, as well as Transjordan. Aside from land, the yishuv also wanted to expand industrially, but capable Jewish factory owners in Holland and Belgium, who feared for their future in light of events in Germany, did not want to invest in Palestine while they lacked faith in securing help from the administration. As for better Arab-Jewish relations, Ben-Gurion ended, he feared that creating a political institution in Palestine at that time would accentuate their differences and not encourage cooperation. As he left the room, Wauchope said: "I wish to promise you again my full sympathy for the Jews of Germany and Poland."[3]

In order to negate HMG's penchant for the Council, Ben-Gurion sent Reuven Zaslani (later Shiloah) to London with a personal message that the Agency Executive office there demand that Jewish and Arab delegates be invited to a Round Table Conference. Ben-Gurion promoted this idea in a long conversation in Jerusalem with Lord Lytton on April

4, arguing that a Royal Commission might aggravate the "unhealthy political tension" in the country still more. It was not right that only the Arabs received an invitation to the Colonial Office. Lytton agreed, even though he and his friends were supporters of Baldwin's government, as he did with Ben-Gurion's championing of parity on a Council. The Arabs, in Lytton's opinion, could not complain of any unfair treatment since the termination of the Great War. The Arabs must be taken as "an entire Arab nation," and not only as Palestinian Arabs, and the Arab nation had received the Kingdom of Arabia, Iraq, and the Emirate of Transjordan after the war. Palestine in its entirety, including Transjordan, was "rightly and justly" given to the Jews, Lytton felt, and no constitutional change should be made that might hinder the fulfillment of the pledge given to the Jewish people.[4]

Unbeknownst to Ben-Gurion and his colleagues, some Palestinian Arabs were taking steps at that moment to stoke fury and resolve yet further. On April 5, leaders of "al-Jihad al-Muqaddas" (Holy War Society), headed by Abd al-Qadir al-Husseini, held a meeting in the Shihada Hassuna house in al-Lud (Lydda). The 29-year old al-Husseini and his associates decided to form *fasa'il* (groups) to fight off Jewish attacks on the Arabs and to cooperate with the *Ikhwan al-Qassam*. Under the leadership of the elderly Sheikh Farhan al-Sa'adi, the latter had been fighting the British in northern Palestine since Qassam's death, and currently resolved to expand their attacks against Jews passing through the Arab "triangle" in the center of Palestine. Ten days later, the *mujahideen* (warriors engaged in a *jihad*) of al-Sa'adi's group would launch their first operation on the Nablus-Tulkarm road.[5]

On April 5, Jabotinsky, then at the New Zionist Organization's headquarters in London, pressed for "decisive action" in light of an "alarming report from Palestine voicing acutest apprehension of anti-Jewish outbreaks" on an "unprecedented scale." These attacks, he warned Wauchope, sought to force Zionist acceptance of the Legislative Council, and experience showed that such developments "inevitably" result in bloodshed, especially considering "scarcity Imperial Troops inefficiency Police" and "absence legalized Jewish self defense." The High Commissioner forwarded this telegram to Thomas three days later, noting that Thomas's invitation to the Arab party leaders "has effected a *détente* in the local political situation for the time being." The Muslims' Nebi Musa annual feast, "when the fanatical crowds can easily be swayed to a pitch of frenzied religious excitement," had passed without violent incident. The danger "will recur if there should be any reversal of policy as regards the Legislative Council," Wauchope cautioned, but the Imperial forces were adequate for the present provided that no "serious deterioration" occurred in Palestine or in Europe. He would not recognize the existence of any armed forces outside of those of HMG. Three days later, Wauchope and his Executive Council decided to take no action towards legalizing illegal immigrants, which the Jewish Agency had regularly requested.[6]

Convinced that Wauchope had engineered Thomas's invitation to the Arabs in order to secure the Council, Ben-Gurion did not share Weizmann's optimism about the deputation's coming appearance in London. He could not overlook the High Commissioner's "obstinacy" and influence, or the propaganda that the delegation would make, supported by the majority of Palestine's population and the sympathy of the Arab/Muslim world. Although Zionists "need not perhaps fear" that any disturbances would occur before the party representatives' departure, it might be assumed that if the group met with little success, it would give a hint that riots should be arranged. Since the invitation reopened the whole Palestine question, Zionists had to press an aggressive expansion plan: develop agriculture and industry; exploit all water resources; open up Transjordan to Jewish settlement; increase the yishuv's strength in the defense forces and the public services generally; and speed up colonization and immigration.

Parity on the High Commissioner's Executive Council, in Ben-Gurion's view, would be a first step towards agreement with the government on the constitutional question. If HMG permitted the entry of at least 500,000 Jews into the country within the next five years, he concluded in a long letter to Brodetsky on April 9, a basis would be established for Arab-Jewish agreement and England would be freed from the "Arab problem." The pressure of British public opinion and Parliament, which were capable of feeling the Jewish tragedy and viewing affairs in Palestine "not as a temporary expedient but as a matter of historic right," could help achieve this fundamental change in policy.[7]

The new turn of events with respect to the Legislative Council did not worry Laski, whose deepest fears just then focused on the issue of Zionist support for the World Jewish Congress. He fully agreed with similar concerns that Waldman had raised at the American Jewish

Committee's annual meeting in January. "Moving heaven and earth" in a successful effort to prevent the Board of Deputies of British Jews from associating itself with the prospective Congress, Laski considered the Zionist domination of Jewish life more than ever "likely to undermine our position in the countries of the Diaspora." To the sympathetic Felix Warburg, he concluded a long letter with this credo:

> The bogey of the international Jew which finds its crudest form in the Protocols [of the Learned Elders of Zion], is, if you will bear with me, definitely assisted both by Zionism and by its offshoot—or, as I have termed it, facet—the World Jewish Congress. We need, except in matters of philanthropy, which belong to humanity, and therefore may be talked of and acted upon in the language of universals, to preserve, emphasize, and indeed reinvigorate, as individuals, our status as citizens of the particular state in which we live, and if, in accordance with the non-Zionist approach to Palestine, we pursue Palestinian work, no one will quarrel with us. If, however, we decline to take this stand, but say that the loyalty of the Jew is a divided or twin loyalty, we shall destroy the Jewish position the world over.[8]

In Palestine, Thomas's invitation to the Arabs to select six representatives to lay their views about the Council directly before him, officially announced in reply to a question from Wedgwood in Parliament on April 8, brought internal squabbles again to the surface. At an all-party meeting one day earlier, Husseini insisted that the Palestine Arab Party have a majority in the delegation, since they were the largest party. He proposed that the 1930 delegation to London should be re-elected, with the addition of Mayor Khalidi in place of the late Musa Kazim Pasha. Haj Amin, Husseini, and Rock would represent his party, joined by Nashashibi, Abd al-Hadi, and Khalidi. Left out of the suggested delegation, Salah vehemently objected. The Nashashibis also rejected Husseini's proposal, demanding that each party be represented by its leader or have a National Congress convened which would elect the delegation.[9]

Other differences swiftly arose in this same meeting, Shertok informed the Mapai Political Committee. In a discussion as to the group's platform, Salah demanded that HMG be told that the delegation was traveling to London in order to call for the repudiation of the Balfour Declaration. Nashashibi characterized this strategy as stupidity, and Salah left the meeting. Both the National Defense Party and the National Bloc Party indirectly argued that the Mufti's supporters insisted on the composition of the delegation because of their reluctance to accept the Council in its present form. In Ben-Gurion's later evaluation to the Agency Executive, he reported that the Palestine Arab Party disguised its fundamental objection to the Council lest the Arab masses accuse it of siding with the Jews. Those favoring the Council dominated the discussion because of the general feeling that Jewish opposition signaled that the proposed body was good for the Arabs. A minority against the Council charged that the delegation at this time would accomplish nothing, recalling that the Syrian deputation had traveled to Paris only after a general strike had forced the French government to surrender and promise the substitution of a treaty for the mandate. The majority responded that it was best to accept the invitation now, and if they saw that they were unsuccessful, they would give a sign so that disturbances would break out in Palestine along the lines of the Syrian model.[10]

As late as April 15, these differences of opinion had pushed off the delegation's departure. Opposition to the trip arose within the Arab community once it heard of the invitation. The Istiqlalists, in particular, continued to think that cooperation with the British was impossible, confrontation the only alternative. Jewish Palestine remained in a state of "suppressed turmoil," wrote Henrietta Szold to her two sisters in the United States.[11] None in the yishuv could foresee a spontaneous outbreak and its three-year aftermath, which would justly be termed the Arab Revolt.

The murder of Yisrael Avraham Hazan on April 15 provided the spark. That Wednesday evening, armed Palestinian Arabs blocked the Nablus-Tulkarm road between Nur Shemesh and Anbata and demanded money from passers by. Three travelers discovered to be Jewish were pulled out of their cars, put in the front seat of a lorry, and shot at point-blank range. Hazan, an elderly Jew from Saloniki who had arrived in the Promised Land one year earlier, died on the spot. A British police company eventually brought his body and the two wounded men to Tel Aviv's Hadassah hospital. In retaliation, the next night two members of the militant Irgun Bet faction of the Hagana approached a tin shack near the Petah Tikva-Yarkona road, and killed Hassan Abu Rass and Selim Al Masri, workers in an orange grove nearby.

Friday morning, Hazan's funeral took on political overtones when right-wing Revisionist Betar youngsters and a roiled crowd, its ranks swelling to 6,000, conveyed the victim's body to the city's old cemetery. Alongside a black-bordered Zionist flag at the head of the procession, speakers attacked the mandatory power, and calls for revenge—"Down to Jaffa"—were heard. After the burial, police succeeded in dispersing a group headed for that predominantly Arab urban center, but stones from balconies and roofs in the southern direction of Nahalat Binyamin Street began to pelt police reinforcements. N. Kramer, an observant Jew then in charge of Tel Aviv's Division of Police, fired two shots into the air. A baton charge, followed by several arrests, finally cleared the area.[12]

Despite this turmoil, Ben-Gurion still rejected the premise that the aspirations of the Jews and Arabs were incompatible. That same day, in a talk with Antonius at Magnes's suggestion, the Agency Executive chairman advocated unrestricted Jewish immigration, parity on a Legislative Council, and a Greater Syria including an autonomous Jewish "Eretz Yisrael" that incorporated Palestine and Transjordan. (He did not consider the Jordan River a boundary, but "a river of Eretz Yisrael.") Antonius responded with a counterproposal for a "United Syria," stretching from the Taurus Mountains to the Sinai Desert, which provided for a Jewish "establishment" extending from Haifa to Gaza and the Jezreel Valley, while Arab Palestine would stretch from Hebron to Nablus. These would not be cantons, but two separate countries. Two subsequent talks that same month could not bring agreement, especially when Antonius stressed that the Arabs "had no option but to fight against the flooding of the country with Jews." Ben-Gurion had already told the Mapai Political Committee on April 16 that "there is no chance for an understanding with the Arabs unless we first reach an understanding with the English that enables us to become the preponderant force in Palestine." Only the fact of a strong yishuv, he argued, could then bring the Arabs to see that an agreement with the Jews was better than strife and war.[13]

Already in 1928 Ben-Gurion had first laid down the maxim "I am not willing to give up even one percent of Zionism for the sake of 'peace'." Magnes had assured him the previous November that serious and influential Arabs would approve of a yishuv numbering 40 percent of

Palestine's population. Ben-Gurion replied that he was prepared to meet with Arabs for negotiations, but only for a joint effort to arrive at a solution satisfactory both to the Jews and to the Arab nation as a whole. The two foundations for this activity had to be a constitutional guarantee that neither people would dominate the other irrespective of numerical strength, and help for the Arab countries outside of Eretz Yisrael. "We should not, we cannot, drive the Arabs out by force," he had told Ussishkin that same month. In March Ben-Gurion had told Magnes that the difference between them was that Magnes was prepared "to sacrifice immigration for peace, while I am not, though peace is dear to me." He went on: "And even if I were prepared to make a concession, the Jews of Poland and Germany would not be, because they have no other choice. For them immigration comes before peace." "Peace for us is a means, not an end," the Agency Executive chairman would soon write to his colleagues. "The end is the fulfillment of Zionism, complete and total fulfillment of Zionism in its maximum scope." For him that entailed unlimited immigration and settlement throughout Palestine.[14]

Coinciding with Ben-Gurion's argument that Polish and German Jewry had no alternative but emigration, a report from the Paris central office of the JDC described the conditions of the distressed Jews in Europe during the past few months. Since the beginning of the year, an additional 7,000 German Jews had been deprived of their livelihood in the newspaper, graphic arts, and printing fields. They were also being eliminated as druggists and veterinarians, while the on-going boycott against Jewish businesses, forcing more and more Jewish firms into "Aryan" hands, led to at least another 1,500 Jewish employees losing their jobs and "facing destitution." An estimated 15,000 Jewish children still in the general public schools would likely be forced to leave their classes during the course of the year. The plight of the German Jewish refugees in France, Holland, and Czechoslovakia was "becoming daily more serious." A "profound depression" had affected Poland's Jews, with Jewish business enterprises continuing to be hard-hit. In Rumania, particularly in districts struck by famine, conditions were as bad as those in Poland. "Abysmal poverty" was reported in Bessarabia, Marmorosch, and other parts of the country. Schools, hospitals, and welfare institutions were "barely able to keep up their miserable existence."[15]

In Palestine, a delegation of Arab leaders finally prepared to depart for talks at the Colonial Office, Nashashibi having informing Wauchope on April 16 that only the Palestine Arab Party was unwilling to accept the Legislative Council if the British refused further concessions. Insisting that this meeting be considered entirely unofficial and confidential, Wauchope pointed out to Nashashibi and Husseini that the delegation's position would be stronger if it presented a unanimous front. In any event, all parties ought to be represented. His own stance had changed in the last month, and Thomas had "quite properly" decided that the Council, immigration, and land sales should be discussed. The High Commissioner could not nominate the delegates, which should have the confidence of all the parties. Since May 4 had been fixed as the date for the first interview with Thomas, Wauchope needed a definite reply in the course of the next two days; postponing the interview would "create a very bad impression." Husseini suggested that the delegation be HMG's guests for the first three days of the visit and independent thereafter, but dropped the idea once Wauchope replied that this would be "both ungracious and unwise." The meeting then came to a close.[16]

Wauchope and other mandatory officials saw no particular reason to anticipate serious trouble in Palestine. The energetic effort of this Highland Covenanter, committed to the Council, land sale restrictions, and limits on Jewish immigration, appeared heading for realization. He cabled to Thomas on April 18 his certainty that if Egypt and Syria were granted "further measure of self-government" and HMG's proposals for a Council were postponed, "it needs no argument from me to prove that Arab discontent in Palestine will be strengthened." In Chief Secretary Hall's later testimony before the Permanent Mandates Commission, there had been "a *détente*" as a result of Thomas's invitation to send an Arab deputation to England. The actual report on April 18 of the Intelligence Branch of the C.I.D. consisted of only two pages, giving no indication of impending violence. Hall, together with the Air Officer Commanding and the Inspector-General of the Police, prepared for a trip to Akaba for a couple of nights. In fact, their kit had been sent on ahead.[17]

Quiet reigned briefly. Instigators failed that same Friday to sway Muslim devotees in Ramleh, currently celebrating the holiday of the legendary traveler and preacher Nebi Tzalach, to assault Jews in response to (false) stories that scores of Arabs had been butchered in Petah Tikva. On Saturday, individual Arabs were attacked in Tel Aviv, and groups of youngsters gathered in the Jewish municipality's streets to proclaim "In

Blood and Fire Judah will Rise!" and sing the "HaTikva." However, tension had subsided sufficiently towards the evening that British troops, summoned earlier by police, could return to their base in Ramleh. The Tel Aviv headquarters of the Jewish Agency's clandestine Hagana defense force, thinking that overt danger to the yishuv had passed, cancelled its status of "on alert" as well.

The explosion of Arab violence occurred early on April 19 in nearby Jaffa, the same day that Zvi Denenberg, Hazan's driver, died of his wounds. Arab agitators from "the Youth" (*Al-Shabab*) and the Scout movement convinced indigent Syrian Hourani day laborers, Bedouin of the southern Negev region, and migrants from neighboring Arab countries that three Houranis and an Arab woman had been killed in Tel Aviv the previous night. The announcement by Arab notables, after visiting the Tel Aviv police station at the District Commissioner's invitation, that these rumors were false had little effect. Knives, daggers, stones, and clubs quickly became weapons of choice against Jews unfortunate to be in the Jaffa area. Arab policemen generally restricted their efforts to bringing victims to local hospitals; many Jews found refuge among Arab friends and in government buildings. By afternoon, police and soldiers had restored order. Jaffa and Tel Aviv came under a night curfew, and the Defense Order-in-Council was proclaimed for the entire country, empowering Wauchope to put Emergency Regulations into effect. The day's toll among the Jewish populace proved heavy: nine killed and close to sixty injured, who were transferred to hospitals in Tel Aviv.[18]

The spontaneous outburst of April 19 gathered momentum in the next several days. While thousands turned out in Tel Aviv to mourn the nine Jewish victims, assaults began on April 20 against Jews living in neighborhoods between Jaffa and the first modern Hebrew city. Seven more Jews died, scores were wounded, and considerable damage was done to property. By the third day, some 7,000 had found shelter in Tel Aviv. While the yishuv kept to a strict position of self-restraint (*havlaga*), the police killed six Arabs and deported hundreds of Houranis beyond Palestine's borders. This proved too late to restore calm, however, as young Arab zealots of the Istiqlal Party seized upon the events in Jaffa to press the older leadership for a firm stand against the mandatory government. The residents of Nablus, fired up by Zu'aiter, independently called for a general strike and set up a National Committee, as did other Arab centers. By the time the five leading Arab parties met again with Wauchope on April 21, they had received Zu'aiter's warning that the delegation had to present one demand: "halt the Zionist immigration," much as the Egyptians' "one word: constitution" had gained their objective from HMG after a lengthy strike. Confronted by this rise in militancy, the party leaders informed Wauchope that their delegation would not depart for London "in compliance with the expressed desire of the nation and in view of the state of anxiety and disorder which now prevails in the country." A committee was then formed to organize a strike of Arab transport in general, Nashashibi reluctantly joining the others in support. "This is a struggle," wrote al-Sakakini in his diary, "for life and for death."[19]

The Arab Higher Committee came into being in Nablus on April 25, uniting the different factions under the control of the extremist Palestine Arab Party and the Istiqlal. Haj Amin, equally taken by surprise at the masses' spontaneous outbreak, became president, with Abd al-Hadi the new group's secretary. A Committee of Ten announced that a non-violent, general strike would continue until HMG granted all of the demands submitted to Wauchope the previous November. If no successful results were forthcoming by May 15, the Committee would next declare a civil revolt, including acts of destruction and terror against the government and Jews alike. The following day, the ten-man executive resolved to send Wauchope a memorandum to this effect, establish connections with National Committees in other towns, encourage the boatmen's strike in Jaffa and Haifa ports, and visit the Arab victims in Jaffa. It also agreed to appeal to the Arab kings and rulers for support, to ask the mandatory about the news that the Jewish Agency was supplying food to Jewish police constables, and to examine closely the question of requiring government Arab officials to join the strike. By the month's end, practically all Arab shops were closed and Arab transport disappeared from the country's roads. Jerusalem's streets were strewn with nails thrown by Arab youngsters; non-Arab traffic passing through Nablus, Tulkarm, and Jenin was conveyed under police escort as far north as Afula.[20]

The Jewish Agency Executive in Jerusalem immediately rose to the emergency. In separate interviews with Hall and Wauchope on April

19, Shertok insisted on the preservation of security, the chief question of the hour. His and Weizmann's quick intervention spurred the High Commissioner to publicize an accurate version of the unprovoked assaults in Jaffa, although twelve days passed before Thomas corrected his own statement to Parliament about "clashes" between Arabs and Jews, similar to the erroneous announcements made officially after the Arab riots of 1921 and 1929. On April 23, with all communication cut off between Tel Aviv and government offices in Jaffa, the Agency Executive requested that HMG create without delay parallel offices in Tel Aviv and open a harbor there. Six days later, it demanded that the strike, which also affected government works and whose Committee included Arabs occupying official positions (the Supreme Muslim Council's Haj Amin and Jerusalem's Mayor Khalidi), should be declared illegal. It also sought extensive funds from world Jewry to prepare a permanent home in Palestine for Jews "for whom there is no hope" in Germany, Poland, and other countries.[21]

The explosion in Jaffa terribly depressed Wauchope. "It was a great tragedy; things were going so well," he told Weizmann on April 21. That morning, he had asked the Arab leaders to use their influence to prevent "all lawless acts," confessed that he had "no doubt" that the Arab policemen had not lived up to their duties, and thought that the Jaffa port would be operative in a day or two. Ben-Gurion privately cautioned the Zionist Organization of America not to attack HMG or the High Commissioner publicly, but Shertok minced no words in conveying to Wauchope the widespread impression that the government "has passively yielded to violence and abdicated its powers to the Strike Committee." He and Ben-Gurion pressed Wauchope on April 29 to adopt sterner measures: open the Jaffa port; safeguard road traffic; warn workers and government officials against joining the strike; renew labor on mandatory and municipal works; enlist additional policemen, including Jews; and impose collective punishment on villages engaged in uprooting trees and burning Jewish fields. To their surprise, the High Commissioner accepted the view of the strongly anti-Zionist Chief Justice, Sir Michael MacDonnell, that the strike was legal, as well as his advisors' opinion that the Arab Higher Committee's Strike Council included "more moderate" men. Wauchope's optimism notwithstanding, Ben-Gurion and Shertok reported to associates in London that the position appeared to be "grave," and that important Arab friends of theirs thought the strike had not yet reached its peak.[22]

"I indeed fear that if discontent is not lessened," Wauchope cabled to Thomas on April 30, Palestine might be faced with "a long period of disorders and civil disobedience in many forms." Accordingly, he again championed his earlier proposals to establish a Legislative Council, restrict sales of land to Jews, and "somewhat reduce" Jewish immigration "not because of Arab pressure," but because these measures were "equitable and just in themselves." If the government could not proceed now with the Council as approved by HMG, however, then he agreed that Thomas's suggestion of a Royal Commission (already made by critics during the March 24 debate in the House of Commons) was the wisest course to adopt. The commission's terms of reference should include Wauchope's three major proposals, and make recommendations for "lessening animosities" and establishing "a feeling of lasting security" in Palestine. That independent body should inquire and offer recommendations as to the government's future immigration policy, including the "serious problem" created by unauthorized Jewish entry. The commission, or perhaps a separate body, ought to investigate as well the causes and process of the "disorders." It should be set up as soon as possible, the secret dispatch concluded.[23]

That same day, Wauchope opened the Levant Fair in Tel Aviv. The event represented a partial victory for the Zionists, who had insisted that it take place despite Arab terrorism and the general strike. In his address, the High Commissioner deplored the loss of life and the lawlessness to date. Yet he showed no indignation, reported Szold, who still thought that "a dose of righteous indignation coming from a righteous man" such as Sir Arthur Wauchope "might do good." Moreover, since the Jaffa port continued to be at a standstill, with no measures yet taken by the administration to have work resume there, considerable amounts of perishable goods and a great part of the exhibits from various nations remained on the docks. As a consequence, the fair's opening was restricted to home produce, lest some countries hit by the stoppage be put at a disadvantage opposite others. With a little firmness on the part of the government authorities, it would have been possible to clear at least those goods already in the port, since a private firm succeeded on its own initiative in clearing a part of the Levant Fair goods from the Jaffa customs station and transferring them to Tel Aviv. Ultimately, insisted the Jewish Community Committee of Tel Aviv and Jaffa, a large port on the Tel Aviv seashore, serving the 250,000 Jews of the city and its environs, was essential. The strike will be kept up, Szold feared, and "Satan will continue to find mischief to be done by idle hands."[24]

The Arab Higher Committee stood firm. On May 1, Haj Amin headed a delegation to Transjordan, noting to Abdullah that the Committee had not started this "popular movement," nor could the party leaders stop it unless HMG made some concessions. In possession of Shertok's confidential request to him one day earlier that he urge the Committee to seek a peaceful settlement, Abdullah advised that the leaders avoid coming into conflict with the police and make every effort to preserve England's friendship. When Haj Amin informed the High Commissioner that the Committee might support illegal measures such as non-payment of taxes, Wauchope summoned its executive on May 5 to warn that they disassociate themselves from all illegal activities, declared that the strike was only harming the poorest Arab class, and suggested that they send a delegation to London. Abd al-Hadi immediately replied by letter, asserting that the Arab people had been aroused to "defend themselves and their national existence" after HMG had acceded to Zionist pressure, instead of granting the just Arab claim for independence. In consequence, "all members of the Arab nation" decided upon a general "peaceful" strike. Yet the government continued to pursue its policy of "judaization," not even halting immigration as had occurred after the "disturbances" of 1921 and 1929, a policy which would compel the Arabs "to evacuate their country and will lead then to extermination (sic)." The Committee "deeply" regretted all the loss in life and property, Abd al-Hadi concluded, but since the causes lay in HMG's continuing this "oppressive" policy, the consequences must be borne by the government alone.[25]

Wauchope wired Thomas the same day that he opposed stopping Jewish immigration indefinitely in return for the Committee's calling off the strike or sending a delegation to London. This would show weakness on the government's part, but he "saw no bridge to assist leaders out of the impossible position in which they now [were] placed." It seemed, he thought, that the strike would continue and the chances of further disorders would grow. (The Italians occupied Addis Ababa that same day, and the resistance of the Ethiopians collapsed.) Wauchope instituted proceedings under the Criminal (Seditious Offenses) Ordinance against the Arab Transport Strike Committee's manifesto of May 2 urging non-payment of taxes and that Arab officials in government cease work. Defiantly, the Arab Higher Committee, spurred on by Haj Amin's speech in Jerusalem to the National Committees, issued a Civil Disobedience Resolution on May 7, refusing to pay taxes if their demands were not accepted in a week's time; one day later, a National Congress of the National Committees called for civil disobedience. Wauchope took no action forthwith to enforce his earlier warning, however, and even told *Palestine Post* editor Gershon Agronsky that Haj Amin's influence in "the present troubles" had been towards moderation. The local agitation, sparked by "exaggerated fear of losing their land," had spread from the towns to villages. Wauchope had no doubt of the "ultimate outcome," but stated that things now were bad and might get worse. "My general impression," Agronsky decided, is that "the H.C. is suffering from fatigue and anxiety, that he is worried more than he cares to admit."[26]

By then, Ben-Gurion grasped that the current "disturbances" radically differed from those of August 1929, when the yishuv had numbered only 150,000. In a long letter to Brandeis, he pointed out that no attacks had occurred since mid-April against Jewish settlements, now doubled or trebled in size and in number. The principal cities contained Jewish majorities; agriculture and industry were flourishing. At the same time, while the murderous 1929 riots had a religious character, Zionists confronted at present "*a serious political struggle*," their adversaries seeking to revoke the Balfour Declaration. To achieve this aim, the Arab leaders were making use of the latest political weapons, the general strike and civil disobedience. Aside from confronting Arab "pertinacity," which threatened not only the yishuv's economy but security across Palestine, Zionists were engaged in "a difficult—perhaps a decisive—political battle." The Jewish National Home had to witness a large increase of immigration and rapid growth. Only thus would the Arabs realize that "they must relinquish their destructive and sterile war against developing the country." Their leaders would then understand, Ben-Gurion ended, that they had to make their peace with a Jewish Palestine, whose presence did not threaten the future, the culture, or the identity of the Arab people, but rather helped them to "raise their material and spiritual welfare."[27]

Arab belligerence persisted, even after Wauchope broadcast on May 11 the arrival of significant reinforcements for the current two British infantry battalions, and declared that the government was determined to suppress lawless outbreaks and punish the offenders. Several acts of murder and repeated attempts at arson continued, some of Qassam's original followers becoming key commanders of local bands. Abd al-Hadi declared to Wauchope on the Committee's behalf that the strike was intended "as a defense of the Arab existence and not," as Thomas declared publicly, "with an intent to threaten" HMG so that it would stop Jewish immigration. For the last eighteen years, Abd al-Hadi noted on May 12, the Arabs had insistently demanded the stoppage of that immigration, which alone could reduce Arab fears and enable a delegation to discuss in London the "fundamental changes" that should be made. Two days later, Wauchope secretly informed a Committee delegation that HMG had accepted the High Commissioner's recommendation to appoint an independent Royal Commission in order to investigate "the cause of unrest in Palestine and the grievances of Arabs and Jews," but only after the reestablishment of civil order in the country. Without an immediate suspension of Jewish immigration, however, the Committee would not welcome a Royal Commission and the strike would continue, Abd al-Hadi going so far as to assert that if a change of policy depended on a commission, "the Arabs could but put their fate in the hands of God." The next day, the Committee published a manifesto supporting the non-payment of taxes.[28]

While Ben-Gurion and Shertok pressed Wauchope to take strong steps against the Committee's directing the activities of "incitement and rebellion," the Agency Executive in London urged members of the Cabinet and Parliament to adopt no decision concerning a rumored Royal Commission until Weizmann's imminent arrival there. "Serious consequences might ensue," Melchett cautioned Thomas, if concessions were made to those "who are embarking on a deliberate campaign of murder, arson, highway sabotage and civil disobedience, with the avowed object of forcing the Government to abandon its mandatory obligations." Weizmann met the Colonial Secretary alone at Claridge's for lunch on May 18, where he charged that Wauchope had failed to take more energetic steps against agitation by the Arab press and the Committee, and noted the Chief Justice's very lenient sentences for two of the strike leaders. He also spoke of a truly strong yishuv aiding HMG's interests in the Eastern Mediterranean, and of Palestine's ability to absorb another two million Jews. Nonetheless, that afternoon Thomas announced in the House of Commons the Cabinet's decision that, subject to the restoration of civil order in Palestine, an inquiry on the spot would be taken by a Royal Commission. It would investigate the causes of unrest and the alleged complaints of either Arabs or Jews; it could also ascertain whether the mandate had been fairly interpreted, but not challenge the mandate itself.[29]

The Arab Revolt stirred far different, deep anxieties within James Rosenberg of the American Jewish Committee and the JDC. Connecting the violence in the Promised Land to the position of fellow non-Zionists Waldman and Laski, he wrote that same day to Wise and Louis Lipsky, vice president of the American Jewish Congress, that the World Jewish Congress gathering scheduled for August "threatens the gravest of tragedies in Palestine." Given the recent outbreak of savage Palestinian Arab attacks, the convening of such an assembly would stimulate and might bring about a widespread Pan-Arab movement in the entire region "with a special anti-Jewish purpose." If the "undisputed facts" presented in McDonald's Letter of Resignation were "so totally without result," he observed, not producing "a ripple of action" from the League or elsewhere, what in the practical matter of protecting Jewish rights did they expect from the nations or the conscience of the world as a result of a World Jewish Congress meeting in Geneva? Getting no satisfaction from Lipsky's reply, Rosenberg reminded Wise of the tremendous achievements over the years of various non-Zionist Jewish relief organizations worldwide, and he charged that the projected Congress, also opposed by the Board of Deputies of British Jews and the Franco-Jewish establishment's Alliance Israelite Universelle, contained "a grave menace to Jewish life."[30]

Wauchope, the individual most responsible for the Royal Commission's creation, again assured Palestine's citizens that no strike and acts of violence would cause HMG to "deflect one jot" from discharging "in full" its mandatory obligations. That commitment included his decision to permit the unloading of cargo at a jetty on the foreshore of Tel Aviv, leading Mayor Dizengoff to hope that this signaled the first step towards a future port even as the yishuv continued its work of "construction and peace." The Jewish Agency also heard on May 18 that a schedule of 4,500 labor certificates had been approved, 1,000 deducted beforehand on account of students leaving educational institutions for work and of illegal immigrants who would probably arrive in the next six months. This did not fully meet the Agency Executive's request for

11,200 certificates, as Shertok would point out to Wauchope, but it did represent a considerable improvement on the schedule granted six months earlier. The High Commissioner was "most reluctant" to deport the Committee of Ten, he informed Thomas the same day, before it was "absolutely necessary" and before he saw a definite advantage in doing so. Haj Amin, Wauchope contended, would automatically be replaced by the "much more extreme" senior member of the Arab Higher Committee, and the same argument applied to those who would succeed the current Committee Executive.[31]

Wauchope's concessions to the Jews infuriated the Arab Higher Committee. It was "extremely astonished" to hear of the 4,500 certificate grant, Abd al-Hadi wrote to the High Commissioner, which showed that HMG still persisted in the application of "its wrong policy which has created the present state of anxiety in the country." The Committee "cannot bear the responsibility arising out of such a challenge" to "the Arab Nation," he emphasized, and it would be difficult for the leadership to continue to discharge its task, "which has reached a most difficult and critical stage." Haj Amin noted the tension caused at Jaffa port by the unloading of cargo aboard Jewish vessels in Tel Aviv, to which Wauchope countered that the administration approved the move because the "unreasonableness" of the Jaffa boatmen had closed that port for one month. HMG, added the High Commissioner, would be forced to take more drastic action if occurences of disorder, such as the fatal shooting on May 16 of three Jews outside of Jerusalem's Edison Theatre, did not decrease. Husseini and Abd al-Hadi told Abdullah that all Committee members had received anonymous death threats if they stopped the strike before obtaining sufficient guarantees that Jewish immigration would end, and Haj Amin informed foreign Arabic interviewers that the strike would continue until the Committee's demands were met. It continued to refuse Wauchope's request to sign a public appeal expressing hatred of murder and demanding that all Arabs refrain forthwith from all violent acts.[32]

The Arab Higher Committee, with increasing public support despite a wave of arrests against strike leaders on May 23, dug in its heels by the month's end. Secretly, it decided to pay three months' salary to Arab government officials if they agreed to strike and were dismissed from office as a result. Zu'aiter unsuccessfully appealed that the Committee of Ten should disband and then "open war" against the British, but

Abd al-Hadi told colleagues that if Arab mayors did join the strike, the Committee would "force" Arabs in the courts and other government institutions to follow suit. He was certain of victory, provided that they stood firm "to the end." He did not think that the "Arab nation" would maintain the strike for so long; some men had been killed, two to three each day, but "no independence occurred without bloodshed." Writing in *Al-Di'fa*, the decade's most important Arab newspaper, Salah declared that the proposal to appoint a Royal Commission was "an Anglo-Jewish ruse" and "a Zionist proposal." Echoing the Committee's sentiment, mayors of the ten chief Arab cities informed Wauchope on May 30 that their people in Palestine were resolved to resist until Jewish immigration stopped, Ramallah's representative concluding that they would demand even more in the future "when our sacrifices increased." The chief spiritual leaders in government service reiterated to the High Commissioner the point that never before had any Arab movement in Palestine been so "strong, widespread and determined," men and women prepared to commit suicide or be shot down by British troops rather than suffer Jews to become dominant.[33]

Matters were becoming "graver and more complicated," Shertok wrote to Ben-Gurion on May 31. The municipalities of Jaffa, Ramleh, and Gaza had gone on strike, and it appeared that Arab civil servants would be next. He heard from sympathetic heads of the police and the air force that Martial Law would likely be proclaimed, leading to a halt in Jewish immigration for six months and damaging all Zionist activities. According to Hagana intelligence, Wauchope had told the Arab mayors that immigration could not be suspended, but he listened "with great attention" to the suggestion of the mayor of Jaffa that the Royal Commission be sent out at once and that, on its arrival, Jewish immigration should be halted and then the strike would be stopped. Wauchope had just asked Ruppin if some leading Jews and Arabs could agree whereby the Arabs would call off the strike and the Jews would agree on their own initiative to a halt in immigration for about six months, pending the conclusions of the commission. In addition, the Arabs had no confidence in the appointment on June 1 of William G. Ormsby-Gore, a long-time Zionist ally, to succeed Thomas; Chief Secretary Hall remarked of the new Colonial Secretary, "another reason for an Arab revolt." The same day, Agency legal advisor Bernard Joseph estimated that the Arabs were spending 3,000 pounds a day on the uprising, with 60,000 British pounds in reserve, Italy clearly supplying funds to this cause.[34]

Wauchope's sudden suggestion for a voluntary halt to Jewish immigration actually emanated from some prominent members of the yishuv. Judge Gad Frumkin of the Supreme Court, after a talk with Alami, joined with Magnes, Rutenberg, Smilansky, and Palestine Potash Ltd. founder Moshe Novomeysky to draw up a Jewish-Arab Agreement for Palestine's future. It included Alami's proposal that the Jews should reach 40 percent of the total population after ten years, together with suggestions regarding labor, land, parity in a Legislative Council, and Palestine and Transjordan combining in one unit that would be invited to join an Arab Federation. Rutenberg urged Wauchope on May 20 to demand that the Jewish Agency try to come to an agreement with the Arabs after law and order were restored, and ten days later he concluded in a memorandum that a voluntary suspension of Jewish immigration should be done as a *"beau geste"* if necessary for reaching that understanding. "The Five" submitted their draft agreement on June 1 to the Agency, the final clause stating that if the Jewish Agency and the Arab Higher Committee agreed on the main points, the strike would end and implementation of the new labor schedule would be postponed.[35]

Only the government's "iron hand" could stop the present anarchy, Rutenberg informed Wauchope, the Arab Higher Committee having lost control of the strike to the implacable Arab youth. During the first week of the strike, he disclosed, one of the Committee had offered to stop it if £25,000 were distributed between eight of the ten executive members and another £25,000 given to settle all the outstanding problems "amicably" in London between the Arabs and the Jews. Weizmann summoned Rutenberg to his home in Rehovot, and the two agreed to proceed, but the scheme fell through owing to the opposition of Ben-Gurion and Shertok.[36] Twice in the past, Rutenberg admitted, he had successfully bribed Arab leaders. At present, however, the government had to arrest immediately 25-30 activist youngsters in each town, and keep them in prison for a few weeks. The Committee members should not be arrested, as that would make them martyrs while a body more competent and efficient would take their place, but the instrument through which they were acting should be disbanded. The roads must be free, the whole press suspended or "preventive censorship" established, and Martial Law should be instituted if necessary. He would use all his personal influence to get the support of Shertok and Ben-Gurion in arriving at a Jewish-Arab agreement. If the attempt were not undertaken, Rutenberg warned Wauchope, the next riots would be more serious, and perhaps "still more grave" if war broke out in Europe.[37]

From their first talk with Alami in 1934, Ben-Gurion and Shertok had realized for the first time that the Arabs would oppose the Jews despite the benefits provided them by the Zionist movement. In May, during two conversations with Bernard Joseph, Alami suggested that the Jews voluntarily agree to cease immigration for a few months, the strike would then be called off, and negotiations for a Palestine settlement would commence. Alternatively, Joseph suggested a development project of 100,000 dunams of land to benefit Jew and Arab, parity in the Executive Council, and a five-year agreement on immigration without the Jews becoming a majority. The principal stumbling block that remained was how to bring "reasonable" Arab and Jewish leaders together without British involvement, Alami observed, and he would try to raise the question again with the Arabs. For his part, Ben-Gurion continued to advance his plan for parity on the Council, speaking to his Agency Executive colleagues on May 19 of a Jewish state of at least 8 million, the state to be part of an Arab Federation.[38]

Wauchope's trial balloon via Ruppin on May 31, including a personal letter asking whether the High Commissioner could be of any help in Jewish-Arab talks that would include a temporary halt to immigration, did not take flight. There was no question of the Agency Executive considering any such proposal, Ruppin immediately replied. Speaking frankly with Wauchope on June 2, Shertok termed the possibility "inconceivable." Dr. Magnes thought it advisable, Shertok went on, but he represented only himself. Such a gesture, moreover, would be hailed by the Arabs and by "enemies outside" who had "no more ardent desire" than to see HMG humiliated in talks with the Arabs, although Shertok entertained "no hope at all" that such contacts would lead to finding a way out of the present crisis. Abd al-Hadi was the "moving spirit" of the Committee, all the while urging greater activity in the terrorist campaign. Shertok advised that Wauchope deport the local leaders on a more comprehensive scale, place armed Jewish escorts on buses, impose additional fines on "turbulent" villages and keep their mukhtars (leaders) under arrest until the real criminals were delivered, and levy very heavy punishments for arson and uprooting of trees. Hearing that the Jews had already counted their twenty-ninth victim, Wauchope intimated that he regarded the outlook as "very gloomy."[39]

Wauchope deemed Palestine by now in "a state of incipient revolution." Although his military advisors advocated proclaiming Martial Law throughout the country if disaffection spread among Arab policemen or the situation worsened, he conveyed to Ormsby-Gore the conviction that this drastic measure should not be instituted unless "a serious deterioration" took place and then possibly only applied in certain districts. After the arrival on June 6 of the three additional battalions for which he had asked, three days after the initial formation of Jewish supernumerary police (*notrim*) to help defend Jewish settlements, Wauchope thought that the methods of "reasonable moderation" should be continued; if order could not be restored, then such "rigorous repressive measures" should be adopted as would intimidate the Arab population sufficiently to bring criminal acts to an end. He rejected Abdullah's appeal that Jewish immigration be suspended at present in order to end the disorders, and the mandatory's Executive Council agreed on more active steps against rising lawlessness. These included demolishing houses from which shots were fired upon British forces or whose occupants were proved guilty of violence; levying fines directly upon offenders without the present system of reference to Wauchope; and sending men from "bad or suspect" villages to detention camps. As to the Committee of Ten, while no ample grounds existed for acting against all the members, Abd al-Hadi would be sent without further delay to the Sarafand detention center.[40]

Yet no end appeared in sight. The Haifa-Lydda railway line came under attack. Wanton murder and burning of crops and houses went on, with several thousand trees ruthlessly destroyed in Mishmar HaEmek alone. The yishuv's financial condition was becoming more difficult from day to day, reported Kaplan to Ben-Gurion, and enormous sums were needed to set the wheels of the economic structure going again "to avoid a catastrophe." Bemoaned Szold: "There is safety nowhere in Palestine," while the growing alienation and "creating race-tight compartments" between Arab and Jew would not destroy "the seeds of race-hatred." The Arabs of Nablus forced the local committee to resign after it issued a proclamation calling for peace, Saleh informed Abdullah, and the Committee could not send emissaries to quiet the villagers, as they would be attacked. Hassan Shukri, the Arab mayor of Haifa, was pressured to sign a declaration that if Arab demands were not satisfied quickly he would leave office. The Committee continued to exist in "a feeble and disunited condition," Wauchope reported to Ormsby-Gore on June 16, yet he saw no weakening in the will and spirit of the Arab people. On the contrary, the High Commissioner thought that resistance was stiffening; supported as it was with large funds, it showed no sign of breaking for the present. Five days later, the first major guerilla engagement took place, when sixty Arabs from Nablus ambushed a convoy of troops; a third of the Arabs died.[41]

Ormsby-Gore, making no secret of the fact that he had been a "keen" Zionist even before the Balfour Declaration, saw his first concern as Secretary of State for the Colonies to be "the prestige and authority of the government as such, particularly in the East." HMG's failure to prevent Mussolini's victory in Abyssinia (Italy formally annexed that country on May 9 and the League voted to discontinue sanctions two months later) had been a "serious blow" to Britain's standing. While the Arab's open rebellion had to be met with force, he wrote to Wauchope, the future required some of Palestine's land to be set aside for Arab and Jewish "reserves," thereby meeting Arab fears of losing "the homes of their fathers and their children." He repeated the idea to the editor of the London *Times*, which devoted a feature story to it one week later.[42]

According to Weizmann's account of a first interview which he had with the new Colonial Secretary on June 16, Ormsby-Gore favored the working out of a development scheme which might convince "reasonable" Arabs and British public opinion that the Jews had no intention of "sweeping the Arabs out of Palestine." Law and order had to be restored first, but there could be "no question" of stopping immigration or reducing the Jewish citizens to permanent minority status in their National Home, Ormsby-Gore stressed to the highly satisfied Zionist leader. A Palestinian Arab delegation then visiting London received the same reply. Three days later, responding to a House of Commons debate which noted that the Arab attacks had left a total of 84 dead and 611 injured to date, he insisted that HMG's first task was the restoration of order, and then an impartial Royal Commission could suggest an equitable solution for all of Palestine's population. Restoring order included blowing up, during the next two weeks, the heart of Old Jaffa.[43]

Meanwhile, the efforts of "The Five" to reach such a settlement had achieved little. Rutenberg reported to the group on June 2 that the Agency's discussion about a temporarily fixed immigration resulted in a split vote, leaving the final decision to Weizmann and Ben-Gurion. He quickly cabled the pair in London to have "The Five" pursue the matter in light of the serious situation in Palestine, only to have Ben-Gurion reply that no negotiation should be conducted on a temporary halt or any limit below the great immigration of 1935. Weizmann appeared to accept Iraqi Foreign Minister Nuri Pasha al-Sa'id's suggestion that the Agency itself offer to suspend immigration for a period in order to help HMG, in turn sparking Ben-Gurion's passionate rejoinder at an Executive meeting that this would not only rend the Zionist movement in two, it would also instantly start civil war within the yishuv. Given the "fundamental" Arab-Jewish political divide, he asserted that only if the Arabs accepted a 60,000-65,000 annual Jewish entry, allowing the Jews to double their number within the next five years, could a basis for eventual agreement be laid. On June 16, Shertok and Kaplan informed Novomeysky that the Agency wished to continue the negotiations on its own. Four days later, Magnes told his colleagues that Alami, with whom he had worked out the original draft, was indignant. Ormsby-Gore's remarks in the House of Commons the previous evening confirmed Alami's belief that while "The Five" talked about informal committees and temporary immigration limits, Zionist leaders in London were trying to secure what advantages they could "behind the backs of the Arabs."[44]

Meetings with Shertok on June 21 and 24 did not allay Alami's suspicions. In the first, Alami declared Zionist leaders uncompromising and stated that Haj Amin was opposed to violence; Shertok stressed that "immigration is our fundamental right." In the second, Shertok opened by inquiring if Alami could obtain the support of those Arab leaders, clearly to include Haj Amin and Husseini, whose agreement was essential for cooperative negotiation with the Jews. If he could not "deliver the goods," the Agency would be wasting its time in discussion. Alami rejoined that it was wiser to wait until the Agency Executive offered a definite proposal which he, "much more moderate" than the others, considered acceptable. The Arabs, he noted, all felt that the Jews were intransigent like Ben-Gurion, who in effect had said to Arslan two years earlier, "You give us all we ask for now and in return we shall at some future date, which might never arrive, help you in the matter of an Arab Confederation." They also regarded Wauchope as "their greatest enemy." According to Joseph's notes, Alami agreed to let Shertok know shortly what response he had received from Committee leaders as to future talks. The same day, Alami confessed to Bentwich his distress at the "lack of foresight" shown by the Jews, whom he had expected to be "greater statesmen" than the Arabs, and at their lack of appreciation of the Arab feeling and point of view.[45]

Ormsby-Gore's thought that Palestine's division into cantons would resolve the land question, which he considered "the root of the matter," met with reserved support from Wauchope and Weizmann. The High Commissioner believed that if some form of Administrative Council could be formed in each canton, this would meet HMG's clear pledges to Jews and to Arabs while possibly muting the fears of each concerning domination by the other. Yet Wauchope considered it "a hard nut to crack" to get the two communities to accept a division of the country when "both claimed the whole," and he did not feel hopeful that Zionists would accept any scheme that appeared to limit considerably the sphere of the National Home in future years. Weizmann thought that the Zionists would consider carefully the idea of self-government in such an administrative area if the Arabs agreed to the Jews' right to acquire an additional million dunams of irrigable land in the plains. In the next 15-20 years, he projected to cantonization advocate Archer Cust, the yishuv would be able to settle perhaps 50,000 families on this land; an additional 100,000 families might be settled in towns on the basis of two in the towns and one in the countryside. The Zionists could thus find homes for a third of the two million Jews who could be said to be homeless in Central Europe.[46]

Haj Amin continued to resist any settlement, reviving at this same moment the religious issue that had figured so prominently in the Arab riots of 1929. As president of the Supreme Muslim Council, he wrote to Wauchope that Palestine was "a Muslim country," and that Britain's persistent policy along with troops' disregard of mosques and *Shari'a* religious courts spelled "great danger to the Muslim Holy Places," including the Mosque of Al Aqsa in Old Jerusalem's Harem-es-Sharif. Asserting that "the Zionist cause is fundamentally a religious cause of the first order," he also imputed to the Jews the design to rebuild their Holy Temple on the site of Al Aqsa. Hall rejoined that this "appeal to religious feelings throughout the Muslim world in order to achieve certain political aims in Palestine" would of necessity have "unfortunate results" when "the minds of large numbers of Arabs are excited by lawless and violent acts." Echoing a strong protest from Shertok, he further observed that even the 1930 Shaw Commission's pro-Arab conclusions had dismissed

Haj Amin's accusation at the time that the Jews entertained designs on Muslim holy sites. HMG, the Chief Secretary went on, consistently protected holy places, while the British had to return fire against shooting which had come from the direction of mosques. Agreeing to forward to Ormsby-Gore Haj Amin's letter, which was published in Arab newspapers, Hall reminded the Mufti again of his responsibility to declare "publicly and emphatically" that he stood on the side of law and order. Haj Amin remained resolute in reply while asking sheikhs and preachers to arouse Muslims to join the *mujahideen*. The Mufti did not fulfill Hall's request, and the strike continued.[47]

Orsmby-Gore shocked the Zionist camp with a proposal on June 30, when he met with Weizmann and Ben-Gurion. Referring to Weizmann's projection to Cust of an annual Jewish immigration of 50,000 for 15-20 years, the Colonial Secretary threw up his hands and remarked that such a figure would be bound to confirm Arab fears of a Jewish majority. He wished the Zionists to consider making a gesture of suspending immigration (with the exception of dependants) while the Royal Commission met. Weizmann suggested in turn that the Jews might not apply for a schedule while the commission was in Palestine, but Ben-Gurion strongly objected in principle to any suspension, especially when the yishuv had not engaged in reprisals against Arab violence that would now be encouraged further. Writing to Orsmby-Gore the next day, Weizmann observed that fixing a yearly immigration maximum in advance "strikes at the very root of the mandate and the National Home," and that suspension during the commission's work represented "a retreat in the face of organized terrorism" while the yishuv had shown discipline and self-restraint. His appeal closed: "May I express the hope that, after the terrible ordeal through which our people are now passing, we shall not in addition have to suffer these cruel and undeserved reverses?"[48]

Ormsby-Gore's reply to that question came first with his recommendation on July 4 to an approving Cabinet that HMG announce a suspension during the commission's work, to be publicized once order had been restored and the commission could leave for Palestine. The Zionists remained under "a cloud of doubt," particularly as he confided in Stephen Wise that there might be "a change in the machinery" of the immigration schedule: England was unhappily governed by the precedents of 1921 and 1929 in suspending Jewish entry when confronted by Arab riots, and some Cabinet members thought of Palestine as just "another nuisance." Wauchope, after cabling to Orsmby-Gore his support of the July 4 memorandum, was cautioned by Shertok on July 12 that any suspension would be a surrender to Arab violence and destroy Jewish confidence in the commission. Two days later, Ormsby-Gore told a Palestinian Arab delegation headed by Husseini that HMG "regarded the two sides of the mandate as of equal weight," and when order had been restored would consider a suspension during the commission's inquiry. Receiving Ormsby-Gore's communication on July 17 that the commission would have to make up its own mind as to the mandate's interpretation and any modifications of policy, after which HMG would render a final decision, Weizmann and Ben-Gurion talked in the London Agency Executive for the first time of possibly placing their resignation before the next World Zionist Congress "as their policy has (apparently) failed."[49]

Ben-Gurion had the definite impression after the interview of June 30 that while Ormsby-Gore personally remained a friend of Zionism, the government was preparing for "a complete reversal of the mandate." Indeed, ten days earlier Foreign Secretary Eden had intervened for the first time in the matter by warning the Cabinet about the "keenest anxiety" with which the neighboring Arab and Muslim countries were watching the recent "troubles" in Palestine. Thinking it of "paramount importance" to HMG that any extension of Italian influence in Saudi or Yemen territory should be prevented, he favored immediate steps to halt Jewish immigration pending the commission's report. Accordingly, whereas the British Minister at Jedda had advised Ibn Saud not to accede to Haj Amin's request for intervention soon after the strike began, the Foreign Office conveyed word to the desert monarch on July 3 that HMG "gladly" accepted his offer to mediate directly with the kings of Yemen and Iraq to end the violence. The Colonial Office was shocked, however, when the other two rulers agreed to do so if all or some of the Arab Higher Committee's demands were met, and especially when the Saudi king suggested suspending immigration until HMG agreed to the commission's eventual findings. Embarrassed, the Foreign Office cut short the Saudi initiative, advising Minister Sheikh Hafez Wahba in London to have Ibn Saud himself write a letter to the Committee. The Cabinet decided not to inform Ibn Saud of its decision to halt immigration once the commission left for Palestine.[50]

Extremely worried that the Cabinet seemed ready to suspend Jewish immigration, Wise cabled the ZOA to contact Senator Robert Wagner (D, NY) and other sympathetic Gentile politicians in order to urge Roosevelt to make an "informal representation" to London against taking this action. Responding from a ship bound for Europe, Wagner asked his former secretary and current law partner, Simon Rifkind, to send the telegram to Roosevelt's lawyer and speech writer, Samuel Rosenman, who forwarded it to the President on July 16. On July 22, Ormsby-Gore declared in Parliament that HMG's decision regarding a possible temporary suspension while the commission was carrying out its investigation would be "taken in due course on the merits of the case," and "there is no question of it being influenced by violence or attempts at intimidation." Five days later, replying to Roosevelt's unprecedented query, Secretary Hull observed that U.S. Consul-General Wadsworth had been most active in demanding protection for the some 10,000 American nationals in Palestine, and "it would seem to be unwise for us to insist that the British follow a particular course of action in their present difficulties." FDR agreed to have U.S. Ambassador Robert Bingham informally convey for Eden's consideration the deep concern of American Jewish circles in this matter, without presuming to interfere with or give advice regarding British policy in Palestine.[51]

Aware that Ormsby-Gore would make a Palestine declaration on July 29, Haj Amin and six other members of the Committee of Ten visited Abdullah on July 26 for several hours in hopes of resolving the crisis to their satisfaction. Yet the Emir insisted, as Shertok had requested of him one month earlier, that the episodes of disorder must be stopped at once, and stated his belief in the commission's "beneficial outcome." To Wauchope, he recommended that Ormsby-Gore's scheduled declaration hint of magnanimous treatment for offenders during the disturbances, and that immigration would be suspended while the commission worked in Palestine. Secretly, as conveyed by Emir advisor Mahmoud al-Unsi to the Jewish Agency Arab Department's Aharon Cohen, Abdullah wished Shertok to have Wauchope intervene with Ormsby-Gore to achieve this end. Shertok quickly reaffirmed to Abdullah the Agency's absolute opposition to any suspension; he could only ask the High Commissioner to recommend that the declaration include a personal and cordial appeal to the Committee's "wisdom and sense of responsibility," inviting the Arab leaders to realize that the strike harmed their people and to call on their followers to desist. Hearing from Shertok on July 28 that Abdullah endorsed the approach as "very helpful," Wauchope replied that he would certainly pass on to Ormsby-Gore the suggestion of this appeal to Arab "statesmanship" without mentioning that it had originated with Abdullah via the Agency.[52]

The Zionists tried other means of influencing Orsmby-Gore's statement in the House of Commons, scheduled for the last day of the Parliamentary session. Jan Smuts wrote letters to Ormsby-Gore, Amery, and Lloyd George (Smuts and Lloyd George the two surviving members of the Imperial War Cabinet that had approved the Balfour Declaration) against a total suspension during the commission's inquiry. Amery informed Abdullah—with Ormsby-Gore's approval—that he had urged a large area of Palestine to be reserved for Arabs, as well as parity of Arab-Jewish votes in any future legislation, and requested that the Emir use his influence to induce the Arabs to abandon violence and present their case to the impartial commission. Frankfurter made the case to Cabinet member Lord Halifax that Arab fears should not be dealt with by making the "obvious concessions," but by "patient elucidation, education and firmness," and that the considerations leading to the Balfour Declaration and the mandate were even more valid now in light of the results achieved and the dreams realized. Ambassador Bingham transmitted the Roosevelt-Hull message "entirely unofficially" to Eden, who thanked him for the information but gave no indication as to what HMG's policy would be.[53]

Ormsby-Gore's declaration on July 29 announced the appointment of the Royal Commission's members and its terms of reference, which he himself had drafted. While reiterating the substance of his Parliamentary statement a week earlier, it directly contradicted his speech of June 19, indicating that the matter would not be made public until law and order returned to Palestine. Alami was not pleased, thinking all the time that the declaration would include some "calming" announcement which would help "quiet the situation." One month earlier, Alami had engineered a memorandum to Wauchope of 137 Arab senior government officials who called for halting Jewish immigration as "the only fair, humane, and honorable solution of the present deadlock," the present unrest deemed "no more than an expression" of "Arab despair," and warned that the Palestinian Arabs' feeling "a loss of faith" in the value of British pledges and assurances could not be "crushed by force." Now Alami advised Khalidi that the commission's immediate arrival in Palestine would at least show that the Arabs had not halted their strike before then, while the Committee could claim that it had not given in to government threats. Shertok sent Abdullah his regrets that Ormsby-Gore's declaration did not contain the suggested appeal to the Arabs. The Emir thanked him for his efforts, and hoped that the two would continue to work "hand-in-hand for the cause of peace and understanding."[54]

Abdullah's progress in talks with the Arab Higher Committee the next month converted Wauchope to endorse a temporary suspension. On August 5, British Resident Cox in Transjordan reported that although Haj Amin insisted that the strike continue until all the Committee's demands were met, Nashashibi and others fully supported the Emir's suggestion that the strike stop, provided that Jewish immigration be halted during the commission's visit to Palestine and pardon be extended to Arab "patriots" who had been punished or were liable to prosecution. On August 21, the High Commissioner informed his superior that Abdullah's efforts had resulted in the creation of "a nucleus of moderate opinion" favoring the cessation of disorder so that the commission could proceed. (Yet, for their favoring mediation by Abdullah, the acting mayor of Hebron and the editor of *Falastin* were killed by Arab insurgents, who also assassinated Arab policemen.) He also reminded Ormsby-Gore that the July 29 statement in the House of Commons "might reasonably be interpreted as indicating that a temporary suspension may possibly be decided upon in due course."[55]

The next day, Wauchope noted to Ormsby-Gore that the additional British troops had failed to restore order, there were no signs of this end in sight, and the rebel forces were stronger and more determined despite the fact that nearly nine hundred of their ranks had been killed or injured. Repressive measures under Martial Law, which his frustrated military advisors strongly advocated, offered the hope that in future years the Arabs would not be so ready to rise against HMG. He suggested that if the Arab leaders publicly appealed to stop lawlessness and a marked diminution of attacks followed, it would be wise for HMG to make a concession to their demands. Talks between Wauchope and Hall with Khalidi led to a draft agreement stipulating that immigration would be suspended within one week of the leaders' public declaration calling off the strike. Ormsby-Gore approved this in a memorandum on August 26 to a receptive Cabinet, making his recommendation conditional on Wauchope's first obtaining the Committee's statement to end the revolt. Disagreeing with a London *Times* editorial which, for the first time, criticized a temporary embargo on immigration as "neither courageous nor logical," Wauchope responded to the Colonial Secretary that while suspension would "wound the feelings" of the Jews, it would also go far to end "their immediate afflictions." Moreover, he asserted, by helping the commission, it "will, we all trust, make their relations with Arabs more secure in future."[56]

Simultaneously, spurred by a British initiative, Iraqi Foreign Minister Nuri Sa'id sought to end the strike and violence through private intervention in Jerusalem. He argued unsuccessfully to Shertok that, given the Arabs' "jailed prisoners" and the government "not budging from its stand," the Jews should make a gesture of stopping immigration in order to end the deadlock and have their sacrifice demonstrate that they "truly sought peace." Nuri achieved more with the Arab Higher Committee, which on August 22 unanimously accepted his activity on the basis of the original three demands of November 1935 and a broad amnesty for offenders. The same day, Nuri reported to Wauchope his hopes to stop the strike by means of a memorandum addressed to the Committee. It would express confidence that Iraq's informal mediation would end the revolt, in return for which "Iraq would use its good offices to see that the mandatory granted the legitimate demands of the Palestinian Arabs." While denying to Shertok any knowledge of Nuri's activity, Wauchope highly recommended to Ormsby-Gore that the memorandum be pursued. The Colonial Secretary objected, asserting that the end of disorders had to be unconditional, and that he would never agree to Nuri's intrusion regarding general government policy in Palestine. Eden concurred, observing that Nuri was creating "maximum amount of elbow room for future Iraqi intervention in Palestine affairs and to further his own pan-Arab ideas."[57]

The Jewish Agency leadership responded forcefully. Shertok requested Wauchope to charge Haj Amin with responsibility for continuation of the terror, and to remove him from the presidency of the Supreme Muslim Council if he declined to publish an appeal for ending the disturbances. He cautioned the new head of the R.A.F. Intelligence Service that Nuri was "obviously staking out a claim for himself and his government permanently" to interfere in the affairs of Palestine, and that a wholesale suspension of immigration would lead to a "most violent" reaction by the Jews. The Agency viewed with "grave concern this unprecedented interference in the internal affairs of Palestine by an unofficial representative of a foreign government," Shertok wrote to Wauchope on August 30, a mission that went against the mandate by its "investing Palestine with the character of an Arab country." In an interview with Ormsby-Gore the following day, Weizmann charged Wauchope with failure because he was discussing "peace terms" with the instigators of terrorism, and had continued, along with the Chief Justice, to hamper action by the British military. Asked about Nuri's involvement, Weizmann indicated a willingness to meet with him and Palestinian Arabs in order to arrive at a *modus vivendi*, but noted that if one concession were made to the Arabs there was no reason to suppose that they would not demand others. Neither Wauchope nor the government had committed themselves to granting any of the demands alleged to have been put forward by the Arab Higher Committee in the course of its discussion with Nuri, Ormsby-Gore responded.[58]

Immediately thereafter, Ormsby-Gore asked Wauchope if Nuri and some Palestinian Arabs would be willing to meet Weizmann at a conference, which might placate the Arabs, but would meet with world Jewry's denunciation. This might "conceivably afford [a] way out of the impasse" and would at least save HMG from having to reject the Nuri overture outright, he added, the only alternative being further military measures to suppress disorders without any concession to "Arab sentiment." Replying on September 1, Wauchope ruled out a Round Table Conference: the Palestinian Arab leaders would almost certainly refuse to attend; the Arabs would insist on suspension of immigration, on which the Jews will not yield; and fundamental questions of policy could not profitably be discussed in anticipation of the Royal Commission. Continuing negotiations via Nuri would place HMG under "a moral obligation" to suspend immigration now or a little later. "Cowing the country" with military operations, on the other hand, would require the dispatch of six additional battalions, applying Martial Law, and a "long and bloody" campaign against the Arabs of Palestine, whose continued revolt would be backed by Arabs of surrounding countries. Wauchope adhered to his earlier position, favoring Nuri's continued talks and a suspension of immigration. If the Cabinet decided on the morrow to reject Nuri's mediation or if his hands were "so tied that there is little prospect of his succeeding," however, then a reinforcement of three battalions should be dispatched at once.[59]

Across the Atlantic, Wise moved swiftly to get the Democratic administration to weigh in against the threatened decree. He got an early morning appointment for September 1 with Hull, thanks to U.S. Postmaster General James Farley, then eager to use Wise's speaking talents in Roosevelt's 1936 presidential campaign. Farley also wired Roosevelt, on his way to Salt Lake City, to telephone Hull in support of the matter Farley had "discussed with Stephen with whom Felix [Frankfurter] and Isaiah [Brandeis] [were] in complete accord." Hull promised to fulfill Wise's requests to communicate with "the Skipper" (FDR) and, if he got Roosevelt's permission, to say to Baldwin or to Ormsby-Gore that the president opposed the suspension, which would bring disaster to the Jewish National Home and to Jews abroad seeking asylum from tyranny. Hull, whom Wise later wrote "could not have been more friendly" and "eager" to be of help, telephoned FDR and then Bingham. Repeating at Roosevelt's request the gist of Wise's appeal, Hull added that the ambassador should tell the British "in a spirit of friendly intercession on humanitarian grounds" that the proposed action would probably harm Anglo-American relations for "long years to come," especially given the personal influence exercised by Wise and his associates. Bingham relayed the urgent message to the Foreign Office, and replied the same afternoon that it would be transmitted to the Cabinet.[60]

A story on September 1 in the *Palestine Post*, leaked by the Zionists, proved most significant for the Cabinet meeting. It published the supposed text of a provisional agreement between Nuri and the Arab Higher Committee, which, in return for ending the strike and terrorist campaign, provided amnesty for offenders and a suspension of immigration until the Royal Commission published its report, with Iraq to represent the Palestinians before the commission. Ormsby-Gore informed Wauchope the same day that in view of the Arabs' continued violence and belligerent attitude, the Committee having just declared that it would continue the strike until its aims had been attained, he could not agree to a temporary suspension before the commission left England. That departure would not occur until the Committee publicly declared an end to the strike and "a more determined military effort" had rounded up the "murderers" and reestablished the administration's authority. Weizmann confronted Ormsby-Gore with the newspaper account, which the Colonial Secretary officially denied to Weizmann on

September 2 along with permission to publish his letter.[61]

Without revealing that the Hagana had tapped Arab Higher Committee telephone conversations and obtained copies of the Wauchope–Ormsby-Gore cable traffic, Shertok told Wauchope the same day that he knew "definitely" that the Arab leaders were "banking with certainty" on immigration being suspended as soon as they called off the strike. Haj Amin, he further observed, was "holding out" in hopes of obtaining further concessions from the government. Wauchope confessed that Nuri's intervention had originated in the Foreign Office, and expressed the conviction that there must be a change: "Either the Arabs must stop all attacks or drastic methods would have to be adopted," a decision which the Cabinet would make that day.[62]

A consensus of the Cabinet on September 2 reversed the policy of August 26, Eden and the Secretary of State for India, the Marquess of Zetland, alone in favor of concessions to the Arabs. The members took into account, Ormsby-Gore informed Wauchope, the original circumstances under which Nuri came to intervene, the "presumptuous and defiant" terms of the Committee's published manifesto on August 31 of maximum demands, and the fact that "outrages" continued. British prestige already having suffered severely as a result of "the Abyssinian imbroglio," the Cabinet also judged that coming to terms with the Committee at present would be interpreted universally as an additional sign of British weakness. Accordingly, it was essential that "more drastic and effective steps be taken now to disarm the "gunmen," bring the criminals to "summary justice," and show the Arab leaders that "we cannot be intimidated into surrender by the continuance of their present tactics." The declaration of Martial Law would therefore be involved, at least in certain areas of Palestine. War Secretary Duff Cooper, following the General Staff's advice, obtained his colleagues' approval to send a complete division from England as soon as possible to deal with the disorders. Together with the troops already there, it would be placed under the command of Lieutenant-General John G. Dill, late Director-General of Military Operations and Intelligence at the War Office.[63]

The predictable reaction of Jew and Arab to the government's *volte-face*, a clear admission that Wauchope's policy had been fruitless, followed swiftly. Hearing from Hull of this "encouraging" development, Wise thanked the U.S. Secretary of State for his personal help, and relayed his and Brandeis's "rejoicing over the temporary postponement in any event of the evil of suspension of immigration." The Cabinet had no alternative but "to cut through all these knots with a strong hand," Weizmann wrote Shertok, in view of Wauchope's bringing Palestine to a point of "grave danger unprecedented in the annals of British Colonial history." In Committee circles, Salah termed this "a Jewish victory," the Jews having forced London to fulfill their wishes. Khalidi reckoned that Martial Law would increase the extremism of Arab youth, and bemoaned that "we have lost everything." "Unable to retreat or even surrender," Haj Amin concluded that "we must give ourselves up into the hands of Providence."[64]

Concurrently, Alami, whose sister had married Husseini, began serving as the Committee's secret liaison in securing funds from Italy for the Arab Revolt. He had recently sold his family's property in the Beisan Valley to the Jewish National Fund, receiving written permission to do so from Fawzi al-Kaukji, commander with Haj Amin's approval and funding of Syrian and Iraqi volunteers in the Arab Revolt and then operating with about three hundred men throughout that area. (The following year, the religious-Zionist kibbutz Tirat Zvi, the valley's southernmost "stockade and tower" (*"homa u'migdal"*) fortified settlement, would be built on those lands.) Alami succeeded in receiving substantial funds from Italy, although he failed to obtain both weapons and technical advisors, the latter meant to sabotage Britain's oil pipeline from Iraq to Haifa and to arrange that Tel Aviv's water supply be "contaminated [*sic*]."[65]

HMG publicly acknowledged on September 8 that a "political" strike called by "a Committee of Arab notables" and maintained by "widespread intimidation" directly challenged the government, which now admitted that "all efforts to introduce a reasonable spirit of accommodation have hitherto failed." The Palestine garrison under Dill's command would be brought up to 17,000, sufficient for Martial Law, although the authorities still hoped that this step would not be necessary. It was Great Britain's "earnest desire" to carry out a policy of "impartial justice" to Arabs and Jews, the government "fully in accord" with the sense of the Permanent Mandates Commission's pronouncement to the Council of the League of Nations in 1930 that the obligations to both "are of equal weight" and "are in no sense irreconcilable." The official statement ended with the further aspiration that the Royal Commission would make recommendations that "will enable His Majesty's Government to bring finality to a situation of doubt and fear on both sides, and that, out of the tragic misunderstandings and the disorder of the last five months, a lasting settlement can be reached." Thus did the Cabinet confirm a keen observation from the pen of England's greatest eighteenth-century poet: "Hope springs eternal in the human breast."[66]

Wishful thinking of this sort led the Colonial Office to support an additional attempt at mediation, the Cabinet's decision notwithstanding. One day after HMG's announcement regarding Martial Law, the king having personally approved an Order-in-Council to this effect, Herbert Samuel presented Ormsby-Gore with a new plan for an Arab-Jewish settlement. It proposed the voluntary consent by Jews not to exceed 40 percent of Palestine's population by 1950; Jewish land purchase and colonization limited to specified areas of the country; substantial expenditure for Arab agriculture and education; Transjordan to be opened to Jews and Palestinian Arabs on conditions acceptable to that government, without the Balfour Declaration's provisions applied there; and a Legislative Council to be created with one-third representation each to Jewish, Arab, and British nominees. It also reaffirmed Muslim rights to their holy places, and advocated a customs union covering Palestine, Iraq, Hejaz, Yemen, and Transjordan, with Arabic the official language. Lord Winterton, who was head of the pro-Arab group in Parliament and also had recently issued a public call for direct Arab negotiations with the Zionists, accompanied Samuel in order to obtain Ormsby-Gore's official stamp for this initiative.[67]

Reiterating the essence of what he had already transmitted to Nuri five days earlier, Ormsby-Gore stressed to Samuel and Winterton that HMG could do nothing further until the disorders were brought to an end and the Royal Commission could proceed. Consequently, the *démarche* had to be private, with no guarantees that their proposals, even if accepted by the Arabs, would be implemented by the government. Winterton contacted his good friend Nuri, who scheduled a meeting in Paris for the three men on September 19. Briefed confidentially by Samuel and Rutenberg, Weizmann cautioned Samuel against a limit lower than 40,000 Jews per annum for the next ten years, and that any agreement with Nuri had to be followed by preliminary Arab-Jewish negotiations before a final ratification of proposals was possible. Rutenberg, whose earlier information to Samuel about the initiative of "The Five" (aborted, he claimed, by the Agency) and about his own draft agreement with Abdullah for a development of Transjordan surfaced now in Samuel's plan, concurred with Weizmann's second stipulation. Ormsby-Gore advised Samuel to keep the proposals distinct from Wauchope's ongoing negotiations with the Committee, and to submit them to Nuri as an "eventual" settlement which Samuel and Winterton personally thought the Arabs might seek to present to the commission and which might be accepted by "*some*" Jews. After further discussion with the Colonial Office and Weizmann, Samuel amended his draft to read "an agreement to be made covering a period of years" and "Jewish immigration into Palestine to be limited on a basis to be arranged."[68]

A "very friendly" (Samuel's characterization) Nuri rejected the proposals without delay, stating he did not consider that they would be "acceptable to the Arabs of Palestine." The Arabs expected that the commission would propose a permanent Jewish minority; if not, then a voluntary restriction would be a concession. Parity on a Legislative Council was "quite unacceptable," while the Jews would prove to be the "real beneficiaries" of an Arab-Jewish colonization of Transjordan. The Arabs were already negotiating a customs union among themselves, but the inclusion of Palestine would again primarily benefit the Jewish industrialists there. In any case, Nuri thought that the disturbances would be brought to an end "almost at once," and nothing could be done until after the Royal Commission had come to its conclusions. Samuel reported the fruitless result to London, adding that Nuri also strongly desired to promote some form of political union between Iraq, Palestine, and Transjordan, thereby enabling the Palestinian Arabs to look upon a large Jewish immigration "with equanimity." Writing to the London *Times* one week later, Winterton considered it "intolerable" that nearly 25,000 British soldiers and a considerable Air Force were required to prevent one section of Palestine's population from "cutting the throats of the other." Only a coming together of the two sides on a basis that HMG not favor one to the injury of the second, he urged, could prevent "great danger."[69]

Wauchope did his best to convince the Palestinian Arab leaders "as a friend of the Arab People" that it was in their interest to end resistance and violence without delay, rather than be forced to do so as a result of Martial Law. Hearing this in individual meetings with the High Commissioner, Haj Amin, Nashashibi, and Abd al-Hadi suggested a radical idea: HMG should invite an appeal from the Arab kings and Abdullah to the Arabs of Palestine. Wauchope met with the Committee of Ten on September 12 to convey the government's decision that such an appeal was not possible. To Haj Amin's query if London would object to their approaching the Arab rulers directly, he replied that it was "naturally open" for them to do so, but neither he nor any of HMG's representatives could give such action any encouragement. Rather than issue an ultimatum, he strongly urged that if this course were to be adopted, it should be done with all speed by telegraph. Dill would take over all the country's military forces tomorrow, he warned, and the High Commissioner could make no promise about clemency towards the Arab guerilla bands in the hills and other offenders.[70]

The next day, after a stormy meeting that revealed deep division within its ranks, the Committee adopted two diametrically opposing steps in response to HMG's latest statement. Publicly, it declared that mandate policy, by favoring the Jews, had led to the disturbances; repeated its three fundamental requirements to halt the strike; and declared that it continued to empower Nuri to negotiate officially on its behalf. The strike would continue pending a confirmation of this decision by a conference of the National Committees, to be held on September 17. Privately, the Committee of Ten agreed to send a draft statement to the different Arab rulers whereby the latter would call on Palestine's Arabs to end the strike and disorder for the sake of peace, with the belief that HMG would act justly and fulfill the Arabs' demands. Haj Amin rejected an individual effort by Abdullah's representative to have the Committee call off the strike at the Emir's request alone and rely on his promise to help the Palestine Arabs in the future.[71]

The intransigence of the Committee and particularly Haj Amin's "getting more extreme" wore even Wauchope's patience thin. He wired Ormsby-Gore on September 12, detailing his increasing conviction that the time was approaching when Haj Amin could be "removed." If deported, the Mufti should remain out of Palestine for a period of years "sufficient to insure his own prestige evaporates" and enough time that his successor could acquire influence and enhanced authority once reforms took place in the Supreme Muslim Council's constitution. An early declaration of Martial Law over the whole country would be required if violence continued, he wired "IMMEDIATE" four days later. The current and projected reality "necessitated severe measures of repression." Accidental deaths of innocent and loyal Arabs were inevitable, but "it is better that they should happen under Martial Law than under the ordinary civil administration." Justice would be administered more speedily, and Arabs not receive encouragement by lenient sentences.

Dill concurred, Wauchope went on, but had stressed that Martial Law could not be fully effective until the First Division arrived in early October. The two officials agreed that should the situation rapidly deteriorate or should the armed bands act with greater aggression and more success, then Martial Law might well have to be declared at an earlier date. Writing to the mandatory's Director of Education one week later from Government House atop the Hill of the Preacher in the south of Jerusalem, Wauchope dejectedly ruminated: "I was up early this morning, and could have wept as I saw the walls of Jerusalem turn golden under the cloudless sky and thought of—what you and I think of every sorrowful day."[72]

Unaware of these developments, Weizmann sought to convey to Eden via Deputy Under-Secretary Alexander Cadogan the same day that the Zionists, contrary to Nuri's statements, had never demanded a "Jewish State." He had told MacDonald in 1931 that however large the Jewish majority might be in Palestine, they would never wish to exercise their power to the detriment of their Arab neighbors. His conception "had always been that Palestine must be a bi-national state," that the two parties "must live side by side, managing their own affairs, with the British Crown as arbiter between them." According to Weizmann's memorandum, permanent political parity would "remove the sting" of political controversy and "leave the field open" to economic cooperation with Arabs in and outside of the country, with membership in the British Commonwealth offering "ultimate security" to the Jews. The Agency desired a conference with the Palestine Arabs under HMG's aegis, he concluded, to discuss the details and practical implications of a compromise based on these principles.[73]

George Rendel, the highly influential head of Whitehall's Eastern Department, would have none of this. He continued to maintain that a suspension of immigration symbolized the "test case" for HMG's future policy in Palestine. The Zionists, Rendel submitted, had always declared their intention to set up a Jewish state, and if curtailing of Jewish entry did not occur, a strong reaction in the Arab and Muslim world would undoubtedly follow. On September 17, Eden asked Rendel if he was correct in thinking that he should work for a temporary suspension once violence had ended and for a "fair deal" from the Royal Commission. His Middle East expert replied: a decision should be arrived at now, before the disorders ceased, to suspend Jewish immigration during the commission's work. Further, the Foreign Office should aim to give assurances that HMG would implement the commission's findings, even if these were favorable to the Arabs. HMG had "two sets" of obligations "of equal validity" under the mandate, he argued when reviewing another pro-Zionist appeal from Smuts to Ormsby-Gore, and it is "not easy to disprove" the Arab contention that HMG "have sacrificed their obligations to the Arabs in favor of those to the Jews."[74]

Khalidi came to the conclusion that with "God, too, having abandoned us," the Palestinian Arabs' "principal hope" lay with the Arab kings. Haj Amin first sought mediation from Ibn Saud, who again asked the Foreign Office's opinion, as he did not wish to take any step that might "cause embarrassment or inconvenience" to HMG. If the government would be prepared after the cessation of violence to issue a general amnesty, the monarch noted, it would be of "the greatest help" in bringing about a rapid settlement. Rendel replied to the Saudi chargé d'affaires on September 16 that HMG's policy remained steadfast: the strike and violence had to stop unconditionally, and Ibn Saud's appeal to the Arab Higher Committee along these lines would be welcome. Nuri received an identical message when obscurely suggesting that the Iraqi government appeal thus to the Palestinian Arabs in return for a "face saving device" to balance their abandonment of demands put forward earlier. Permanent Under-Secretary Lord Vansittart relayed to Eden on September 22 that the Whitehall staff agreed to respond to a similar request from Iraq's King Ghazi (and to the other kings if they wished to participate) along the lines of Rendel's statement for Ibn Saud, making corrections to Nuri's draft for this purpose. Yet when the Saudi delegate put to the Committee the same day his ruler's request that it end violence and disorder "at once," he was told that it awaited Ibn Saud's appeal with the stipulation that HMG prove its good intention by granting a general amnesty after the restoration of order and suspending immigration until the commission reached its conclusions. Iraq's prime minister received the same message.[75]

In light of the Committee's apparent preparedness to "procrastinate indefinitely," as the mandatory police's C.I.D. reported, the Colonial and War Offices shifted to oppose any concessions to Arab violence. Making it clear to Weizmann and Namier that he did not like the Arab kings' intervention, Ormsby-Gore now rejected any suspension of immigration. On October 2, War Secretary Alfred Duff Cooper privately urged the Colonial Secretary that Dill should at once be authorized to declare that if the rebellion was not called off by October 5, Martial Law would be declared the next day. Ormsby-Gore demurred with Whitehall's approval, thinking the ultimatum "most embarrassing" at a time when the Arab rulers were still actively trying to stop the revolt. Indeed, the Foreign Office heard on October 2 that Haj Amin had pledged to the Iraqis that when King Ghazi's appeal was published, the Committee would not declare that it had received any "assurance" regarding HMG's future Palestine policy. An impatient Dill, who earlier told an Agency liaison that he had "not come for an Anglo-Jewish war against the Arabs," wired Duff Cooper on October 6 to help "force the pace" to end the "parleys" with Arab kings. The First Division, the Lieutenant-General noted, "having arrived with great flourish of trumpets, strong action should immediately follow." The role of "paper tiger for the army is neither dignified nor effective," and he felt that "Martial Law will in any event be necessary to restore order here."[76]

Highly critical of Wauchope's "bazaar politics" with the Arabs, Weizmann advised Ormsby-Gore that he wished to get in touch with Jewish and Arab opinion in Cairo, the object a conference based on a manifesto endorsing political parity between the two peoples in Palestine under a British administration within the British Empire. Wauchope doubted that such an initiative would do anything to allay Arab fears or improve the current situation. Rendel responded that Weizmann actually wished to see Palestine a Jewish state, an ideal "hardly likely to be facilitated by an early settlement of present troubles between us and the Arabs"; Vansittart considered Weizmann an "extremist bent on his goal" who would not mind if "we ruined our whole position" to get to it, unlike Samuel's taking the "longer and wiser" view, while HMG had an "admitted duty" to the Arabs under the mandate. The Agency Executive in London received encouragement from some leading newspaper editors for the political parity idea, which already had been touted by Amery and Winterton, viewing it as a "firm platform" on which the Zionist movement could take its stand. Ben-Gurion and Shertok thought this "inadmissible" without the authority of the movement's Smaller Actions Committee in Palestine, however, and asked Weizmann to come to Palestine and help in preparing the Agency's case for the Royal Commission.[77]

On October 5, Ambassador Clark Kerr in Baghdad sent Eden a cable, repeated to his colleagues in Jerusalem, Geneva, Jedda, and Cairo, containing the proposed Arabic text with a translation of Ghazi's letter "to our sons the Arabs of Palestine." Prepared in agreement with "our brother Kings and the Amir," it noted the Yemeni monarch's "great distress" caused by the present situation in Palestine, and appealed to the Committee to "restore tranquility in order to prevent further bloodshed, relying on the good intentions of the British Government and their declared desire to see that justice is done." "Be assured," the call ended, "that we shall continue our endeavours to help you." Three days later, the ambassador relayed that Ibn Saud agreed immediately to the text, and the Arab rulers issued it publicly on October 10. Wauchope warned Abdullah that if the strike and the campaign of violence did not cease before October 14, "it will be essential to adopt more active military measures" under Martial Law. HMG's representatives communicated in like vein to the other Arab governments. Informing Wauchope that the crisis would end "within the coming two days," Abd al-Hadi asserted once again that the Palestinian Arabs would not agree to a policy that denied their natural right to independence, and suggested that the suspension of Jewish immigration and a general amnesty would "diminish the effects" of the Arabs' "overwhelming pain."[78]

On October 11, Wauchope sent a message marked "CONFIDENTIAL" to the Arab Higher Committee that he was "very glad" to hear that it had just issued an appeal to call off the strike and end all disorder. (Secretly, the Committee urged the militia band leaders to "stop activity until needed": "If the Royal Commission comes and judges equitably and gives us all our rights, well and good. If not, the field of battle lies before us.") The High Commissioner expressed his certainty that this step would benefit the whole country, including Palestine's Arabs, and put an end to "the deplorable loss of life and disorders that have been occurring during the past few months." He was confident that the Committee members would insure that the call was made "fully and promptly effective," because if disturbances did not patently cease before October 14, his instructions were to delegate his powers to General Dill under the new Martial Law Order-in-Council. The cessation of the strike, editorialized the *Palestine Post* that same day, "may, if its lesson has been fully learned, be the beginning of a new and brighter era for the Holy Land."[79]

The following morning, after 175 days, the Committee called off the strike. All the Arab newspapers except Nashashibi's *Falastin* (which published the statement without comment) hailed it as "a historic day in Palestine." The notes struck ranged from "We are victorious" to exhortations to be prepared to continue the struggle after the "truce." In fact, Arab government workers had continued at their posts, Jewish settlements stood firm, and Tel Aviv witnessed the beginnings of a new port. Thanks to Mayor Hassan Shukri, the mixed city of Haifa carried on as usual, even after he departed for Lebanon because the Mufti had accused him of treason and two attempts on his life by Arab "patriots" followed. Two of his wife's brothers were murdered in front of their home. The number of casualties to that date in the Arab rebellion well exceeded 1,000, including 224 Arabs, 80 Jews, and 39 Britons killed, leading Szold to a mordant conclusion: "The patience of the Government has been godlike, but the results have been hellish." Haj Amin and followers declared that the end arrived because of the appeals of the Arab rulers, but the London *Times* more dispassionately attributed it to the threat of Martial Law, with the kings' appeals offering Haj Amin and his followers "an opportunity to escape from their predicament." Disagreeing with the terms of Dill's Order of the Day announcing that resolute British military action had brought about the result, Wauchope had suppressed its publication, but the declaration was ultimately publicized on the BBC airwaves.[80]

The very next day, Wauchope could wire Ormsby-Gore that since "a very marked diminution of disorders" had taken place—clearly indicating the Committee's control, Dill thought that no need existed to issue the proclamation of Martial Law. The High Commissioner also suggested that it would be hard to warrant the proposal to deport Haj Amin if order was completely restored throughout the country during the week; Palestine's Arabs would certainly protest a decree of exile and the Mufti's enemies would be obliged to join in such expressions. At the same time, it would be justifiable to curtail Haj Amin's powers with a closer mandatory control of administering the funds of the Waqf, more easily done if recommended by the Royal Commission. The Colonial

Secretary replied that in view of the altered situation, he considered that the proposal to deport Haj Amin and others "must be abandoned." The Executive Council agreed to recommend to Ormsby-Gore that steps be taken to disarm the population by paying Arabs for weapons given over, while getting the Agency to disband the illegal Hagana in return for 3,000 serviceable rifles placed at the disposal of selected Jewish auxiliary or special constables for the purpose of defense. This process should begin in mid-November, Wauchope suggested, to coincide with the commission's arrival, although the possibility existed that disarmament at any time might lead to an Arab boycott of that investigatory group.[81]

Wauchope broached the possibility of "a gentleman's agreement" with Ben-Gurion and Shertok on October 16, arranging that the Hagana's weapons be handed over in exchange for the continued presence of Jewish supernumerary police in exposed Jewish villages and districts in mixed towns. The Agency, Ben-Gurion replied, had nothing to do with secret arming, but it was "quite natural" for Jews to try to provide for their own security after they had been "bitterly and repeatedly disappointed" at the government's failure to do so. Unlike the Arabs, Shertok observed, the Jews had only used their weapons in self-defense, and never attacked a single Arab village throughout the disturbances. Ben-Gurion made it clear: If HMG effectively disarmed the terrorist bands, established an adequate system of defense, and made provision for the proper participation of the Jews in the defense and security forces, the proposed agreement might be discussed. Wauchope agreed with Shertok's argument in principle, but noted that if the Jews "set a good example," it would make "infinitely easier" the administration's task of getting the Arabs to deliver their weapons. The yishuv pair remained skeptical, and sharply differed with Wauchope's assertion that it was "a very hard matter to fix direct responsibility" for the campaign of violence on Haj Amin and the Committee.[82]

Harry P. Rice, head of the C.I.D., agreed with Ben-Gurion and Shertok about Haj Amin's decisive part in fanning the flames of the revolt. One month earlier, a C.I.D. report had observed that the Arab Higher Committee conducted propaganda in order to encourage the Arab villages to "maintain violence." On October 27 Rice informed Hall's deputy that Haj Amin's agents "watched" those like Nashashibi who "do not happen to be in his good books," and had intended that Suleiman

Bey Toukan, the mayor of Nablus, "should be put out of the way." There was "every reason to believe" that Aref el Jaouny, the organizer of intimidation and assassination around Jerusalem, did nothing without Haj Amin's knowledge, and had found a hiding place together with other "undesirables" in Jerusalem's Harem-es-Sharif (to Jews, the Temple Mount) during the rebellion. Some of the stolen weapons from the Police Armory the previous year were secreted in the Harem-es-Sharif, and Rice believed that Haj Amin knew everything which went on there. A considerable amount of the funds, usually termed "Distress" or "Relief," that were sent to Haj Amin from abroad "undoubtedly" contributed towards the upkeep of the armed gangs and the purchase of weapons. The bandit movement in the hills, Rice concluded, was clearly "encouraged" by the Committee as well.[83]

The Committee continued to adhere to its principles. On October 16, Haj Amin's newspaper *Al Liwa* called for a boycott of Jewish goods, much to Wauchope's regret. In a meeting with the High Commissioner the following week, the Mufti requested that detainees be released and the Emergency Regulations repealed. He further suggested that all Jewish supernumerary police be dismissed, the Tel Aviv port closed, and all rebel fighters given a general amnesty. The grant of a new immigration schedule, Haj Amin added, "may endanger the peace of the country." Shortly thereafter, Wauchope broadcast his desire for peace in Palestine, seeing in the commission "a great opportunity for both communities to find a common agreement." Abd al-Hadi immediately responded by expressing the Arabs' surprise that the speech contained no reference to immigration. Since they held a "general belief" that the government would announce a halt to Jewish entry before the commission's arrival, he feared that "the people may take a negative attitude towards the Royal Commission" if the stoppage of such immigration was delayed for a long time.[84]

Ormsby-Gore, however, contended in the Cabinet on October 28 that any concessions once the Palestinian Arab disturbances had ceased would give the impression that a "deal" existed between HMG and the Arab rulers. Rendel had advised, by contrast, that the present Arab-Jewish population ratio should be kept stable while the commission met. He also observed that the Colonial Secretary's memorandum hardly contained any allusion to probable "risings" in the Muslim world or to Italian "intrigues" if immigration were not suspended now, an argument that seemed "unanswerable" to Vansittart. Indeed, Haj Amin asked Wauchope on November 3 for a complete stop to Jewish immigration "in order to prepare a peaceful atmosphere" in which the commission could work "most satisfactorily." Told by Ormsby-Gore the same day that HMG wished to keep the actual numbers of Jewish immigrants down to "a minimum" in the next few months, Weizmann begged that the Jews receive a labor schedule of 3,000 plus an unrestricted flow for the next six months of those who qualified as "capitalists," exercised as he was over "the imminent fate of European Jewry." Ultimately, the Cabinet decided on November 4 that there would be "no change of policy" and no "total" (thanks to Whitehall's amendment) suspension of immigration for "political reasons."[85]

Hearing of Ormsby-Gore's announcement to Parliament the next day of a half-year labor schedule for 1,800 Jews, including his statement that any change in the status quo might prejudice the commission's findings, the Arab Higher Committee decided on November 6 to boycott the Royal Commission. That same evening, Wauchope persuaded Haj Amin to withdraw publication of the boycott manifesto, which had already appeared in the Arabic press in Palestine, Egypt, and Syria, and he met with some of the Committee's leaders the next morning to note the "folly" of their decision. The commission, he urged as one who always felt "very deeply for the welfare" of Palestine's Arabs, would undoubtedly examine the situation "conscientiously and impartially." Haj Amin countered that "there was no place in Palestine for two races," and the Jews, who "left Palestine 2,000 years ago," should go to other "wide, vacant spaces" in the world. "Whether twenty Jews or 20,000 were admitted was of no moment," Husseini added, the Arabs standing for the principle of "no more Jews." Wauchope's arguments, including that HMG "will not allow the Jews to make a Jewish state in Palestine," failed to move the Committee. It re-issued its declaration on the evening of November 8.[86]

"The calls for patience on the High Commissioner are great," Wauchope observed to Ormsby-Gore the day of the Cabinet's decision, but "most navigators these days, whether patient or hurrying, sail on stormy seas." Since the Agency told him that it could not "do anything" to induce the illegally armed Jews to surrender their weapons, the attempt at a quick disarmament of the Arabs enjoyed "even less prospect of success." To attain the latter, it would be wiser and lead to greater results "to spend a little money than much blood to achieve our purpose." As to the "undue power" of Haj Amin, in whose mind "the wicked Dr. Jekyll has become more and more dominant over the moderate Mr. Hyde" during the past few months, Wauchope advised that it be curtailed. As Mufti, permanent President of the Supreme Muslim Council, and Chairman of the general Waqf Committee, Haj Amin wielded "excessive" influence and authority that dangerously "mixed politics with religion." The government now had to secure the close control of Wakf funds and the effective independence of the *Shari'a* Courts, over which a large measure of independence had been given in 1921 to the Muslim community, Wauchope concluded.[87]

Wauchope looked forward to the commission's coming as "an event of historical importance," but others viewed the *dénouement* with concern. Dill lamented to the War Office that local civil justice had been "only tardily and ineffectively imposed" against the Arab murderers; because Wauchope's policy had not given British forces a free hand under Martial Law, he told a Jewish Agency liaison, the task would have to be faced at a later date when far fewer troops would be available. The Arab kings objected to the Committee's proclaimed boycott, Ibn Saud going so far as to send Haj Amin a cable reprimanding that if the decision about the commission stood, he would "disappear from the mediation." Winterton expressed to Laski his regret that Arab "extremists" had for some time gained the "upper hand"; considered the boycott "a very grave mistake" and the Arab political claims based upon alleged treaty arrangements with HMG "grossly exaggerated"; and still hoped to get moderates on both sides to achieve justice for both Arab and Jew. Certain that the Colonial Office and the Palestine administration would "keep the letter of the mandate and avoid its spirit," Melchett believed that only "the utter necessity of dealing with the European Jewish problem" could counteract this policy. That meant, as his new book advocated, a self-governing British dominion of 3 million Jews in Palestine and Transjordan, which would remove forever the possibility of a successful armed uprising to destroy the effects of the mandate.[88]

For Ben-Gurion, as he put it in a lengthy address to a yishuv conference on November 10, Zionists were about to enter "a battle much more severe and pregnant with dangers" than the one which had ended "for the time being" one month earlier. Although none of the Royal Commission's members had a prior connection to Palestinian affairs or bore an internationally known name, each had experience in their respective fields, and their recommendations would carry "great, perhaps decisive," weight. The Arabs and Jews embraced directly opposing objectives, the first wishing to free themselves as soon as possible from England and the mandate, the second wanting the British administration to continue and to live up to that document in full. Yet the Jews' "starting point" in their relationship to Palestine rested not on the mandate, Ben-Gurion stressed, but on three basic foundations: the historical bond between the Jewish people and Eretz Yisrael; the distress of Jewry in the Exile; and the land's great economic potential. Zionism's demands for immigration and settlement "without political limitations or numerical restrictions" were rooted in Jewry's historical connection to Palestine, the mandate, and the developing National Home's ability to serve as "the sole outlet" for the distress of the Jewish masses abroad. The entire yishuv and every Jew called before the commission, Ben-Gurion ended, had to champion these principles.[89]

On November 11, the Royal Commission, chaired by William Robert Wellesley, the first Earl Peel and a former Secretary of State for India, arrived in the Holy Land. Melchett looked upon Peel, an old friend and board colleague on Barclay's Bank, as "a practical and sensible man and by no means unsympathetic to our tribulations." Pessimism dominated Ben-Gurion's thoughts that Wednesday, however, for he wrote to Ussishkin that in this "insane era," when every government wished to be rid of the Jews—"pleasantly or by force," the Jewish people suffered from "a deficient national sense." A rising "pan-Arabic movement" concurrently revealed great strength, and that "ferment" would certainly increase. Jewry should therefore make every effort, Ben-Gurion insisted, to augment the friendship and help of England, presenting to HMG shared political interests instead of relying on pleas for supreme justice or on pledges eventually to be broken. Yet, on that very same day, Whitehall endorsed the judgment by one of its Middle East experts that it did not lie in HMG's true interest to have Palestine "relieve" Central Europe of its "serious" problem, "however much may hang on the fate of the Jews," at the expense of "intensifying" the Jewish problem in a part of the world which did "directly and vitally" affect Great Britain.[90]

Jabotinsky reluctantly concluded that "the British phase of Zionism is virtually over," but he did not know which "Sancho Panza" could serve as a substitute to carry out "a pledge given by Don Quixote." Having been the first to warn HMG in early April of a Palestinian Arab assault on an unprecedented scale, Jabotinsky supported the Agency's policy of forbearance and static defense, viewing these outbreaks as the opportunity to have Britain sanction legal battalions via the Jewish Legion that he and Joseph Trumpeldor had spearheaded in World War I. His independent New Zionist Organization also urged an internationally sponsored Ten Year Plan for Palestine's development to settle at least 1.5 million Jews on both sides of the Jordan River within the next decade. (A few months later, he would assert that this "Evacuation Plan" was needed "to save Jewry from the onrush of lava.") Abba Ahimeir challenged Jabotinsky's endorsement of *havlaga*, demanding at Betar's conference in July that Palestinian Jewish youth follow the example of Pilsudski's soldiers and the Arabs themselves in a commitment to ultimate sacrifice, to become "a generation of heroes" rather than one of "holy martyrs." By the end of August, Jabotinsky admitted that restraint had been harmful in the face of increased Arab rebellion, and on October 1 he wrote to a close associate: "Our *Los von England* tendency cannot, for the present, go further than something like this: a big last attempt to get what we need from *this* partner; and, if it fails, then..." Beyond, he could not yet envision "the big main road."[91]

After six months of rebellion, not one of the Arab Higher Committee's three cardinal demands had been met. Its obduracy and ultimata finally pushed the Cabinet to reassert British authority in Palestine. The emerging seeds of civil war, reflected dramatically in the murder that August of Hevron's vice-mayor Nasser al-Din by extremists because of his support of Nashashibi and Abdullah, weakened the Palestinian Arab community and led Khalidi to tell an associate that "we are mired in muck from which we do not know how to extricate ourselves." Unemployment rose sharply. Rebel bands from foreign lands, including supreme commander Kaukji, departed by November. Although Kaukji and his men had been surrounded by British detachments "with every prospect of being destroyed in battle," Wauchope decided that the former be permitted to withdraw unmolested "in order to avoid bloodshed" provided that he left British mandate territory within a certain time.[92]

The yishuv's commerce and industry suffered a severe, if lesser, economic shock, yet it determinedly hewed to a policy of self-restraint. While suffering 80 dead and 396 wounded (110 severely), it only abandoned two small settlements. Increasingly, the slogan "there is no choice" (*ein breira*) surfaced, a fatalistic sense that the yishuv was predestined to live by the sword. Almost 3,000 supernumerary Jewish police received weapons and training while the underground Hagana, caught unprepared (as in 1929) by the initial, spontaneous outburst in Jaffa, began to go on the offensive and to be transformed into a closely-knit national militia. In Palestine and in London, Weizmann, Ben-Gurion, and Shertok vigorously defended their cause. American Zionists played an important role in helping to check a suspension of Jewish entry into Palestine.[93]

Yet a palpable transformation within the Arab camp could not be denied. A heightened sense of Palestinian Arab nationalism began to assert itself, especially among radicalized youth, spurred on by measures of freedom that had been gained in Iraq, and more recently in Egypt and Syria. Abd al-Hadi privately confessed his own surprise that the peasant masses ardently continued to follow the Arab Higher Committee's strike call. Moderates like Alami and Nashashibi would not acquiesce to a Palestinian Jewish majority either, nor would the Arab kings. Even Abdullah thought it "highly meritorious," reported the British Residency in Cairo after the strike ended, that "the Arab world would have no objection to entry of Jews over sixty years of age who came solely in order to be buried there."[94]

Weizmann justifiably observed that the Arab population had increased by 40 percent in recent years, rebutting the charge that Zionism was crowding out the non-Jewish population, but Husseini articulated a growing consensus when telling Wauchope that the Arabs stood on the principle of "no more Jews." "This is an uprising of an entire nation," Ben-Gurion observed to the Agency Executive in July, "fighting and ready to be destroyed." With the strike over, the often vacillating High Commissioner had King Edward VIII informed that however exaggerated the Arab fear of eventual subjugation by the Jews, "it is perfectly genuine and cannot be neglected if we are to have peace and freedom from riots in this country, and avoid the growth of anti-English feeling in neighboring Arab countries."[95] The latter anxiety spurred the Foreign Office for the first time to intervene actively in mandate affairs by bringing in the Arab rulers and pressing for concessions. Appeasement of violence and terror followed.

As a consequence, the Committee's declaration to end the revolt signaled no guarantee of law and order. The fact that the Arab Revolt was not forcefully suppressed and Martial Law not instituted, subsequently concluded both War Office Military Intelligence and

Ormsby-Gore, and that no direct measures were taken against Haj Amin and the Committee had "left them with their power and prestige largely unimpaired." General Dill feared this, as did Ben-Gurion, who thought that the rebellion would erupt again, especially if the Peel Commission did not satisfy the Arabs. He therefore informed the Agency Executive on October 25 that Wauchope's suggestion about the Hagana's voluntarily surrendering its weapons could not be accepted. As for the Arab monarchs, Namier pointedly warned Ormsby-Gore of the obvious when challenging these rulers' unprecedented intercession: "If on one occasion, they enjoined the Palestine Arabs to stop a strike, they acquire a right on another occasion to advise them to start one." In light of this volatile uncertainty, Wauchope thought that Bentwich's saying rang true: "Blood is easily spilt but terribly indelible."[96] Now an official six-man British delegation would seek to ascertain the underlying causes of the revolt, as well as the possible grievances of Arab and Jew regarding the mandate's implementation, and make recommendations for the removal of these complaints and the prevention of their recurrence. A new chapter in Palestine's very troubled history was about to unfold.

Endnotes

1   Cabinet meeting, Apr. 1, 1936, Cabinet (CAB) records, 23/83; Wauchope to Thomas, Apr. 1, 1936, CO 733/307/75438/1; both in PRO; Nashashibi to Wauchope, Apr. 1, 1936, S25/22723, CZA.
2   Wauchope-Arab leaders interview, Apr. 2, 1936, S25/22723, CZA. The five were Nashashibi, Husseini, Salah, Ghussein, and the Reform Party's Mahmoud Abu Khadra.
3   Ben-Gurion, *Zikhronot* 3, 103-109.
4   Ibid., 103, 116-117.
5   Taysir Jbara, *Palestinian Leader Hajj Amin al-Husayni, Mufti of Jerusalem* (Princeton, 1985), 141; Elpeleg, *The Grand Mufti*, 38. Abd al-Qadir, operating in the Bethlehem hills, was captured on October 7 but escaped to Syria

Porath, *The Palestinian Arab National Movement*, 131-132, 179, 182.

6   Wauchope to Thomas, Apr. 8, 1936, S25/22711, CZA; Executive Council, Apr. 11, 1936, file M-4754/32, ISA.

7   Ben-Gurion to Brodetsky, Apr. 9, 1936, file C14/9/7, BDA.

8   Laski to Warburg, Apr. 9, 1936, microfilm 1933, Warburg MSS; see also Laski letter, Mar. 18, 1936, file P-13/2/11, CAHJP; Laski to N. Laski, Mar. 24, 1937, Foreign Countries/Palestine file, AJCA.

9   *Parliamentary Debates, House of Commons*, 310, col. 2760, Apr. 8, 1936; C.I.D. reports, Apr. 11, 1936, and May 6, 1936; both in FO 371/20018, PRO.

10   Sharett, *Yoman Medini*, 1: 1936 (Tel Aviv, 1976), 71, 77; Wauchope to Thomas, Apr. 23, 26, and 28, 1936; all in CO 733/310/75528/I, PRO; Ben-Gurion, *Zikhronot*, 133.

11   Ben-Gurion, *Zikhronot*, 173; Wauchope to Thomas, Apr. 18, 1936, CO 733/297/75156/II, Wauchope to Thomas, Apr. 21, 1936, CO 733/307/75438/I, both in PRO; Joint Bureau News, Apr. 16, 1936, S25/3139, CZA; Szold to sisters, Apr. 10, 1936, H. Szold MSS.

12   Slutsky, *Sefer Toldot HaHagana*, 632-633; Kramer report, June 22, 1936, S25/22742, CZA. While providing the names of the two men killed on the night of April 16, a female Arab nationalist would depict the cold-blooded murders of April 15 as perpetrated by "a number of ordinary highwaymen" engaged in robbery, rather than the action of al-Sa'adi's terrorist group. Matiel E.T. Mogannam, *The Arab Woman and the Palestine Problem* (London, 1937), 292-293.

13   Ben-Gurion, *My Talks With Arab Leaders*, 42-62; Ben-Gurion at Mapai Political Committee, Apr. 16, 1936, Labor Party Archives.

14   Ben-Gurion, *Zikhronot* 2, 526, 509; Teveth, *Ben-Gurion*, 539; Ben-Gurion, *Zikhronot* 3, 255.

15   Summary of Confidential Report, Apr. 1936, microfilm #25, Brandeis MSS. The JDC's David Bressler, "knowing the uncompromising attitude of the Zionist-Nationalist mentality," warned Warburg at this time that it would be "a hopeless task" to limit the preponderantly Zionist influence in the Council for German Jewry. Warburg conveyed similar disappointment about the Council to Bentwich soon thereafter (Bressler to Warburg, Apr. 3, 1936; Warburg to Bentwich, Apr. 6, 1936; both in microfilm #1935, Warburg MSS).

16   Wauchope-Nashashibi-Husseini interview, Apr. 16, 1936, S25/22789, CZA.

17   Wauchope to Thomas, Apr. 18, 1936, CO 733/297/75156/II, PRO; Hall's testimony, Aug. 3 and 7, 1937, *League of Nations, Permanent Mandates Commission, Minutes of the Thirty-Second (Extraordinary) Session* (Geneva, 1937), 107, 60.

18   Brakha Habas, ed., *Meoraot Tartsav* (Tel Aviv, 1937), 1-32, 419-427; Slutsky, *Sefer Toldot HaHagana*, 633-634; Hall testimony, Aug. 3, 1937, *League of Nations, Permanent Mandates Commission, Minutes of the Thirty-Second (Extraordinary) Session*, 63-64. The Hagana, founded in 1920, began in Jerusalem when Vladimir Jabotinsky and Pinhas Rutenberg led a hastily assembled force of 200 Jews to resist Arab attackers. The underground

group was placed under the control of the World Zionist Organization. In the spring of 1931, a group of Hagana commanders founded the Irgun Tsva'i Leumi (Hagana Bet), which favored a more militant response to Arab assaults against the yishuv. They remained independent until 1937, when half of the members merged with the Hagana; the other half, ideologically tied to the Revisionist Zionist Party, created the (second) Irgun Tsva'i Leumi one year later.

19   Slutsky, *Sefer Toldot HaHagana*, 636-637; Palestinian Arab newspapers cited in Cohen memorandum, Nov. 25, 1936, J1/4139, CZA; Wauchope to Thomas, Apr. 21, 1936, CO 733/307/75438/1, PRO; Nashashibi *et al.* to Wauchope, Apr. 22, 1936, S25/22789, CZA; al-Sakakini, "*KaZeh Ani, Rabotai!*," 184-185. Ben-Gurion called for restraint and self-defense on the very first day of the disturbances (JAEJ, Apr. 19, 1936, CZA). For Zu'aiter's militancy and its impact, see Kabha, *Itonut B'Ein HaSe'ara*, and Matthews, *Constructing an Empire, passim*. The camps housing these Jewish refugees from Jaffa were only liquidated six months later. Szold to sisters, Nov. 14, 1936, H. Szold MSS.

20   Air Intelligence report, Apr. 1936, S25/11741, CZA; Yehuda Taggar, *The Mufti of Jerusalem and Palestinian Arab Politics, 1930-1937* (New York, 1988), 320-375; Slutsky, *Sefer Toldot HaHagana*, 638. The spontaneous outbreak had taken the Mufti by surprise as well. See Yuval Arnon-Ohana, *Herev MiBayit, HaMa'avak HaP'nimi BaTenua HaLeumit HaPalistinit* (Tel- Aviv, 1989), 252.

21   Moshe Sharett, *Yoman Medini*, 80-90; Shertok statement for Reuters, Apr. 20, 1936, file C14/9/6, BDA; Weizmann to Wauchope, Apr. 21 and 24, 1936, WA; *Palestine Post*, Apr. 24, 1936.

22   Wauchope-Weizmann interview, Apr. 21, 1936, microfilm #1934, Warburg MSS; Wauchope Apr. 21, 1936, statement to Arabs, quoted in Locker to Gillies, May 14, 1936, International Sub-Committee MSS, Labour Party Archives; Ben-Gurion–Rothenberg telephone conversation, Apr. 23, 1936, Box 116, Wise MSS; Shertok to Wauchope, Apr. 29, 1936, microfilm #1934; Ben-Gurion to London Executive, Apr. 29, 1936, microfilm #1933; both in Warburg MSS. For MacDonnell, see CO 733/75528/24, PRO; Tom Bowden, *The Breakdown of Public Security: The Case of Ireland 1916-1921 and Palestine 1936-1939* (London, 1977), 222-228.

23   Wauchope to Thomas, Apr. 30, 1936, S25/22725, CZA.

24   Szold to her sisters, May 1, 1936, file 1, H. Szold MSS; Locker to Gillies, May 14, 1936, International Sub-Committee MSS, Labour Party Archives; Knesset Israel committee statement, Apr. 30, 1936, A340/15, CZA.

25   May 2, 1936, report, S25/22726; Shertok to Abdullah, Apr. 30, 1936; Abdullah to Shertok, May 6, 1936; both in A24/197; Abd al-Hadi to Wauchope, May 5, 1936, S25/22704; all in CZA.

26   Wauchope to Thomas, May 5, 1936, S25/22725, and Shertok at Va'ad HaLeumi meeting, May 5, 1936, J1/7236, both in CZA; Jbara, *Palestinian Leader Hajj Amin al-Husseini*, 143; Agronsky note, May 8, 1936, A209/2, CZA Wauchope also permitted Haj Amin to travel around Northern Palestine, thinking that

he would be a moderate influence on Arab agitation. Keith-Roach, *The Pasha of Jerusalem*, 185.

27   Ben-Gurion to Brandeis, May 7, 1936, microfilm #25, Brandeis MSS. In a memorandum at this time to the League of Nations' Permanent Mandates Commission, Weizmann claimed that Palestinian Jewish industry represented an investment of £7 million, that by the end of 1934 it had reached an annual output of £6.5 million (an increase of 160 percent in the course of four years), and employed over 25,000 workers. It therefore could be classed as the most important single factor in the country's economic life (Weizmann to Wauchope, Apr. 30, 1936, microfilm #1933, Warburg MSS).

28   *Palestine Post*, May 12, 1936; Porath, *The Palestinian Arab National Movement*, 183; Abd al-Hadi to Wauchope, May 12, 1936; Wauchope–Arab delegation meeting, May 14, 1936; Abd al-Hadi to Wauchope, May 14, 1936; all in S25/22704, CZA.

29   Ben-Gurion and Shertok to Wauchope, May 14, 1936, microfilm #25, Brandeis MSS; Melchett to Thomas, May 12, 1936; Lourie to Shertok, May 13, 15, and 18, 1936; Thomas-Weizmann interview, May 18, 1936; all in A24/196, CZA; *Parliamentary Debates, House of Commons*, 312, col. 837, May 18, 1936.

30   Rosenberg to Wise and Lipsky, May 18, 1936, PAC files, McDonald MSS; Lipsky to Rosenberg, May 22, 1936, file P-672, Box 3, Louis Lipsky MSS, AJHS; Rosenberg to Wise, May 18, 1936, PAC files, McDonald MSS. Rosenberg would expand on these convictions in a 40-page letter six years later, by which time he had become an anti-Zionist. Rosenberg to Waldman, July 22, 1942, Rosenberg file, AJCA.

31   *Palestine Post*, May 16, 1936; Wauchope-Shertok interview, May 19, 1936, microfilm #1934, Warburg MSS; Wauchope to Thomas, May 18, 1936, S25/22708, CZA. For the beginnings of the Tel Aviv port, see Avidan, *BaDerekh LeTsahal*, 81-82.

32   Abd al-Hadi to Wauchope, May 19, 1936, Wauchope-Haj Amin interview, May 19, 1926, both in S25/22704; Cohen interview with M.U. (Mahmoud Unsi), May 25, 1936, and Sasson note, June 2, 1936, both in J1/4139; Wauchope to Abd al-Hadi, May 23, 1936, S25/22704; all in CZA.

33   Committee telephone conversations of May 28, 30, and 31, 1936, S25/22836; Hall to Haj Amin, May 29, 1936, S25/22704; Wauchope note, n.d., S25/22725; all in CZA. E.E. (Epstein) memorandum, May 31, 1936, file P-1056/7, ISA. Wauchope's Private Secretary, thinking the Arab demands "reasonable" and opposing the administration's new repressive measures against the strike, resigned (E. C. Hodgkin, ed., *Thomas Hodgkin, Letters from Palestine 1932-1936* (London, 1986), 164-165, 186-188).

34   Shertok to Ben-Gurion, May 31, 1936, file C14/9/8, BDA; Ruppin memorandum, May 31, 1936, A24/196, JAEJ, May 31, 1936, and memorandum, May 30, 1936, S25/22704, all in CZA. The Italian radio station in Bari broadcast pro-Arab propaganda on a regular basis as well. Thomas was forced to resign from politics. It was revealed that he had been entertained

by stock exchange speculators and had dropped heavy hints as to tax changes planned in the budget. For example, while playing gold, he shouted "Tee up!", which was taken as a suggestion that the duties on Tea were to rise.

35   Gad Frumkin, *Derekh Shofet B'Yerushalayim* (Tel Aviv, 1954), 325-326; Frumkin memorandum, n.d. (May 1936), file P-1056/7, ISA; Smilansky, *T'kuma V'Shoa*, 187-194; Wauchope-Rutenberg interview, May 20, 1936, file 9001/115, and Rutenberg diary, May 24-June 1, 1936 , file 9003/116, both in Rutenberg MSS; Memorandum, May 30, 1936, file P-1056/7, ISA; Memorandum, June 1, 1936, S25/9795, CZA.

36   Smilansky's subsequent memoir, a novel with himself cast as "Yehuda," fleshes out Rutenberg's disclosure. In this account, he and Tufiq Bey Ghusayn, whose son Yacoub was a member of the Supreme Muslim Council, agreed that monies paid to the council would make possible the agreement to be drawn up by the "idealists" Magnes and Alami. Abd al- Hadi and some of his colleagues eventually agreed on £50,000 to be paid to eight of the council executive. (This excluded Haj Amin, because he was receiving enormous sums from the Italians and the Germans, while "foolish" principled Husseini would not take money.) Rutenberg, whose company had already suffered because of the strike and who would likely be hurt further by its continuation, agreed to give half the sum. Smilansky persuaded Weizmann, although the WZO president had a tense relationship with Rutenberg, to invite Rutenberg to Rehovot for a discussion of the matter. Rutenberg consented to give half the funds if the Jewish Agency provided the other half. Weizmann failed, however, to persuade the Executive. Smilansky did not get the sum from Wauchope, either, and thus ended his private efforts (Smilansky, *T'kuma V'Shoa*, 194-196).

37   Wauchope-Rutenberg interview, May 20, 1936, file 9001/115, Rutenberg MSS, IECA.

38   Ben-Gurion, *My Talks With Arab Leaders*, 14-17, 25-40; Furlonge, *Palestine is My Country*, 231; Joseph-Alami talks, May 11 and 28, 1936, file P-1056/7, ISA; JAEJ, May 19, 1936, CZA.

39   JAEJ, June 2, 1936, CZA; Wauchope–Shertok interview, June 2, 1936, microfilm #24, Brandeis MSS. Ruppin also wrote to the new Colonial Secretary, observing that the influx of Jews had witnessed a remarkable rise in the non-Jewish population's standard of living. "Almost unlimited" possibilities of development lay ahead, notably in the area of underground water resources, by which both the native Arab population and Jewish immigrants would benefit. Realizing that "political troubles" were apt to check economic progress, Ruppin concluded with the hope that the Palestine government "will be strengthened by you in its zealous endeavours to bring back peace to the country." Ruppin to Ormsby-Gore, June 1, 1936, A107/98, CZA. Ruppin believed that Palestine could absorb an additional 2,000,000 individuals, giving the Jews a majority of the population. Va'ad HaPo'el HaMetsumtsam, Oct. 14, 1936, A107/302, CZA. An advocate of bi-nationalism in the 1920s, Ruppin concluded by the end of April 1936 that "we are living in a sort of

latent state of war with the Arabs which makes loss of life inevitable" (*A. Ruppin*, 277).

40 Wauchope to Ormsby-Gore, June 2, 1936; Wauchope note, June 3, 1936; both in S25/22725, CZA; Executive Council meeting, June 6, 1936, file M-4754/32, ISA; Wauchope to Abdullah, June 10, 1936, S25/22726, CZA. According to Ragheb Nashashibi's account, Abd al-Hadi's arrest had been engineered by Haj Amin, who, together with Jerusalem's Mayor Khalidi, had refused Abd al-Hadi's appeal that they endorse the strike and persuade Arab government officials to do likewise. Haj Amin then told Wauchope of Abd al-Hadi's approaching an Arab official on the government judiciary to take this step, and the deportation followed (June 18, 1936 report received, file P-1056/7, ISA).

41 Szold to her sisters, June 5, 1936, H. Szold MSS; Kaplan to Ben-Gurion, June 11, 1936, file 20, Mack MSS; Police intelligence report, June 8, 1936, S25/22726, CZA; Shertok to Wauchope, June 6, 1936, microfilm #24, Brandeis MSS; Wauchope to Ormsby-Gore, June 16, 1936, S25/22725, CZA; Lesch, *Arab Politics in Palestine*, 219.

42 Ormsby-Gore to Wauchope, June 10, 1936, S25/22725; Lourie to Weizmann, June 23, 1936, A24/186; both in CZA. After work on the Arab Bureau in Cairo (1916-1917), Ormsby-Gore served as political officer on behalf of the British government on the first Zionist Commission in Palestine under Weizmann during April 1918. In 1919 he served on the Foreign Office staff at the peace conference in Versailles, then became the first British member of the Permanent Mandates Commission when the Mandates for Palestine and Iraq first came up to the League.

43 Ormsby-Gore–Weizmann interview, June 16, 1936, microfilm #24, Brandeis MSS; Izzat Tannous, *The Palestinians* (New York, 1988), 182-183. Aside from saying that the Jews would cooperate "heartedly" with the Royal Commission, Weizmann requested that fullest use be made of the new powers taken under the Order-in-Council against the Arab Revolt, that distribution of strike funds from outside sources be halted, and that Jews be armed under British officers for defense of the yishuv's colonies. Ormsby-Gore to Wauchope, June 17, 1936, S25/22725, CZA; London *Times*, June 20, 1936; Brandeis MSS; Matthew Hughes, "Britain's Suppression of the 1936-39 Arab Revolt in Palestine," *Journal of Palestine Studies* 39.2 (2010): 6-22.

44 Rutenberg diary, June 2-16, 1936, file 9003/116, Rutenberg MSS; Ben-Gurion to Jewish Agency Executive Jerusalem, June 9, 1936, Jewish Agency 1934-1936 files, ZA; *Baffy*, 21; Rutenberg diary, June 20, 1936, file 9003/116, Rutenberg MSS.

45 Sharett, *Yoman Medini*, 176-179; Ben-Gurion, *My Talks With Arab Leaders*, 93-97; Alami to Bentwich, June 24, 1936, A255/294, CZA. Alami's version of the June conversations, as retold to Magnes two months later, is in Magnes to Shertok, Aug. 20, 1936, S25/2960, CZA.

46 Wauchope to Ormsby-Gore, June 24, 1936, S25/22725, CZA; Weizmann to

Cust, June 9, 1936, WA; Lourie to Shertok, June 26, 1936, S49/389, CZA; Cust memorandum, June 28, 1936, CO 733/297/75156/3, PRO. Having first publicized his own plan in February, Cust would elaborate on his views in *Great Britain and the East*, July 23, 1936. Meanwhile, A.C. Crossley MP had spoken in the House of Commons for cantonization, which the *Spectator* endorsed in May (*JTA*, May 24, 1936).

47   Hall to Haj Amin, June 27, 1936, S25/22784, and Shertok to Hall, June 28, 1936, A24/196, both in CZA; *Palestine Post*, June 28, 1936; Jbara, *Palestinian Leader*, 147; Haj Amin to Wauchope, July 1, 1936, S25/22704, CZA. Sir Walter Shaw's Commission, established to investigate the Arab riots of 1929, suggested restrictions on Jewish immigration and land purchase. For the response of yishuv rabbis to Haj Amin's charge about Jews wishing to take over Jerusalem's Holy Mount, see S25/3414, CZA.

48   Ormsby-Gore–Weizmann–Ben-Gurion interview, June 30, 1936, CO 733/297/75156/3, PRO; microfilm #24, Brandeis MSS; Weizmann to Ormsby-Gore, July 1, 1936, FO 371/20021, PRO.

49   Orsmby-Gore memorandum, July 4, 1936, FO 371/20021, PRO; Cabinet meeting, July 4, 1936, CAB 23/85, PRO; Wise memorandum, July 8, 1936, Box 118, Wise MSS.; Wauchope to Ormsby-Gore, July 9, 1936, S25/22725, CZA; Wauchope–Ben-Gurion–Shertok interview, July 9, 1936, microfilm #24, Brandeis MSS; Shertok to Wauchope, July 12, 1936, A24/200, CZA; Ormsby-Gore–Arab delegation interview, July 14, 1936, CO 733/289/75054, PRO; Ormsby-Gore to Weizmann, July 17, 1936, A24/199, CZA; *Baffy*, 26.

50   Political Advisory Committee meeting, July 1, 1936, Robert Szold MSS; Eden memorandum, June 20, 1936; Note, June 18, 1936; both in FO 371/20021; Ryan to Foreign Office, Apr. 30, 1936, CO 733/314/75528/44/1; all in PRO; Eden to Wauchope, July 7, 10, and 14, 1936, S25/22726, CZA; Oliphant–Hafez Wahba interview, July 14, 1936; Parkinson memorandum, July 16, 1936; both in CO 733/314/75528/44/1, PRO.

51   Meeting, July 27, 1936, ZOA Executive minutes, ZA; Rosenman to Roosevelt, July 16, 1936; Hull to Roosevelt, July 27, 1936; both in PSF Great Britain, Box 25, FDRL. Consulted by a ZOA delegation, Brandeis advised that the Jewish Agency press advance the principle of Palestine's absorptive capacity and not agree to any fixed number of immigrants, and demand that the yishuv be compensated for damages sustained during the Arab uprising but not charged for any cost of the Jewish constables or police force required (Meeting, July 27, 1936, ZOA Executive minutes, ZA).

52   Cohen to Unsi, June 28, 1936; Unsi to Cohen, July 3, 1936; both in J1/4139; Memorandum, July 26, 1936, S25/22726; all in CZA. Cohen memorandum, July 28, 1936, file P173, CAHJP; Wauchope-Shertok interview, July 28, 1936, microfilm #24, Brandeis MSS.

53   Smuts to Lloyd George, July 23, 1936, file G/18/6/10, Lloyd George MSS; Smuts to Weizmann, July 24, 1936, microfilm #25, Brandeis MSS; Ormsby-Gore to Amery, July 28, 1936, Leopold Amery MSS, London; Halifax-Frankfurter

interview, July 28, 1936, A264/57, CZA. My thanks to the late Julian Amery for permission to examine his father's papers. Lloyd George had conveyed his fervent pro-Zionist views to Weizmann and Ben-Gurion during lunch at his country home one month earlier. See David Ben-Gurion, *Letters to Paula*, trans. A. Hodes (London, 1971), 96-98.

54 *Parliamentary Debates, House of Commons*, 315, col. 1511, July 29, 1936; Furlonge, *Palestine is My Country*, 109; *Palestine Post*, July 10, 1936; London *Times*, July 10, 1936; Alami-Khalidi telephone conversation, July 29, 1936, S25/22836, CZA; Shertok note, July 29, 1936, microfilm #24, Brandeis MSS. In protesting the Arab officials' memorandum, Shertok asked Wauchope to have those District Officers who signed the statement replaced in zones of Jewish settlement with Jews or such Arab officers who did not sign it (Shertok to Wauchope, July 28, 1936, Jewish Agency MSS., file 15/1, ZA). Hall, by contrast, responded by citing Ormsby-Gore's July 22 statement in Parliament, then conveyed the Colonial Secretary's understanding of their "very delicate" position, his "grateful recognition" of the loyalty they had shown in this trying time," and his confidence that they would "continue to maintain the loyalty which is traditional in the Public Service" (Hall to Mustafa Bey el Khalidi, Aug. 14, 1936, S25/22783, CZA).

55 Haj Amin telephone conversations with Fuad and Khalidi, Aug. 3, 1936, S25/22836; Cox to Wauchope, Aug. 5, 1936, S22726; Wauchope to Gore, Aug. 21, 1936, S25/22764; all in CZA; Hillel Cohen, *Army of Shadows, Palestinian Collaboration With Zionism, 1917-1948*, trans. H. Watzman (Berkeley, 2008), 104-107.

56 Wauchope to Ormsby-Gore, Aug. 22, 1936, S25/22764, and Khalidi-Hall agreement, Aug. 26, 1936, S25/1033, both in, CZA; Ormsby-Gore memorandum, Aug. 26, 1936, CAB 24/263, PRO; Ormsby-Gore to Wauchope, Aug. 26, 1936, CO 733/297/75156, PRO; London *Times*, Aug. 19, 1936; Wauchope to Ormsby-Gore, Aug. 29, 1936, S25/22725, CZA.

57 Jbara, *Palestinian Leader*, 150; Sharett, *Yoman Medini*, 271-276; Arab Higher Committee meeting, Aug. 22, 1936, file P-3221/18, ISA; Committee telephone conversations, Aug. 23-25, 1936, S25/22836, CZA; Ormsby-Gore to Wauchope, Aug. 25, 27, and 29, 1936, in CO 733/314/75528/44/1, PRO; *Palcor*, Aug. 30, 1936; Wauchope to Ormsby-Gore, Aug. 30, 1936, and Eden to Baghdad and Jerusalem, Aug. 31, 1936 both in S25/22726, CZA. The previous March, a concerned Whitehall was fully aware of Nuri's desire to unite Transjordan and Iraq, as well as about Abdullah's wish to become king over Transjordan and Syria. Rendel to Clark-Kerr, Mar. 8, 1936, FO 371/18965, PRO; Cox to Wauchope, Mar. 26, 1936, S25/22779, CZA.

58 Sharett, *Yoman Medini*, 262-268; Shertok–R.A.F. officers conversation, Aug. 27, 1936, microfilm #37, and Shertok to Wauchope, Aug. 30, 1936, microfilm #25, both in Brandeis MSS.; Ormsby-Gore–Weizmann–Ben-Gurion interview, Aug. 31, 1936, FO 371/20024, PRO.

59 Ormsby-Gore to Wauchope, Aug. 31, 1936, S25/22726; Wauchope to

Ormsby-Gore, Sept. 1, 1936, S25/22725; both in CZA.

60   Wise to Brandeis, Sept. 1, 1936, Box 106; Wise-Weizmann telephone conver-
      sation, Sept. 1, 1936, Box 122; both in Wise MSS. Hull-Bingham telephone
      conversations, Sept. 1, 1936, Box 66, Cordell Hull MSS, LC; Brandeis to Wise,
      Sept. 4, 1936, Box 104, Wise MSS. Roosevelt fondly referred to Brandeis as
      "Old Isaiah," while Frankfurter was one of FDR's trusted, unofficial advisors.
      Brandeis and Frankfurter strongly opposed Wise's idea of taking the matter
      to the League of Nations' Council, arguing that the risks of adverse opinion
      were too serious and the possible advantage of any positive opinion too slight
      (Frankfurter to Wise, Sept. 4, 1936, Box 109, Wise MSS).

61   *Palestine Post*, Sept. 1, 1936; Ormsby-Gore to Wauchope, Sept. 1, 1936, CO
      733/297/75156/4, PRO; Sharett, *Yoman Medini*, 302-304; Ormsby-Gore to
      Weizmann, Sept. 2, 1936, S25/6329, CZA.

62   Sharett, *Yoman Medini*, 291-296. Shertok also informed Wauchope that his
      private talks with "a certain gentleman" (Shertok knew that Wauchope was
      aware of his talks with Alami) about possible Agency negotiations with the
      Committee had yielded nothing because that individual apparently could not
      get his people "to agree to anything." Covering up his failure, Shertok added,
      this Arab told various people that the Jews were not sincere and just pretend-
      ing in declarations of their desire for peace.

63   Sept. 2, 1936, CAB 23/85, PRO; Ormsby-Gore to Wauchope, Sept. 3, 1936,
      S25/22726, CZA. For the later impact of Italy's victory on War Office plan-
      ning, see Michael J. Cohen, "British Strategy in the Middle East in the Wake of
      the Abyssinian Crisis, 1936-1939," in Michael J. Cohen and Martin Kolinsky,
      eds., *Britain and the Middle East in the 1930s: Security Problems, 1935-39*
      (London, 1992), 21-40.

64   Margolies to Wise, Sept. 4, 1936, Box 116; Wise to Hull, Sept. 9, 1936, Box
      66; both in Wise MSS. Weizmann to Shertok, Sept. 6, 1936, WA; Committee
      telephone conversations, Sept. 4, 1936, S25/22836, CZA.

65   Nir Arielli, "Italian Involvement in the Arab Revolt in Palestine, 1936-1939,"
      British Journal of Middle Eastern Studies 35 (Aug. 2008): 190-194, 196; Eliyahu
      Eilat, *MiBa'ad L'Arafel HaYamim, Pirkei Zikhronot* (Jerusalem, 1989), 164;
      Jbara, *Palestinian Leader*, 151; Ilana Arieli-Meir, ed., *Homa U'Migdal, Perakim
      B'Toldot HaYishuv* (Tel Aviv, 1983). Mussolini personally approved these re-
      quests from Alami, but the relevant Italian records do not reveal that the plan
      for such technical advisors was vigorously pursued. From September 1936
      until June 1938, when Rome halted payments, Italian financial support for
      the Arab Revolt totaled £138,000.

66   Sept. 8, 1936, HMG statement, *League of Nations Official Journal*, 17.2
      (Geneva, 1936): 1357-1358; Alexander Pope, *An Essay on Man, Epistle I* (1733).
      A British representative to the Permanent Mandates Commission, referring
      to a statement by Prime Minister MacDonald in the House of Commons on
      April 3, 1930, had first used the term "equal weight." At that extraordinary
      seventeenth session of the Commission on the 1929 Arab disturbances,

the idea of two obligations of equal weight assumed its present form. That statement by the Permanent Mandates Commission was accepted "with satisfaction" in the Passfield White Paper of October 1930. The subsequent Royal Commission report (p. 39) would revert to the earlier understanding that "the *primary purpose* of the mandate as expressed in its preamble and its articles is to promote the establishment of the Jewish National Home" (Van Asbeck statement, Aug. 12, 1937, *League of Nations, Permanent Mandates Commission, Minutes of the Thirty-Second [Extraordinary] Session*, 164).

67 *League of Nations, Permanent Mandates Commission, Minutes of the Thirty-Second (Extraordinary) Session*, 172; Samuel memorandum, Sept. 8, 1936, CO 733/315/75528, PRO; London *Times*, Sept. 4, 1936.

68 Ormsby-Gore to Istanbul (for Nuri Pasha), Sept. 3, 1936, S25/22726, CZA; Ormsby-Gore interview with Samuel-Winterton, Sept. 8, 1936, CO 733/315/75528/315, PRO; Weizmann to Samuel, Sept. 4, 1936; Weizmann to Samuel, Sept. 14, 1936; Samuel to Weizmann, Sept. 15, 1936; all in WA; Ormsby-Gore to Wauchope, Sept. 14, 1936, S25/22726, CZA; Ormsby-Gore to Samuel, Sept. 15, 1936, WA; Samuel final draft (Sept. 1936), file P-649/18, ISA. From Weizmann's report, Shertok concluded that Rutenberg was behind Samuel's scheme. JAEJ, Sept. 20, 1936, CZA. For Rutenberg's letters in this regard during the summer, see Rutenberg to Abdullah and memorandum, July 12, 1936; Abdullah to Rutenberg, July 17, 1936; Rutenberg to Samuel, July 10, 1936; Rutenberg to Samuel, Aug. 7, 1936; all in file 9011/181, Rutenberg MSS. Samuel chaired the Palestine Electric Company's board of directors.

69 Samuel note, Sept. 20, 1936, FO 371/20026, PRO; Winterton letter, Sept. 26, 1936, Z4/17441, CZA; Namier (LBN) note, Dec. 16, 1936, WA; Nuri's summary to the Iraqi prime minister of the talks, dated Sept. 26, 1936, is in FO 371/20028, PRO. The Agency obtained a copy. See in S25/22719, CZA.

70 Wauchope interviews with Haj Amin and Nashashibi, Sept. 9, 1936; Wauchope–Abd al-Hadi interview, Sept. 10, 1936; all in S25/22704, CZA; Wauchope–Committee interview, Sept. 12, 1936, FO 371/20027, PRO. Wauchope informed Shertok of the first two interviews. Wauchope-Shertok interview, Sept. 9, 1936, file 17/1, Jewish Agency files, ZA. The Agency obtained a copy of the Committee interview. See in S25/22776, CZA.

71 Committee meeting, Sept. 13, 1936, file P-3221/18, ISA; *Palcor*, Sept. 13, 1936; Khalidi telephone conversations, Sept. 13, 1936, S25/22836, CZA. Haj Amin, Husseini, Khalidi, and Fuad Saba wished to stop the strike and disorders after the Arab rulers' appeal, provided that the local National Committees agreed; Nashashibi and Rock were ready to act on a call from Abdullah but only if the rest of the Committee would act with them; Abd al-Hadi, Ghusayn, and Hilmi Pasha wished to act after the Arab rulers' appeal without taking council of the local committees (Cox to Wauchope, Sept. 19, 1936, S25/22704, CZA).

72 Wauchope to Ormsby-Gore, Sept. 12, 1936; Wauchope to Ormsby-Gore, Sept. 16, 1936; both in S25/22725, CZA. A.J. Sherman, *Mandate Days: British Lives in Palestine, 1918-1948* (New York, 1997), 101.

73   Weizmann-Cadogan interview and Weizmann memorandum, Sept. 19, 1936, FO 371/20025, PRO. In response to a newspaper interview in which Weizmann indicated that he had "no understanding and no sympathy for a Jewish majority in Palestine," the WZO Congress in 1931 passed a resolution which spoke of "reviving in Eretz Israel a national life with all the characteristic features of the normal life of a nation."

74   Rendel minute, Sept. 14, 1936, FO 371/371/19983; Rendel minute, Sept. 17, 1936, FO 371/20025; Rendel minute, Sept. 24, 1936, FO 371/20026; all in PRO. For Rendel's seminal influence, see Elie Kedourie, *Islam in the Modern World and Other Studies* (London, 1980), 93-170.

75   Khalidi telephone conversation, Sept. 15, 1936, S25/22836; Ormsby-Gore to Wauchope, Sept. 21, 1936, S25/22706; both in CZA. FO 371/20026, PRO; Ormsby-Gore to Wauchope, Sept. 22, 1936, S25/22726, CZA; Committee meeting, Sept. 22, 1936, file P-3221/18, ISA; Eden to Wauchope, Sept. 30, 1936 and Bateman to Wauchope, Sept. 28, 1936, both in S25/22726, CZA.

76   C.I.D. report, Sept. 25, 1936, S25/22741; Ormsby-Gore–Weizmann–Namier interview, Sept. 30, 1936, A24/199; both in CZA. Ormsby-Gore memorandum, Oct. 1, 1936, CAB 24/264, PRO; Ormsby-Gore to Wauchope, Oct. 2, 1936, S25/22726, CZA; Rendel minute, Oct. 3, 1936, and Ormsby-Gore to Wauchope, Oct. 5, 1936; both in FO 371/20027, PRO; Committee meeting, Oct. 3, 1936, file P-3221/18, ISA; Clark-Kerr to Eden, Oct. 2, 1936, FO 371/20026, PRO; Agronsky to Weizmann, Sept. 25, 1936, A209/2, Simson-Kisch interview, Oct. 4, 1936, A24/199, and Dill to Duff-Cooper, Oct. 5, 1936, S25/22726, all in CZA.

77   Ormsby-Gore–Weizmann–Namier interview, Sept. 30, 1936, A24/199; Wauchope to Ormsby-Gore, Oct. 2, 1936, S25/22726; both in CZA. Rendel minutes, Oct. 9, 1936; Vansittart minutes, Oct. 10, 1936; both in FO 371/20027, PRO; Lourie to Ben-Gurion, Sept. 29, 1936; JAEJ, Oct. 4, 1936, and Ben-Gurion–Shertok to Weizmann, Oct. 6, 1936, A24/199, both in CZA; Sharett, *Yoman Medini*, 324-325. The American Zionist leadership also opposed the parity declaration. See Wise to Frankfurter, Oct. 10, 1936, Box 109, and Wise to Weizmann, Oct. 26, 1936, Box 122, both in Wise MSS.

78   Clark-Kerr to Eden and Arab capitals, Oct. 5, 1936, S25/22726, CZA; Clark-Kerr to Eden, Oct. 8, 1936, CO 733/314/75528/44, PRO; Abdullah to Committee, Oct. 8, 1936, file P-3221/18, ISA; Wauchope to Abdullah, Oct. 9, 1936; Abd al-Hadi to Wauchope, Oct. 9, 1936; both in S25/22726, CZA. Egypt, its prime minister informed HMG's ambassador to Cairo, had not participated in the appeal of the Arab rulers because HMG had not acceded to his request that Jewish immigration to Palestine be provisionally suspended. Lampson to Eden, Nov. 9, 1936, FO 371/20028, PRO.

79   Wauchope message, Oct. 11, 1936, S25/22704; CZA; A.A. (Epstein) report, Oct. 1, 1936; "Text of a Secret Proclamation," n.d., both in S25/3441, CZA; *Palestine Post*, Oct. 11, 1936.

80   *Palestine Post*, Oct. 12, 1936; Joseph Nevo, "Palestinian-Arab Violent Activity

during the 1930s," in M.J. Cohen and M. Kolinsky, eds., *Britain and the Middle East in the l930s: Security Problems 1935-39* (New York, 1992), 177; Slutski, *Sefer Toldot HaHagana*, 641, 650; H.J. Simson, *British Rule, and Rebellion* (Edinburgh, 1937), 286; Szold to her sisters, Oct. 9, 1936, file 1, H. Szold MSS; London *Times*, Oct. 14, 1936; Keith-Roach, *Pasha of Jerusalem*, 186.

81   Wauchope to Ormsby-Gore, two letters, Oct. 13, 1936, S25/22726; Ormsby-Gore to Wauchope, Oct. 14, 1936, S25/22704; both in CZA. Executive Council, Oct. 15, 1936, file M-4754/32, ISA.

82   Sharett, *Yoman Medini*, 333-338, 348-350. Asked by the Agency Executive in Jerusalem if Ormsby-Gore should be pressed on the disarmament of the Arabs, its London counterpart strongly objected on the grounds that the step would not achieve anything effectual and would require HMG to disarm the Jews simultaneously. Lourie to Shertok, Oct. 13, 1936, A24/199, CZA.

83   C.I. D. report, Sept. 25, 1936, S25/22741; Rice to Moody, Oct. 27, 1936, S25/22725; both in CZA. See also Porath, *The Palestinian Arab National Movement*, 194-195. For Nashashibi's wish to break with Haj Amin after the strike had ended, see telephone conversation, Oct. 17, 1936, S25/22836, CZA.

84   *Palestine Post*, Oct. 16, 1936; Wauchope-Committee interview, Oct. 24, 1936, S25/22704, CZA; *Palestine Post*, Oct. 30, 1936; Abd al-Hadi to Wauchope, Oct. 30, 1936, S25/22726, CZA.

85   Cabinet meeting, Oct. 28, 1936, CAB 23/86, PRO; Rendel memorandum, Oct. 21, 1936; Rendel and Vansittart minutes, Oct. 22, 1936; all in FO 371/20028, PRO; Haj Amin to Wauchope, Nov. 3, 1936, S25/22704, CZA; Ormsby-Gore—Weizmann interview, Nov. 3, 1936, Premier (hereafter PREM) records, file 1/352, PRO; Cabinet meeting, Nov. 4, 1936, CAB 23/86, PRO.

86   Committee statement, Oct. 6, 1936, file P-3221/18, ISA; Wauchope-Committee interview, Nov. 7, 1936; Wauchope to Ormsby-Gore, Nov. 8, 1936; both in S25/22704, CZA.

87   Wauchope to Ormsby-Gore, Nov. 4, 1936, PREM 1/352, PRO; Wauchope to Ormsby-Gore, Nov. 5 or 7, 1936, S25/22784, CZA.

88   *Palestine Post*, Oct. 30, 1936; Wauchope to Ormsby-Gore, Nov. 4, 1936, PREM 1/352, PRO; Dill report to War Office, Oct. 30, 1936, CO 733/371/1, PRO; Dill-Kisch interview, Nov. 6, 1936, microfilm #25, Brandeis MSS; Nashashibi telephone conversations, Nov. 10 and 11, 1936, S25/22836, CZA; Winterton-Laski interview, Nov. 11, 1936, Foreign Countries/Palestine files, AJCA; Melchett to Wise, Box 116, Wise MSS; Lord Melchett, *Thy Neighbor* (London, 1936).

89   David Ben-Gurion, *Zikhronot* 3, 482-493. The danger of world war, including the threat of Arab armies and the possibility of Hitler's forces reaching Palestine, convinced Ben-Gurion that Zionism had to augment the yishuv's strengths quickly and to gain England's support. Va'ad HaPoel HaMetsumtsam, Oct. 26, 1936, S5/287, CZA.

90   Melchett to Wise, Nov. 9, 1936, Box 116, Wise MSS; Ben-Gurion to

Ussishkin, Nov. 11, 1936, A24/247, CZA; Bennet note, with Oliphant and Vansittart comments, Nov. 11, 1936 (and Eden's approval, Nov. 13, 1936), FO 371/20028, PRO.

91   Joseph B. Schechtman, *Fighter and Prophet: The Vladimir Jabotinsky Story; The Last Years* (New York 1961), 302-304, 346; Jabotinsky press conference, May 21, 1936, A330/779, CZA; Abba Ahimeir, "Giborim V'Lo K'doshim!," in Abba Ahimeir, *HaTsiyonut HaMahapkhanit* (Tel Aviv, 1966), 98-100. The Warsaw foreign office organ, *Gazeta Polska*, endorsed Jabotinsky's Ten Year plan, adding that new areas for Jewish emigration had yet to be found (*JTA*, Nov. 10, 1936).

92   Khalidi-Issa telephone conversations, Aug. 14 and 25, 1936, S25/22836, CZA; Hurewitz, *The Struggle for Palestine*, 70-71; Alec S. Kirkbride, *A Crackle of Thorns: Experiences in the Middle East* (London, 1956), 155; Roger Courtney, *Palestine Policeman* (London, 1939), 72-73.

93   Slutski, *Sefer Toldot HaHagana*, 652, 657-689, 696; Anita Shapira, *Land and Power: The Zionist Resort to Force, 1881-1948* (New York, 1992), 223; Eliyahu Ben-Hur, *LaTset Et HaGeder* (Tel Aviv, 1985), 68-88.

94   Abd al-Hadi-Tsalah telephone conversation, May 31, 1936, S25/22836, CZA; Residency Cairo to Foreign Office, Oct. 28, 1936, S25/22726, CZA, and FO 371/20028 PRO. The French-Syrian treaty of September 9 (ratified in December) stipulated that the mandate would end within three years and Syria admitted to the League, with the Lebanon to retain its individuality. The Anglo-Egyptian treaty of August 26 (ratified in December) restricted British forces to the Suez Canal; accepted a British naval base at Alexandria for not more than eight years; permitted an unlimited Egyptian immigration into Sudan along with troops and Egypt to enter the League; and confirmed an alliance for twenty years, after which the agreement was to be reexamined.

95   Chaim Weizmann, "Where We Stand," *Masada*, Nov. 1936, 3-4; JAEJ, July 6, 1936, CZA; Wauchope–Committee interview, Nov. 7, 1936, S25/22704, and Wauchope to Harding, Nov. 5, 1936, S25/22725; both in CZA.

96   Michael J. Cohen, *Palestine: Retreat from the Mandate , The Making of British Policy, 1936-45* (New York, 1978), 31; Simson, *British Rule, and Rebellion*, 286 and chap. 18; Porath, *The Palestinian Arab National Movement*, 216; JAEJ, Oct. 25, 1936, Ormsby-Gore–Weizmann–Namier interview, Sept. 30, 1936, A24/199, and Wauchope to Bentwich, June 5, 1936, A255/294, all in CZA.

www.ingramcontent.com/pod-product-compliance
Lightning Source LLC
Chambersburg PA
CBHW050333270326
41926CB00016B/3432